# THE CANONICAL APPROACH

*A Critical Reconstruction of
the Hermeneutics of Brevard S. Childs*

# BIBLICAL
# INTERPRETATION
# SERIES

*Editors*
R. ALAN CULPEPPER
ROLF RENDTORFF

*Assistant Editor*
DAVID E. ORTON

*Editorial Advisory Board*

VOLUME 16

# THE CANONICAL APPROACH

*A Critical Reconstruction of*
*the Hermeneutics of Brevard S. Childs*

BY

PAUL R. NOBLE

E.J. BRILL
LEIDEN · NEW YORK · KÖLN
1995

The paper in this book meets the guidelines for permanence and durability of the Committee on Production Guidelines for Book Longevity of the Council on Library Resources.

**Library of Congress Cataloging-in-Publication Data**

The CIP-data has been applied for.

ISSN  0928-0731
ISBN  90 04 10151 9

PRINTED IN THE NETHERLANDS

## CONTENTS

# ACKNOWLEDGEMENTS

The present book is a revised and expanded version of my doctoral dissertation, which was submitted to the University of Cambridge in March 1991. Naturally, it has inherited a number of debts from its predecessor.

First and foremost, I would like to thank my research supervisor, Dr. G.I. Davies, both for his many valuable comments on my work and for encouraging me to pursue it beyond the traditional boundaries of Old Testament research. During Dr. Davies' leave of absence, I was temporarily supervised by Professor N.L.A. Lash.

Parts of chapters 2 and 3 were read at the Cambridge Old Testament Seminar, and I am grateful to those present for their interesting questions and comments. I also wish to thank Dr. S.G.F. Jones for reading an earlier draft of chapters 8 and 9, and Dr. Mark G. Brett for making a copy of his thesis available to me. Special thanks are also due to Professor Brevard S. Childs for discussing his work with me during his time in Cambridge in 1987.

While undertaking my doctoral research, I was supported financially by a Research Studentship from Trinity College, Cambridge (1987–90), and by a Crosse Studentship from the Divinity School, University of Cambridge (1990–91), and am grateful to both these institutions for their generosity.

# ABBREVIATIONS

| | |
|---|---|
| *ATR* | *Anglican Theological Review* |
| *BI* | *Biblical Interpretation* |
| *BQT* | *Basic Questions in Theology* (Pannenberg) |
| BTCon | 'Biblical Theology, Contemporary' (Stendahl) |
| *BTCri* | *Biblical Theology in Crisis* (Childs) |
| *BTONT* | *Biblical Theology of the Old and New Testaments* (Childs) |
| *CAOTS* | *The Canonical Approach to Old Testament Study* (Brett) |
| *EC* | *Exodus: A Commentary* (Childs) |
| *ExpTim* | *The Expository Times* |
| *HBT* | *Horizons in Biblical Theology* |
| *HeyJ* | *Heythrop Journal* |
| *HS* | *Holy Scripture* (Barr) |
| *IAC* | *Isaiah and the Assyrian Crisis* (Childs) |
| *IDB* | *Interpreter's Dictionary of the Bible* |
| IF | 'Interpretation in Faith' (Childs) |
| IFal | 'The Intentional Fallacy' (Wimsatt and Beardsley) |
| *Int* | *Interpretation* |
| *IOTS* | *Introduction to the Old Testament as Scripture* (Childs) |
| *JAAR* | *Journal of the American Academy of Religion* |
| *JBL* | *Journal of Biblical Literature* |
| *JPhil* | *Journal of Philosophy* |
| *JLT* | *Journal of Literature and Theology* |
| *JTC* | *Journal for Theology and the Church* |
| *JTS* | *Journal of Theological Studies* |
| *JSOT* | *Journal for the Study of the Old Testament* |
| *JSOTS* | *Journal for the Study of the Old Testament*—Supplement Series |
| KH | 'Kerygma and History' (Pannenberg) |
| *MTI* | *Memory and Tradition in Israel* (Childs) |
| *NHH* | *New Horizons in Hermeneutics* (Thiselton) |
| *NTCI* | *The New Testament as Canon: An Introduction* (Childs) |
| OBT | Overtures to Biblical Theology |
| OTL | Old Testament Library |
| *OTTCC* | *Old Testament Theology in a Canonical Context* (Childs) |
| *Proof* | *Prooftexts: A Journal of Jewish Literary History* |
| *RaH* | *Revelation as History* (Pannenberg) |
| REH | 'Redemptive Event and History' (Pannenberg) |
| *RelStud* | *Religious Studies* |
| *RelSRev* | *Religious Studies Review* |
| SBT | Studies in Biblical Theology |
| *SJT* | *Scottish Journal of Theology* |
| SLS | 'The Sensus Literalis of Scripture' (Childs) |
| *TM* | *Truth and Method* (Gadamer) |
| *TToday* | *Theology Today* |
| *VTSup* | *Vetus Testamentum*—Supplements |

CHAPTER ONE

# INTRODUCTION

It is now more than thirty years since Brevard S. Childs published his programmatic essay 'Interpretation in Faith',[1] in which he argued that biblical studies needs to be reoriented in a number of fundamental ways. For much of the subsequent period, and especially since the publication of Childs' *Introduction to the Old Testament as Scripture*[2] in 1979, these proposals have been the subject of intense debate.[3]

Reactions to Childs' work have been extremely diverse. On the one hand, there are a number of scholars who seem intent on demolishing Childs' programme root and branch: according to their assessment it is shot through with fundamental flaws, and has few positive virtues to offset them. On the other hand, however, Childs has not been completely without support. Over the years there has been a slender trickle of publications which have sought to defend Childs' work from its critics,[4] or have engaged in some aspect of biblical studies from a perspective akin to Childs' own.[5] Despite the length and intensity of the debate, however, no clear consensus has emerged concerning the viability of Childs' 'canonical approach' or the contribution it might make to biblical studies. Meanwhile Childs himself has continued to develop and implement his initial sketch, sometimes modifying or further articulating the position set out in 'IF', but generally remaining close to its distinctive tenets. These have been applied in turn to the tasks of Old Testament commentary,

---

[1] 'Interpretation in Faith: The Theological Responsibility of an Old Testament Commentary', *Int* 18 (1964), pp. 432–49.

[2] London: SCM, 1979.

[3] For a lucid exposition of Childs' methodology, which helpfully sets his work in the context of the modern scholarly debate, see R.W.L. Moberly, 'The Church's Use of the Bible: The Work of Brevard Childs', *ExpTim* 99 (1988), pp. 104–109. For a complete bibliography of Childs' writings (to 1988), see John B. Trotti, 'Brevard Spring Childs: A Bibliography', in Gene M. Tucker *et al.*, *Canon, Theology, and Old Testament Interpretation* (Philadelphia: Fortress, 1988), pp. 329–36.

[4] See, for example, Gerald T. Sheppard, 'Barr on Canon and Childs', *Theological Students Fellowship Bulletin* 7 (1983), pp. 2–4.

[5] Most notable here, perhaps, is Rolf Rendtorff's *The Old Testament: An Introduction* (London: SCM, 1985).

Old and New Testament Introduction, and Old Testament Theology; most recently they have found expression in his very substantial *Biblical Theology of the Old and New Testaments*,[6] which finally implements Childs' methodological proposals in their fullest extent.

Childs will no doubt continue to develop and refine various aspects of his programme. Nonetheless, with his work having reached a natural completeness with the publication of *BTONT*, and yet there still being little agreement as to how it should be assessed, this is a particularly apposite moment at which to make a detailed analysis and evaluation of his canonical methodology.

Since the present book is a further addition to a long-running debate, it is appropriate to begin with a survey of previous contributions. Childs' major works have been the subject of numerous reviews,[7] which naturally reflect a wide variety of perspectives.[8] The inherent limitations of even an extended review article, however, generally prevent them from making a full-scale assessment of Childs' work. Thus restrictions of length and the necessity of concentrating upon a single work, mean that they have often been better at raising pertinent questions than discussing the fundamental issues in any depth.

Frank Spina's comparison of Childs and Sanders usefully highlights both the similarities and the major differences between these scholars.[9] Spina reviews Childs' major works (to 1982) in chronological order, but seems not to have sufficiently appreciated that there have been important developments in Childs' thought.[10] Spina concludes by putting a series of perceptive questions to Childs (p. 187); but as he himself observes, however, 'The issues being dealt with . . . are of such substance and complexity that any attempt to solve them here is out of the question' (p. 165).

---

[6] *Biblical Theology of the Old and New Testaments: Theological Reflection on the Christian Bible* (London: SCM, 1992).

[7] For a bibliography of secondary literature on Childs (to 1987), see Charles Joseph Scalise, *Canonical Hermeneutics: The Theological Basis and Implications of the Thought of Brevard S. Childs* (Unpublished Ph.D. thesis; Southern Baptist Theological Seminary, 1987), pp. 222–47.

[8] For a summary of recurrent criticisms see Frank A. Spina, 'Canonical Criticism: Childs Versus Sanders', in W. McCown and J.B. Massey (eds.), *Interpreting God's Word for Today* (Indiana: Warner, 1982), pp. 181–83.

[9] 'Canonical Criticism', pp. 183–86. Since for the themes that will be considered in this book the differences are far more significant than the similarities, I shall have little to say about Sanders.

[10] Better in this respect is Gerald T. Sheppard's 'Canon Criticism: The Proposal of Brevard Childs and an Assessment for Evangelical Hermeneutics', *Studia Biblica et Theologica* 4 (1974), pp. 3–17.

Turning, then, to the more extensive discussions of Childs' programme, there are four scholars whose work should be particularly mentioned. Firstly, John Barton has made an important assessment of Childs' methodology from a literary perspective. Barton construes Childs' canonical principle as a hermeneutics that focuses on how the Bible should be *read* (namely, as a unified whole) rather than upon the intentions of the original writers,[11] and therefore tries to assess the viability of Childs' methodology by comparing his work with various anti-intentionalist schools of literary criticism (especially New Criticism and Structuralism). I shall argue presently, however, that this gives an unbalanced construal of Childs' work, which overlooks the substantial role that historical-critical considerations play within his programme.[12] Nonetheless, Barton's literary discussions are also of some importance for Childs, and have been helpful in clarifying the issues raised by 'interpretation in the context of the canon'— although he has made rather less progress towards resolving them.

The second book to mention here is James Barr's *Holy Scripture*.[13] Insofar as this discusses Childs—which it does at considerable length— it is a quite peculiar piece of work. Although Barr is highly critical of Childs, he shows little comprehension of the structure and goals of Childs' programme; on the contrary, his expositions of Childs often descend into caricature and misrepresentation.[14] Nonetheless, Barr has a surer instinct than most other scholars for what the important issues are; and although his inability to understand Childs means that his comments are often very wide of the mark, he is usually commenting on something important. I shall take up a number of specific points in subsequent chapters; for now it suffices to note that Barr is particularly concerned that Childs is marginalizing the historical-

---

[11] *Reading the Old Testament: Method in Biblical Study* (London: DLT, 1984), p. 81.

[12] See section 3.2 below.

[13] *Holy Scripture: Canon, Authority, Criticism* (Oxford: OUP, 1983). Cf. also his 'Childs' *Introduction to the Old Testament as Scripture*', *JSOT* 16 (1980), pp. 12–23, which anticipates several of the points he develops in *HS*. Several of Barr's criticisms have been reiterated by Manfred Oeming in his very negative evaluation of Childs, *Gesamtbiblische Theologien der Gegenwart* (Stuttgart: Kohlhammer, 1985).

[14] As Childs himself comments, with some justice: 'I come away from reading Barr's book with the impression that the major concerns of my Introduction have been badly misinterpreted. . . . It is troubling when an author scarcely recognises his own profile in another's mirror. . . . I feel strongly that Barr has misconstrued my approach and consistently read my book against the grain' ('Review of *Holy Scripture: Canon, Authority, Criticism* by James Barr', *Int* 38 (1984), p. 67). Cf. Sheppard, 'Barr on Canon and Childs'; unfortunately much of Sheppard's response to Barr is unduly *ad hominem*, and does little to clarify the issues.

critical approach to Scripture,[15] and that questions of truth, and of 'what really happened', are thereby being neglected.

Thirdly, Charles J. Scalise has looked at the theological background to Childs' work in his doctoral dissertation, *Canonical Hermeneutics: The Theological Basis and Implications of the Thought of Brevard S. Childs.* According to Scalise, 'The canonical approach of Brevard S. Childs is in large measure an extension of the theological hermeneutics of Karl Barth' (p. 4); and in adopting this approach he is clearly tackling issues that are central to Childs' own concerns. As is well known, Childs has often commended Barth for his serious theological engagement with the Bible, and is clearly indebted to him for much of his own methodology.[16] Moreover, Barth has offered numerous examples of theological exegesis at the 'canonical level', and has also been subjected to many of the criticisms which are now being levelled against Childs (particularly concerning his alleged neglect of historical-critical issues). One might therefore hope that an analysis of Barth's hermeneutical and exegetical methodology would yield much that could illuminate Childs' work. Unfortunately, however, Scalise's book is marred by the shallowness of his discussion, with his understanding of Childs being generally accurate but without depth. Consequently, his comparison between these two great scholars rarely does more than point out some fairly obvious similarities and differences (usually with a heavy dependence upon the secondary literature). There nonetheless remains an important task here to be tackled, although it will not be pursued in the present book.

Finally, there are two works by Mark G. Brett to consider: his doctoral dissertation, *The Canonical Approach to Old Testament Study*, and the book derived from it, *Biblical Criticism in Crisis?*[17] In *CAOTS* Brett draws upon recent discussions of sociological theory in order to clarify the aims of the canonical approach. The distinction between 'emic'

---

[15] Cf. Sean McEvenue, 'The Old Testament, Scripture or Theology?', *Int* 35 (1981), pp. 229–42.

[16] See especially Childs' 'Karl Barth as Interpreter of Scripture', in D.L. Dickerman (ed.), *Karl Barth and the Future of Theology: A Memorial Colloquium Held at Yale Divinity School January 28, 1969* (New Haven: Yale Divinity School Association, 1969), where many of Childs' characterizations of Barth's work read uncannily like descriptions of his own canonical approach.

[17] *CAOTS* (Unpublished Ph.D. thesis; Sheffield University, 1988); *Biblical Criticism in Crisis?: The Impact of the Canonical Approach on Old Testament Studies* (Cambridge: CUP, 1991) The latter has been reviewed in some detail by James Barr in *JTS* 43 (1992), pp. 135–41.

and 'etic' studies is used to differentiate between the various kinds of 'interpretative interests' that scholars may have,[18] with Brett arguing that 'Childs advocates *an emic approach to the final form of biblical texts*'.[19] Unfortunately however, this does not, in my view, prove to be a particularly illuminating perspective from which to view Childs' work. The problem is well illustrated by the following passage:

> The task of emic description presents a number of problems which are still hotly debated. . . . (1) can we be certain that anthropologists have not projected a feature of their own culture . . . upon the society being interpreted? (2) How can one determine the reliability of individual 'informants'? (3) Can, indeed, *individuals* give a faithful picture of a whole culture? (4) What bearing does an informant's behaviour have on the interpretation of what he or she is saying? In Old Testament studies we ask similar questions. (1) Can we be certain that biblical scholars have not projected a feature of their own culture . . . upon ancient Israel? (2) How does one determine the reliability of individual author-informants? (3) Can, indeed, *individuals* give a faithful picture of beliefs, practices, or events . . . ? (4) What bearing do reconstructions of social practices and historical events—'informant behaviour'—have on un-derstanding the content of Israelite tradition?[20]

Brett's second set of questions helpfully identify a number of important issues in Old Testament studies, and his suggestion that they might be clarified through considering parallel issues in sociological meth-odology is an interesting one. Apart from the first question, however, this angle of investigation only impinges somewhat tangentially upon *Childs'* specific concerns; consequently, some of the central elements in the canonical approach are handled quite inaccurately, with little feeling for the details and nuances of Childs' thought. (This is par-ticularly the case with historical-critical questions, which, since they are concerned with etic issues, make little contact with Bretts' essen-tially emic construal of Childs.) In other words, the emic/etic cat-egories are too broad, and are too preoccupied with concerns which run athwart Childs' own, for them really to serve Brett's purposes. Thus although he works hard to distinguish between different kinds of emic description, and to grapple with the theoretical problems

---

[18] Cf. Brett's 'Four or Five Things to Do with Texts: A Taxonomy of Interpre-tative Interests', in David J.A. Clines *et al.* (eds.), *The Bible in Three Dimensions* (JSOTS 87; Sheffield: Sheffield Academic Press, 1990), pp. 357–77.

[19] *CAOTS*, p. 98; Brett's italics.

[20] Pp. 50–51; Brett's italics.

they raise, the insight which this offers into Childs' work is generally quite moderate.

Although the emic/etic distinction continues to play an important role in *Crisis?*, Brett has by this stage become more cautious in his use of it. Childs' canonical approach is now described as 'a new type of interpretative interest (most closely related to, but distinguishable from, emic description) which . . . seeks to interpret texts in their final form' (p. 27). As one might expect from this parenthesizing of the emic, it is no longer used to illuminate the tangled methodological web that it was introduced with in *CAOTS*. In *Crisis?*, rather, there is a redirecting of the argument towards Brett's thesis that biblical studies should follow a policy of 'hermeneutical pluralism', in which different interpretative interests are allowed to flourish in relative isolation from one another.[21] Brett sees Childs as being sometimes a pluralist but on other occasions a 'hermeneutical monist', who would like all biblical scholars to adopt his own interpretative interests. The principal aim of *Crisis?*, therefore, is to remodel the canonical approach along consistently pluralist lines. In my view, however, this project is misconceived in a number of respects: Brett's monistic/pluralistic distinction is confused and confusing; the hermeneutical pluralism he advocates is untenable; and his attempted accommodation of Childs' programme to his own pluralistic methodology quickly leads to him giving a distorted presentation of Childs' work.[22] As with *CAOTS*, one comes away from *Crisis?* feeling that Brett has not really grasped what Childs' distinctive 'interpretative interests' actually are.

The major discussions of Childs' work to have appeared thus far, then, are generally disappointing. One important theme that keeps recurring throughout the secondary literature, however, is that Childs' own methodological foundations are insufficient for the superstructure he wishes to build upon them; and this has naturally led to various thinkers and schools of thought being suggested as providing the theoretical underpinning which Childs' work needs.[23] In my view

---

[21] This was already present in *CAOTS* (compare especially *CAOTS* pp. 116–28 with *Crisis?* pp. 41–52); but in the later work it is developed more fully and given a more prominent role.

[22] I shall discuss these points fully in section 6.5 below.

[23] In addition to the writings of Barton, Scalise, and Brett discussed above, see Stephen Fowl's 'The Canonical Approach of Brevard Childs', *ExpTim* 96 (1985), in which comparisons are drawn between Childs and H-G Gadamer. This has subsequently been taken up by Scalise and Brett.

this is a potentially valuable way of trying to rectify what is, I believe, a significant defect in Childs' own presentations of his work. Much of the present book, therefore, will also adopt this strategy. Unfortunately, however, the manner in which it has hitherto been pursued has not always been helpful. In some cases at least, it is difficult to escape the impression that the 'external system(s)' which are canvassed as possible aids for Childs have too readily been regarded as established reference points in their own right. The consequences of this are, on the one hand, an undue haste in criticizing and reconstructing Childs' programme along the lines suggested by the external system, without his work being given sufficient opportunity to explain itself *on its own terms*; and on the other hand, there is a tendency towards accepting the methodology of the external system as an 'assured result' which is simply invoked, rather than itself being critically tested. Not surprisingly, discussions of Childs' work which follow these lines tend to be unilluminating.

Despite, then, the volume of previous discussion, most of the major issues raised by Childs' work still await an adequate analysis. In the present book, therefore, I shall first assess the viability of Childs' canonical approach 'on its own terms', and then suggest how certain weaknesses that emerge from this assessment might be overcome. The next two chapters will offer a detailed analysis of Childs' canonical methodology as it has developed from 'IF' to *BTONT*. This will argue that (i) Childs' earlier discussions are marked by a number of methodological tensions—in particular, between faith and reason, between the descriptive and the normative/constructive tasks, and between the original and the canonical contexts; and that (ii) these tensions have continued to haunt his later work, and are significant factors in his *Biblical Theology* falling some way short of Childs' goals.

Having thus identified a number of problems that are internal to Childs' programme, subsequent chapters will explore various ways in which they might be either avoided or solved. This will broaden out the discussion to cover a number of central issues in biblical methodology and hermeneutics, which will in turn have to be assessed in their own right. In the light of these considerations, various suggestions will be made as to how Childs' programme might be 'reconstructed'. For the most part, however, this will preserve the main objectives and principles of Childs' programme, but will argue that they can be achieved—or at least, that it may be possible to work towards them[24]—in ways that often differ somewhat from those which Childs envisages.

The present book, then, hopes to make a significant contribution both to the assessment of Childs' work and to a number of important issues in biblical methodology and hermeneutics. The place to begin, however, is with an analysis of how Childs has presented his programme.

---

[24] For a programme as complex and diverse as Childs, I am naturally more confident about the defensibility of some aspects than of others.

# CHAPTER TWO

# CHILDS' METHODOLOGY:
# SOME FUNDAMENTAL ELEMENTS

The purpose of this and the following chapter is to identify the key hermeneutical and methodological issues that are raised by Brevard Childs' canonical approach to biblical interpretation, and to trace their development through his publications. Childs' hermeneutics is one strand in a long-running and complex debate, to which many scholars have contributed; so to set his work in some sort of perspective, I shall first review the contrasting methodologies of James D. Smart and Krister Stendahl. This will highlight a number of themes which are of central importance to Childs' own programme. Let us begin, then, with Smart.

## 1. *The Hermeneutical Context*

Smart uses 'Biblical Theology' quite broadly, to denote such study of the Bible as wrestles with its theological dimensions. If 'biblical science' is to do justice to the documents it studies, then (Smart stresses) it must be well-equipped to handle not only literary and historical questions, but theological problems also.[1] In this sense, 'Biblical Theology' is clearly not a distinctively modern development. Smart expresses great admiration for the biblical theology of Luther and Calvin (i.e., for the theological penetration of their exegetical work, p. 49), but notes that their freshness and creativity was stifled in the post-Reformation period by the rigidity of Protestant Orthodoxy. This

---

[1] *The Past, Present, and Future of Biblical Theology* (Philadelphia: Westminster, 1979), p. 11. Smart is critical of Childs' delineation of a distinct American Biblical Theology Movement that spectacularly collapsed in the early 1960s, particularly for his failure to appreciate that this was part of an international interest in biblical theology that has continued to flourish (pp. 22–30). However, Smart is largely talking at cross-purposes to Childs who, while recognizing affinities between scholars on different continents, defines this Movement in terms of a specific set of beliefs (e.g., revelation in history; a distinctive Hebrew mentality, etc.). Cf. Childs' review of Smart's book in *JBL* 100 (1981), pp. 252–53.

was in turn broken by the Enlightenment, with the rise of biblical
criticism; but the new theologies which then resulted were very much
the product of their own day—those influenced by the Enlightenment's
rationalism portrayed Moses and Jesus as great rationalistic teachers,
whereas those who reacted against this aspect of the Enlightenment
produced very different theologies. In time an uneasy recognition
began to grow that each 'biblical' theology bore an uncanny resemblance to the theological stance of its author; and when this led to
radical thinkers such as H.S. Reimarus and D.F. Strauss writing
scandalously unorthodox lives of Jesus, a reaction against biblical
theology set in. From the middle of the nineteenth century attempts
were made to model theological methodology more closely upon that
of the natural sciences, so as to exclude the personal biases of the
investigator and thus arrive at objective truths. In particular, this meant
(Smart reminds us) that theological concerns had to be excluded:
'The biblical scholar was to be purely a historian. Involvement in
theology would endanger the objective scientific character of his investigation' (p. 50). Thus biblical theology was gradually replaced by
history of religion, which studied the history of Israel and the church
as human developments of religious ideas and institutions.

The *religionsgeschichtliche Schule* was dominant, according to Smart,
from about 1875 until the 1930s; yet despite its adherents' disavow-
als, its supposedly objective, purely historical findings were still strongly
coloured by the theological ethos of the period. Smart speaks of 'an
amazing theological naivety among [these] religious experts' (p. 55),
pointing out (pp. 100–102) how easily we can now recognize that
the Pauline theologies of Johannes Weiss and Wilhelm Wrede, ostensibly discovered through impartial historical research, were in fact
strongly influenced by the liberal-theological presuppositions of their
authors' day. Smart therefore warns us that

> we must not divide the twentieth century in biblical science into two
> periods, one purely scientific and untheological, the other primarily
> theological. The interpretation of Scripture never takes place in a theo-
> logical or cultural vacuum, and that larger context with its influence
> must be an essential part of the story of each period. (p. 57)

Nonetheless, while the History of Religions school was in the ascendancy theological interests did go underground, disavowed and unac-
knowledged by most scholars (even though they continued, unwittingly, to be influenced by the prevailing theological liberalism of

their day). Thus it was a major hermeneutical achievement of Karl Barth, particularly in (the much-revised, 1922 version of) his commentary on Romans, to bring the theological questions into the centre of the arena once more. Although Barth had been thoroughly trained in the historical-critical methodology of such men as Johannes Weiss and Adolf Jülicher (his New Testament professors at Marburg), when he came to write his commentary

> he was not content to spell out what the text meant when it was written. He could not separate this from what the text meant now in the midst of a war-torn Europe and in a church sharply divided between a complacent liberalism and a complacent pietism.[2]

These political, social, and ecclesiastical crises awakened Barth to the bankruptcy of the liberal-Protestant theology of his day. The outcome was Barth's development of a new outlook, in which the fundamental concept was God's self-revelation. This revelation 'was hidden in the text of Scripture',[3] and therefore a new approach to the interpretation of Scripture, which could handle this revelatory dimension, was needed. This new approach was Barth's threefold methodology of *Nachdenken*, *Mitdenken*, and *Selberdenken*, which Smart describes thus:

> *Nachdenken* is the whole historical process by which we enter imaginatively into the original situation of the text and think the author's thoughts after him.... *Mitdenken* signifies a second stage in which, consciously or unconsciously, there takes place a mingling of our own thoughts with those of the author. The text speaks, but the hearer also speaks.... He comes to the dialogue with the author with his own present theology, his theory of knowledge, his philosophy.... At the third stage, *Selberdenken*, the interpreter has become so identified with the author that in spite of all differences between the two he almost forgets that he is not himself the author. And now he undertakes to restate the content of the text in the language and thought forms that are most readily comprehensible in his own day. (pp. 66–67)

Insofar as this recognizes that interpretation is not a purely historical task but has a theological component also, Smart considers it to have been a major improvement upon the methodology of the *religionsgeschichtliche Schule*.

It is not necessary for our present purposes to trace the history further, but this account clearly raises a number of methodological

---

[2] Smart, p. 65.
[3] Smart, p. 66.

and hermeneutical questions that are of some importance to Childs—
e.g., concerning the role of one's presuppositions in biblical exegesis,
the (im)possibility of interpretative objectivity, and the relationship
between the historical and the theological tasks. Before discussing
Childs' own views, however, let us first review the very different
methodology of Krister Stendahl. In 'Method in the Study of Biblical Theology', Stendahl succinctly summarises his position as

> the conviction that in the study of biblical theology we must make a
> definite distinction between the descriptive study of the actual theology
> and theologies to be found in the Bible, and any attempt at a norma-
> tive and systematic theology which could be called 'biblical'.[4]

Stendahl sets out this distinction between the descriptive and the
normative more fully, however, in his celebrated article, 'Biblical
Theology, Contemporary'. Like Smart, Stendahl also sees great significance in the *religionsgeschichtliche Schule* setting aside theological questions to concentrate on the historical, but for reasons that are diametrically opposed to Smart's. By bracketing out

> questions about relevance for present-day religion and faith ... the
> *religionsgeschichtliche Schule* had drastically widened the hiatus between our
> time and that of the Bible, between West and East, between the ques-
> tions self-evidently raised in modern minds, and those presupposed,
> raised, and answered in the Scriptures. Thereby a radically new stage
> was set for biblical interpretation. The question of meaning was split
> up in two tenses: 'What *did* it mean?' and 'What *does* it mean?' These
> questions were kept apart long enough for the descriptive task to be
> considered in its own right.[5]

Stendahl is in no doubt that this bifurcation was a Good Thing. By
distinguishing 'then' from 'now', modern theology has developed a
'radical concern for the original *in its own terms*';[6] and it is for this
reason that the descriptive task is capable of being an objective, scientific undertaking whose findings should be acceptable to all scholars, irrespective of their own religious or theological beliefs (p. 422).

  For Stendahl, then, Biblical Theology is to be a purely descriptive
explication of 'what it meant'. This, of course, is not the whole task
of theology, which is also concerned with what, in the light of the

---

[4] 'Method in the Study of Biblical Theology', in J.P. Hyatt (ed.), *The Bible in Modern Scholarship* (London: Carey Kingsgate, 1966), pp. 198–99.
[5] 'Biblical Theology, Contemporary', *IDB* I, p. 419; Stendahl's italics.
[6] 'BTCon', p. 430; Stendahl's italics.

biblical witness, the modern church ought to believe, and how it ought to live. Answering questions about 'what it means' for today, however, is not the business of Biblical but of Systematic theology. This would require a 'translation' (to use Stendahl's metaphor) of what the New Testament meant into what it means for us today, which would involve very different kinds of consideration from those that were needed for the descriptive task. Stendahl illustrates his point from the use that is sometimes made of the distinction between 'the *historische* Jesus . . . i.e., the picture we can reconstruct . . . about when and where he was born, what he did and said [etc.]' and 'the *geschichtliche* Jesus', namely, 'what he became in the subsequent history . . . the Jesus tradition as it came to play a meaningful role in the life of the church and in history at large'.[7] Both the *historische* and the *geschichtliche* Jesus (Stendahl observes, p. 201) 'can be studied by the same historical methods'; yet we pass beyond historical description when it is suggested (whether on account of the immense difficulties in recovering the *historische* Jesus or for some other reason) 'that what really matters is *Geschichte*' (p. 201). Stendahl allows that 'It may well be that this method of relating faith to history has its merits'; but his methodological point is that 'If [this is] so, [it] can only be evaluated and assessed within the disciplines of metaphysics or systematic theology' (*ibid.*), because it is the *systematician's* task to make a critical evaluation of the biblical writings, conducted in the light of whatever philosophical, scientific, and other considerations seem to bear upon the matter. It is the systematician rather than the biblical scholar who is equipped for this task (p. 205). Stendahl's basic point, then, is that there are two different kinds of question that can be asked, and each needs its own distinctive types of categories and methods if it is to be properly handled.[8]

That Stendahl's views have been so influential is perhaps due in no small measure to their *prima facie* success in giving a rationale for a long-standing division of labour within theology.[9] Smart, however, (who describes Stendahl as 'one element in the confusion that

---

[7] 'Method', pp. 200–201.

[8] For a thorough discussion of Stendahl's dichotomy see Ben C. Ollenburger, 'What Krister Stendahl "Meant"—A Normative Critique of "Descriptive Biblical Theology"', *HBT* 8 (1986), pp. 61–98. For further bibliography see Ollenburger, p. 91 note 2. I shall take up some of Ollenburger's criticisms of Stendahl in section 12.2 below; my purpose in this and the following section is to consider Stendahl's methodology vis-à-vis those of Smart and Childs.

[9] Cf. Ollenburger, pp. 61–62. According to Childs, 'Stendahl's ['BTCon'] article

constituted and still constitutes the crisis [in Biblical Theology]', p. 41)
has objected to this dichotomy on hermeneutical grounds: Being largely
unaware either of his own theological and cultural presuppositions
or of the extent to which they influence one's exegesis, Stendahl has
a confidence in the ability of the historical-critical methods to discover
objectively 'what it meant' that the hermeneutical insights of Barth
and Bultmann, not to mention the unfortunate examples of the
'objective' historical studies of Weiss and Wrede, show to be quite
unwarranted:

> The scholar, as R.G. Collingwood, Bultmann and others have shown,
> has no access to the original meaning unless the text has some mean-
> ing for him now. Exegesis is a dialogue between the Then and the
> Now. (p. 43)

This, according to Smart, is because the interpreter does not start in
'neutral' but begins from a particular cultural perspective that cannot be shed (p. 103); therefore Stendahl's vision of objective exegesis, with the atheist and believer working together on a purely objective description of 'what it meant', is an impossible ideal, unattainable
not just in practice but as a matter of fundamental principle. In a
passage which, but for its succinct clarity, could have been written
by H-G Gadamer, Smart tells us that

> the biblical scholar who thinks to simplify his task and to guarantee his
> scientific integrity by claiming that he is responsible only to determine
> what the text meant in its original situation sets himself in an irrespon-
> sible isolation. . . . He has no access to the original meanings of the
> text except as the text speaks to him in his twentieth-century world.
> And he takes with him in his investigation of it a mind and a complex
> of cultural and theological traditions other than those of his author.
> His methodology does not make him master of the text, able to declare
> with reasonable finality what it meant, from which can then be de-
> duced by others what it means.[10]

Stendahl, however, has anticipated this objection, and made two points
in reply. Firstly, 'the material itself gives us means to check whether
our interpretation is correct or not'[11]—having formulated our interpretation of a particular text we can carefully compare it with the

---

received such a ready response because he advocated what was, in fact, happening'
(*Biblical Theology in Crisis* (Philadelphia: Westminster, 1970), p. 79).
   [10] Pp. 143–44; I shall discuss these and related aspects of Gadamer's hermeneutics
in chapters 8 and 9 below.
   [11] 'BTCon', p. 422.

text once more to see if this is really what it says. And secondly, different interpreters will be influenced by different biases. Believers will have a natural empathy with the text but be inclined towards reading their own beliefs into it; atheists will not be tempted in this way, but will find it harder to enter into the text's thought-world. Each, however, can engage in 'mutual criticism' of the other, pointing out where their particular biases have led their interpretation astray and thus opening the way for them to be corrected (*ibid.*).

Smart, surprisingly, does not really allow for these replies, although the great majority of scholars (including Gadamer) recognize that there are various 'control mechanisms' by which our presuppositions can be corrected—at least to the extent that interpretation does not degenerate into individualistic accounts of 'how it seems to me'. A question still remains, however, as to whether these controls are 'tight' enough for Stendahl's quest for objective descriptions to be viable, or whether the fact that interpreters begin from a wide diversity of historical and cultural standpoints means that, even when all controls have been allowed for, an irreducible plurality of readings will inevitably remain. I shall return to such questions in subsequent chapters; but for our present purposes sufficient background has now been sketched for us to begin our analysis of Brevard Childs' canonical hermeneutics. This I shall introduce through reviewing Childs' long-running joust with Stendahl.

## 2. *Childs and Stendahl*

We shall see as our exposition progresses that Childs explicitly or implicitly attacks Stendahl's dichotomy in several of his writings (including his most recent work); but by far his most extended discussion occurs in his programmatic essay, 'Interpretation in Faith'.[12] Moreover, Stendahl has briefly responded to this in 'Method', where he comments:

---

[12] This essay is generally recognized as marking a new departure in Childs' thought (see, for example, Spina, 'Canonical Criticism' p. 166; Barr, *HS* p. 153). There are nonetheless important thematic links between Childs' earlier and later work, which have been explored in Brett's insightful discussion of Childs' 1960s monographs (*Crisis?*, pp. 28–38//*CAOTS*, pp. 101–12).

> Childs [thinks] that the descriptive task cannot be seen as a 'neutral'
> preparatory stage to exegesis. This, he says, destroys from the outset
> the possibility of genuine theological exegesis. (p. 203, n. 13)

Having summarized what he takes to be Childs' three main reasons
for this (each of which concerns Childs' belief that the text witnesses
to a divine reality beyond itself), Stendahl continues, 'I fail to see
any of these reasons . . . [as being] capable of substantiating his main
point, i.e., the fallacy in isolating the descriptive task' (*ibid.*).

   Stendahl's comments are tantalizingly brief, but he seems to read
Childs as rejecting a two-stage methodology in which there is a distinct, neutral, descriptive task. Yet although this captures some important aspects of Childs' programme, it does not do full justice to
his thought. On the one hand, there are a number of passages in
'IF' which, *prima facie*, support Stendahl's reading—perhaps most clearly
when Childs tells us that

> The descriptive task lies at the heart of the theological task and is
> never something prior to or outside of the theological endeavour. It is
> not a neutral ground but a part of the exegetical responsibility of studying
> the Bible to hear the Word of God. (p. 438)

This close conjoining of the descriptive, the theological, and the hearing
of God's Word does sound like a rejection of Stendahl's two-stage
procedure. Yet on the other hand there is another strand running
through 'IF' in which Childs does not so much want to reject
Stendahl's dichotomy as to radically question both his conception of
the descriptive task and his account of how the descriptive and normative tasks are related. Childs is, in fact, able to use two-stage language himself in formulating his own methodology:

> Does not theology need normative *as well as* descriptive categories in
> order to execute its task? In other words, many theologians feel the
> need of *going beyond* the historian's task of describing Israel's faith, so
> as . . . to employ the Old Testament witness in building a constructive
> theology.[13]
>
>    A theological commentary has a genuine responsibility to *go beyond*
> describing the changing witness within Israel's tradition; it has *not only*
> a descriptive task but a normative one.[14]

This aspect of his thought becomes clearest, however, when Childs

---

[13] P. 433; italics added.
[14] P. 443; italics added.

discusses his three hermeneutical circles, namely, between the single text and the whole Old Testament, between the Old Testament and the New, and between the Old Testament witness and the theological reality itself (pp. 438–44). There is much in Childs' account of (especially) the first and (also the) second circles which sounds like a new version of the descriptive task, whereas the third circle is concerned with passing beyond this to the constructive/normative.[15] Thus in explaining his first circle Childs emphasizes that the biblical texts are the product of particular historical situations and processes which have left their marks upon them, and therefore affirms the necessity of source- and form-criticism to bring the text 'into sharpest focus' (p. 439); and likewise of his second circle Childs says that 'The central role is to be the historical study of the text' (p. 442). In discussing his third circle, on the other hand, Childs tells us that 'The theological task cannot end with an analysis of a historical witness but must penetrate to that reality which called forth the witness' (p. 444), adding that this is what 'makes possible the penetration of the descriptive categories by normative ones' (*ibid.*). Thus the third circle seems to parallel Stendahl's own transition from the descriptive to the normative.

How these diverse elements are supposed to form a coherent programme will be discussed more fully below; but first there is an obvious objection to Childs which needs to be considered: If interpretation must proceed from faith, is there not a serious danger that each scholar's 'description' of the biblical material becoming a more-or-less overt reading into the texts of his or her own beliefs? Childs, of course, is well aware of this problem, and it is precisely in response to the fear that his plea for faith is 'a gigantic step backwards to the pre-Gabler days when preconceived theological systems silenced the literal meaning of the text' (p. 438) that Childs introduces his three hermeneutical circles, and insists (in filling out the circle between individual text and Old Testament context) that '*there is a descriptive task!*'.[16] But if Childs' circles are capable of exercising this degree of critical control over the claims of faith, are not the latter in danger of becoming so marginalized as to play no substantive role in the exegete's work after all? In that case, however, Childs would

---

[15] Stendahl in fact recognizes this (*ibid.*); but in citing the two-stage elements in Childs against Childs' rejection of a neutral descriptive task he has failed to grasp the alternative methodology that Childs is proposing.

[16] *Ibid.*; Childs' italics.

have reverted to an essentially Stendahlian conception of a neutral description of 'what it meant', with faith only being allowed to play a substantive role at the second stage. Certainly Childs does not intend to marginalize faith—in setting out his first circle he insists that description 'is not a neutral ground' (p. 438)—and yet it is difficult to see what faith is supposed to contribute.

It seems, then, that at the heart of Childs' proposals lies a modern version of the age-old problem of Faith and Reason: If religion can be defended on rational grounds then there appears to be no place for faith; and conversely, if religion claims that faith is 'above' reason, or appeals to a special 'logic of faith',[17] then faith seems to be in imminent danger of degenerating into irrationalism or subjectivism. In other words, is not the very notion of an 'Interpretation in Faith' inherently self-contradictory?

Resolving this difficulty will be one of the major aims of the present book; but at this point it is appropriate to look more closely at how Childs conceives the descriptive task in 'IF'. Childs believes that its nature has been misunderstood by most critical scholars, of whom he sees Stendahl as typical. Symptomatic of this is the failure of many modern commentaries to deal with the *theological* dimension of the Bible.[18] According to Childs, this is a consequence of them using a flawed methodology:

> The fundamental error lies in the starting point. It is commonly assumed that the responsible exegete must start with the descriptive task and then establish a bridge to the theological problem. It is felt that the real problem lies with the second task. Rather, the reverse is true. The basic issue revolves about the definition of the descriptive task. What is the content that is being described and what are the tools commensurate with the task? This is far from obvious. In fact, the answer to this question determines in large measure the character of the entire task of exegesis. (p. 437)

To explore this further, let us look more closely at the two questions

---

[17] As Childs does in answering certain of James Barr's objections ('Response to Reviewers of *Introduction to the Old Testament as Scripture*', *JSOT* 16 (1980), p. 56). In *BTCri* Childs remarks that 'The interpreter is anxious to show the nature of the logic of faith. The joining of the two Testaments does not result in an arbitrary construct . . .', and briefly summarizes some aspects of their 'compatibility' (p. 112). But would a faith that had been demonstrated still be faith?

[18] *The Interpreter's Bible* and the *Biblischer Kommentar* come in for particular criticism, pp. 434–35.

Childs poses here, and particularly note how his answers relate to Stendahl's:

(i) 'What is the content that is being described?' Given the importance of the descriptive task for Stendahl, his answer to this is surprisingly ambivalent. He appears to give a clear-cut response when he describes his methodology as '[making] a definite distinction between the descriptive study *of the actual theology and theologies to be found in the Bible . . .*';[19] i.e., he seems to envisage the descriptive task as primarily theological, and one would therefore expect that the principal objects of study would be the larger, theologically significant units, such as Mark's Gospel or the Deuteronomistic History. This is not borne out by either of his articles, however. On the contrary, the stress in 'BTCon', far from being on these 'higher' levels, is firmly on the original context:

> The first and crucial task of biblical theology—i.e., its descriptive function—. . . yields the original in its own terms, limiting the interpretation to what it meant in its own setting. (p. 425)

Stendahl spells this out quite fully for the Old Testament, where the descriptive task is charged with investigating the 'layers of meaning' that have accumulated through the transmission of the Old Testament traditions (p. 422). Not only must each layer be interpreted in its own setting, but the development of the tradition must be studied within the ongoing life of Israel; therefore the interpretation of a certain layer of the tradition is an investigation into what it meant for a specific community, within the larger history (pp. 422–23). Thus it is not surprising that he particularly praises the works of G.E. Wright and Gerhard von Rad, in which theology is closely allied to historical development (p. 423).

In view of his stress on the original setting, it is hardly surprising that Stendahl is quite dismissive of the biblical canon:

> As far as the descriptive approach goes, the canon can have no crucial significance. . . . In order to grasp the meaning of an OT or NT text in its own time, the comparative material—e.g., the intertestamental literature [etc.]—is of equal or even greater significance than some canonical material. The revival of biblical theology in our own generation depends greatly on the way in which such material was brought to bear on the original meaning of the biblical texts. (p. 428)

---

[19] 'Method', p. 198; italics added.

This conception of the descriptive task, which would clearly create major problems for Childs' hermeneutics, will be assessed in subsequent chapters. For the present, however, I will simply set out Childs' own answer to his question, 'What is the content that is being described?'.[20] In one respect this is very similar to Stendahl's response, namely, in stressing the importance of the original context:

> The biblical text has been transmitted through generations of scribes and bears all the signs of this historical process. To study the text means undertaking a descriptive analysis of this area. (p. 439)
>
> The form-critical method is . . . essential to the descriptive task and is a tool commensurate with the fact that the Bible is a deposit of traditional material, treasured by a community of faith. The framework of faith takes seriously its confession that theological reality is found only in the witness of this historical people whose character is stamped in every detail of existence by common Near Eastern institutions.[21]

Such statements are not typical, however, of Childs' work as a whole. Rather, he is more positive in 'IF' than in his subsequent writings about the *direct* relevance of the history of tradition and the original context, and also, therefore, about the value of the literary-critical tools (although he continues to find a positive role for them in his more recent work). In this respect, Childs is closer to Stendahl here than he will be subsequently.

But turning now to the ways in which Childs differs from Stendahl, there are two main points to notice. Firstly, they disagree over the role of the New Testament. Stendahl sets out his own view in the following passage (which Childs quotes on p. 434):

> The crucial question arises when we ask what impact the NT should have on the presentation of OT theology. When biblical theology allows for such impact, it goes beyond its descriptive task, unless what is being attempted is merely a description of how the early church understood the unity between the OT and its fulfilment in what came to be the NT. But if the biblical theologian should go on to say that this is consequently what the OT text meant, he would be making a statement, either of his own faith or a statement about the faith of the NT.[22]

---

[20] In his later writings a dominant factor will be 'the final (canonical) form of the text'; but this idea plays little part in 'IF'.

[21] *Ibid.* There are some interesting pointers to the future here in the phrases 'historical process' (in the first quotation) and 'community of faith' (in the second); subsequently they will be drawn much closer together in Childs' notion of a canonical process, although here little is made of them.

[22] 'BTCon', p. 424.

Childs vehemently rejects this. His second hermeneutical circle asserts that 'The exegete interprets the Old Testament in the light of the New Testament and, vice versa, he understands the New Testament in the light of the Old' (p. 440), and in the subsequent discussion he is at pains to stress that the relationship is genuinely two-way. The connection between them is not only historical (i.e., with the Old Testament being part of the background against which the New Testament is interpreted) but also ontological (as Childs calls it)—both bear witness to the same God, and therefore 'the exegete seeks to understand the one purpose of God by hearing the dual witness of the Old and New Testaments' (p. 441). Childs' reply to Stendahl thus rests explicitly on a faith-claim: A Christian believes that both Testaments bear witness to the same God (this seems to be part of Childs' definition of 'Christian'), and cannot, in all integrity, simply forget this when she becomes an exegete; rather, she must interpret the Scriptures in a way that accords with what she knows (by faith, or as one who has faith) their true nature to be.

The second way in which Childs' conception of what is to be described differs from Stendahl's is his concentration upon the text rather than the historical events. Admittedly this is implicit rather than explicit—Childs does not actually deny that such description has a place. And yet it is striking that, although he has much to say about textual description, nothing is said about the description of historical events or persons being a significant task. Of course, this does not mean that Childs is completely indifferent to historical questions—on the contrary, when discussing his similarities to Stendahl we noted his (unusually full) commitment to historical-critical research. Nonetheless, historical studies do not seem to progress beyond being 'for the sake of the text' to assume importance in their own right. Instead, the focus is upon investigating (for example) military techniques in the early monarchy so that we can better understand the military allusions in Samuel, rather than showing any interest in reconstructing the life of the historical David.[23] In contrast, Stendahl groups together the reconstruction of the historical Jesus and of the growth of the traditions about him as both being included in the historical-descriptive task, and both being amenable to the same historical

---

[23] 'The descriptive task within the framework of faith seeks to learn everything relevant to the historical background of the text', 'IF' p. 439.

methods.[24] This naturally leads on to Childs' second question:

(ii) 'What are the tools commensurate with the [descriptive] task
[thus conceived]?' Childs' main points here are (1) that the usual
historical-critical tools are *not* adequate for this task; and (2) this is
because they are 'neutral'—i.e., lacking a specifically Christian faith-
commitment. Therefore a new kind of methodology is needed:

> We are arguing that the genuine theological task can be carried on
> successfully only when it begins from within an explicit framework of
> faith. Only from this starting point can there be carried on the exegetical
> task which has as its goal the penetration of the theological dimension
> of the Old Testament. Approaches which start from a neutral ground
> never can do full justice to the theological substance because there is
> no way to build a bridge from the neutral descriptive content to the
> theological reality. (p. 438)

Yet although this makes the general direction of Childs' thought fairly
clear, a certain ambivalence emerges when he tries to explain more
precisely what he considers to be wrong with the historical-critical
methods. Sometimes the problem seems to be that the critical tools
can only do part of the job: The Old Testament is 'a record of
Israel's faith', and therefore needs to be studied in ways that are
capable of capturing this dimension of the text (p. 433), which Childs
clearly thinks the critical tools cannot do.[25] Yet if this were his sole
complaint then his disagreement would not be with the critical methods
as such but with those scholars whose concentration upon the critical aspects of biblical studies leads them to neglect the theological
dimension. That is not Childs' fundamental point however. Rather,
it is that the very nature of the critical approach is such as to make
the theological task virtually impossible:

> The majority of commentators understand the descriptive task as be-
> longing largely to an objective discipline. One starts on neutral ground,
> without being committed to a theological position, and deals with tex-
> tual, historical, and philological problems of the biblical sources before
> raising the theological issue. But, in point of fact, in defining the Bible
> as a 'source' for objective research the nature of the content to be
> described has already been determined. *A priori*, it has become a part

---

[24] 'Method', pp. 200–202.

[25] Nor, of course, is Childs alone in this opinion. Thus, for example, although
John Barton sees many problems in the 'canonical approach', he nevertheless gives
it a cautious welcome insofar as it can handle aspects of the Old Testament that
elude the historical-critical tools (*Reading*, pp. 77–83, 101).

of a larger category of phenomena. The possibility of genuine theological exegesis has been destroyed from the outset. (p. 437)

'Objective' and 'neutral', of course, are the terms which Stendahl uses to commend his descriptive task; but Childs' claim is that they are deeply misleading: Methods which are sufficiently 'neutral' for an atheist happily to use them are not really neutral at all but implicitly *anti*-theological, and are thus quite unsuited for Christian biblical studies. The latter, rather, should start from a 'framework of faith' which

> resists the abuse of an allegedly neutral criticism which would seek to define in advance the nature of biblical reality. The application of dogmatic laws, whether of universal development or of existential self-understanding, prevents one's hearing the full range of notes belonging to the witnesses,[26]

by which, of course, Childs means the theological notes in particular.

Childs' purpose in 'IF', then, is not to *deny* that a distinction can be drawn between the descriptive and the normative but to *relativize* it.[27] His basic methodological objection to Stendahl is that conceiving of these tasks as fundamentally different in kind has inadvertently drawn an iron curtain between them which makes it impossible to pass from the former to the latter. What Childs instead proposes, therefore, is that the descriptive task is also faith-informed, so that there is an essential continuity of character between the descriptive and the normative tasks. Thus it is in explicating his first hermeneutical circle, in which his commitment to historical research is most fully expressed, that Childs makes his most frequent appeals to the 'framework of faith',[28] because only if the descriptive task is understood in this way (Childs claims) can the theological task be properly executed. Or to put it another way (although here, in order to relate 'IF' to Childs' later work, I am indulging in a certain amount of *Selberdenken*) the difference between Introduction and Biblical Theology is primarily a question as to which part of the single theological enterprise

---

[26] P. 439; note also Childs' rejection here of Hegelian or existentialist 'input' into biblical studies.

[27] As Childs himself was to remark a few years later, 'The descriptive and constructive [i.e., normative] aspects of interpretation may well be distinguished, but never separated when doing Biblical Theology according to this model' (*BTCri*, p. 100).

[28] See pp. 439–40, where this phrase occurs six times in the course of Childs' brief delineation of 'the descriptive task within the framework of faith' (p. 439).

one is focusing upon. And because they are both parts of the one
project they must both be undertaken from the same methodological
perspective: A faith-interpretation of the Scriptures that bear witness
to God.

It is appropriate at this point to set out more fully how this broader
project is conceived in 'IF', since Childs lays down a number of
principles here that will later prove to be important for his *Biblical
Theology*. Basically there are three points to make. Firstly, we have
already noted Childs' faith-claim that both Testaments bear witness
to the one God. Secondly, however, each Testament does so in its
own distinctive way, which must not be blurred through unwarranted
harmonizations, or through the New Testament being read back into
the Old. Childs is well aware that theology has hitherto been led
astray by typological exegesis, and is careful to distance his own
approach from it (although he allows that 'There is an analogical
relationship between the action of God in both Testaments', p. 441).
But thirdly, the exegete-theologian must pass beyond the witness of
the scriptures to the reality to which they point:

> The theological task cannot be adequately done when the exegete is
> satisfied only to analyse the witness of scripture and to trace its differ-
> ent levels within the tradition. The final task of exegesis is to seek to
> hear the Word of God, which means that the witness of Moses and
> Jeremiah, of Paul and John, must become a vehicle for another Word.
> The exegete must come to wrestle with the kerygmatic substance which
> brought into being the witness. (p. 443)

This is the ultimate reason why exegesis must proceed from faith,
and why Biblical Theology is a *normative* discipline.

'Interpretation in Faith', then, sets out a wide-ranging theological
programme which, in a number of respects, poses a radical challenge to prevailing wisdom. Some of its proposals (particularly Childs'
comments about passing from witness to divine reality) are very
obscure, and others raise problems to which 'IF' does not itself give
adequate answers: Can a faith-interpretation of the Old Testament
really avoid degenerating into Christian eisegesis? How is such interpretation to proceed?—what is the exegete actually to do in making
a Christian interpretation of Genesis or Hosea? And is it possible for
Childs to maintain his commitment to historical-critical research
without so fragmenting the Old Testament and driving such a wedge
between Old Testament and New as to undermine his claim that
the whole bears witness (albeit in diverse ways) to the one God?

These are issues with which Childs continues to wrestle in his subsequent writings, and will be major themes in the present book.

### 3. *The First Sketch of a New Biblical Theology*[29]

Childs continues to affirm the importance of faith throughout his
subsequent writings, yet in a much more low-key way than in 'IF',
where it dominates the whole discussion. The reasons for this change
of emphasis are not clear, although it is perhaps not unrelated to the
fact that, as James Barr has pointed out, Childs has been unable to
show what concrete contribution faith commitment actually makes
to his programme: 'No aspect that is really dependent on personal
religious commitment is built into the structure or proceedings of
canonical criticism'.[30] Moreover, we shall see that the tensions we
discovered in 'IF' continue to plague his work. And yet faith-commitment is so woven into the fabric of his programme that it cannot
be removed without the whole project being torn apart: For Childs
to call upon the academic community (as he does in 'IF') to interpret the Old and New Testaments as together bearing witness to
God, to pass beyond the witness to engage with the reality to which
it points, and to hear through the human words the Word of God
just *is* to exhort us to engage in faith-interpretation. The hermeneutical
challenge, then, is to transform these general prescriptions into workable exegetical procedures.

Childs' next major methodological work was his 1970 book, *Biblical
Theology in Crisis*. This has many points of continuity with 'IF', including the rejection of Stendahl's dichotomy (pp. 141–42) and an
explicit appeal to faith in setting out the guiding principles of his
new approach (pp. 99, 112, etc.). There are at least two respects,
however, in which important new ground is broken. Firstly, Childs
introduces in *BTCri* the question of the proper *context* for doing Biblical
Theology. Interpretation can be done from many different contexts,
and Childs points to the study of Hebrew grammar within the family

---

[29] Cf. Childs' own description of *BTCri* in his *Biblical Theology of the Old and New
Testaments*, p. xv.

[30] *HS*, p. 111. One should not overlook, however, Childs' important (though very
sketchy) attempts to fill out 'faith commitment' through appealing to Calvin's doctrine of the Holy Spirit illuminating the biblical interpreter. I shall discuss this fully
in chapter 10 below.

of Semitic languages, and to the comparison of biblical genres with those of Babylon and Egypt, as examples of 'fully legitimate contexts from which to interpret the Bible' (p. 97). His distinctive thesis in *BTCri*, however, is that 'the canon of the Christian church is the most appropriate context from which to do Biblical Theology'.[31] As Childs draws out the implications of this, 'canonical context' becomes a 'bracket' within which he groups his principal themes (most of which are already familiar from 'IF')—to do Biblical Theology in the context of the Christian canon means that the Old and New Testaments are together the Scriptures of the Church, that they are to be interpreted as the medium through which God reveals himself, that they are theologically normative, etc.[32]

Having thus clarified what canonical interpretation involves, Childs next poses the vital question,

> How does the alleged context of the canon relate to the other contexts in which the Bible can be read? Or to put this same question in another form, what is the role of the historicocritical method for the doing of Biblical Theology? (p. 107)

The main point in Childs' answer is the importance of the original setting: The biblical witnesses 'bear all the marks of their historical conditioning', and this not only legitimatizes but necessitates the employment of the critical tools in order that the witnesses be heard from their proper historical setting (p. 112). Yet running through the same section is an equally firm insistence that the Old Testament has a new meaning through being placed in the context of the completed canon—Biblical Theology is concerned with the meaning that the Old Testament has when it is read in the light of the New, and

---

[31] P. 99. This was anticipated, to some extent, by his first two hermeneutical circles in 'IF', which likewise focus our attention upon the 'intertextuality' of interpretation; but in *BTCri* (and subsequent writings) this is both put forward more explicitly and given a much more fundamental role in Childs' programme.

[32] A further implication that Childs draws from his Canonical Principle (as I shall call this giving of priority to the canonical context) is that Biblical Theology should 'take the Biblical text seriously in its canonical form' (p. 102). *Prima facie* this seems very close to 'the normativity of the final form of the text', which becomes a central principle in his later writings; but in fact Childs puts it in opposition here not to earlier forms of the tradition but to approaches that find theologically significant data outside the biblical text (e.g., in the actual historical events). In *BTCri* 'the final form' has not yet become a major element in Childs' thought (although 'canonical context' is clearly moving towards it); nor can it do so until certain changes also occur in Childs' conception of the critical tools. This will be discussed more fully in the next chapter.

Childs particularly commends the work of Calvin and Barth in this respect (pp. 109–11). Yet how these very different approaches to meaning are to be reconciled is left in total obscurity—'original context' and 'canonical context' are simply juxtaposed, with both affirmed as indispensable.

This is clearly inadequate, and in the next chapter we shall see that in his later writings Childs himself significantly modifies this aspect of his thought. But continuing here with *BTCri*, a second way in which it breaks new ground is in its fuller account of how a new Biblical Theology should proceed.[33] Methodologically this is very similar to the position set out in 'IF', but now the rather abstract discussion of principles is supplemented with some extended exegetical examples. The acid test of a Biblical Theology, of course, is its ability to bring the two Testaments together in an illuminating way, and Childs has firmly pinned his colours to this mast by insisting that each Testament should be read in the light of the other, and that both bear witness together to the one divine reality. But reflecting now more concretely on how this might be done, Childs suggests that there are a number of advantages in '[beginning] with specific Old Testament passages within the New Testament':[34] The New Testament thereby provides a warrant for doing Biblical Theology in this way; beginning with a text provides one with biblical categories; it makes clear the dependence of meaning on context; etc.[35]

Childs' approach is best understood from one of his examples, the canonical interpretation of Psalm 8.[36] The first step towards this consists in a study of the psalm in its Old Testament context. Drawing upon the work of Gunkel, Childs first classifies Psalm 8 as a hymn and outlines its threefold structure, before moving on to consider its

---

[33] See especially pp. 111–18.

[34] Pp. 114–15. Childs makes it clear, however, that this is only one of a number of approaches that might be used, and elsewhere suggests that Biblical Theology could also proceed through drawing together passages that have clusters of similar vocabulary (p. 191), or are related through 'conceptual analogies and affinities of subject matter' (p. 195). Childs' concern throughout it to provide safeguards against superficial connections being made with irrelevant parts of the canon, which would only blur the biblical witness.

[35] See p. 115. In his more recent work Childs is quite critical of certain aspects of these proposals (*BTONT*, pp. xv, 76); nonetheless, there remains a strong continuity between his earlier and later conceptions of Biblical Theology.

[36] For interesting discussions of Childs' example see Barton, *Reading* pp. 83–86; Bonnie Kittel, 'Brevard Childs' Development of the Canonical Approach', *JSOT* 16 (1980), pp. 6–8.

relationship to other parts of the Old Testament (p. 152). Here Childs
notes the dependence of Psalm 8 upon the Priestly traditions reflected
in Genesis 1, but is particularly interested in the distinctive use which
has been made of this material. The psalmist has in fact been very
selective, focusing exclusively upon 'the role of man in relation to
God his Creator' (p. 153). In his own reflections upon this theme,
however, the psalmist passes beyond the Genesis traditions in seeing
considerable tension between, on the one hand, man's role as the
lord of creation, and, on the other hand, his insignificance in comparison to the vastness of that creation. Yet the psalmist responds to
this 'clash' not with scepticism but with adoration of God, and with
an affirmation that 'man has indeed been given dominion over all
things'. This, however, 'rests on an act of divine grace' (*ibid.*).

Turning next to the interpretation of Psalm 8 in Hebrews 2, Childs
notes that the New Testament author's use of the Septuagint's translation of this Psalm 'made possible a new direction of interpretation
that had not been available to the reader of the Hebrew text' (p. 156).
The Hebrew had portrayed man as only *a little less exalted* than the
Elohim (which in this instance Childs understands as referring, via
an allusion to the heavenly court, to the image of God in Genesis 1).
The Greek translation, however, used a word with a broader semantic range, which opened up the possibility of this psalm meaning
that man was 'for a little time' less exalted than the Elohim, who are
now interpreted by the Septuagint as the angels. Using these translations, Psalm 8 is now read as a witness to the humiliation and
exaltation of 'the Son of man', which the Christian writer naturally
interprets as a reference to Jesus. By '[reading] into the psalm a full
Christology' (*ibid.*), the author of Hebrews finds that the exalted Christ,
as 'the representative for mankind' (p. 157), fulfils the original promise of man's dominion over creation.

Thus far Childs has been tackling 'the . . . descriptive task' (p. 158);
but Christian theology must 'move from the descriptive task to the
constructive, reflective task of interpreting Ps. 8' (p. 160). Childs gives
a couple of general indications as to how this is to be done: It will
proceed christologically, yet in such a way that the distinctively Old
Testament witness of the psalm is not obliterated through having
New Testament doctrine read back into it (pp. 158–59); and it will
try to hear the two witnesses in relation to one another, and 'grapple
with the reality that called both of them forth' (p. 160). Childs begins by noting that the tension in Psalm 8 between insignificance

and lordship is a common Old Testament theme; but whereas in this psalm it issues in praise of the Creator, elsewhere 'Hebrew man finds himself so overwhelmed by the powers of the world as to threaten any sense of his special role in God's creation' (*ibid.*). When Psalm 8 is seen against this background, however, a substantive continuity emerges between the psalm and Hebrews 2 in their common affirmation that 'man's role in the creation is not simply an idea or wishful thinking on his part' (p. 162). But the author of Hebrews, as a *New* Testament witness, goes beyond this to deal with the tension (to which both Testaments call attention) between the actual and the promised state of man. This he does

> by testifying to God's work in Jesus, the Son of Man. Only when one understands man in the light of the man, Jesus Christ, can he see what God intended humanity to be. . . . This is to say, the New Testament now sees the basic problem that lies behind the Old Testament witness in the light of Jesus Christ, and gives its own clear witness.[37]

The psalmist's witness to man having a special role in creation is reaffirmed, but the New Testament witness adds that the way in which man attains this role is through entering 'the new world to come'. This is the world which Jesus Christ is 'bringing into fulfilment' (*ibid.*).

From the viewpoint of traditional scholarship there are a number of objections that might be raised against Childs: Is it legitimate for him to bring in the broader Old Testament context? Does this not make Psalm 8 and Hebrews 2 appear to be more similar than they really are through blurring their distinctive viewpoints? And has not Childs been tendentiously selective in his use of the Old Testament?— one can find many other parts that show little or no sign of the *angst* he identifies. And granted that the New Testament writer is seeking to resolve certain tensions christologically, has not Childs failed to get to grips with what the central problem really is, namely, that this author bears his christological witness through finding a meaning in Psalm 8 that is simply not justified by what the Hebrew text actually says (whatever context it is read in); and that if this is so, might it not make some difference to our assessment of its witness, and of the possibility of working it into a coherent Biblical Theology?

Such questions will be considered in later chapters (particularly in

---

[37] P. 162; Childs also considers (p. 163) how the New Testament witness is to be read in the light of the Old, but it is unnecessary to review this here.

connection with Childs' *Biblical Theology*); but the immediate task is
to compare what Childs does in this example with his methodological statements. In reviewing Childs' study of Psalm 8, we have seen
him undertaking first a 'descriptive' and then a 'constructive' task.
Childs' willingness to use this Stendahlian vocabulary of his own work
confirms that his basic intention is not to abolish this distinction but
to modify it in certain ways; and yet when we look more closely at
what Childs does at each stage, certain problems appear: His descriptive task seems in fact to be indistinguishable from Stendahl's;
and his constructive task suffers from problems of faith and reason.
Thus as regards the first stage, although Childs eschews discussion of
the dating and possible liturgical functions of Psalm 8 in favour of
delineating its structure and theology, this still falls within Stendahl's
conception of a neutral explication of 'what it meant'.[38] It is difficult
to point to anything that Childs does here that an atheist could not,
in principle, also do—*prima facie*, there seems to be no more reason
why one would need to believe in the Christian God in order to
describe the Old Testament accurately (including its theology) than
one would need to worship Baal in order to give an accurate description of Canaanite religious beliefs and practices. By contrast,
Childs' execution of the constructive/normative task does proceed
from a definite faith commitment, yet in ways that apparently separate faith from reason or even set them against each other. Thus
there would seem to be little point in affirming that '[the] . . . writer
of Hebrews . . . finds in . . . psalm [8] a witness to the humiliation
and exaltation of Jesus through whose suffering man's salvation was
won' (p. 160) if sound exegetical reason shows that the Hebrew text
of this psalm means no such thing. In other words, Childs has not
adequately shown that this *is* a reasonable 'faith interpretation' of
Psalm 8, rather than a christologically motivated misinterpretation
which hears in this text things that it does not actually say.

To summarise, then: In *BTCri* Childs sets out a conception of Biblical Theology in which there is an indispensable faith component,
but has not been able to give an adequate account of how it actually
functions.

This is also an appropriate point at which to say something about
the role of biblical inspiration in Childs' programme. Although,
officially, 'canonical context' is the fundamental principle of his ap-

---

[38] Cf. Stendahl's own comments on Childs in 'Method', p. 203 n. 13.

proach, what often seems to be doing the real work (although from just below the surface) is a belief in the 'inspiration' (in quite a strong sense) of the canonical text: If the Old and New Testaments are both inspired by God then it follows immediately that the interpreter ought to read them as dual witnesses to the one divine reality, accept them as theologically normative, eschew searches for a 'positivity behind the text', etc. In other words, granted a suitable doctrine of inspiration, the rest of Childs' programme flows naturally from it.

These thoughts can be made more precise by reviewing James Barr's insightful characterization of Childs' relationship to the American Biblical Theology Movement (the demise of which Childs analysed in *BTCri*). Although this movement made little overt appeal to the concept of the canon, Barr sees this as having been one of its central concerns:

> The earnest emphasis of the movement on the unity and distinctive-
> ness of the Bible was an implicit welcome to the idea of the canon as
> boundary of a highly special area. . . . What was within was (in some
> way) revelation, what was outside was something different.[39]

Given this canonical orientation, Barr makes the interesting suggestion that much of the movement's activity can be seen as a quest for some principle or concept that would mark off just these writings as normative Scripture, with *Heilsgeschichte*, Hebrew mentality, existential self-understanding, and the like, being the various candidates that were proposed. Each of these candidates (Barr observes) was a *material* principle, i.e., it sought to '[locate] biblical uniqueness in some aspect of its *content*';[40] but unfortunately they all failed to mark out the unique-ness of just those writings that the church accepted as canonical. So, for example, even if *Heilsgeschichte* was a valid way of presenting the historical writings as normative Scripture, it could do little with the Wisdom material; Hebrew mentality turned out to be not so differ-ent from that of other ancient Near Eastern peoples, and thus largely failed to mark off the Scriptures as the unique locus of God's revela-tion; etc. Thus Biblical Theology fell into a state of crisis because it repeatedly failed to locate a viable distinguishing principle.

Relating this to Childs' programme, Barr rightly sees Childs as sharing many of the values and concerns of the old Biblical Theology

---

[39] *HS*, p. 134.
[40] P. 135, Barr's italics.

Movement, and thus in large measure trying to carry on essentially the same programme, though by very different means. Childs' major departure from the old movement, however, is that instead of seeking a new material principle, he has proposed a *formal* principle, namely, the canon. This, Barr observes, solves for him the major problems of the old movement at a stroke:

> By its own nature it coincides exactly with the boundary of scripture. . . . By taking the canon as principle one was no longer forced to argue that there was an absolute difference in content, in ideas, in thought patterns, between the Bible and the rest of the world. . . . The biblical material was normative, not because it was necessarily different in content, but because the canon separated it off and gave it its distinctive shape. (p. 135)

Thus 'The canon was the Grail for which the American Biblical Theology Movement had been the Quest' (p. 136).

To my mind the main question raised by Barr's illuminating discussion is whether a formal principle is capable of fulfilling the same role as a material one; and in particular, what bearing this has upon the question of revelation. The various material principles, precisely because they were concerned with the *content* of the Bible, were also (to a greater or lesser extent) accounts of how God revealed himself. This is particularly clear in the case of *Heilsgeschichte*; and yet existential encounter, Hebrew mentality, and the rest, were each in their own way an attempt to mark out some special sphere or aspect of the world through which God has made himself known. And because of this, each of these principles, if it had solved the boundary problem adequately, would also have been theologically self-justifying—if God has revealed himself through the history of Israel and the life of Jesus as the *Heilsgeschichte* theologians envisaged, then this obviously has to be the central, organizing, and unifying principle of one's theology. Such is not the case, however, with a formal principle. Since this is *not* based on (some aspect of) the Bible's contents, it is not self-justifying—when Childs offers 'canonical context' as the fundamental principle for biblical interpretation, we are left asking for some further justification—Why these particular writings? Why in their final form?—in a way that we are not so left by a material principle. In other words: Canon, as a formal principle, is able to tell us *what* we ought to do (read each passage in the context of the whole, etc.) but not *why* we should do so, or why we are able to do so. Such questions can only be answered by a principle that is based upon the material content of the Scriptures.

Childs himself shows some awareness of these problems when, criticising the Biblical Theology Movement for replacing 'the theology of the inspiration of Scripture . . . by a theology of Scripture as revelation', he suggests that

> the effort to take seriously the confession of a canon offers another alternative in respect of the inspiration of Scripture. . . . [namely,] the claim for the inspiration of Scripture is the claim for the uniqueness of the canonical context of the church through which the Holy Spirit works.[41]

This is decidedly vague; yet Barr's formal/material distinction points to a useful division of labour in developing a more precise theory of inspiration. On the one hand, the material aspect of the theory, being concerned with the substantive content of God's relationship to the Bible, would raise a host of difficult theological problems (concerning, for example, the 'mechanics' of how inspiration 'works'). To discuss these issues is far beyond the scope of this book. In section 12.3, however, I shall develop a formal theory of inspiration through suggesting an exegetical model which mirrors Childs' notion of canonical context, and which thus explicates it in such a way as to have significant exegetical consequences.

## 4. Re-Assessing Critical Exegesis

We have seen, then, that Childs' earlier conceptions of a new Biblical Theology are beset with a number of difficult problems. Childs himself was not unaware of this, and the appearance in 1979 of his Old Testament *Introduction* marked some important reconceptions of his programme (particularly with regard to the historical-critical tools). Significant steps towards this had already been taken, however, with the publication of Childs' commentary on Exodus, and with the appearance in 1976 (when work on *IOTS* was presumably well under way) of Childs' important article on 'The Sensus Literalis of Scripture'.[42] The purpose of the present section, therefore, is to review these works.

---

[41] *BTCri*, p. 104.

[42] 'The Sensus Literalis of Scripture: An Ancient and Modern Problem', in Herbert Donner (ed.), *Beiträge zur Alttestamentlichen Theologie. FS für Walther Zimmerli zum 70. Geburtstag* (Göttingen: Vandenhoek & Ruprecht, 1977), pp. 80–93. This article has

Although *Exodus: A Commentary*[43] was published in 1974, Childs'
interests in Exodus extended back some twenty years prior to this,
and he was actively at work on the commentary over a period of ten
years. Much of it was presumably written, therefore, in and around
the period from 'IF' to *BTCri* which we have been considering, and
methodologically it does appear, for the most part, to be closely related
to these works. *EC* is a complex and wide-ranging book which, in
addition to the philological and historical-critical discussions that one
would expect to find in a modern scholarly commentary, also has
extensive sections on such topics as the New Testament's use of
Exodus, and on the history of its exegesis. Moreover, Childs himself
identifies 'the heart of the commentary' as lying not in the philological and critical material but in '[t]he sections on Old Testament
context, New Testament context, and theological reflection [in the
context of the canon]' (p. xvi). From his explanations of the purposes
of these sections (pp. xiv–xvi), it becomes clear that they are meant
to perform, respectively, the Old and New Testament descriptive tasks
and the constructive/normative task that we have already seen Childs
tackling in *BTCri*. Childs' intention in these sections of *EC*, then, is
to extend the sort of study that he had made of Psalm 8 in *BTCri* to
the whole of Exodus.[44]

The great diversity of material in *EC* itself raises an important
methodological question as to how this is to be structured into a
coherent whole. It is in this connection that Childs introduces a new
principle which will prove to be highly significant for his subsequent
work. We saw in section 3 that one of the major unresolved issues
in *BTCri* was the relationship between studying a text in its original
context and its canonical context. Childs now proposes that there
should be a definite subordinating of the interests of the one to the
other, with the primary purpose of the former (at least, in a canonical

---

been heavily criticized by James Barr, 'The Literal, the Allegorical, and Modern
Biblical Scholarship', *JSOT* 44 (1989), pp. 3–17; cf. Barr's articles on Benjamin
Jowett (with whom Childs had taken issue in 'SLS'): 'Jowett and the Reading of the
Bible "Like Any Other Book"', *HBT* 4 (1988), pp. 1–44; and 'Jowett and the "Original
Meaning" of Scripture', *RelStud* 18 (1982), pp. 433–37. Childs has replied to 'Lit-
eral' in 'Critical Reflections on James Barr's Understanding of the Literal and the
Allegorical', *JSOT* 46 (1990), pp. 3–9, and I have discussed their debate in 'The
*Sensus Literalis*: Jowett, Childs, and Barr', *JTS* 44 (1993), pp. 1–23.

[43] OTL; London: SCM, 1974. For the following points see p. x.
[44] This is implicitly confirmed by the section in *EC* on Moses' slaying of the
Egyptian taskmaster (pp. 27–46), which largely reproduces the study of this pericope
that Childs had published in chapter 10 of *BTCri*.

commentary) being to aid the latter: 'In my judgement, the study of the prehistory has its proper function within exegesis only in illuminating the final text' (p. xv). Unfortunately, however, the bulk of the commentary does not observe this principle, there being numerous cases in which, as Childs himself admits, 'the prehistory is quite irrelevant to understanding the synchronistic dimension of the biblical text' (p. xiv). This results in the 'Traditio-Historical Problems' and 'Old Testament Context' sections often being virtually unrelated.[45] One gets the impression, in fact, that much of the historical-critical work in *EC* was done before Childs had clearly formulated his ideas on just how this was to serve the larger goals of his work.

There is one further comment to make on the 'Old Testament Context' sections. It will be recalled that in 'IF' Childs' first hermeneutical circle proposed that the individual text was to be interpreted in the context of the whole of the Old Testament, and the heading to these sections in *EC* suggests that Childs is now going to address himself to this important task. In practice, however, his aim is much more modest. As Brett has aptly observed, these sections could have been more accurately entitled 'Exodus Context', since 'many of the references to other books in the Old Testament are simply comparative in nature, and they have no direct bearing on the final form interpretation'.[46] For 'final form interpretation' on the scale that 'IF' envisages, one has to await the publication of Childs' *Old Testament Theology*.

In summary, then, *EC* shows that Childs was now hard at work in many different fields, and had also taken certain steps towards tackling the residual methodological problems of *BTCri*. At this stage, however, the latter had not made sufficient progress to enable him to organize into a coherent programme the many disparate factors which, in his view, ought to be part of a 'new biblical theology'. The result is that *EC* too often reads like a number of separate books

---

[45] Similar comments also apply to the 'History of Exegesis' sections. These clearly reflect Childs' long-standing orientation towards the Old Testament as the Scriptures of the church, and more specifically, are intended to show how 'the questions which are brought to bear [upon Exodus] by subsequent generations of interpreters influenced the answers which they received' (p. xv). Serious doubts have been raised, however, both as to how successful Childs is in achieving this goal and as to whether a commentary is the right place even to attempt such an exercise. See Barr, *HS* pp. 162–64; Brett, *Crisis?* pp. 52–57 // *CAOTS* pp. 129–34.

[46] *Crisis?*, p. 39 // *CAOTS*, p. 113; cf. James Wharton, 'Splendid Failure or Flawed Success?', *Int* 29 (1975), p. 274.

that have been interleaved with one another. Clearly, more work is still needed on the methodological issues.

This brings us next to Childs' *Sensus Literalis* article. Tracing the different conceptions of 'literal meaning' that have been offered by various scholars, both Christian and Jewish, Childs finds a high-point in the work of the Reformers, and especially of Calvin. Calvin's exegesis focused on the text itself, rather than trying to penetrate behind it,

> because for him the text was the faithful vehicle for communicating the oracles of God. Calvin does not therefore need to add a secondary or spiritual meaning to the text because the literal sense is its own witness to God's divine plan. (p. 87)

That is, he understood 'the single true sense of the text' to be 'both literal and spiritual' (*ibid.*); or, as Childs explains in *BTCri*, Calvin could frequently speak of Christ when interpreting the Old Testament because for him this *was* the plain sense of the text, when interpreted in its full canonical context (p. 110).

This understanding of the matter, however, did not survive the rise of the historical-critical approach. Drawing heavily upon Hans Frei's *The Eclipse of Biblical Narrative*,[47] Childs outlines how the 'literal meaning' of the text subsequently came to be much more narrowly conceived as the meaning it had in its original historical context. I shall discuss this in section 11.2 below; but for now we can note that, according to Childs, one consequence of this change is that

> an almost insurmountable gap has arisen between the historical sense of the text, now fully anchored in the historical past, and the search for its present relevance for the modern age.[48]

This, of course, is another stab at Stendahl; and yet a very significant shift has occured from 'IF' and *BTCri*. There the insurmountability of the gap was variously blamed on interpretation not being done from a faith stance, or on the neglect of the theological dimension of the texts; but now this problem is blamed much more directly upon the quest for the original meaning. Having found it, Childs claims, scholars were stuck with it, unable to move from there to a meaning for the present. Summing up, Childs makes the devastating judge-

---

[47] *The Eclipse of Biblical Narrative: A Study in Eighteenth and Nineteenth Century Hermeneutics* (New Haven: Yale University Press, 1974).
[48] 'SLS', p. 91.

ment that, while the intention of the historical-critical method had been 'to free the text from the allegedly heavy hand of tradition and dogma', in fact 'the effect was actually to destroy the significance, integrity, and confidence in the literal sense of the text' (pp. 91–92). This is a much more negative evaluation of the critical approach than Childs had made hitherto.

Unfortunately 'SLS' gives far more attention to analyzing the problem than to developing a solution; but it is a clear sign that by this stage a major rethinking of Childs' programme was in progress.

# CHAPTER THREE

# FROM CANONICAL INTRODUCTION TO
# BIBLICAL THEOLOGY

The rumblings of discontent with which the previous chapter ended soon bore abundant fruit in Childs' significantly entitled *Introduction to the Old Testament* As Scripture.[1] Childs has himself pointed out that *IOTS* marks a significant shift in his conception of Biblical Theology, it having been born (following the publication of *BTCri*) of a growing conviction that 'biblical theology could not be done . . . by adding a layer of icing on the historical critical Introduction.'[2] Therefore in *IOTS* Childs set himself to 'reexamine the foundations' of his theological programme (p. 199).

## 1. *Canonical Context and Canonical Process*

We saw in section 2.3 above that *BTCri* had raised but not solved the problem of how canonical context was related to original context, and what contribution, therefore, the critical tools were expected to make to Childs' theological programme. In *IOTS* Childs works out in detail a solution to this problem that has far-reaching consequences for his subsequent work. Although he continues to recognise that the biblical writings can legitimately be studied in many different contexts, he now sets off the canonical context from the others much more sharply than in *BTCri* through asking *for whom* is each context legitimate?, and *for what purpose?*. In a brief but very important aside, Childs remarks:

> Of course, it is legitimate and fully necessary *for the historian of the ancient Near East* to use his written evidence in a different manner [from the

---

[1] Useful epitomes of *IOTS* are provided by Childs' articles, 'The Exegetical Significance of Canon for the Study of the Old Testament', *VTSup* 29 (1978), pp. 66–80 and 'The Canonical Shape of the Prophetic Literature', *Int* 32 (1978), pp. 46–50, both of which summarize the methodology of *IOTS* and give some pertinent illustrations.

[2] 'A Response [to James Mays *et al.*]', *HBT* 2 (1980), p. 206.

theologian], often reading his texts obliquely, but *his enterprise is of a different order* from the interpretation of sacred scripture which we are seeking to describe.[3]

Childs is here making the straightforward but nonetheless important point that *how* one studies the Scriptures—whether one analyzes the Pentateuch into underlying documents, which are then used to re-construct the development of Israel's religion, or whether one inter-prets it in its final, canonical form—will depend upon the *purpose* for which the study is undertaken. Experts from different disciplines therefore need to consider how the Scriptures might best be studied in order to attain their own scholarly goals. The answers given may well vary considerably from one discipline to another.

This 'Relevance Principle' (as I shall call it) is fundamental to *IOTS*, because it enables Childs to perform what Anthony Thiselton calls a 'metacritical ranking' of the various interpretative tasks.[4] For any particular Old Testament writing there are many different kinds of question one could ask about its underlying sources, their use of older traditions, the redactor's *tendenz*, etc. If Childs' Introduction had at-tempted to review all these issues 'on a par', and had also analyzed the canonical shape of the literature's final form, the result would almost certainly have been a highly diverse collection of material with little internal coherence or overall shape, precisely because these different kinds of study are undertaken in different contexts and for different ends.[5] In Childs' view, this sort of failure to consider *why* one is engaging in this or that critical pursuit is one of the principle reasons why critical studies of the Old and New Testaments have often hindered rather than helped Biblical Theology. What is needed, therefore, is a fundamental reassessment of their role. This, then, is the main problem which Childs is tackling in *IOTS*, which can thus be characterized as an extended plea for us to rethink the relevance of the critical approaches to the broader theological enterprise.[6]

This brings us to consider more closely the role which Childs assigns to the historical-critical tools within his overall programme.[7] According

---

[3] *IOTS* p. 76, italics added. A very similar point has been made by Gerhard von Rad, *Old Testament Theology* I (London: SCM, 1975), pp. 105–106.

[4] *New Horizons in Hermeneutics* (London: Harper-Collins, 1992), pp. 315–18, etc.

[5] We have seen, in fact, that Childs' own *EC* provides some good illustrations of this.

[6] Cf. *IOTS*, pp. 13, 45, 83, etc.

[7] Childs emphasises throughout *IOTS* the positive contribution which the critical tools make to his work, thus setting off canonical hermeneutics from precritical interpretation.

to Childs, the critical approach has performed an indispensable service
for biblical studies by bringing to light the many problematic features of the text (e.g., changes of style and outlook, dislocations in
the line of thought, schematizing and idealizing tendencies, etc.). These
were largely unknown to pre-critical scholars, and are glossed over
by anti-critical scholars only through an unacceptable *sacrificium
intellectus*. In both cases this has resulted in unduly 'flat' readings of
the Bible, which fail to take seriously the character of the text which
is being interpreted. Illustrating his case from Habakkuk, Childs first
reviews the critical study of this book and then comments,

> In my judgement, the genuine contribution of this history of scholar-
> ship has been to point out a variety of difficult problems which, when
> once seen, prevent all efforts at glossing over homiletically. (p. 450)

At this stage in his development, then, Childs apparently has no
reservations about the intrinsic soundness of the critical methods or
the value of the results they are capable of producing. What he does
take issue with, however, is the (as he sees it) unduly destructive,
anti- (or at least a-) theological bias that has typically characterised
their use.[8] A 'doctrinaire application of historical criticism . . . [raises]
a series of wrong questions', and thereby 'effectively blocks true insight' into the material it is studying (p. 455).

What Childs tries to do in *IOTS*, therefore, is to find a new role
for the fruits of critical research, by which they can make a positive,
constructive contribution to the theological reading of the Bible as
scripture.[9] Unlike the anti-critical approach Childs refuses to gloss
over the inconcinities that critical research has uncovered; but unlike
the usual critical approach he will not use its tools to refocus attention upon the reconstructed traditions and/or events behind the text
(a procedure which, for reasons that I will return to shortly, he believes to be destructive of the text *as Scripture*). Rather, Childs' aim is

---

[8] Unfortunately Childs is sometimes unduly negative in his portrayal of mainline
critical scholarship, tending to speak as though the historical orientation of the
*Religionsgeschichte Schule* was typical of scholarship as a whole. Elsewhere Childs does
express his appreciation of the theological dimension in the work of such scholars as
Wolff, Zimmerli, and von Rad; nonetheless, he claims that they achieved this apart
from (or perhaps even despite) their use of the critical tools, rather than through it.
See, for example, 'A Response', p. 208.

[9] In his comments on the critical study of the Pentateuch Childs describes his
approach as 'post-critical' (p. 127), in that it fully accepts the critical results but,
through building upon them, tries to pass beyond them.

to understand how the various tensions which critical studies has discovered in the biblical writings contribute to the meaning of the text as we now have it, in its canonical form. Thus commenting on Exodus he writes,

> A literary analysis of sources is frequently of great help in hearing precisely the different witnesses within a passage. However, when the attempt is made to treat the sources as separate theological entities, an assumption of an isolation between sources is at work which runs counter to the canonical traditioning process and which disregards the way the material was used authoritatively within a community of faith and practice.[10]

Childs' aim, then, is to resolve the tension that arose in *BTCri* between 'original context' and 'canonical context' by using the critical study of the text's prehistory to illuminate the meaning of the text in its final form. The former is thus subordinated to the latter in order to achieve Childs' ultimate theological goal.

## 2. *The Final Form of the Text*

This brings us to the best known aspect of Childs' *Introduction*, namely, that 'Canonical analysis focuses its attention on the final form of the text itself. . . . It treats the literature with its own integrity' (p. 73). In some respects this is a less contentious claim than it was when *IOTS* first appeared in 1979—'literary approaches' to the Bible, which generally (though not always) focus upon the text in its final form, now have a well-established place in Biblical Studies. Childs' own approach to the final form, however, remains quite distinctive in a number of ways. Firstly, literary approaches generally have little interest in the critical reconstructions of traditional scholarship, finding its methods and results largely irrelevant to their own literary

---

[10] P. 177; cf. the similar comment on redaction criticism on p. 383. The distinction that Childs is apparently trying to draw between 'witnesses' and 'theological entities' is far from clear, but it may be that the latter (which Childs associates here with 'sources' and contrasts unfavourably with the diverse 'witnesses' within a passage) may be alluding to, for example, redaction-critical studies of 'the theology of J' which explicate it solely as historically conditioned, human thoughts about God, which arise from the author's particular social and political circumstances. Childs' point in this passage, then, would seem to be that although we can recognize a plurality of voices within Exodus they are to be heard as a polyphonic chorus of witnesses to God, not as spokesmen for a plurality of political parties.

concerns[11]—boundaries between sources, if noted at all, are freely
read across; questions of 'what really happened' are not raised; etc.
Childs, by contrast, comes to the canonical text with an acute awareness of these matters, and tries (as we have just seen) to incorporate
the results of critical research into his readings of the final form.
And secondly, whereas literary studies are for the most part taken
up with questions of character, plot development, narrative technique,
and the like, Childs' concern is first and foremost with the final form
of the text as *theologically normative*. This necessarily orientates his work
towards various specifically theological and historical debates. It means,
for example, that Childs needs to defend his giving of priority to the
final form against those who find the primary *locus* of God's revelation in Israel's developing traditions, or against those who see the
canonical texts as the product not primarily of theological reflection
but of political and sociological forces. This again takes Childs into
territory quite different from the literary critic's.

In view, then, of the distinctive character of Childs' concern for
the final form, it is worth looking at his specifically theological reasons for according it priority. One such reason turns on a certain
conception of the relationship between Israel's encounters with God
and the canonical process which shaped the Scriptures. As Childs
explains it,

> The reason for insisting on the final form of scripture lies in the pecu-
> liar relationship between text and people of God which is constitutive
> of the canon. The shape of the biblical text reflects a history of en-
> counter between God and Israel. The canon serves to describe this
> peculiar relationship and to define the scope of this history by estab-
> lishing a beginning and an end to the process.... The significance of
> the final form of the biblical text is that it alone bears witness to the
> full history of revelation.[12]

Childs admits that earlier stages of the text were also once regarded
as canonical; yet they are not to be so regarded today, or made the
object of theological study, precisely because the canonical process
moved on past that stage. Therefore to recover the separate theologies
of J and P is to prescind from the full witness to God's revelation, in
favour of a partial witness that has long since been superseded.

---

[11] See, for example, David Gunn and Danna Fewell's recent introduction, *Narrative in the Hebrew Bible* (The Oxford Bible Series; Oxford: OUP, 1993), pp. 11–12.

[12] Pp. 75–76; almost identical passages also occur in 'Canonical Shape' (p. 47)
and 'Exegetical Significance' (p. 69).

Another consideration to which Childs sometimes appeals is that it is the final form which has functioned as the scriptures of the church. Childs is troubled by the

> enormous hiatus between the description of the critically reconstructed literature and the actual canonical text which has been received and used as authoritative scripture by the community,[13]

and therefore proposes that it is the final form which should be accepted as theologically normative. I cannot see, however, that this argument carries much weight. For most of its history the church has had no choice but to use the final form of the text, simply because this was the only form available. If however, like Childs, we believe that critical studies has in some cases recovered the underlying sources then a choice now *is* available, and it has to be made in the light of the relative merits of each option. If instead such matters were decided simply by appealing to what, *de facto*, has hitherto prevailed, then a good case could surely be made for the Septuagint and/or Vulgate rather than the Hebrew text being accepted as the canonical Old Testament; but as Childs himself argues for this latter case, there may be other grounds upon which the church's actual usage can be criticized and corrected.[14] The primary question to be asked with regard to the final form, therefore, is whether, in the light of recent discoveries, the church's current practice should now be reformed; therefore in appealing to this practice as simply 'given' Childs is putting the cart before the horse.

A further argument that can be reviewed here turns on the observation that reconstructions of the traditions behind the text is necessarily hypothetical and often quite uncertain; studying the final form, by contrast, gives one a definite text to interpret.[15] In my view, how-

---

[13] *IOTS*, p. 40.

[14] See *IOTS* pp. 97–99, 664–65. Whether or not the arguments Childs rehearses here establish the particular position he favours is not germane to the present discussion.

[15] See, for example, R.W.L. Moberley, *At the Mountain of God: Story and Theology in Exodus 32–34* (*JSOTS* 22; Sheffield: *JSOT* Press, 1983), p. 21. Moberly claims (*ibid.*) that Childs himself uses this as an argument for the priority of the final form; cf. David P. Polk, 'Brevard Childs' *Introduction to the Old Testament as Scripture*', *HBT* 2 (1980), pp. 168–69; and Brett, *Crisis?* p. 62. This appears to be an overstatement, however. Childs does, of course, frequently point out that arguments about the underlying traditions have been inconclusive, and he also reminds us that previous attempts at Old Testament theology have sometimes foundered because scholars have subsequently lost confidence in the historical reconstructions upon which the theologizing was based (e.g., *IOTS* pp. 74–75). But although Childs (like many other

ever, this is again a weak argument, because it wrongly subordinates questions of intrinsic theological value to those of scholarly convenience. The point can be made by seeing how this argument would fail to cut any ice with someone holding a view contrary to Childs'. Suppose, for example, it were believed that God has primarily revealed himself through real, historical events; then this would, *prima facie*, put a high premium upon recovering what actually happened. Such reconstructions may be very uncertain, but at least they would be uncertain quests for something of high theological value. By contrast, the most assured exegesis of the final form would, according to this view of revelation, yield results whose theological value was quite uncertain, because their relationship to the real events cannot be determined simply from an exegesis of the canonical text. In other words, questions about the relative priority one gives to the final form vis-à-vis its prehistory are, when asked in the context of a theological programme such as Childs', themselves fundamentally theological questions, and therefore have to be decided through the appropriate theological considerations. There would simply be no point in pursuing a programme which, by its intrinsic nature, could not reach the desired goal.

Much stronger than the preceding arguments, however, is Childs' claim that studying the final form of the text reveals a fullness of meaning—and, in particular, of theological meaning—that is simply lost if the canonical text is dismembered into its component sources.[16] Since this is a very significant argument I shall look in more detail at how Childs develops it by reviewing his discussion of the portrayal of David in 2 Samuel.[17] Examining von Rad's thesis that during the 'Solomonic Enlightenment' a new conception of history emerged in Israel, in which Yahweh was believed to control the course of events through a hidden, providential shaping of history, Childs notes

---

scholars) finds this unsatisfactory, it is less than clear, in my view, that he would extrapolate from these cautionary examples an important general argument such as Moberly and Brett attribute to him. Childs, in fact, is much more concerned to find a positive role for historical reconstructions than one would realize from Moberly's comments on pp. 20–21.

[16] A closely related idea is Childs' claim that it is through the canonical shape given to the final form that the ancient text is 'actualized' for the modern church. I shall introduce Childs' views on this later in the section.

[17] I have taken this example from Childs' *Old Testament Theology in a Canonical Context* (London: SCM, 1985) rather than from *IOTS* as it illustrates the point I wish to make in a particularly clear-cut way. For a similar (though more complex) example from *IOTS* itself, see Childs' exposition of Josh. 1–12 (pp. 247–50).

that von Rad found in Rost's theory of a 'Succession Narrative' an example that strongly supported his own view. This meant, however, having to excise 2 Samuel 21–24 as 'an unfortunate intrusion into the otherwise brilliantly conceived narrative of the succession'.[18] But although (Childs allows) von Rad was thus able to make some 'brilliant observations' on the literary character of Samuel he was unable to grasp the deeper theological dimension of this passage, since this has been decisively shaped through the inclusion of chapters 21–24. According to Childs, these chapters

> offer a highly reflective, theological interpretation of David's whole career as adumbrating the messianic hope. . . . Although David's human weaknesses are not suppressed within the tradition, his final role as the ideal, righteous king emerges with great clarity. (p. 119)

Unfortunately Childs does not spell out his argument in detail, but his main point seems to be that the tension between the real and the ideal arouses a hope for a better king in the future.[19] In other words, the canonical form of Samuel has used subtle literary means in order to portray the history of David's kingship as a theological model that points beyond itself; therefore to unpick the literary design through separating out the underlying sources will necessarily result in a grave theological impoverishment.[20]

Although examples such as this provide a pragmatic rather than a theoretical justification for studying the final form, it is nonetheless an important consideration. Working through the exegetical sections of Childs' Old Testament *Introduction*, it is difficult to escape the impression that, in some cases at least, a careful reading at the canonical level uncovers a wealth of meaning which would otherwise be missed. Moreover, with the theoretical debate about meaning, context, author's intention, and the like, currently being in a state of

---

[18] *OTTCC*, p. 118.

[19] It is, of course, possible to raise questions here at an exegetical level. To keep the discussion focused upon the methodological issues however, I shall (in this and other examples) simply take Childs' readings as 'given'.

[20] Childs perhaps overplays the divergence between himself and von Rad, who also argued that the 'confessional' value of the developed traditions should not be bypassed in a search for a historically reliable core; see especially his discussions of saga (*Old Testament Theology* II (London: SCM, 1975), pp. 420–22; *Genesis: A Commentary* (OTL; London: SCM, Revised 1972), pp. 31–43). It would be more accurate, therefore, to see Childs as applying von Rad's insights more consistently, i.e., in arguing that the confessional/theological value of the final form should not be sacrificed to the less developed viewpoint of an underlying source.

considerable flux, identifying a number of persuasive exegetical examples can provide an essential 'reference point' for alternative theories to be tested against. Some of Childs' own methodological proposals (such as his views on historical referentiality, or 'canonical intentionality') are, of course, highly controversial; and as biblical scholars have become increasingly interested in 'literary approaches' to the Bible it is hardly surprising to see the theoretical debates that are currently raging in literary circles also finding their way into theological discussions. Yet even if one has reservations about some of the reasons that scholars such as Childs offer in defence of what they are doing, the exegetical results can still stand on their own feet, providing useful insights in their own right and suggesting further avenues that might be profitably explored.

Another aspect of Childs' concern with final form to note here is his views on actualization. Childs sees the canonical process which shaped the traditions as having 'loosened up' their exclusive attachment to a particular historical situation, so as to present them in a form in which they are able to 'speak' to situations far removed from the circumstances in which they originated.[21] This has the important corollary that undoing the canonical shaping renders the Scriptures dumb:

> The modern hermeneutical impasse which has found itself unable successfully to bridge the gap between the past and the present, has arisen in large measure from its disregard of the canonical shaping. The usual critical method of biblical exegesis is, first, to seek to restore an original historical setting by stripping away those very elements which constitute the canonical shape. Little wonder that once the biblical text has been securely anchored in the historical past by 'decanonizing' it, the interpreter has difficulty applying it to the modern religious context.[22]

Since canonical hermeneutics aims to interpret the Old Testament as God's address to the modern church this is an issue of some importance for Childs. We can best grasp his point through reviewing some examples—not least to see the variety of ways in which he

---

[21] This, of course, is not an original idea of Childs', who himself traces it back especially to Mowinckel's *Psalmenstudien* II; see Childs' *Memory and Tradition in Israel* (SBT 37; London: SCM, 1962), p. 75 n. 2 and pp. 81ff.

[22] *IOTS*, p. 79. In section 2.4 above we saw that already in 'SLS' Childs blamed the inability of the Scriptures to 'speak' to the modern church upon the quest for original meanings; but in *IOTS* it becomes much clearer how, in his view, this comes about.

conceives it as operating. According to Childs, actualization is one of the major concerns of Deuteronomy—how is the law that was given at Sinai to function for this new generation? Childs finds a number of different strategies being used. Sometimes the law was modified to fit the new historical circumstances;[23] on the other hand, Childs also points out (following von Rad) the timeless, idealized quality of Deuteronomy which, while not obliterating the 'historical specificity' of many of the elements, renders them applicable to all generations.[24]

In Ezekiel actualization takes a theological form. Childs points to 'Ezekiel's radical theological orientation', which led him to describe 'the plan of God for Israel in terms completely freed from temporal limitation' (p. 361); likewise the fact that he often portrayed his addressees in highly theological terms, together with his frequent use of symbols, allegories, and visions, also has the effect of partially detaching his message from specific historical circumstances. In other words, the message is given in such a form as to confront both present and future generations with 'the unchanging will of God' (p. 363).

A quite different procedure was adopted by the redactors of Amos, however, who preserved the prophet's oracles as rooted in their specific historical circumstances. In this case actualization was achieved through the redactors inserting commentary, doxologies, and eschatological material of their own (p. 410). Thus actualization does not necessarily mean 'dehistorisizing' the material—sometime it can be achieved through showing how the historically particular has a future-orientated significance.

Historical particularity also plays a part in the actualization of the Davidic psalms, yet in a way quite different from Amos. Childs notes that the psalms whose titles attach them to an incident in David's life are related to him not as the king but simply as a man. 'The emphasis is made to fall on the inner life of the psalmist' (p. 521), so that in vividly portraying the reactions of this man of God to the diverse circumstances through which he passed, the psalms take on an immediate relevance for the modern believer.

In *some* cases, then, it seems that Childs can present a good *prima facie* case for the theological value of studying the text in its final form. What is far less clear, however, is whether there are sufficient

---

[23] E.g., the law about tithes in a situation in which 'the way is too long for you' (Deut. 14).
[24] *IOTS*, p. 222.

grounds for his elevation of the priority of the final form into a *general hermeneutical principle* that governs the interpretation of every text. In fact there is a major problem at this point. Childs himself accepts, in significant measure, the standard critical reconstructions of the traditions behind the text (particularly as regards literary sources); but when the same reconstructions also show that the dominant influences in the formation of these traditions, and hence in the shaping of the final text, were such factors as political infighting, poor historiographical methodology, misunderstandings of the material, or sheer antiquarianism, it is far from clear why priority should still be accorded to the canonical form. On the contrary, in circumstances such as this it would seem far more reasonable for someone like Childs, who is particularly concerned to hear the text's *theological* testimony, to go back behind the canonical text in the hope of recovering a layer of tradition for which theological motivations *were* the dominant concerns in its shaping. In cases such as these we might wonder if Childs' own Relevance Principle convicts him of unduly neglecting the critical reconstruction of the traditions.

Childs, of course, is aware of these problems, and I shall now outline three ways in which he responds to them. The first is his claim that only the final form bears witness to 'the full history of revelation', which we have already noted. A second response is to concede that the standard critical reconstructions do pose genuine difficulties for his programme, but then to suggest that they can be resolved historico-critically. So, for example,[25] in reviewing Wellhausen's reconstruction of how the priestly offices arose and developed in Israel, Childs notes that, according to this account, the canonical portrayal of priesthood has been substantially influenced by non-theological, political factors. Childs concedes that if this were in fact the case then

> it would be virtually meaningless to focus on the religious use of authoritative traditions in order to form a theological witness if the forces at work were really of a radically different sort. . . . It runs directly in the face of a canonical understanding to assume that the present form of the text is really a cover for the real political forces which lie behind it, or to posit that the later theological use transformed the tradition into something different in kind from the original secular function. (p. 148)

---

[25] Again it is more convenient to take an illustration from *OTTCC* (pp. 145–49) than from *IOTS*. Childs makes a similar point in reply to Barr: See Barr, 'Childs' *Introduction*', pp. 15–16; Childs, 'Response to Reviewers', p. 56.

For theologically significant literature to arise in this way is about as plausible, Childs suggests (*ibid.*), as something akin to Augustine's *Confessions* coming out of Richard Nixon's Watergate tapes!

Having recognized this as a traditio-critical problem, Childs duly attempts a traditio-critical solution, appealing in particular to an alternative reconstruction of Gunneweg's. Childs' point is not, of course, that Gunneweg's account vindicates the biblical portrayal of priesthood as historically accurate—on the contrary, one of the cardinal tenets of *IOTS* (and subsequent writings) is that there is no simple correlation between the historical veracity of a text and its theological value. What Gunneweg's reconstruction (if correct) shows, however, is that the biblical portrayal was shaped through predominantly religious concerns; and granted this, Childs thinks it legitimate to make a final-form study of priesthood.

Childs' third response to the problems posed by critical reconstruction is to separate meaning from author's intention:

> It is not clear to what extent the ordering of oral and written material into a canonical form always involved an *intentional* decision. At times there is clear evidence for an intentional blurring of the original historical setting. . . . At other times the canonical shaping depends largely upon what appear to be *unintentional* factors. . . . But *irrespective of intentionality* the effect of the canonical process was to render the tradition accessible to the future generation by means of a 'canonical intentionality', which is coextensive with the meaning of the biblical text.[26]

Unfortunately Childs nowhere explains what he means by 'canonical intentionality'. Barr has dubbed it a 'mystic phrase',[27] and it is certainly a little peculiar to ascribe intentionality to a text rather than to an author. Nonetheless, when read in context it seems tolerably clear what Childs means, and Barr himself is not far wrong when he suggests that it indicates a desire 'to know the meaning of the text, not the intention of the writer' (*ibid.*). More precisely, Childs seems to be exhorting us to take the canonical text 'on its own terms', reading it as an integral whole without worrying about whether these meanings were intended by the tradents/redactors or whether they

---

[26] *IOTS* pp. 78–79, italics added; cf. Childs' important reaffirmation of this point in rebutting David Polk's claim that 'Central to Childs' position is the understanding that the final edited form of the canonical text is always somehow intentional' (Polk, 'Childs' *Introduction*' p. 167; Childs, 'A Response' pp. 206–207).

[27] 'Childs' *Introduction*', p. 13.

arose through accidental, unintended circumstances.[28]

Such, then, are Childs' three main responses to the difficulties raised by critical reconstruction. None of them, in my view, are entirely unproblematic, and in subsequent chapters I shall consider them in greater detail. At this point, however, there are two general comments to make in relation to Childs' second and third responses (which I shall generally refer to hereafter as, respectively, the Intentionalist and the Anti-intentionalist strands in Childs' thought). Firstly, it is important for a full understanding of Childs' views, as Childs himself presents them, to realize that *both* these responses are important factors in his programme. Unfortunately, Childs' work has received a seriously one-sided presentation in this respect from John Barton, who focuses almost exclusively upon the anti-intentionalist strand. According to Barton, the canonical approach is 'a proposal about how biblical texts ought to be read, *as opposed* to being interested in what their authors meant by them'.[29] Childs regards the biblical texts as forming a unified canon, which ought to be interpreted in accordance with the following 'prescription':

> Read all these texts as if they were written by one author (say, God) at a single sitting; set out what he must have meant by each of them if he also wrote all the others, and had a consistent purpose in doing so; then delete all references to the author from your final statement of their meaning. We know (from historical criticism) that the biblical texts did not in fact have a single author; but the meaning they have as a canon is the meaning they *would* have had if they *had* had a single author.[30]

Barton therefore finds canonical hermeneutics to have important affinities with structuralism, and suggests that Childs might look to this school of literary thought in order to find theoretical support for his own work.

---

[28] Cf. *IOTS* pp. 300, 486, and 645, where 'the intention of the text' appears to be used with a similar meaning. The distinction between canonical meaning and author's intention is given greater prominence in Childs' *The New Testament as Canon: An Introduction* (London: SCM, 1984), e.g., pp. 38, 49, 83–84, 162, 172–73, 185–86, 291–92, 427, 461, etc.

[29] *Reading*, p. 81; italics added.

[30] P. 102, Barton's italics; unfortunately an element of parody creeps in with the apparent implication that Childs' approach is close to viewing the Bible as divinely dictated (cf. Barton's very similar description of the Fundamentalist theory of inspiration on p. 85). Although we shall see a number of reasons why Childs does seem to need *some sort* of theory of inspiration to undergird his programme, it is not necessary to saddle him with this thoroughly discredited version.

Given the obscurity of Childs' comments on 'canonical intentionality', this is an interesting suggestion as to how *this particular notion*
might be further elucidated. Barton goes badly astray, however, in
characterizing Childs' programme *as a whole* as structuralist, because
there are many other important aspects of his work that cannot be
fitted under this umbrella. There are three aspects of this which can
be noted here. The first is seen in Childs' conception of the canonical
process, by which the traditions were developed into the final form.
Although he allows that accidental factors played *some* part, his main
stress is upon the religious community and successive redactors intentionally shaping the traditions in ways that are highly reflective.
One should not overlook the fact that, particularly in *EC* and the
two *Introductions*, Childs has devoted several hundred pages to reconstructing these historical processes. This would be largely wasted labour
if he were the thoroughgoing anti-intentionalist whom Barton portrays.

Secondly, Childs has a much more positive attitude towards critical
studies than Barton realises. Unfortunately, Barton has not understood that Childs' aim is to *reorient* the critical tools so that they make
a positive contribution to biblical theology;[31] rather, he speaks of 'the
"anti-critical" stance of Childs' [Old Testament] *Introduction*' (p. 98),
and of the particular vigour with which 'canon criticism' (as he insists on calling Childs' work) tries to 'abolish' preceding methodologies (p. 206), such as form- and source-criticism. And thirdly, Barton
has overlooked Childs' commitment to extra-textual questions of 'what
really happened'. Childs has himself raised this point against Barton:

> Because the biblical text continually bears witness to events and reac-
> tions in the life of Israel, the literature cannot be isolated from its
> ostensive reference. In view of these factors alone it is a basic misun-
> derstanding to try to describe a canonical approach simply as a form
> of structuralism (*contra* Barton).[32]

Barton's construal of Childs' views on author's intention, then, is badly
one-sided.

The second comment to make on Childs' second and third responses, however, is that there is considerable tension between them,
although care must be taken to identify the problem accurately. To
assist with this, it is helpful to recall Quentin Skinner's distinction

---

[31] Cf. section 1 above.
[32] *OTTCC*, p. 6.

between 'motives' and '(communicative) intentions', which Mark Brett
has recently brought to the attention of biblical scholars.[33] As Brett
explains,

> [O]ne ought to distinguish between *what* an author is trying to say
> (which might be called a 'communicative intention') and *why* it is being
> said (which might be called a 'motive').[34]

Thus the motives behind the production of a certain text might include such things as the author's desire to inform or amuse the reader,
or to make money; whereas the author's communicative intention is
concerned with such matters as verbal meaning, language, and genre.

Applying this distinction to Childs' second and third responses,
the Wellhausen-Gunneweg example is clearly concerned with the
tradents' *motives*—these scholars differ as to whether the traditions
were shaped primarily to serve political or religious ends, and Childs
affirms that this is relevant to the viability of a canonical theology.
Things are less clear-cut with Childs' third response, however. In the
passage I quoted there from *IOTS* pp. 78–79, the orientation towards 'the meaning of the biblical text' is reminiscent of formalist
theories of meaning; and it is primarily in this way that Childs does
in fact use the idea of 'canonical intentionality' in *NTCI*, where he
defends the legitimacy of finding meanings at the canonical level which
no-one intentionally authored. In other words, Childs is separating
textual meaning from communicative intention. In *IOTS* itself, however, this passage is clearly meant to deal with the problem of *motives*: It appears in a section headed 'The Canonical Process and the
Shaping of Scripture' (p. 77), which is concerned with '[t]he motivations behind the canonical process' (p. 78); and it is clear from the
context that 'motivations' here refers to the same sorts of factors as
Skinner and Brett call 'motives'. One such motive, which (Childs
notes) the Scriptures themselves profess, is to transmit the authoritative traditions to future generations; yet scholarly research has shown
that the traditions were also shaped by other motives, such as rival-
ries between different political parties. In response to this, Childs

---

[33] Skinner, 'Motives, Intentions, and the Interpretation of Texts', *New Literary History*
3 (1972), pp. 393–408; Brett, 'Motives and Intentions in Genesis 1', *JTS* 42 (1991),
pp. 1–16. Skinner does not claim to have originated this distinction, but assumes
that it is already commonly accepted (although in practice not always observed; see
p. 395, n. 10). 'Communicative intention' is Brett's term, which I shall generally
adopt here.
[34] P. 5; Brett's italics.

suggests that (in ways which he leaves far from clear) the effect of these motives were somehow 'filtered out' by the tradition process, to produce a canonical text that stands largely untainted by the motives lying behind it, and may therefore be read without taking them into account (p. 79).

What, then, Childs seems to be proposing here is a formalist reading of the canonical text which discounts both the communicative intentions *and* the motives which produced it: If (Childs seems to be saying) the final form proposes a certain understanding of priesthood, then that is what we should accept as the theologically significant datum. Construed in this way, however, the intentionalist and anti-intentionalist strands in Childs' thought appear to conflict: If it is legitimate to read the canonical text simply as 'given', 'irrespective of [the] intentionality [i.e., motivation]' of those who shaped it, then there is no reason why Wellhausen's reconstruction of the priesthood traditions should trouble Childs—even if the tradents *were* impelled by political concerns, this would not bar the church from reading their work as its own Scriptures. Thus Childs' various arguments in defence of the final form appear not to be mutually consistent.

So then, the priority of the canonical text is clearly a central element in Childs' programme from *IOTS* onwards, and we have now seen that he draws upon a number of diverse considerations in defending it. These will have to be discussed more fully in subsequent chapters.


### 3. *Faith and Description*

One particularly surprising feature of *IOTS* is its account of the descriptive task, which this *Introduction* is to perform for the Old Testament literature. Contrary to what he had previously argued, Childs now tells us that

> The approach which is being proposed [here] . . . is descriptive in nature. It is *not confessional* in the sense of consciously assuming the tenets of Christian theology, but rather it seeks to describe as objectively as possible the canonical literature of ancient Israel,[35]

adding later that this does not require a faith-commitment, because

---

[35] P. 14, italics added; this is essentially what he in fact did in his Ps. 8 example in *BTCri*, which we discussed in section 2.3 above.

what is being described is 'the literature of Israel's faith, not that of the reader' (p. 72). Whether or not the reader wishes to identify with the faith thus described can be decided after the description has been completed (*ibid.*).

Taken on its own this seems to indicate a significant move towards accepting Stendahl's two-stage methodology,[36] with faith only being brought in after the descriptive stage has been completed— although significant differences from Stendahl would still remain, especially in Childs' subordination of the original to the canonical context. Somewhat in tension with this 'new objectivism', however, is Childs' subsequent claim that 'The [canonical] approach seeks to work descriptively within a broad theological framework'.[37] The breadth of this framework is indicated by the immediate context, in which Childs envisages the descriptive task being jointly undertaken by Protestant, Catholic, and Jewish scholars; but this seems to be a curious half-way house. Why is this much of a faith-commitment needed (so that atheists and Buddhists, for example, are excluded even from describing Israel's faith), and yet nothing stronger (such as a specifically Christian, or Protestant, or Reformed theological framework)? Childs does not explain, and one is left wondering to what extent his comments have been guided by external considerations (such as a desire to encourage greater cooperation between a broad spectrum of Jewish and Christian scholars), rather than by the internal logic of his programme.

This flirtation with neo-Stendahlianism does not last long, however. In *The New Testament as Canon: An Introduction*[38] Childs brings his conception of the descriptive task almost full circle: The tension

---

[36] *Contra* Brett, who sees an essential continuity between *IOTS* and Childs' earlier writings in their conception of the descriptive task (*Crisis?*, pp. 59–61). This stems from him misunderstanding Childs' position prior to *IOTS*; thus, for example, while correctly noting that in 'IF' Childs calls the interpreting of the single text in the light of the whole Old Testament a 'descriptive task', Brett overlooks the fact that, precisely in explicating the historical-critical dimensions of this task, Childs repeatedly affirms that it must be done within a 'framework of faith' ('IF', pp. 439–40). It is precisely this confessional orientation of the descriptive task that is denied in *IOTS*, however.

[37] P. 81; cf. p. 83, where Childs insists that the interpreter must '[view] the exegetical task as constructive as well as descriptive'.

[38] The methodological position of *NTCI* is very similar to that of *IOTS*; Childs is in fact performing the same task in *NTCI* for the New Testament as he had already undertaken in *IOTS* for the Old (see *NTCI*, p. xv). I shall therefore only discuss those aspects of *NTCI* that mark significant developments from *IOTS*.

between Faith and Reason/description which permeated 'IF' reappears in *NTCI*, where Childs oscillates between them. Affirming (with a clear stab at Stendahl, once more) that 'the descriptive and hermeneutical task of interpretation cannot be held apart, as if to determine what a text meant and what a text means could be neatly isolated' (pp. 36–37), Childs observes that such affirmations have sometimes led to his programme being charged with 'fideism' or even 'uncontrolled subjectivity' (p. 37). Childs responds by stressing the descriptive task—so much so, that in essentially repeating from *IOTS* the claim that what is being described is the faith not of the modern reader but of the first Christians (*ibid.*) he comes perilously close to reinstating Stendahl's dichotomy. Childs soon becomes uneasy, however, that perhaps this unduly minimises faith, and asks whether the descriptive task can be carried through 'regardless of religious commitment' (p. 38). His answer is that, in principle, it *can* (he is clearly intent on rebutting the charge of fideism); but in practice, he observes, it is rare to get penetrating theological commentary from a scholar who does not share something of the faith of the New Testament, because his 'scale of priorities' are different from those of the text (p. 39).

With faith thus reintroduced, however, Childs soon moves on to the much stronger claim that '[it] belongs to the exegetical task that the modern reader takes his point of standing within the authoritative tradition by which to establish his identity with the Christian church' (p. 40), and even claims that part of the proper context for biblical interpretation is 'an expectation of understanding through the promise of the Spirit to the believer' (*ibid.*). Why this does not after all lead into fideism, or how the unbeliever can, in principle, undertake such studies, is not explained; the descriptive task as Childs had first characterized it has now dropped from view. In sum, Childs' discussion of faith and reason is marked by an uneasy alternation between them, without ever showing us what a unified 'description in faith' (or 'Interpretation in Faith') might be. Or to put the problem more generally: What Childs wants is a form of interpretation that proceeds from a *specific* standpoint (i.e., of faith), but yields interpretations that can be *generally* recognised as reasonable (i.e., which are not just 'reasonable to those who have faith', which would be fideistic). Unfortunately Childs has made little progress towards accomplishing this; on the contrary, the reviews in this and the preceding chapter have shown that the tensions in 'IF' have not been resolved but heightened in his subsequent works, as the disparate elements have each been more sharply formulated.

Nonetheless, *NTCI* also brings a new twist to this tale by appropriating from reader-response theory the idea that the meaning of a text is a function of how it is read.[39] Although Childs does not explicitly appeal to reader-response theory as justifying his own approach, a number of important methodological formulations in *NTCI* seem indebted to this school of literary criticism, particularly when Childs is arguing for the necessity of faith. Thus, for example:

> The theological issue turns on the Christian church's claim for the integrity of *a special reading* which interprets the Bible within an established theological context and towards a particular end;[40]

or again,

> The hermeneutical task of interpreting scripture requires ... *an act of construal on the part of the reader*. This interaction between text and reader comprises every true interpretation;[41]

and similarly, Childs claims that the 'literary analysis of the canonical corpus' requires 'not only an understanding of the church's construal of its scriptures, but also an important element of "reader competence" in forming a modern construal'.[42] In the same vein, Childs criticizes conservative biblical studies for adhering to a standard of objectivity that does not reckon with how the traditions are received by the Christian community (p. 543; cf. p. 26).

It is not difficult to see that, *prima facie*, reader-response theory may have much to offer Childs: (i) It ovecomes Stendahl's sharp dichotomy between 'what it meant' and 'what it means'—what was written 'then' has meaning only as it is read 'now', from a contemporary standpoint;[43] (ii) It enables Childs to fill out his cryptic claims that the Scriptures must be read from a particular faith-stance, by

---

[39] This first appears explicitly in the Preface to the Second Edition of *IOTS*, where Childs says that 'I would now assign more significance to the role of "reader competence" than I did in the [first edition of this] book' (p. 17). Nonetheless, reader competence has obvious affinities with his concern for the role of the community in shaping Israel's traditions through using them as their Scriptures, and with his notion of canonical intentionality.
[40] P. 37, italics added.
[41] P. 40, italics added.
[42] Pp. 529–30; cf. p. 163.
[43] Cf. James Smart's criticism of Stendahl, reviewed in section 2.1 above. This

explaining this as a certain kind of reader-competence, or as a reading strategy of the faith community; (iii) It gives Childs a theoretical
framework from which to answer those who claim that canonical
interpretation rides roughshod over the original meaning of a passage—the reader-response theorist would reply that such criticisms
assume an untenable objectivism about 'the meaning of the text',
which in fact can never be separated from the way in which it is
actually read; and (iv) It also enables Childs to answer the charge
that canonical hermeneutics is a new kind of fideism, which allows
each interpreter to read his or her own faith into the text—reader-
response theory (in most of its forms) resists the accusation that, in
any significant sense, it is individualistic or arbitrary. What Childs is
suggesting in *NTCI*, then, is that 'interpretation in faith' is a particular kind of reader-competence, and this appears to be a potentially
very promising development in his programme. The fulfilment of this
promise, however, depends upon one finding a version of reader-
response theory which is both capable of performing the various
theoretical tasks that Childs' programme would ask of it and is a
viable literary theory in its own right. In section 7.3 I shall look at
one version of reader-response theory which appears to offer Childs
substantial help—namely, that of Stanley Fish.

## 4. *Towards Biblical Theology*

Within the broader framework of Childs' overall programme, the
main purpose of his Old and New Testament *Introductions* was to
perform the descriptive task—from a canonical perspective, of course—
in preparation for the constructive task of Biblical Theology. Before
looking at Childs' execution of the latter, however, there are three
more things to do: To take stock of Childs' changing views on the
historical-critical tools; to introduce the closely related subject of 'historical referentiality'; and to see how Childs' views on Biblical Theology were developing subsequent to *BTCri*.

Beginning, then, with the historical-critical tools, something further needs to be said here about Childs' views on (i) whether they
are methodologically sound, and (ii) what their role should be. Childs'

also has affinities with Gadamer's notion of 'the fusion of horizons', which will be
discussed in chapter 9 below.

thoughts on both these matters have fluctuated considerably. In 'IF'
he expressed significant reservations about the soundness of the critical
methods, claiming that their supposed neutrality was in fact anti-
theological. Childs therefore wanted to develop an approach which
was more thoroughly faith-informed; nonetheless, he still envisaged it
as recovering 'original meanings' in a way which, as we saw, has
strong similarities to Stendahl's conception of the descriptive task.
Some traces of these reservations about the soundness of the critical
tools can also be found in *BTCri* (e.g., p. 102) but they are now more
muted; and by the time *IOTS* was published all such reservations
seem to have disappeared. Moreover, it is also in *IOTS* that Childs
makes his radical new proposals about what the critical tools should
be used *for*—original context is now subordinated to canonical context
in such a way that the critical tools are given a supporting rather
than a central role. (Of course, since a concern for the original is
intrinsic to historical criticism, Childs is, at least implicitly, affirming
that 'original context' still has *some* importance for his work.) This
reconception of their role is continued in the New Testament *Introduction*; and yet *NTCI* also reintroduces doubts about the inherent
soundness of the critical tools that are reminiscent of his earlier
works—Stuhlmacher is criticized for '[assuming] that the critical
method is basically sound' and needs only to be supplemented, therefore, by a further 'dimension' that is 'different in kind from . . .
historical exegesis';[44] and a few pages later the historical critic is
faulted for

> [presuming] to stand above the text, outside the circle of tradition,
> and from this detached vantage point [to] adjudicate the truth and
> error of the New Testament's time-conditionality. (p. 51)

By contrast, the canonical interpreter works from within the context
of the received tradition (*ibid.*). In summary, then, although the subordination of original to canonical context marks a definite development in Childs' methodology, his thoughts on the role of faith vis-à-
vis the critical methods, and on the inherent soundness of these
methods, remain obscure.

Secondly, this is an appropriate place at which to introduce Childs'

---

[44] P. 46; recall that Childs' fundamental objection to Stendahl in 'IF' is that by
(wrongly) conceiving description as faith-neutral he made it different in kind from
the constructive task.

views on historical referentiality. Broadly speaking, his point is that the theological value of a text is generally related, at best, only indirectly to questions of historical veracity.[45] Childs almost invariably uses this idea polemically, to oppose the high value that modern biblical studies generally accords to historical reconstruction;[46] and it is therefore hardly surprising that Childs gives far more attention to the canonical portrayals of Moses and David than to attempted recoveries of them as historical individuals. But how far does Childs pursue these 'ahistorical' leanings?

According to Barr, Childs takes them to extremes, and thereby neglects something very important. On Barr's reading of *IOTS*,

> [Childs'] basic [epistemological] conviction seems to be the belief that one must not take up a hermeneutical base *extrinsic* to the text. Any such extrinsic vantage-point—whether it be a canon within the canon, a set of actual events, a history, a history of tradition, or a sociological situation—is vehemently opposed. . . . A truly theological reading of scripture, he seems to think, must be based not on any reconstructed entity outside scripture . . . but on the totality of canonical scripture alone;[47]

and a few pages later he adds (somewhat patronisingly) that if Childs had allowed the New Testament a little more influence in *IOTS*, then

> It might have suggested the importance of extrinsic realities for interpretation: there is no question that Jesus 'canonically' rose from the dead, but it is the extrinsic resurrection that matters for faith. (p. 21)

Stated as baldly as that, however, (and Barr does not add any significant qualifications) this is a badly skewed account of Childs' work. Childs himself flatly rejects it in his reply to Barr:

> Of course, Israel's own testimony continually points outside itself to extrinsic reality. It speaks of God's intervention in time and space, of institutions and offices, of politics and nations.[48]

Childs in fact made it clear at several points in *IOTS* that he recognised the importance of extrinsic reality,[49] as he had in his previous works

---

[45] I have expressed this rather vaguely because, as I shall argue in the next chapter, Childs is actually tackling a number of distinct problems under this broad heading.

[46] E.g., *IOTS* pp. 41, 199–200, 237, 252, 328, 460, 485, etc.; cf. *OTTCC* pp. 129–30, 147–49.

[47] 'Childs' *Introduction*', p. 15; Barr's italics.

[48] 'Response to Reviewers', p. 57.

[49] E.g., pp. 71, 75, 289, 298–99.

also,[50] and has continued to do so since. Barr would no doubt affirm
that

> The New Testament bears witness to realities outside itself. The prophets
> and apostles spoke of things which they saw and events which they
> experienced. . . . Christians have always understood that we are saved,
> not by the biblical text, but by the life, death, and resurrection of Jesus
> Christ who entered into the world of time and space;

but in fact it was Childs who wrote these words.[51]

And yet, there is also a problematic side to Childs' commitment
to historical reference. Firstly, he has been extraordinarily reluctant
to act upon the obvious implications of these programmatic statements—with the exception of *IAC*, it is very rare to find Childs trying to reconstruct 'what really happened' in the history of Israel or
in 'the life, death, and resurrection of Jesus Christ'. Even though the
significance of these events is clearly affirmed, Childs seems to have
little interest in finding out about them. Generally he concerns himself only with the canonical picture of Jesus or Moses, without asking
whether the biblical incidents really did happen in 'the world of time
and space'. And secondly, questions of historical factuality never, in
practice, seem to make any impact upon Childs' assessments of the
Old or New Testaments 'as Scripture'. Of course, one must be careful here not to beg the question: Childs is explicitly rejecting the
idea that there is a *direct* relationship between history and theology.
Yet it often seems as though, in practice, Childs has fallen back into
*non*-referentiality: The theology of a text is expounded *just as if* everything had happened as the text portrays it, with no significance being allowed to the question of whether it really did or not. These
issues will be explored more fully in the next chapter.

Turning now to Childs' views on Biblical Theology, I begin with
Barr's criticism of *IOTS* for failing to be a specifically *Christian* Introduction to the Old Testament—given Childs' hermeneutical principle that the canon is the proper context for interpretation, and
that for Christians the New Testament is a major component in their
canon, one would have expected (Barr argues) that *IOTS* would
have been more overtly christological in its readings of the Old

---

[50] E.g., *BTCri* pp. 105, 112; *Isaiah and the Assyrian Crisis* (SBT Second Series 3;
London: SCM, 1967), *passim.*
[51] *NTCI*, p. 545; cf. *OTTCC* p. 6, *BTONT* p. 665.

Testament.[52] Childs has replied that his purpose in *IOTS* was not to write a biblical theology but 'an introduction to the Hebrew Scriptures';[53] but in my view the problem is a little more complex than either Childs or Barr have realized. On the one hand, Childs has always been sensitive to the dangers of arbitrarily 'christianizing' the Old Testament, and has therefore insisted that the distinctive witness of each Testament needs to be heard 'on its own terms'. This is clearly Childs' purpose in *IOTS*, which therefore accords much better with his previously declared methodology than Barr realizes. On the other hand, however, Childs' principal objection to Stendahl was that making the descriptive task different in kind from the constructive/normative task wrecks the theological enterprise; and it is therefore quite correct of Barr to question whether Childs should, within his (sc. Childs') own terms of reference, attempt to describe the Old Testament in isolation from the New. In other words, it seems questionable whether Childs has in fact left himself enough methodological scope for him to describe the Old Testament 'non-confessionally'[54] without making his own programme subject to the same criticisms that he has levelled against Stendahl. Once again, there appear to be unresolved problems of Faith and Reason gnawing away at the foundations of Childs' programme.

The wider questions of biblical theology find almost no place in *IOTS*, being confined to the briefest of affirmations on the final page that the integrity of the Old Testament must be respected, that the Christian church finds a witness to Christ in both Testaments, and that the two Testaments together form a 'new theological context . . . for understanding both parts which differs from hearing each Testament in isolation' (p. 671). A couple of further points are added, however, in Childs' responses to reviewers of *IOTS*. Firstly, James A. Sanders' 'Canonical Context and Canonical Criticism' has elicited from Childs an explanation of how, in his view, the New Testament writers regarded the Old Testament:[55] They inherited from Judaism both a 'wholistic understanding' of the Hebrew canon and various 'hermeneutical techniques' such as midrash and pesher. By these means 'Christians sought to justify their confession' from the Scriptures which Jews and Christians alike recognized as authoritative; however, this

---

[52] *HS*, pp. 151–52.
[53] 'Review of *HS*', p. 70.
[54] Recall *IOTS* pp. 14, 72.
[55] See 'A Response', pp. 203–204.

does not imply that modern interpretations of the Old Testament are 'restricted to the hermeneutical practices of the N.T.', because the emergence of the New Testament alongside the Old puts us in a position different from the apostles.

Since much of the New Testament's use of the Old—including its resorting to midrash and pesher—is now widely regarded as exegetically unsatisfactory, questions clearly need to be asked about how Childs' account of this use is to be integrated into his canonical programme. In his New Testament *Introduction* Childs frequently discusses how the various New Testament writings draw upon the Old Testament;[56] but since his purposes in *NTCI* are descriptive rather than normative Childs confines himself to delineating what each author does, without discussing the possible implications for the constructive task. These questions are of central importance to his conception of Biblical Theology, however, and will therefore be taken up again later.

A second major issue to emerge from the reviews of *IOTS* was raised by Douglas A. Knight's question, 'What role does the category of authority play in Childs' understanding of the canon?'.[57] Authority (Knight observes) is at present a poorly analysed concept; and although Childs is no worse than other scholars in his handling of it, it does present a particular problem for him because he has '[made] this category fundamental to his understanding of canon' (*ibid.*). Quoting a passage from *IOTS* in which Childs suggests that there is a dialectical relationship between the development of the religious community and of its authoritative traditions, Knight asks

> whether in Childs' opinion the source for the literature's authority rests in the literature itself by virtue of some special character it has, or in the community which chooses to vest the literature with authority, or in some other source (such as the deity) external to these other two. (*ibid.*)

In his reply to Knight, Childs suggests that this subject is best approached through an exegesis of the relevant biblical passages. Taking 2 Kings 22 as an example, Childs discovers that

> According to this account, authority rested in the book which was discovered, but it was also acknowledged as such by a community of recipients who attributed its imperatives to God as its true source.[58]

---

[56] See pp. 69–71, 113–16, 136–37, 258–60, 509, etc.
[57] 'Canon and the History of Tradition', p. 140.
[58] 'A Response', p. 209.

This seems to raise as many problems as it solves, however. On the one hand, Childs explains that although it is 'the book' which is authoritative, this in turn is due to its contents being given by God. In other words, Childs is proposing something quite similar to a traditional understanding of the Bible's authority as deriving from its 'divine inspiration'; and although 'inspiration' is itself a problematic concept, Childs' comments thus far at least help to clarify what *kind* of account he would give of the canon's normativity. On the other hand, however, there is considerable tension in Childs claiming both that the community 'acknowledged' the book's authority and that it 'attributed' its origin to God. Insofar as this provides a response to Knight's question about 'whether . . . the source for the literature's authority rests in the literature itself . . . or in the community which chooses to vest the literature with authority' Childs' answer is Both; but in the absence of a fuller explanation it is difficult to see how the different elements in Childs' account are supposed to fit together coherently, and Knight is able to raise a host of questions to which Childs has no obvious answers: How does authority operate (e.g., by coercion or inculcation)?; how is it related to the content of the message?; etc.

The final thing to do in this section is to introduce Childs' views on the interpretation of the Hebrew scriptures in Judaism. When discussing *IOTS* we noted Childs' desire that Jewish scholars should participate in the descriptive task, and a similarly positive attitude towards Jewish exegesis had already been expressed in 'IF' (pp. 444–49) and *BTCri* (pp. 120–22). These earlier discussions particularly emphasize that Jewish interpretation must be heard on its own terms, being understood and assessed, in the first instance, in relation to the outlook and concerns of Judaism, rather then being faulted for not meeting the predefined criteria of Christianity.[59] The way in which Childs develops this point, however, appears to have some disconcerting implications for his own canonical programme. Both Jews and Christians, Childs points out, interpret the Old Testament in the light of another normative tradition ( Jewish oral traditions; the Christian New Testament), which significantly affects the way in which the Hebrew canon is heard. In his desire to respect both of these approaches, however, Childs seems close to undermining the 'meaningfulness' of the Old Testament itself:

---

[59] 'IF', pp. 445–46.

> The Old Testament does not 'naturally' unfold into the faith of the
> New Testament. It does not lean toward the New Testament, but the
> Christian interpretation is fully dependent upon the radical new ele-
> ment in Jesus Christ;[60]

and *mutatis mutandis*, presumably, the Old Testament does not 'naturally' lean towards a Jewish interpretation either. But although most
scholars would accept that meaning is *to some degree* dependent upon
context, Childs seems perilously close here to pushing this principle
to extremes, virtually conceding that all Christian interpretation is
ultimately an eisegetical reading of the New Testament into the Old
(and similarly, again, for Jewish interpretation with respect to *its*
normative traditions). This, however, would reduce interpretation to
little more than a wresting of the text to fit one's preconceived beliefs.

   Childs, of course, would strongly resist this construal of his position. Immediately after the passage I quoted above he adds that
'Nevertheless, it is equally true that there is a continuity between the
Old Testament and the New, which the Christian claims is not arbitrary but essential' (*ibid.*); yet in my view it is far from clear that,
given his accommodation to Jewish exegesis, he can still maintain
sufficient safeguards to prevent interpretation descending into eisegesis.
Childs' second hermeneutical circle, it will be recalled, was supposed
to prevent interpretation descending into 'a morasse of theological
subjectivity' by insisting that each Testament be read in the light of
the other, yet in such a way that '[the] character of both Testaments
as independent witnesses must be maintained'.[61] Childs' discussion of
Jewish exegesis, however, seems to make the Old Testament so pa-
tient of divergent interpretations that it is difficult to see how the
independence of its witness can be maintained, and how, therefore,
this hermeneutical circle is to function as a critical corrective.

   Furthermore, Childs' comments on the context-dependence of
meaning seem to have a much wider application than he has realized.
The New Testament also is never read in a vacuum; and if it too
were as willing as (on Childs' account) the Old Testament is to adapt
itself to the contours of its interpretative context then it seems to
follow that we would have to accept an irreducible plurality of New
Testaments, each reflecting back the distinctive characteristics of the
ecclesiastical tradition or social philosophy of its interpreters. Again

---

[60] 'IF', p. 448.
[61] 'IF', p. 441.

Childs would not be happy with this conclusion, but it is difficult to see how he could avoid it. Once more, then, we find him running into serious problems when he attempts to relate exegesis to a faith community.

## 5. *The Canonical Theologies*

With *IOTS* and *NTCI* having tackled the descriptive task for each Testament, the ground was now prepared for the constructive task of writing a biblical theology. This, as we have seen, has been a long-standing concern of Childs', and the publication of his *Biblical Theology of the Old and New Testaments* is thus a major landmark in the development of his programme. It is with *BTONT* that we shall be chiefly concerned in the present section; but before turning to this, there are some comments to make on its Old Testament forerunner, the *Old Testament Theology in a Canonical Context*.

Our discussion of *OTTCC* can be brief, since on the one hand it is methodologically close to *IOTS*, and on the other hand its exclusive focus upon the Old Testament means that, in contrast to *BTONT*, it is not concerned with the relationship between the Testaments. The main point to comment on here is the sense in which *OTTCC* is an *Old Testament* theology. Childs begins his theological reflections by emphasizing that he comes to these ancient writings as a Christian (pp. 28–29), having previously explained how this affects his conception of the task:

> [T]he task of Old Testament theology is to reflect theologically on only the one portion of the Christian canon, but as Christian scripture.... [T]he Old Testament functions within Christian scripture as a witness to Jesus Christ precisely in its pre-Christian form. The task of Old Testament theology is ... to hear [the Old Testament's] own theological testimony to the God of Israel whom the church confesses also to worship. (p. 9)

That the Old Testament bears witness to Christ is a claim that Childs had already made in a number of previous works,[62] and it remains a central theme in *BTONT*. Unfortunately, however, the contents of *OTTCC* offer little to substantiate his claim, or to show how his

---

[62] E.g., *BTCri* pp. 110–11; *IOTS* p. 671.

programmatic statements about Old Testament Theology being a Christian enterprise can actually be implemented. On the contrary, even when full allowance is made for his quite proper concern to respect the *Old* Testament character of these texts, it is generally very difficult to see how Childs' expositions are distinctively Christian. What, in fact, *OTTCC* seems to show is that Childs has thus far been unable to convert his 'description within a framework of faith' formula, which we saw him using extensively in 'IF', into a workable exegetical methodology. On the contrary, in *OTTCC* its two components rather clearly come apart: The initial methodological discussions make a clear Christian faith-affirmation but offer no exegesis, whereas the balance of the book performs an exegetical-descriptive task which does not appear to be distinctively Christian.

This does not bode well for Childs' *Biblical Theology*,[63] whose purpose is to reflect upon the dual witness of the Old and New Testaments. Childs sees the task of Biblical Theology as being set by the particular way in which the New Testament writers responded to their encounter with Christ:

> [T]he New Testament makes its own witness. It tells its own story of the new redemptive intervention of God in Jesus Christ. . . . Yet the complexity of the problem [for Biblical Theology] arises because the New Testament bears its totally new witness in terms of the old, and thereby transforms the Old Testament. Frequently the Old Testament is heard on a different level from its original or literal sense, and in countless figurative ways it reinterprets the Old to testify to Jesus Christ.[64]

Because of this, Childs thinks that the task of Biblical Theology is 'to reflect on the whole Christian Bible with its two very different voices, both of which the church confesses bear witness to Christ' (p. 78).

The relationship between the Testaments is thus a central issue in *BTONT*, and Childs has much to say about it, both positively and negatively. Negatively, Childs distances himself from a number of accounts which he considers to be inadequate. In his Introductions Childs had tackled the problem of canonical shaping by tracing the redactional layering of the traditions; but this approach is largely inapplicable to the formation of the Christian Bible as a whole. On the contrary, there is an almost total absence of Christian redaction-

---

[63] For an analysis of the structure and contents of *BTONT*, together with some perceptive criticism, see the review by Richard Bauckham, *BI* 2 (1994), pp. 246–50.
[64] *BTONT*, p. 78; cf. p. 93.

al work upon the Hebrew text—the church did not, for example, bracket Old Testament books with extracts from the Gospels but preserved them in their integrity. Again, the New Testament is not a further redactional layer upon or midrashic interpretation of the Hebrew Scriptures; nor is it the final chapter in an ongoing story. Childs is therefore critical of scholars such as Gese who trace an unbroken traditio-historical trajectory from Old Testament to New, because they fail to grasp the essential *newness* of the New Testament's witness.[65]

The Old Testament, then, was taken into the Christian canon as a closed collection, with the New Testament writings being added as another, distinct, collection (p. 75). Nonetheless, the two are not merely juxtaposed, in a way analogous to the collecting of the four Gospels within the New Testament canon[66]—on the contrary, the Old Testament is frequently referred to in the New. Or again, Childs takes issue particularly with Bultmann and his followers for overplaying the discontinuity between the Testaments—the Old Testament is not just 'a testimony to miscarriage and failure' but is itself a true witness to the divine reality.[67]

Turning now to the positive side of Childs' account, the distinctive task of Biblical Theology, as he conceives it, is determined by the fact that '[b]oth testaments make a discrete witness to Jesus Christ which must be heard, both separately and in concert' (p. 78). As Childs explains this more fully a number of points emerge. Firstly, the integrity of each Testament must be respected. With this Childs is particularly taking issue with allegorical and other 'christianizing' interpretations of the Old Testament which read the fullness of the New Testament witness back into these pre-Christian writings. This, Childs contends, is illegitimate, because it fails to respect their character as *Old* Testament.[68]

Secondly, however, the two witnesses must be heard together, and this has important hermeneutical implications. According to Childs,

---

[65] See pp. 76, 211–12; cf. Childs' comments on von Rad on p. 720.

[66] Pp. 75–76; Childs is referring here to his discussion in *NTCI*, in which he claims that the juxtaposing of the Gospels within the canon led to the emergence of theologically significant new meanings, despite the lack of redactional intentionality.

[67] See pp. 76–77, 212.

[68] P. 77; cf. pp. 91–93. This has been a recurrent theme throughout Childs' writings; see 'IF' pp. 441–42; *BTCri* p. 111; *OTTCC* pp. 8, 9. In *BTONT*, however, Childs does add an important qualification, to which I shall return shortly.

[T]he New Testament bears its totally new witness in terms of the old, and thereby *transforms* the Old Testament. Frequently the Old Testament is heard on a different level from its original or literal sense, and in countless figurative ways it reinterprets the Old to testify to Jesus Christ. This description is not to suggest that the plain sense of the Old Testament is always disregarded by the New Testament, but only that the New Testament most characteristically comes to the Old Testament from the perspective of the gospel and freely renders the Old as a transparency of the New.[69]

This raises at least two problems, however. Firstly, how do these 'transformed' meanings of the Old Testament relate to its 'original or literal' meanings, by which Childs is presumably referring to the meanings that emerge when the Old Testament is read as a discrete witness in its own right? We have seen that a similar difficulty had already surfaced in *BTCri*, but that in *EC* and *IOTS* Childs apparently resolved it by subordinating original to canonical context. With *BTONT* resuming *BTCri*'s orientation towards Biblical Theology, however, it appears that Childs' 'subordination principle' only tackles part of the problem: It directs us to use the original meanings of, say, the traditions behind Genesis to illuminate the meaning of the canonical book, but it offers us no advice about the relationship between the meaning of the canonical Genesis when read in its original historical context, and whatever meanings may accrue from reading it in a canonical context that includes the New Testament. Further clarification, then, is still needed.

The second problem to be noted here for a canonical exegesis which 'transforms' the meaning of the Old Testament pertains to the New Testament's own interpretations of the Old. It is now widely agreed that the New Testament writers often used midrashic and other techniques which modern scholarship regards as methodologically dubious. But given, then, that their reading of the Old Testament often made little contact with its original meaning, does this not raise considerable problems for their place within a canonical Biblical Theology?

Childs, of course, is aware of these difficulties, and insists that the interpretative procedures of the New Testament authors cannot be adopted by modern interpreters of the Old Testament—'Paul was an Apostle; we are not!'.[70] It is far from clear, however, whether

---

[69] P. 78, italics added; cf. pp. 65, 93.
[70] P. 705; cf. pp. 66, 84–85, 381.

such a sharp distinction can be made between 'us' and 'them'. If one concedes that the New Testament writers used a variety of *intrinsically unsound* methodologies in reading the Old Testament, does this not affect the status of their readings, and hence of their own theological witness? Clearly there are some important issues at stake here, which will have to be discussed more fully in subsequent chapters.

The third aspect of Childs' views on the witness of the two Testaments to be introduced here is that Biblical Theology must move beyond the texts to the divine reality to which they point. The multitude of witnesses have a 'partial' and 'fragmentary' grasp of reality, from which the biblical theologian must pass to 'the full reality which the Christian church confesses to have found in Jesus Christ' (p. 85). Childs, then, is proposing a kind of *Sachkritik*, i.e., 'a critique in terms of . . . content'; yet this content must itself be conceived in a way that comports with the biblical witnesses.[71] In other words, there is a dialectical movement between text and reality, much as Childs had previously outlined in the third of his hermeneutical circles in 'IF' (pp. 443–44).

The movement between text and reality performs a number of important functions in Childs' conception of Biblical Theology. Firstly, it is in this way that Childs handles the diversity of the biblical materials. One of the major concerns of *BTONT* is to describe the different streams of tradition within each Testament and to trace the divergent ways in which the Old Testament trajectories were taken up (or not taken up) by the various New Testament writers. Yet if one is writing a Biblical Theology (rather than a history of theological thought) some sort of overall consistency or coherence needs to be found. Childs' solution is to find the required unity in the one divine reality to which the diverse witnesses testify.

A second important contribution which the movement from text to reality makes to Childs' programme concerns the necessity of interpreting the Old Testament 'typologically'. Once one has passed from witness to substance and reflected theologically upon the nature of the divine reality, there must then be a movement in the reverse direction from reality to biblical witness. Now this may sound (Childs observes, p. 87) as though the allegorizing which he had previously rejected is finally being readmitted; but this is not in fact so, because the motivation for such interpretation and the kind of

---

[71] *Ibid.*; cf. p. 721.

interpretation which it therefore allows is quite different. Allegorizing, in the inadmissible sense, 'assumes that the original meaning of the Old Testament has lost its theological significance', and therefore replaces it with the revelation of the New Testament. The 'typological interpretation' which Childs advocates, however, respects the integrity of the Old Testament and yet, regarding it as a witness to Christ, believes that a 'fuller' meaning can be found through reading it in the light of our knowledge of him.[72] In this sense, then, typological interpretation is a Christian necessity.

The Christian interpretation of the Old Testament, including 'typological' interpretations of various kinds, has long been recognized as an extremely complex and difficult subject. We summarized some of the problems when reviewing Childs' canonical interpretation of Psalm 8 in *BTCri*, and saw that he did not then appear to have satisfactory solutions to them. The methodological discussions in *BTONT* show that Childs has continued to reflect intensively upon this subject, and in fact offer a useful outline of what the problem is: One wishes to make a distinctively Christian reading of these pre-Christian writings, and yet still respect them as pre-Christian. What is rather less clear from *BTONT*, however, is whether Childs has made any significant progress towards actually doing this satisfactorily. On the contrary, one might plausibly argue that his clarifications have finally shown the problem to be indistinguishable from that of trying both to have one's cake and eat it, and that we should therefore heed the advice of those scholars who argue against such interpretation even being attempted.

These issues are clearly of central importance to Childs' conception of Biblical Theology, and will be discussed more fully in subsequent chapters. For the present, however, I wish to put some flesh upon these methodological bones by summarizing some examples from *BTONT* of how biblical-theological reflection, as Childs conceives it, is actually to proceed.

The methodology of *BTONT* is well illustrated by the first chapter of Part 6, which discusses 'The Identity of God'. Childs begins the Old Testament Witness section by recalling that many different names are used to designate God; but whatever their origins may have been, they now function as 'attributes of the one God' (p. 352). Turning

---

[72] *Ibid.*; cf. Childs' section on 'Allegorical or Typological Approaches' in his chapter surveying 'Current Models for Biblical Theology', pp. 13–14.

then to the 'insights into Israel's understanding of God' afforded by the Old Testament narratives (*ibid.*), Childs notes that sometimes Yahweh's identity is seen through his direct interventions in human affairs, but that often he works in an indirect, hidden way. Various aspects of God's identity in the psalms, the legal materials, and the prophetic writings are then likewise reviewed in turn. This leads Childs to observe that Israel's understanding of God was extremely diverse, but he nonetheless suggests that 'there are clearly some unifying themes, some characteristic patterns, and some strong elements of unity' running through the whole (p. 354): That God discloses himself through a personal name, which gains its content from what he does; that he is Israel's God because he freely chose to bind himself to them; etc. (pp. 354–56). Finally, Childs ends this section by considering whether God suffers, with material from all over the Old Testament being collected around the twin poles of God's sovereign freedom and his involvement with humanity.

Turning now to the New Testament Witness,[73] Childs first traces the continuities and discontinuities between the Testaments. Under the former, Childs notes that the Synoptic Gospels portray Jesus against a Jewish background (pp. 361–62), that Paul likewise affirms the continuity with Jewish monotheism (but often in a more conscious and polemical way, p. 362), etc. Nonetheless, this is a 'Continuity within a Christology' (p. 363), rather than a simple identity. The New Testament frequently turns to the Old 'to interpret God's relation to Jesus Christ' (*ibid.*), to whom it also applies the Old Testament designations and characteristic functions of God. Moreover, there are some passages—particularly those using triadic formulae—in which 'both the unity and the diversity between God and Christ are mentioned' (p. 364), and in which Childs sees the 'roots' of the doctrine of the Trinity.

In the light of this survey, Childs argues that when the church, starting from its encounter with Jesus Christ, reflected upon his relationship to God, it saw no need to modify the Old Testament's doctrine of God. Rather, it formulated this relationship by drawing upon the Old Testament's portrayal of God's activities. Nonetheless, it assigned different roles to each agent:

---

[73] Childs in fact precedes this with a section on 'Early Judaism's Understanding of God' (pp. 359–60), but it is not necessary to review that here.

God sent the Son and raised him from the dead. The relationship was
never the reverse. God called the world into being by his creative will.
Yet Christ participated in creation. (p. 367)

Or again, the relationship was explicated through drawing upon the
imagery of the Old Testament, with John 1, for example, using the
concepts of the word of creation and of wisdom 'to bear witness to
the unity and diversity within the Godhead' (*ibid.*). Childs sees the
church's struggles to understand this relationship as '[laying] at the
heart of the development of Trinitarian theology' (p. 368).

Turning next to the section dealing with Biblical Theological
Reflection, Childs discusses here a number of 'The Attributes of God
within the Witness of Scripture' (p. 371): He 'has revealed himself
both as creator and redeemer' (p. 372); 'as a God of righteousness
and mercy' (p. 373); as holy (p. 374); etc. To grasp Childs' methodology it is necessary to look only at one of these discussions; and
since his style becomes so dense here that it is impossible to summarize, I shall simply quote a typical passage:

> God's identity has been made known through his name. It is ... en-
> countered in an event. Jesus is the 'name above every name' (Phil.
> 2:9) ... He identified himself with the external[74] presence of the God
> of Israel as 'I am' (John 8:58). The divine reality has entered history:
> 'Behold your God; the Lord God comes with might (Isa. 40:9f). God
> said to Moses: 'I am Yahweh—this is my name for ever' (Ex. 6:2;
> 3:15). Also Matthew announces Jesus by name: 'You shall call his name
> Jesus, for he will save his people from their sins' (1:21). The revealing
> of the name prevents one envisioning the God of the Bible as a part
> of a 'symbol system'.... Rather, according to both testaments, God
> graciously made known his true being as the One whom he has re-
> vealed. 'I am who I am' (Ex. 3:14). 'Philip said, Lord show us the
> Father ... Jesus said: He who has seen me has seen the Father' (John
> 14:9). (p. 371)

Childs ends his chapter on the identity of God with a section entitled 'From Biblical Theology to Dogmatics: Trinitarian Theology'
(p. 375), in which he asks whether the Scriptures can now be read
in the light of the 'subject matter' to which the preceding sections
have led us—namely, the triunity of God and 'the reality of Jesus
Christ' (p. 379). Unfortunately, however, this consists of little more
than a reiteration of the methodological points he has made else-

---

[74] *Sic*; presumably this is a misprinting of 'eternal'.

where in *BTONT*, with virtually no attempt being made to actually reinterpret the Bible in the way proposed.[75]

Childs' approach to Biblical Theology, then, is quite complex. Its main strengths, I would suggest, are firstly, that Childs fully respects the diversity of the biblical materials—his work has never had the harmonizing tendencies of which it is sometimes accused—and secondly, that he is nonetheless able to suggest some interesting foci around which one can at least begin to order this diversity. On the other hand, however, the examples we have just reviewed raise (or rather, reiterate) a problem which strikes at the very heart of Childs' project: He still seems to have made little progress towards setting the reading of the Old Testament as Christian Scripture on a methodologically sound basis. And likewise, therefore, he has made little progress towards hearing the two Testaments as co-witnesses to the one divine reality. These problems show themselves in a number of ways:

(i) The Old Testament (Childs has repeatedly told us), even in its discrete identity apart from the New Testament, bears witness to Christ. In keeping with this he ends the Old Testament Witness section we reviewed above with the following comment:

> It is not by chance that the early church struggled with the Old Testament when it sought to bear witness to the sheer mystery of the God of Israel who in Jesus Christ 'emptied himself, taking the form of a servant, and became obedient unto death'. Jesus brought no new concept of God, but he demonstrated in action the full extent of God's redemptive will for the world which was from the beginning. (p. 358)

It is perhaps appropriate at this point to say that I am largely sympathetic towards what Childs is attempting in his *Biblical Theology*; and yet it is difficult to see how, within their context in Childs' discussion, the comments I have just quoted amount to anything more than an arbitrary 'christianizing' gloss upon the Hebrew Scriptures. The preceding paragraphs, it will be recalled, are a descriptive survey of the Old Testament materials relating to God's suffering; and since this particularly concerns his involvement with humanity, it is not

---

[75] The one exception occurs on p. 382, where Childs quotes from Isa. 53 and comments: 'This canonical text addresses the suffering community of historical Israel within the context of the old covenant.... Yet to know the will of God in Jesus Christ opens up a profoundly new vista on this prophetic testimony.... For those who confess the Lordship of Jesus Christ there is an immediate morphological fit'. This barely even begins to address Childs' claims about further levels of meaning, however.

surprising that (as Childs remarks) the early church was drawn to
such passages when trying to understand Jesus in the light of its
Scriptures. This, however, is no more than a *historical statement* about
the early church. For it to become a *theological* statement something
further is required—at the very least, it needs to be shown that
in referring these Scriptures to Jesus one is not merely appropriating them for an alien purpose but is, in some sense, truly hearing
their witness.

This point is of considerable importance for assessing Childs' *Biblical Theology*, and is therefore worth developing more fully. Thus it is
one thing, for example, to cite Isa. 63:9 (as Childs does on p. 357)
as a witness to God's suffering-redemptive involvement with humanity—or, more precisely, to Yahweh's involvement with Israel. It is
something else, however, to claim that Yahweh's suffering-redemptive
involvement with humanity took the specific form of him becoming
incarnate in Jesus; and it is yet something else again to claim that
the former, as an anticipation[76] of the latter, is in some sense a prior
witness to it. This is not to say that it is wrong to pass from the first
claim to the second or the third. On the other hand, however, there
is certainly no *obvious* inconsistency in affirming the first claim but
denying the others; therefore the burden of proof clearly rests upon
those who believe that it is possible to pass from one to the other.
The weakness in Childs' position at this point, then, is that he makes
no attempt to bear this burden, nor even shows much awareness
that it needs to be borne. Rather, he has devoted his exegetical skills
to the descriptive questions which relate to the first claim and then
passed by some sort of unexplained leap[77] to the distinctively Christian claims, without really showing us that we are still hearing a
legitimate witness of these Old Testament texts.

(ii) Similar problems also recur, not surprisingly, in the New Testament Witness and the Biblical Theological Reflection sections. In
the former, having summarized the continuities and discontinuities
between the Testaments Childs comments:

---

[76] Or 'as an aspect', or 'a generalization'—Childs does not make it clear what
sort of relationship he has in mind.

[77] The passage where the transition is made (in the first full paragraph on p. 358)
leans heavily on 'Israel' 'his [sc. God's] people' and 'the world' being used inter-
changeably, and 'salvation' being used in an undefined sense which is assumed to
cover 'what God does' in relation to each of these distinct groups.

> In sum, the New Testament writers even in the process of developing their christologies, see no real tension between the Old Testament's understanding of God and their own understanding of Jesus Christ. (p. 364)

Yet whatever one might think of this as a descriptive-historical statement about the New Testament writers, it is difficult to accept it as a theological witness when questions about whether they were *right* to see 'no real tension' here, or whether, on the contrary, this means that they had essentially stifled the Old Testament's witness with their own preoccupations, are not even raised. Or again, the lengthy passage I quoted from the Biblical Theological Reflection does little more than juxtapose verses from the Old and New Testaments on the slender 'catchword' principle that they are concerned with the self-revelatory names of Jesus or the God of Israel.[78] Here also Childs does not even ask the crucial questions as to whether this produces a largely fortuitous concatenation of data which has little theological significance—and it cannot lightly be set aside that catchword exegesis is generally looked upon askance by modern scholarship—or whether this does in some way yield a genuine witness of the two Testaments in unison.

(iii) As we saw in the case of *OTTCC*, so also in *BTONT* one finds relatively little overtly christological exegesis of the Old Testament, and what there is tends to be very general and low-key. Besides the chapter on 'The Identity of God', there is one entitled 'Christ, the Lord' (pp. 452–84); but again the Old Testament discussions are very thin. The Old Testament Witness section briefly summarizes the diverse strands in Israel's messianic hopes. As Childs explicitly notes (p. 453), he is here largely following the studies in Old Testament theology of Eichrodt and others; thus it appears that, in this most central area of Biblical Theology, his methodological statements about the distinctiveness of the canonical approach to the Old Testament do not in fact lead to anything very new or original. The corresponding Biblical Theological Reflection is also very brief (pp. 476–80). After about a page of methodological discussions there is a two page survey of different aspects of God's presence with Israel, and again it is difficult to see anything here that is distinctive of his canonical approach. Nor is it clear why this material should be

---

[78] Cf. his similar handling, in the same section, of God revealing himself 'as a God of righteousness and mercy' (p. 373).

included in a chapter specifically on christology, or why it is presented as a contribution to Biblical Theology rather than Old Testament Theology. Then finally in this section there is juxtaposed to the Old Testament material a one page summary of how the New Testament regarded God to be present in Jesus, and how it drew upon the Old Testament offices of king, priest, and prophet to express this. Once more, however, the crucial theological question of whether, or in what sense, this was a valid hearing of the Old Testament is not addressed.

In sum: Although Childs' *Biblical Theology of the Old and New Testaments* certainly makes a number of valuable contributions to the discipline, it falls a long way short of being the Biblical Theology which Childs has been aiming to produce, and does so in ways that point to his programme being beset by fundamental methodological problems.

## 6. *Canonical Hermeneutics in Crisis?*

Our lengthy analysis of Childs' work, then, has finally brought us full circle. When we discussed the programme for a new Biblical Theology which Childs set out in 'Interpretation in Faith' and *Biblical Theology in Crisis* we saw that it was fraught with unresolved tensions between faith and reason, between the descriptive and the normative/constructive tasks, and between the original and the canonical contexts. In the *Introductions*, however, the extent of these problems was substantially masked[79] by the restricted nature of the task they were tackling—an Old Testament Introduction is primarily oriented towards describing the Hebrew writings as ancient literature, rather than making a significant contribution to constructive theology, or showing how Genesis is to be read in the light of the New Testament witness to Christ. The full range of issues, however, is taken up again in the canonical *Theologies*; moreover, their nature is such that the argument has to be carried mainly by the exegetical studies of the biblical texts rather than by the methodological discus-

---

[79] They are rather more evident in *EC*, which (as we saw in section 2.4) attempts to apply the programme of 'IF' and *BTCri* to the theological study of Exodus. I have not discussed the problems of *EC* in much detail, however, as this would largely repeat points which can generally be made more clearly in analysing Childs' other works.

sions. As we have now seen, however, this quickly leads to the previously unresolved methodological problems resurfacing again. In view of this, therefore, it is not going too far to say that Childs' programme is currently in a state of crisis: It has long-standing methodological problems that greatly hinder its implementation, and which it has made little progress towards resolving.

In the remainder of this book I will explore various ways in which the problems identified in this and the previous chapter might be solved, or at least mitigated. To round off the present discussion, however, I wish to review a couple of examples, drawn from Karl Barth's *Church Dogmatics*, which attempt to provide something like the distinctively Christian interpretations of the Old Testament that Childs has long been advocating but never quite producing. (Turning to Barth for help with this is particularly apposite in view of the many favourable comments, spanning much of his career, that Childs himself has made on Barth's theological approach to biblical interpretation.)[80] As with our previous interpretative examples, the primary objective is not to defend the actual exegesis—in fact I would not endorse these interpretations without at least adding some significant qualifications—but to see what methodological issues they raise.[81]

Let us begin, then, with Barth's trinitarian interpretation of Gen. 1:26–27. Modern scholars have usually explained the 'us' and 'our' of v. 26 with reference to the heavenly court;[82] yet whatever merit this may have as a reconstruction of their 'original meaning', the further question can be asked as to what they now mean when read in their present canonical context, and in the light of the full canonical witness to the character of God. On this Barth makes the following pertinent observations:

> Those addressed here are not merely consulted by the one who speaks but are summoned to . . . an act of creation, the creation of man, in concert with the One who speaks. . . . How could non-divine beings

---

[80] See especially Childs' article, 'Karl Barth as an Interpreter of Scripture', *passim*. For earlier favourable comments see 'IF' p. 437 n. 14, p. 443 n. 19, and *BTCri* pp. 110–11; in *BTONT* Childs claims that 'Karl Barth's interpretation of many biblical narratives from both testaments remain often unparalleled in power and insight' (p. 708). The work of Childs and Barth is compared and contrasted in chapter 2 of Charles Scalise's *Canonical Hermeneutics*.

[81] These will be discussed more fully in section 12.3 below.

[82] E.g., Gerhard von Rad, *Genesis*, pp. 58–59. Alternatively, Westermann describes it as 'a plural of deliberation', for which he cites various alleged parallels from elsewhere in the Old Testament (*Genesis 1–11* (London: SPCK, 1984), p. 145).

even assist in an advisory capacity in an act of creation, let alone have an active part in the creation of man, as we are expressly told?[83]

Yet although this act of creation is contemplated as the action of a plurality (*wayyōmer 'ĕlōhîm na'ăseh 'ādām* 'And Elohim said, "Let *us* make man"', v. 26), its implementation is described as the action of a singularity (*wayyibrā' 'ĕlōhîm 'et hā'ādām* 'And Elohim [*he*] created man', v. 27). In other words, 'Elohim' occurs here, in close juxtaposition, as the subject of both a singular and a plural verb. Similarly, God's 'image' is ascribed to him through both singular and plural possessive pronouns (*bĕṣalmēnû kidmûtēnû* 'in our image, according to our likeness', v. 26; *bĕṣalmô* 'in his image', v. 27). Elohim seems to be, in some sense, both a singular and a plural being.

This is further underlined when we consider what 'the image of God' actually is. Without reviewing the numerous alternatives that have been suggested, it suffices for our present purposes to suggest that the emphatic parallelism between the three *bārā'* clauses in v. 27 makes it natural to understand the creation of *hā'ādām* as male and female as an explication of what it is for them to be created in God's image. This at least makes plausible Barth's contention that 'God . . . has created man male and female, and in this way in his own image and likeness' (p. 187). Again the point can be put grammatically: As male and female humankind is the plural object of God's creative act (*bārā' 'ōtām* 'he created them', v. 27); yet in the closest juxtaposition to this humankind is also the singular object of God's creation (*bārā' 'ōtô* 'he created him', *ibid.*). In other words, humankind is presented here as, in some sense, both a singular and a plural being,[84] and in this very respect is created in the image of God.

Barth also discusses the image of God in the New Testament, which he finds to be closely related to his interpretations of Genesis 1 and 2.[85] Unfortunately the details are rather obscure, but the main thrust seems to be this: There are a number of references in the New Testament to Christ and to Christians bearing the image of God, and in some cases they are alluding to the creation narratives in Genesis; but how, more precisely, is this related to the image envis-

---

[83] *Church Dogmatics* III.1 (Edinburgh: T&T Clark, 1958), p. 192.

[84] This is hinted at again in 2:18–24. Male and female are 'of the same substance' ('bone of my bones, and flesh of my flesh', becoming 'one flesh' in marriage) and yet two different, but complementary, forms of humanity, so that humanity only reaches its fullness in their union. Cf. Barth, pp. 288–311 *passim*.

[85] Pp. 201–206, 320–29, *passim*.

aged in Gen. 1:26–27? Barth finds the key in (i) Col. 1:15–18, where Christ is characterized both as 'the image of the invisible God' and as the 'head of the body, the church'; together with (ii) 1 Cor. 11:3–12 and Eph. 5:22–33, which (with explicit reference to Genesis 2) portray Christ's relationship to the church in terms of human marriage. In the light of the full canonical witness, therefore, Barth understands the image of God to be borne by the unity and plurality of Christ's 'marriage' to his bride, the church, with the connection between them established through the imagery of human sexuality: The image of God as explicated in Gen. 1:26–27 as unity and plurality is mirrored in the creation of humankind as male and female, and more particularly in the sexual union of the two becoming one. This imagery is then drawn upon in portraying Christ's relationship to the church.

Using this as a hermeneutical bridge between Genesis and the New Testament, Barth offers a remarkable Christian interpretation of Genesis 2:

> Why could not man be content with the co-existence of the animals? Why could he recognize in the woman alone the helpmeet which he lacked? From the standpoint of the New Testament we must answer that it is because the calling and ingathering of the Church of Jesus Christ ... was to be a matter of His own free election.... Why did the first man have to fall into that deep sleep when the work of God was done in which the woman had her origin? From the standpoint of the New Testament it is because the Church of Jesus Christ was to have its origin in His mortal sleep and to stand complete before Him in his resurrection. (p. 321)

There is clearly no doubt in Barth's mind that the Old Testament is to be read as Christian Scripture!

In comparing this with Childs, it would of course be wrong simply to present Barth's work as a 'gold standard' that Childs has fallen short of. Barth's interpretations have themselves been severely criticized by many biblical scholars, and there are aspects of the preceding from which Childs might well want to distance himself—one can certainly query, for example, whether the christological interpretation of Genesis 2 has really respected this as a passage from the *Old* Testament. And yet, possible excesses apart, this does seem to be much closer to the spirit of Childs' proposals than his own, christologically very thin, discussion of the identity of God. Moreover, Barth makes a sustained attempt to show that, even though his interpretations of Genesis 1–2 are indebted to the New Testament, they are none-theless grounded in the Old Testament texts.[86] In other words, he is less dependent than Childs upon claims of what the Old Testament *comes* to mean when read with Christian hindsight—a procedure which, as our examples from *BTONT* have suggested, can all too readily appear arbitrary and eisegetical—and is therefore in a better posi-tion to claim that he is hearing the witness *of the Old Testament* to the God whom the Christian church confesses. So could one perhaps find in Barth's work exegetical principles or procedures which could be beneficially ingrafted into Childs' theological hermeneutics?

The analysis of Childs' canonical programme, then, in this and the preceding chapter has suggested that it raises a number of important methodological and hermeneutical issues. These will be discussed more fully in the remainder of the book.

---

[86] *Contra* Westermann, who brushes aside Barth's trinitarian interpretation of Gen. 1:26 as simply echoing 'a dogmatic judgement' of the early church (*Genesis 1–11*, p. 144).

CHAPTER FOUR

# REFERENCE, FACT, AND INTERPRETATION

It was suggested in section 3.4 that 'historical referentiality' covered several different problems in Childs' programme; so in the first section of this chapter I shall try to distinguish between them. The remainder of this chapter and the next will then consider in some detail one central aspect of referentiality, namely, the reconstruction of (alleged) historical events that are explicitly referred to in the biblical texts. (Other aspects of referentiality will be discussed in subsequent chapters.) For *this* kind of referentiality, I shall argue from Childs' own Relevance Principle that he does not allow historical reconstruction as significant a place in his programme as he ought.

This naturally raises the question as to how, from a canonical perspective—and particularly in view of Childs' claim that scholarship ought to work 'from faith'—an investigation into 'what really happened' ought to proceed. In subsequent sections, therefore, I shall develop a 'faith informed' historical methodology, defend it against a number of critical arguments, and assess its significance for Childs' programme.

## 1. *Two Terminological Distinctions*

Broadly speaking, Childs' position on referentiality is that our understanding of a text should not be uniformly tied to questions of historical reference: The referentiality of the biblical texts is very variable, with some giving precise and detailed accounts of, say, specific military engagements, while others speak only in very general terms about conflict and destruction. Taking the text's canonical shape as normative entails that we should respect this variability, and not undermine it through, for example, trying to reconstruct a text's precise historical circumstances when the text itself has obscured them. Childs faults both liberal and conservative scholars for going against the canonical shaping in this respect.[1]

---

[1] E.g., *IOTS* pp. 16–17, 133.

To clarify the different issues at stake within this broad thesis I wish to draw a couple of terminological distinctions. The first concerns two senses of 'understanding the final form of the text': (i) Semantic Understanding, and (ii) Genetic Understanding. (i) Puzzled by Saul's enigmatic encounter with the young maidens coming to draw water (1 Sam. 9:11–12), we come across Robert Alter's explanation of it[2] as a generally propitious type-scene that is here broken off prematurely, thus casting an ominous shadow over Saul. Our puzzlement is resolved through Alter showing us (if we are persuaded by him) a *meaning of the text* that fits it smoothly and appropriately into its context. (ii) Puzzled by the extremely repetitious nature of the Flood narrative, we come across Wellhausen's explanation of it as an editorial conflation of two originally independent accounts, each essentially complete in itself. Our puzzlement is resolved through Wellhausen showing us (if we are persuaded by him) a *genesis of the text* that accounts for this problematic feature.[3] Yet although, broadly speaking, we can say that Wellhausen's analysis helps us to understand the final form of the text, this is clearly an understanding quite different in kind from a semantic understanding of its meaning.

Now when Childs asserts that we should understand the final form as the Scriptures of the church it is clearly semantic understanding that he intends. This is not to say that understanding the text's genesis is of no account—on the contrary, Childs' Intentionalist stance is a clear affirmation that the underlying factors which influenced the text's production are of considerable importance for his canonical programme. Nonetheless, Childs clearly regards the Scriptures as addressing the modern church through the message of their final form; therefore it is semantic understanding which is the primary concern of the canonical approach.

The second (related) distinction to be drawn is between 'referentiality *behind* the text' and 'referentiality *in* the text'. By the former I mean (reconstructed) references to things which are not as such referred to in the canonical text—for example, the original historical setting of a prophetic oracle when this has been largely obscured by the final

---

[2] *The Art of Biblical Narrative* (Hemel Hempstead: George Allen & Unwin, 1981), pp. 60–61.

[3] Of course, genetic understanding may have to reckon with a broad mixture of literary, religious, cultural, and political factors in accounting for a text's formation. I will use 'genetic understanding' to cover all such explanations.

form, or the cultic ceremonies that scholars reconstruct as the original *sitzen im Leben* of many psalms. By 'referentiality *in* the text', on the other hand, I mean those references that the biblical writers themselves overtly make to (what they took to be) real historical persons and events—the authors of Kings or the synoptic Gospels were not, *prima facie*, writing parables or historical novels, but were telling us about things which (they believed) really happened. It is this kind of referentiality that we shall chiefly be concerned with in the present chapter.

These distinctions of understanding and reference are clearly related to each other, although in a rather complex way. Attempting to understand a text's genesis will obviously raise issues of the referentiality behind it; but if one is only interested in a semantic understanding of the text's final form will this also involve one in questions of what lies behind it? On the one hand, Childs is clearly right in arguing that *some* questions of this sort are excluded—a commentary that discusses incubation rites and the primeval chaos will add little to our semantic understanding of the psalms precisely because references to them have been largely 'demythologized' and/or expunged from the final form. Using the psalms to reconstruct the 'myth and ritual' of the cult is simply a different task from understanding these texts semantically. Yet on the other hand, Childs also wants to maintain that semantic understanding is not *completely* independent of referentiality behind the text. As we saw in section 3.1, he believes that one use of the critical tools (which are essentially concerned with this kind of referentiality) is to further our semantic understanding of the final form. Childs' outlines of the text's canonical shape in fact make frequent references to reconstructed entities (such as the Deuteronomistic redactors, or the J source); and conversely, it is the neglect of these matters by pre- and anti-critical scholars which is blamed for making their exegesis 'flat'. So then, the relationship between these kinds of referentiality and understanding is complex.

I shall return to these issues in later chapters; they are raised here in order to set them off from the main subject of the present chapter, which is the overt references of the biblical texts to allegedly historical persons and events. This poses much more immediate problems for Childs than does referentiality behind the text, because, by Childs' own insistence upon the normativity of the canon, it would seem that we ought to take seriously its *prima facie* intention to give us historical information about ancient Israel and Jesus of Nazareth.

But what should we do, then, if critical studies show us that this information is sometimes incorrect?


## 2. *Historical Reference and Theological Value*

One important strand in Childs' solution to the problem I have just outlined is his decoupling of a text's religious and theological value from its historical veracity. Although Childs has not (as far as I am aware) developed this point at any length, his scattered comments and his way of handling specific instances suggest that, if pressed, he would argue along the following lines: Although liberal and conservative scholars differ widely in their estimates of the accuracy of the biblical texts, the importance they both attach to historical reconstruction is due to them implicitly agreeing that a text's value is quite directly correlated with its veracity. In Childs' view, however, the relationship between historical accuracy and theological value is extremely variable. In some cases the interdependence is high—as we saw in section 3.4, Childs is unequivocal in affirming that the salvific power of the gospel is dependent upon 'the life, death, and resurrection of Jesus Christ who entered into the world of time and space'.[4] In many other instances, however, the connection is very weak; and in such cases it follows that (i) the text may retain its theological value even if it has little historical worth, and (ii) resolving the historical issues has little significance for the biblical scholar as such, however important they may be for other scholars. The theologian's goals are different from theirs, and are often only loosely related to 'what really happened'.

Because Childs is arguing for a *variable* dependence of value upon history it is difficult to discuss his views in general terms. To clarify his position, therefore, I shall look at his handling of three specific cases: The Mosaic authorship of the Pentateuch; Solomon's authorship of Proverbs; and the deliverance of Jerusalem from Sennacherib. Starting, then, with Mosaic authorship, Childs suggests that liberals and conservatives share a common error in regarding this as an important issue. In Childs' view, the theologically pertinent question is not whether Moses really wrote these books, but what the 'canonical function' is of (major portions of) the Pentateuch being ascribed

---

[4] *NTCI*, p. 545.

to him—in other words, the important issues are not those of his-torical authorship but of (what we might call) 'canonical [ascriptions of] authorship'. Childs' discussion of the latter hinges upon his ob-servation that, according to the presentation in the Pentateuch, Moses is commissioned to *write down* the law of God. According to Childs, the significance of this becomes particularly clear in Deuteronomy 31, where it is shown that the law, which is a witness to God's will, is to be binding upon all future generations—though Moses is about to die, his witness will abide.

Childs particularly emphasises the connection between Mosaic canonical authorship and the *authority* of the law: '[L]aws attributed to Moses were deemed authoritative, and conversely authoritative laws were attributed to Moses'.[5] This attribution was not, in the modern sense, a historical judgement; nor was the law authoritative because Moses (really, historically) wrote it. Rather, it was deemed to have been written by him because it had already been recognized by the community as authoritative, and was attributed to Moses as an ex-pression of this.

Childs, then, is trying to find theological value in an ascription of authorship that most scholars can no longer accept historically; but in my view, this particular attempt to separate theology from history encounters a number of serious problems. Firstly, if Moses were the historical author of the law then this would *justify* its claim to be authoritative—in the context of Sinai, it gives the law a direct, di-vine legitimation as an expression of God's will. Moses being the canonical author of the law, however, only *expresses* this claim, leav-ing it unsupported; and this reopens the question about the true status of the law. With Mosaic historical authorship denied, other grounds for accepting it as an authoritative expression of the divine will would have to be found.

For the central moral laws (such as the prohibitions of killing, steal-ing, and bearing false witness) one might plausibly argue that they have a natural authority of their own, and therefore do not need to be externally authorized. However, there are other parts of the law where legitimation poses a much more difficult problem. Was the community right, for example, to regard the food laws, or the sacrificial rituals, as binding upon them as the law of God? Were they really an aspect of how Yahweh expected his people to live before him, or

---

[5] *IOTS*, p. 134.

were they 'traditions of men' that bore no relation to the character
and purposes of God, and which are therefore of no value to the
modern theologian? Once Mosaic historical authorship has been
rejected, questions about the origins of Israel's laws have to be answered in some other way; and it is difficult to see why the theological significance of the law should be held, *a priori*, to be independent
of how these questions are answered.

Secondly, the canonical writings portray the law as central to the
relationship between Yahweh and a real, historical people, and as a
key factor, therefore, in shaping the course which the history of that
people actually took. Thus, to take one example, the division of the
kingdom upon Solomon's death—which was undoubtedly a real,
historical event—is interpreted theologically by the Deuteronomists
as a punishment for Solomon violating Yahweh's prohibition of intermarriage with the surrounding nations and for worshipping other
gods (1 Kgs. 11:1–13). For this to be a coherent explanation, however,
it must take cognizance of the law *as it actually was* at the relevant
time—it would make little sense to claim that God divided the kingdom because Solomon had broken laws that did not in fact exist at
that time. In other words, there are some reconstructions of Israel's
*history* that are incompatible with the Deuteronomistic *theology*; therefore once the Mosaic origin of the pertinent legal codes is denied it
becomes an open question as to the extent to which the Deuteronomistic theology is still tenable. How this question should be answered will then depend very much upon what alternative account
of the law is to replace the canonical portrayal. Thus the tenability
of the theology is heavily dependent upon critical reconstructions of
'what really happened'.

Childs shows some awareness of these problems in *IOTS*, and tries
to defend the Deuteronomists against the charge that their standards
for assessing the kings were anachronistic. Childs' main point appears
to be that Deuteronomy is representative of an interpretation of 'the
Torah of Moses' that was eventually accepted by the whole religious
community—in other words, that although the Deuteronomist's evaluations of Israel's kings are made retrospectively they are nonetheless
legitimate, because they proceed from canonical norms.[6] Yet although
one might allow that there are some cases where retrospective evaluations are legitimate (one would not wish to assess, say, the Nazis'

---

[6] See *IOTS*, p. 291.

treatment of the Jews solely in terms of the Nazi legislation pertaining at that time), it is far from clear whether this really solves the Deuteronomistic problem. If at the time of Solomon God had not prohibited intermarriage with foreigners then it is difficult to see how Solomon's marriages could have been sinful, or how Yahweh could have justly punished him for contracting such marriages. In sum, the tenability of the Deuteronomists' theology does seem to be dependent upon referential questions about Israel's history.

Thirdly, doubts about Mosaic historical authorship call into question the theological status of Childs' interesting observations on the relationship of law and grace. According to the canonical presentation (Childs argues), the law was given at Sinai to a people whom God had already redeemed from Egypt and made his own, and is set within a context of the people's disobedience. The law, therefore, is not a means of self-salvation; rather, the people have already been placed in a state of holiness by God, who has given them the law as a means by which they can respond appropriately to their Godgiven status.[7] Again, however, this theology seems to depend heavily upon the history. If the principal events really did unfold as the canon presents them, then that would give a direct justification for Childs' theological conclusions; but this would hardly be the case if it could be shown that, for example, Israel was *already* observing the Mosaic law while still captive in Egypt. Once again, therefore, we have to conclude that if the law had its origins in circumstances that differ significantly from those depicted in the canon, then our primary theological question has to be, What do *those* circumstances imply about the status of the law?[8]

---

[7] See *IOTS*, pp. 173–74, 185–87.

[8] Unfortunately Childs' discussions of these subjects often seem to be somewhat equivocal; for example: 'In the book of Leviticus one historical moment in Israel's life [namely, 'the divine will made known to Moses at Sinai'] has become the norm by which all subsequent history of the nation is measured' (p. 186). By 'all subsequent history' Childs apparently means what really happened to the historical nation, Israel; yet it is far from clear that he would really want to describe the events at Sinai as 'historical' in this sense. Or again: 'The Old Testament's understanding of God was set forth in a series of revelatory events which entered Israel's time and space. The Old Testament bears witness to the beginning of creation, the call of Abraham, the exodus from Egypt, the revelation at Sinai, the possession of the land, the establishment of the monarchy, the destruction of Jerusalem, exile and restoration' (*BTONT*, pp. 91–92). Without trying to guess Childs' own views on the historicity of these events, one can at least say that for some items on his list there are many scholars who would have severe reservations about describing them as 'events which entered Israel's time and space' if this meant affirming that, for example,

It seems to me, then, that Childs' discussion of Mosaic authorship largely misses the mark. Once Mosaic historical authorship is rejected it has to be asked how Israel's law did in fact develop; and for the reasons we have just discussed, our assessment of the canonical theologies is dependent upon the historical answers we find to this question. If it could be shown, for example, that much of the Pentateuchal legislation can be traced back (not to Sinai but) to the covenant ceremony depicted in Joshua 24 then most of the theology would perhaps still stand. Yet if the bulk of this legal material had its origins in the last years of the monarchy then much of the Deuteronomistic theology would surely be no more than a radical misinterpretation of Israel's history. In the case of Mosaic authorship, then, theology and historical referentiality cannot be decoupled—one cannot regard the law, for theological purposes, as having been given by Moses while also admitting that in fact it was not.

In contrast to this, however, Childs' discussion of Solomon's authorship of Proverbs is much more successful. This canonical ascription of authorship, Childs points out, is *transparently* fictitious: Proverbs itself assigns some of its parts to other authors (30:1; 31:1), and recognises that other portions only attained their present form long after Solomon's death (25:1). Clearly, then, the superscription is not a historical claim that Solomon wrote the whole book, and the way is therefore naturally opened up for us to ask about its canonical purpose without having to be greatly concerned with questions of referentiality.

According to Childs, the initial superscription indicates the 'perspective' from which Proverbs is to be read:

> [It] guards against forcing the proverbs into a context foreign to wisdom, such as the decalogue.... The title serves canonically to preserve the uniqueness of the sapiential witness against the attempts to merge it with more dominant biblical themes. (p. 552)

Or again, the connection of Proverbs with Solomon (as well as the superscriptions in Prov. 30:1 and 31:1) link this material with international wisdom, and thereby 'offer a canonical warrant' for comparing them with foreign material (*ibid.*).

---

Abraham really was a historical individual who, at some definite (though now unknown) date was called by God to leave his home in Haran, etc. One wishes that it were clearer what Childs is actually committing himself to, historically, when he makes such claims as these.

Childs indicates in passing that he sees the issues of Solomonic and Mosaic authorship as quite similar: 'The proverbs were assigned to Solomon who was the traditional source of Israel's sapiential learning (as Moses was of Torah . . .)'.[9] But whatever value this comparison may have as a historical reconstruction of the shaping of the respective bodies of literature, it seems to me that the very different character of the material involved in each case make Solomonic canonical authorship a much more viable concept, theologically, than is Mosaic canonical authorship. Firstly, wisdom generally has a 'self-authenticating' character which the legal material often lacks—one can recognise the 'rightness' of many of the aphorisms and similes of Proverbs simply by pondering upon them in the light of one's experience of life, whereas deciding upon the 'rightness' of the food laws or the Day of Atonement legislation is much more problematic. Since, therefore, wisdom sayings stand in less need of 'external' justification than the legal material, a denial of Solomonic historical authorship of the proverbs is of much less consequence for their status. And secondly, the proverbs are not particularly connected with the biblical portrayal and evaluation of the historical course of Israel's life; therefore questions about the true dating and origin of the proverbs have much less radical consequences than they do for the law. It would make little difference to the status of the proverbs if half of them were post-exilic or inherited from Egypt, whereas it could have radical theological implications if half the Mosaic legislation were post-exilic or inherited from the Canaanites.

The third example of historical referentiality to consider here is taken from Childs' *Isaiah and the Assyrian Crisis*. This is the only full-scale attempt that Childs has made thus far to reconstruct a historical event, and it is therefore somewhat ironic that, having subjected the various biblical sources to a thorough form-critical analysis, he concludes that their character precludes us from making such a reconstruction.[10] Childs nonetheless wishes to affirm the theological value of these texts, and yet to do so in a way that respects the historical forces which contributed to their production. Thus in discussing $B^2$ Childs suggests that it has been strongly influenced by the Zion tradition. This had its origins in myths about the primeval overthrow of

---

[9] P. 551; this, of course, is a standard critical point.
[10] *IAC*, pp. 118–20; to avoid overcomplicating the discussion I shall concentrate on Childs' treatment of the $B^2$ source (sc. 2 Kgs. 19:9b–35//Isa. 37:9b–36).

Chaos, although it had been 'historicized' at an early stage in its development, with the chaotic waters becoming the enemies of Israel. Childs sees B² as resulting from further developments of this kind, through the impact of traditions stemming from the crisis of 701:

> The enemy is . . . removed from its former position as the unidentified evil horde which occupied an undetermined place between heaven and earth, and has been identified with Sennacherib's army. The legend is not satisfied with the assurance of divine destruction of the enemy. It knows the exact manner of its execution . . ., and the precise effect on the army. . . . Moreover, the motivation for the defence of the city is spelled out. It is for Yahweh's own sake and for the sake of David. (p. 102)

But how, then, is this legend supposed to be of theological value? Childs, rather surprisingly, says virtually nothing about this;[11] but we might consider two alternatives: It could be read as a paradigmatic instance, or 'type', of Yahweh's deliverance of his people from an impossible situation;[12] or it might be viewed as a parable. Each approach has its own contrasting attractions and problems. As a type, its theological value would be clear and immediate: If Yahweh delivered Jerusalem in this way then it gives us an unusually direct insight into his character, his power, and his relationship to his chosen people; and it would therefore provide the modern scholar with extremely valuable material for theological reflection. Yet these theological advantages come only at the price of a far greater commitment to historical veracity than Childs feels able to make in this case—for B² to function typologically it would have to give a reasonably accurate portrayal of (the relevant aspects of) the events of 701. If the historical reality behind this 'deliverance by Yahweh' was in fact an unconditional surrender by Hezekiah ('whatever you impose on me I will bear', 2 Kgs. 18:14) then in presenting it as a triumph of Yahweh's power (19:35) B² has fundamentally misunderstood and/ or misrepresented the situation. Victory and abject surrender are totally

---

[11] His concluding section on 'The Theological Problem' (pp. 121–27) is mainly concerned with theological norms, and has little to say about how a text such as B² (which Childs describes as 'the legend of the righteous king', p. 121) is to function theologically.

[12] Childs himself suggests that in Isaiah 33 'the Assyrian crisis has become a type of a recurrent threat' (p. 116); and elsewhere he explains the theological significance of Nahum in terms of it portraying Nineveh as 'a type of a larger recurring phenomenon in history against which God exercises his eternal power and judgement' ('Exegetical Significance', p. 73).

antithetical, and it is impossible for the latter to be legitimately portrayed as the former. $B^2$, then, could only be used as a type if the
distinction between the interpretation and the *mis*interpretation of
historical events were virtually eliminated; and it is difficult to see
how theology could accept this without completely losing its intellectual integrity.

In view of these problems, it may seem preferable to regard $B^2$ as
a parable of salvation which, though originally inspired by certain
(now irrecoverable) historical events, makes its theological point without
calling for any particular commitment to its historical veracity. The
fact that (in contrast to the Sinai narratives) the deliverance of
Hezekiah's Jerusalem was not a 'foundation charter', with significant
implications for the subsequent course of Israel's history, probably
makes a parabolic approach less problematic here than it was for
the Mosaic case; yet it also has its difficulties. Firstly, there is again
the problem of justification: If Yahweh really did slay 185,000
Assyrians in a single night, this would give a direct theological insight into his power to shape history; whereas a parable in which
Yahweh slays 185,000 Assyrians, while effectively expressing a belief
in his power, leaves open the theologically important question, Is
this belief *true*? Is Yahweh really like that? This is not, of course, to
deny that parables may have real theological value; yet this is often
quite different in kind from that of a type. Thus we are again led to
the conclusion that theological value is often less easily detached from
questions of historical referentiality than Childs realizes.

Secondly, I cannot altogether escape the feeling that resorting to
parables in a case such as this is a very artificial manoeuvre. Childs
has himself argued persuasively for the historical character of Kings,
pointing out that to characterize these texts as 'story' (following James
Barr) or as 'history-like narrative' (Hans Frei) is inadequate, because
these descriptions give insufficient recognition to the specifically historical interests of the text, such as its attention to chronological details,
its relating of Israel's 'story' to that of the surrounding nations, and
its frequent citing of sources.[13] Although not all of these considerations apply directly to $B^2$, it seems difficult to deny that, through
integrating it into the ongoing story of Israel and her neighbours, its

---

[13] See *IOTS*, pp. 297–99. It is not altogether clear whether Childs intends to
affirm the historical character of Kings *in contrast* to other Old Testament books,
although similar points could presumably be made about some of the narratives in,
say, Exodus or Chronicles.

author intended to tell us 'what really happened' when Sennacherib attacked Jerusalem (including the miraculous deliverance).[14] Thus although a parabolic reading may be possible, and (to some degree) theologically profitable, it is hardly the most natural way to interpret this text. Or to express the point in a more Childsian way, such a reading seems to go against the text's own canonical intentionality.

What seems to emerge from this discussion, then, is that (i) Childs' general principle of the variable relationship between theological value and historical referentiality is essentially correct; but (ii) its application is not as intrinsically helpful to Childs' programme as he apparently thinks. In some cases at least, our theological problems do not arise from a misguided attempt at reconstructing historical references which the canonical text has obscured, but from the reservations of many modern scholars about affirming the historical statements which the texts themselves clearly make, and upon which the authors of those texts based their theology. Unfortunately, the dependence of a text's theological value upon its historical referentiality does not invariably fall to zero in cases for which scholars have doubts about the text's historical veracity. On the contrary, in such cases as the Sinai narratives I would suggest that Childs' adherence to the theology of the canonical text is rather too easy. If he wishes to uphold this theology then he needs to enter far more deeply into the historical issues, either to dispute the current reconstructions and substitute his own, or at least to show that, contrary to the arguments developed here, the theology is not undermined by the critically reconstructed history.

The fundamental problem here is that theological claims are *truth*-claims, whose truth value therefore has to be assessed. Because Childs has not adequately faced this point, his discussions often achieve less than he thinks. So, for example, his observations on law and grace helpfully outline the theological *claims* of the exodus and Sinai narratives; but these claims only become fully-fledged theological statements that are normative for the church's life and beliefs if it can be affirmed that they give a *true* account of the relationship between law

---

[14] Childs' classification of B[2] as a 'legend' is valuable as a form-critical judgement insofar as it calls attention to certain characteristics of the text (such as the prominent position given to Hezekiah as an exemplary faithful king). It is another question again, however, as to whether the author of B[2] intended, in and through these generic characteristics, to record (albeit in a theologically interpreted way) what really happened. This raises questions about the relationship between 'fact' and 'interpretation', which will be discussed in sections 4.4 and 5.3 below.

and grace. In summary, then, Childs' own Relevance Principle convicts him of neglecting a serious issue: Questions of 'what really happened' are often of considerably greater relevance to his own conception of theology than he has realized, and ought therefore to be given a more central role in his programme.

How Childs might do this—and, in particular, whether history ought to (or can) be studied from a neutral perspective or from a prior faith-commitment—will be considered at length in the following sections. I shall end this section, however, by introducing one more piece of terminology, namely, E.D. Hirsch's distinction between *meaning* and *significance*. Hirsch defines his terms as follows:

> *Meaning* is that which is represented by a text ... it is what the signs represent. *Significance*, on the other hand, names a relationship between that meaning and a person, or a conception, or a situation, or indeed anything imaginable. . . . Significance always implies a relationship, and one constant, unchanging pole of that relationship is what the text means.[15]

Hirsch conceives of meaning as an objective and unalterable characteristic of 'the text itself', whereas the text's significance may vary considerably as that to which it is related varies.[16] So, for example, Ptolemy's *Almagest* was highly valued by the medieval scholar as a scientific text, which established the (then) currently reigning paradigm within which astronomical research was conducted. Today, by contrast, its scientific value is virtually nill, although it is still an important text for scholars interested in the history of astronomy, or in the philosophy of science. Thus the significance of the *Almagest* has fluctuated considerably as the scholarly beliefs and interests to which it is related have changed, whereas its meaning (e.g., that the sun describes an orbit about the Earth) has remained constant.

Using Hirsch's terminology, we can summarize the conclusions of this section by saying that although the *meaning* of a text is independent

---

[15] *Validity in Interpretation* (New Haven: Yale University Press, 1967), p. 8. The first excision that I have made reads, 'it is what the author meant by his use of a particular sign sequence'. Hirsch's views on author's intention have been heavily criticised, and I will argue for a position different from his in chapter 7. For my present purposes, however, it is unnecessary to introduce this added complication.

[16] It follows from this, of course, that there are many different aspects to a text's significance, as its meaning is related to many other things. It should also be noted that a text's veracity is one aspect of its significance, since historical truth is concerned with the relationship between the meaning of the text and those aspects of the world to which it allegedly refers.

94 CHAPTER FOUR

of its historical veracity, its *theological significance*, in general, is not. For such cases as the Sinai narratives, one cannot make affirmations about their theological significance without considering questions of 'what really happened'.

The reader has perhaps noticed that there is an important similarity between Hirsch's distinction and Stendahl's dichotomy, in that each distinguishes between, on the one hand, a 'meaning' which is 'there in itself' and which may therefore be studied objectively, and, on the other hand, a 'significance' which is concerned with how other things relate to that 'meaning'. It is not surprising, therefore, that Hirsch has been criticized in much the same way as Smart has criticized Stendahl: Failing to reckon seriously enough with the influence of the interpreter's own presuppositions upon his or her exegesis, Hirsch has an unwarrantable faith in the objectivity of meaning. The question of presuppositions and objectivity will be discussed at some length in chapters 8 and 9 below; but for now I will simply suggest that the ground we have covered in the present section has at least shown that the Hirsch-Stendahl distinction is natural and plausible—what a text claims, and the evaluation that we make of its claims, do appear to be two quite different issues, with different considerations bearing upon each.

### 3. *Childs on Historical Methodology*

Having now clarified what is at stake with this particular aspect of referentiality, the next question to tackle concerns the methodology that one ought to use in studying (allegedly) historical events to which the text explicitly refers. How should the modern biblical scholar, working from a canonical perspective, set about an investigation of, say, the exodus from Egypt, the Babylonian exile, or the resurrection of Jesus from the dead?

Through much of his career Childs has been particularly unhappy about this aspect of the historical-critical approach. Childs' main objection is that the standard methodology is theologically inadequate, because it treats the biblical text as a 'source' for the neutral reconstruction of past events rather than as a 'witness' to God's entering into Israel's history. I shall begin, therefore, by reviewing Childs' main discussions of this subject, starting with his early monograph, *Memory and Tradition in Israel*. In this monograph Childs sets out his views on historical methodology in the context of a discussion of actualization. The Old Testament bears witness to a series of redemptive events, through which Israel was brought into existence. Childs particularly stresses the truly historical character of these events:

> [They] shared a genuine chronology. They appeared in history at a given moment, which entry can be dated. There is a once-for-all character to these events in the sense that they never repeated themselves in the same fashion. (p. 83)

These events had an ongoing effect on subsequent history as successive generations felt their influence and wrestled with their meaning. But beyond this, Childs claims that there was also 'an immediate encounter, an actual participation in the great acts of redemption' by later Israelites through 'the memory of the tradition' (p. 84). This was possible because 'the events [became] a vehicle for a [redemptive] reality which then continued throughout Israel's history' (*ibid.*), and into which she was thus able to enter.

This naturally prompts one to ask how the 'remembered events' relate to the 'original event' (p. 85); but according to Childs this is the wrong way to pose the question, because the Old Testament does not give us 'an original event':

> What we have are various witnesses to an event.... We are not in a position to ask how the interpreted event relates to the 'objective event'. Rather we are forced to ask: How do the successive interpretations of an event relate to the primary witness of that event? One cannot 'get behind' the witness. There are no other avenues to this event except through the witness.[17]

As the last sentence implies, Childs is particularly taking issue with the standard historical-critical approach to studying Israel's history,[18] which he faults on two counts: First, it regards an interpretation as something that is 'added on' to the event, with the event itself being recoverable (as an uninterpreted 'brute fact') through objective, historical research (p. 86). Appealing to R.G. Collingwood, Childs dismisses this as 'a distortion of the essence of history' (*ibid.*). And secondly, even where there is an extra-biblical parallel to a biblical account of an event, it is only the latter which bears witness to it as

---

[17] P. 85; cf. 'IF' p. 440; *BTCri* p. 102.
[18] W.F. Albright's *From the Stone Age to Christianity* is cited as a specific example (*MTI*, p. 85 n. 1).

Yahweh's redemption.[19] Childs combines these points in the very significant claim that

> [t]he faith response, the interpretation, was not something added to the real event, but constituted the event itself. We maintain, therefore, that it is a fundamental error in interpretation to conceive of redemptive history as a series of scientifically verifiable, historical data to which a religious interpretation has been added.[20]

Childs immediately affirms that historical research must nonetheless 'be employed with the utmost rigour' (*ibid.*); yet it must be pursued on a new basis: 'We resist the effort to identify historical research with the philosophical presuppositions of historicism'.[21]

Unfortunately Childs does not explain in *MTI* what alternative presuppositions should be put in their place; but in *EC* his answer, of course, is 'canonical context'. Stressing that 'canon' entails the acceptance of the Scriptures as the unique, normative witness to God's self-disclosure, it therefore follows that the canonical approach

> does not seek to attribute to the biblical witness a quality of historicity which can be controlled objectively, that is, outside the community of faith. However, it rejects the suggestion that the biblical witness arose simply as a projection of human imagination. The integrity of the canon is maintained without calling into question legitimate areas in which the judgement of human reason is appropriate.[22]

Childs immediately adds that the judgement of reason and the canonical witness are not to be held apart as separate areas; but his discussion here is not very illuminating. On the contrary, it raises a number of critical questions to which he has no obvious answers: If faith and objectivity are opposed to each other, is this not tantamount to admitting that 'interpretation in faith' is a form of eisegesis? Does not the normativity of the canon really mean that, whatever results historical enquiry may establish, they will not be allowed, ultimately, to make any difference? Why is the judgement of human reason legitimate *only* in certain areas? And does not this expose the 'illegitimate areas' to charges of irrationalism? Or how does one dis-

---

[19] *Ibid.*; cf. *EC* p. 301.

[20] *MTI*, p. 86; cf. p. 89.

[21] P. 87; cf. *EC* p. 300, where Childs characterizes the standard critical approach as a form of rationalism which 'suffers from assuming that its criteria are adequate to test all reality', and 'eliminates the basic theological issue by definition'.

[22] P. 300; it is a significant index to Childs' thought that 'faith' and 'objectivity' are here set in mutual opposition.

tinguish between the canonical witness interpreting and misinterpreting an event?

These earlier discussions, then, were not altogether satisfactory. The issues have nonetheless continued to be of considerable importance for Childs' work, and he has recently taken them up again in his *Biblical Theology*.[23] A canonical theology has the task of

> hearing the peculiar form of the Old Testament witness through the form which the historical tradents of the traditions gave the material rather than seeing the uninterpreted historical events themselves as the avenues to an understanding of God's intent.[24]

Childs strongly affirms the once-for-all, historical character of the revelatory events, but adds that what we have in the Old Testament is a *theological testimony* to these events, which have been interpreted and reinterpreted in the developing traditions as 'an ongoing witness to Israel's life with God' (p. 92). For some events (such as the conquest) this has anchored them firmly in the past by emphasizing their unrepeatability, whereas others are interpreted in such a way as to give them a future orientation—David's historical kingship is rendered eschatologically by the traditions as foreshadowing the Messiah (*ibid.*). A canonical theology should respect these interpretations.

Childs further develops these ideas by making an important distinction between treating a biblical text as 'source' or as 'witness'. The former approach regards the text as providing data for a neutral, phenomenological reconstruction of Israel's societal life. In response to the challenge posed by the Enlightenment, most biblical scholars have come to regard this as the *only* legitimate way of studying Israel's history, with Israel's own record being allowed no privileged status. Through applying the various critical tools to the biblical sources, the modern scholar claims to have an independent means of access to the historical events. In this way the biblical traditions can be sifted and corrected.

The preceding, of course, is a summary of the standard critical approach to history. This, however, is what Childs rejects.[25] Instead

---

[23] See especially *BTONT* pp. 91–93, 97–103, 143–46, 196–206.

[24] P. 92; cf. pp. 97–98.

[25] Childs does not at this point spell out why he rejects it, although a hint is given in his comment that 'Usually among these [liberal] theologians using the tools of critical research on the Bible some form of a philosophical system was also employed in an effort to escape radical religious relativism such as idealism, existentialism, or

he proposes that biblical texts should be studied as witnesses to Israel's encounter with God. The canonical approach regards Israel's history as having both an 'outer dimension', which is viewed from a neutral, phenomenological standpoint, and an 'inner dimension', which is viewed from the confessional perspective of a faith-community (p. 100). In Childs' view, the complexity of the problems facing contemporary biblical hermeneutics stems from the fact that these two dimensions are subtly interrelated, so that neither can be dispensed with. The scholar must reckon with 'both divine and human agency' in Israel's history (*ibid.*), while also recognizing that the relative contribution of each will vary considerably from one instance to another.

Childs underlines these points by contrasting his own approach with that of various other scholars. Thus Frank M. Cross' *Canaanite Myth and Hebrew Epic* is criticized for 'read[ing] the Old Testament as a form of cultural expression no different from any Ugaritic text' (p. 102), i.e., for regarding the Old Testament purely as a source. Cross' 'reductionism', Childs suggests, leaves no room for genuine theology. By contrast, von Rad is praised for his sensitive delineations of the Old Testament witnesses; yet he is faulted both for his self-confessed inability to relate his 'kerygmatic approach' to the real (i.e., critically reconstructed) history of Israel, and also for nonetheless basing his interpretation of Israel's witness upon these reconstructions.[26] Thus '[t]he subtle dialectical relation between Israel's inner and outer history . . . is seriously undercut' by von Rad (p. 103).

Summing up, then, we can say that the core of Childs' proposals concerns the legitimacy of viewing historical facts—some of which (such as Jerusalem being conquered by the Babylonians, or Jesus' crucifixion under Pontius Pilate) could be agreed upon by all competent scholars—of viewing such facts through the interpretative perspective of the believing community, whose faith-stance would not be shared by all. It is a question, then, of the relationship between (historical) fact and (faith-) interpretation, and of a methodol-

---

social functionalism' (p. 99). This is reminiscent of his fundamental objection to Stendahl's dichotomy, namely, that an objective, neutral study of 'what the text meant' anchors it so firmly in the past as to render it theologically useless for the modern church. Idealism, existentialism, and social functionalism are here representative of the (in Childs' view, inadequate) bridges that have been thrown across the resulting chasm between 'then' and 'now'.

[26] See *BTONT* p. 103; cf. pp. 92, 145, 200. It is not altogether clear to me whether Childs is entitled to criticize von Rad on *both* these counts.

ogy which can bring this relationship to bear upon the work of the biblical scholar.

Childs' discussions of these subjects, it has to be said, are better at setting out programmatic aims than at showing how they might be achieved. His ideas are nonetheless of considerable importance both for his own approach and for the wider methodological discussion; so to see how they might be further developed I shall next discuss the work of another scholar who has gone considerably further than Childs in working out the details of a methodology which is intended to do justice to God's historical acts of revelation, and who, like Childs, has been motivated to do so by a desire to overcome the supposed dichotomy between fact and interpretation. I turn next, then, to the work of Wolfhart Pannenberg.

## 4. *The Unity of Fact and Interpretation*

Pannenberg develops his views on historical methodology in dialogue with certain other trends in modern theology, which he considers to be understandable but misguided reactions to 'the problem of history'. This (insofar as it impinges upon our present concerns) had its origins in the growing conviction among scholars in the nineteenth century—and particularly as a result of the numerous 'lives of Jesus' which it produced—that critical reconstructions of 'what really happened' were fundamentally incapable of helping us to understand the biblical texts:

> There was no possible bridge from the man Jesus, whose biography and religion was the object of this research, and the apostolic witness to him as the Christ. . . . Thus the problem of the historical Jesus brought to light in an exemplary way something that was for the most part valid for the rest of the biblical writings.[27]

It was with some justice, therefore, that theologians such as Martin Kähler called attention to the kerygmatic character of the biblical documents; and yet Pannenberg sees the *way* in which they did so as unfortunate, as it soon led to a separation between kerygma and history. This had certainly not been the intention of Kähler, who maintained that the Christian faith was founded upon the events of

---

[27] Pannenberg, 'Kerygma and History', in *BQT* I (London: SCM, 1970), pp. 84–85.

history. Indeed, the kerygma itself pointed to these events; but in addition to this, Kähler maintained, 'the reports about the historical fact are always accompanied by a testimony to its revelatory value, which is supplementary to it and exists precisely for faith alone'.[28] Yet it is just this conception of revelation as *supplementary* to the historical facts which, Pannenberg claims, is unacceptable, because this lack of intrinsic connection makes it inevitable that the two will come apart. This is precisely what happened as subsequent kerygma theologians increasingly rejected the question of whether the events which the kerygma proclaimed had actually happened;[29] but Gogarten has pointed out very clearly the fundamental problem in this approach: Faith is simply not capable of *giving* historical facts suprahistorical significance; rather, '[the] suprahistorical significance must belong to the historical itself, granted that the latter is to be the basis of faith'.[30] If faith is not faith in the revelatory and redemptive value of the facts themselves, then no appeal to the historical facts is capable of acting as an objective control upon faith, to protect it from drifting into wishful thinking and self-delusion.

According to Pannenberg, this unity of historical fact and revelatory value has very significant consequences for theology, namely, that '[t]he revelatory character of the redemptive event must be contained in this event itself *as the historian portrays it*'.[31] Historical research is not just a good method for gaining knowledge of the past; it is the *only* proper method for doing this. Pannenberg speaks of 'the monopoly of historical method for historical knowledge' (p. 50)—what cannot be known in this way simply cannot be known: 'In no case is theology ... in the position of being able to say what was actually the case regarding contents which remain opaque to the historian' (*ibid.*).

It might seem as though this would take us straight back to the theologically mute 'life of Jesus' research which the kerygma theologians reacted against; but according to Pannenberg, the reason why nineteenth century historicism largely bypassed the kerygmatic content of the Gospels did not stem from any inherent limitations in

---

[28] Kähler; quoted in 'KH', p. 86. Cf. Walther Künneth's contention that 'Revelation is therefore always more than history, not only history, but not without history'; quoted in Pannenberg, 'Redemptive Event and History', in *BQT* I, p. 60.

[29] Pannenberg sees Bultmann as the most systematic exponent of this position; 'KH', p. 87.

[30] Pannenberg, 'REH' p. 60.

[31] P. 66; italics added.

historical studies as such. Rather, this was due to its faulty methodology, which was incapable of handling the supranatural dimension
of the events which it investigated. The way forward, therefore, is to
replace this flawed methodology with one that is more appropriate
to its subject-matter.

The details of this new methodology, and the objections which
might be raised against it, will be discussed in the next chapter; but
here I wish to consider 'the fact and interpretation issue' more closely.
Although the unity of fact and interpretation is a key element in
Pannenberg's programme he actually offers very little in support of
it beyond a few rhetorical questions,[32] and the interesting but highly
abstract claim that 'only if the revelatory significance is enclosed in
the events themselves will one be able to speak here of Incarnation,
an entrance of God into our mode of existence'.[33] One would, I
think, already have to be well-disposed towards the unity of fact and
interpretation to be persuaded by considerations as general as these.
Fortunately, however, there is much more that can be added in
support of Pannenberg,[34] and reviewing the main arguments here
will help us considerably when we return to Childs. The cardinal
point to grasp is that facts and interpretations are *essentially the same*

---

[32] E.g., 'Does not [Kähler's] argument accept all too uncritically the neo-Kantian
distinction between being and value?'; 'KH' p. 86.

[33] 'REH', p. 61.

[34] These issues have been extensively discussed in the philosophy of the natural
sciences. A sharp dichotomy between fact and interpretation was one of the central
tenets of Logical Positivism (or Logical Empiricism), but from the late 1950s this
view has been subjected to severe and (as is now universally recognised) highly effective
criticism. The Positivist dichotomy has now been superseded by the recognition that
(to cite the standard formula) 'all observation is theory-laden'; i.e., that it is impossible to make an observation which simply gives us uninterpreted 'bare facts', because there necessarily has to be extensive 'theoretical input' in the making of any
observation (in, for example, deciding what is worth observing, in designing the
apparatus, and in describing what one sees through it). For influential discussions of
the theory/observation issue see Norwood Russell Hanson, *Patterns of Discovery* (Cambridge: CUP, 1958); Karl R. Popper, *The Logic of Scientific Discovery* (London:
Hutchinson, Tenth impression (revised) 1980); *ibid., Conjectures and Refutations: The
Growth of Scientific Knowledge* (London: RKP, Fourth edition (revised) 1972); Mary B.
Hesse, 'Theory and Observation', in Hesse, *Revolutions and Reconstructions in the Philosophy of Science* (Brighton: Harvester, 1980); Thomas S. Kuhn, *The Structure of Scientific Revolutions* (Chicago: Chicago University Press, Second Edition, enlarged 1970).
The demise of Logical Empiricism has been discussed at length by Frederick Suppe,
'The Search for Understanding in Scientific Theories', in Suppe (ed.), *The Structure
of Scientific Theories* (Urbana: University of Illinois Press, 1974), pp. 1–241. Unfortunately space does not allow me to review these debates, although they will be implicitly guiding much of the subsequent methodological discussion.

*kind of things*; thus although it is often convenient to make a distinction between them, this is not a division into two different sorts of entities. Therefore there is really no problem about 'how they are to be brought (or held) together', because there is already a natural unity between them.

These claims depend, of course, upon how one conceives interpretation. In defending this thesis I shall therefore begin by defining 'interpretation', and showing that this definition does capture something important about its nature. I shall then offer some philosophical arguments for the unity of fact and interpretation. Beginning, then, with a definition, I suggest that *a true interpretation simply states the facts*; to claim that 'The true interpretation of these data is X' is also and thereby to claim that 'X is in fact the case'. And correspondingly, a misinterpretation (assuming that it is sincerely offered) is an *attempt* to state the facts which actually gets them wrong.

To grasp the point of this definition, consider two detectives who are examining the evidence at the scene of a murder. One infers from this and other circumstantial evidence that the butler did it; the other that the murderer was the dead man's son. One way of describing this situation would be to say that the detectives disagree over the correct interpretation of the evidence; another way, however, would be to say that they disagree over who in fact committed the murder. The important point to grasp is that these are *equivalent* descriptions of *the same thing*. Thus in resolving their dispute, the detectives do not first try to reach agreement concerning the correct interpretation of the evidence and then, as a second stage, go on to argue about who committed the murder; on the contrary, to argue that the correct interpretation of the evidence is that 'the butler did it' *is in itself* to argue that in fact the butler did it. The correct interpretation simply states the facts.

What this example suggests, then, is that one cannot distinguish between such claims as 'The fact is, the butler did it' and 'According to my interpretation of the evidence, the butler did it' in terms of their metaphysical status—the difference is not that the former claim, when legitimate, deals with the objective, the 'really real', or that which is 'simply there', whereas the latter gives us, at best, no more than insubstantial, subjective opinion ('that's *merely* his interpretation'). The difference, rather, concerns not their metaphysical but their epistemological status. 'According to my interpretation . . .' acknowledges that there is a respectable body of contrary opinion, and will

therefore usually be accompanied by substantive arguments to persuade the hearers that this is the correct interpretation; whereas 'the
fact is . . .' generally introduces something about which (at least among
those being addressed) virtually all are agreed, and the accompany-
ing arguments, if given at all, will therefore be no more than cursory
summaries of the main points.[35] *Both* locutions are used, however, to
state what (as the speaker believes) is the case.

This brief illustration, then—to which the reader could doubtless
add many more, drawn from different fields of study and investigation—suggests that the proposed definition helps one give an intuitively
plausible account of 'what we are arguing about' in disputes over
facts and interpretations. Having established this, it is now appropriate to proceed to some more formal arguments for the unity of fact
and interpretation.

Although visual observation is somewhat removed from the kind
of historical interpretation which is the primary subject of this chapter
I shall nonetheless begin with some comments on the visual case,
both because this is where much of the philosophical discussion has
been concentrated and also because the distinction between fact and
interpretation can seem particularly plausible here—seeing with our
own eyes appears to simply 'give us the facts'. That this is not so,
however, has now been demonstrated by numerous discussions. It is
perhaps most clearly seen from gestalt diagrams such as the wire
cube or the wineglass and two faces. Someone viewing such a figure
may see different things from one moment to another, although the
diagram itself remains the same. The change comes not from alter-
ations in one's 'sense data' but through the lines and shapes being
*organized* in different ways, with first this part being construed as the
foreground and then that. Or looking around a room, one does not
see a kaleidoscope of coloured patches all 'on a par' with one another;
rather, one sees this subset of one's visual phenomena as a distinct
object, having an integrity of its own and being set off from (yet also
related to) a host of other such objects. Even in the most straightforward cases, then, there is more to seeing than a blank, undifferentiated
perception of whatever shapes and colours fall upon our retina. Over
and above this, there is the integrating and structuring of these 'sense

---

[35] There are also, of course, various non-standard and rhetorical uses of these
phrases—a speaker may, for example, introduce a highly dubious claim with 'the
fact is . . .' precisely to disguise its debatability.

data' into a visual field.[36] The visual facts are *already interpreted* facts.

Once the unity of fact and interpretation has been grasped for the visual case, it is easily recognized in the historical case also. One way of demonstrating this is by showing that there is no non-arbitrary way of 'drawing a line' through a historical event such that all the interpretation is 'above' the line and all the facts 'below' it. Or to put it another way, as one level of interpretation is stripped off further levels of interpretation are invariably found beneath it—one never comes down to a core of uninterpreted 'hard facts'. Consider, for example, God's bringing of Israel out of Egypt. Someone who believes in a difference in kind between fact and interpretation might draw the distinction here by claiming that 'Israel escaped from Egypt' states the 'hard facts', whereas 'God brought Israel out of Egypt' is a theological interpretation that has been added to those facts.[37] A moment's reflection soon reveals, however, that these 'hard facts' themselves involve considerable interpretation: Designating a certain group as 'Israel' implicitly interprets them as a nation (rather than just an agglomeration of disparate individuals), and thus tacitly assumes the existence of the sorts of shared values and goals, institutions, social structures and other relationships that maintain the cohesiveness of nationhood. Or again, to describe Israel as 'escaping from' Egypt (rather than 'departing from' or 'being ejected by') is to give a particular interpretation of the relationship that existed between those nations. 'Israel escaped from Egypt', then, is clearly not an uninterpreted fact but the product of a vast amount of interpretative work.

Now of course, once this has been recognized these further interpretative factors can in turn be stripped off; so one might now try to draw the fact/interpretation distinction along the lines, 'That Moses, Aaron, Miriam, [etc.] passed along a certain route, followed by

---

[36] This is brought out particularly well by Hanson (*Patterns*, ch. 1), although he is reluctant for this to be described as, say, a diagram being *interpreted* now as a wineglass and now as two faces (pp. 9–11). This, however, seems to be no more than a verbal quibble about the correct usage of the word.

[37] The empiricist affinities of the fact/interpretation dichotomy become plain when (in terms of the present example) it is argued for along the lines, 'What would you have *actually seen* if you had been there? You would not, as such, have seen God bringing Israel out; all you would have actually seen is Israel escaping from Egypt. That, therefore, is the "hard facts" of the case; that God brought it about is then an interpretation added to the facts'. For a classic example of such an argument, see Hume's analysis of causation: *An Enquiry Concerning Human Understanding*, section VII; *A Treatise of Human Nature*, section I.iii.

Pharaoh, the commander of the army, [etc.] is the "hard facts" of the case; that one nation was escaping from another, and that this was a divine deliverance, are interpretations of these facts'.[38] But again these 'hard facts' are heavily laden with implicit interpretations: 'Followed by' implies intent on the Egyptian's part (rather than their taking the same route being a mere coincidence); naming a certain character as 'Moses' implies that the person who looks like Moses (which is all that one 'actually sees') really is he (rather than, say, an actor impersonating him); etc.

These interpretations could also be stripped off, of course; but it should be clear by now that however far one pursues this pruning, further interpretations will always be found underneath—right down, ultimately, to metaphysical assumptions about the reality of the external world, the nature of the past, etc. At no point does one stop interpreting and start dealing simply with 'the facts themselves'.[39] Or to put it another way: *whichever* level the investigation is pitched at, one is still dealing with facts, whether they be the fact of Israel's nationhood, or of Yahweh's deliverance of Israel. These are never just 'plain facts' in a sense that would contrast them with interpretations; but that there is an interpretation involved in claiming that Israel's exodus from Egypt was a divine deliverance is no reason at all for viewing this as somehow 'less real' or 'less factual' than the historical fact of Israel's nationhood. Interpretation is involved at *every* level, and every level deals with facts.

The difference between nationhood and divine deliverance, then, is a difference not of kind but of the *scope* of the interpretations involved: Identifying Israel as an autonomous nation involves making interpretations at the level of social, cultural, and political relationships; whereas identifying her as the elect nation of Yahweh involves, in addition, making interpretations which concern the relationship between certain historical events and the purposes and plans of God. Making interpretations at these higher levels will naturally be more

---

[38] Or in terms that make the empiricism more explicit: 'All you would have *actually seen* would be Moses, Aaron . . .'.

[39] Except, perhaps, (and then in a greatly weakened sense) when one resorts to simply reporting one's own sensations, provided that these reports are taken entirely solipsistically (see Hesse, 'Theory' especially section 2). But 'red appearance now' (with no implications about whether there is really anything red 'out there') is hardly the kind of hard fact that the theologian deals with; and one important reason for the demise of Logical Positivism was that the philosopher could not do anything with this sort of fact either.

difficult, and the results more tentative; but even at the highest level
the interpretation, if true, simply states the facts. In the latter case,
however, the facts concern not only this-worldly reality but embrace
the divine realm also.

There is still some distance to go before we can assess Childs'
views on 'referentiality in the text'; but already we can see that his
protest against theology's constructive task being viewed as a 'mere'
homiletical topping that is added onto the results of the standard
historical-critical reconstruction[40]—as though it were only the latter
which dealt with the 'really real'—does identify a significant methodological error. Thus although, for example, it is a truism of New
Testament research that the Gospels are not neutral biographies of
Jesus but kerygmatic confessions, written from the perspective of post-
resurrection faith, one cannot use this to draw ontological distinctions between 'Jesus died on the cross' and 'Christ died for our sins',
as though it were only the former—and more generally, only what
can be discovered through the standard historical-critical procedures—
which deals with solid fact, whereas the latter, as one particular interpretation that has been put upon these facts, cannot be enter-
tained as a claim about objective truth. If the arguments of this section
are correct, then 'Jesus died on the cross' and 'Christ died for our
sins' are both interpretative claims, and both, if true, are fact-stating
(although the latter involves a much broader range of facts than the
former). Thus the mere identification of a certain statement as an
interpretation of the early church cannot be taken as, in and of itself, a sufficient reason to strip it away as 'secondary'—as though
this would automatically bring one nearer to what the true facts really
are. The question that has to be asked, rather, is whether the church's
interpretations give us deeper insight into what really happened at
the cross and resurrection. If it does, then this is obviously the preferable form of the tradition. Childs is quite right, therefore, to protest against this sort of automatic devaluation of highly-interpreted
—and especially theologically-interpreted—statements about incidents
in the life of Jesus; and he is also right, I would suggest, to see this
as one reason why the modern church often has difficulty in hearing
the Bible speak to it as Holy Scripture: It is much harder to preach
from 'Jesus died on the cross' than from 'Christ died for our sins'.

Our discussion, then, has taken an important step towards vindi-

---

[40] *BTCri*, p. 141.

cating Pannenberg's version of revelation-in-history: If the correct interpretation of the relevant evidence is that God raised Jesus from the dead then this is to be accepted as a bona fide factual statement about reality, including divine reality. This naturally raises the question, however, as to what sort of methodology is capable of making such interpretations, or, equivalently, of investigating reality in both its natural and its divine dimensions. We saw in section 2.2 that in his earlier writings Childs hinted that the critical methodology should be revised in such a way that its investigations started from a faith-commitment, but unfortunately he never showed how this might be done. Pannenberg, however, *has* taken significant steps in this direction. It is time, therefore, to look at this more closely.

# CHAPTER FIVE

# HISTORICAL METHODOLOGY

We saw in section 4.4 above that, according to Wolfhart Pannenberg, God has revealed himself through the events of history; and that these events therefore, *as revelatory of God*, should be the object of the theologian's historical studies. Thus for Pannenberg, historical investigation is inherently theological; and since this clearly has affinities with Childs' views on the necessity of starting from a faith-commitment, a study of Pannenberg's historical methodology is potentially of considerable value for Childs' canonical programme.

Pannenberg's views on this subject, it must be said, are very much a minority opinion (at least among English-speaking specialists in Biblical Studies); so the first question to consider here is why critical historiography is generally thought to be incapable of investigating such matters as whether Yahweh delivered Israel from Egypt. According to Mark Brett, the fundamental reason is that historiography is an *empirical* discipline:

> [T]he events that are being reflected upon in the biblical tradition have an inexpungable religious dimension which could not be empirically verified, even by ideal eye-witnesses. For example, would a newsreel report of the exodus event record the intervention of Yahweh, or at most, a sequence of coincidences which turned out to favour the Israelites? . . . I would suggest that no eye-witness or historian could verify statements like this without first believing that Yahweh existed and could be active in history. In short, many of the central concerns of the Hebrew Bible *could not be verified by a purely empirical historiography*.[1]

The question that needs to be asked, however, is whether historiography *should* be 'purely empirical' in this sense. Brett is obviously correct in pointing out that acts of God are not the sort of thing that can be observed, as such, by an eye-witness; yet his questions about what would be seen by an ideal observer or reported by a newsreel are clearly moving beyond this uncontroversial claim towards a version of Humean empiricism, which virtually equates the knowable with

---

[1] *Crisis?*, p. 162 (Brett's italics); cf. *CAOTS*, p. 272.

the sensible. As we saw in section 4.4, however, when the question of what one *actually sees* is pressed with this sort of stringency, it turns out that one 'actually sees' very little. Thus the ideal witness is not even capable (*contra* Brett) of observing 'a sequence of coincidences which turned out to favour the Israelites'—as we have seen, 'the Israelites', for example, denotes an entity which is no more observable than an act of God. Or again, the newsreel camera ultimately captures nothing more than patches of colour and shade—anything beyond this is an interpretation which we put upon these patches when viewing the newsreel, and this holds equally for such interpretations as 'Israel escapes from Egypt' as for 'God rescues his people'. Followed through consistently, Brett's positivistic criterion would, if valid, put not only acts of God outside the historian's domain but virtually everything else as well. As the Logical Positivists discovered to their great discomfort, once one retreats to the security of one's own sense-data there is no way of advancing beyond them again to re-establish contact with the real world.[2]

But given, then, that the secular historian *is* capable, in principle, of investigating such matters as 'Did Israel escape form Egypt?', or 'When did Israel become a nation?', the issues that need to be looked at are how the historian handles such 'unobservables' as nationhood, and whether acts of God might be handled in a similar way. This in fact raises a number of important epistemological questions, which will be considered more fully in section 2 below. For now, however, the following 'common sense' answer is sufficient: Historians are able to investigate these 'unobservables' because they can draw inferences that go beyond what an eyewitness reports. So, for example, if the relevant sources show that certain tribes[3] frequently gave military aid to one another, that they shared the same religious sanctuaries, that they had many common traditions, etc., then this may give the historian reasonable grounds for inferring that these tribes were parts of a single nation. Such (interpretative) inferences are clearly essential to the historian's work; but granted their legitimacy, they seem also

---

[2] The Logical Positivists had hoped to provide a secure basis for all genuine knowledge through analysing such 'real world' statements as 'There is a table in the next room' into statements about the observer's (potential) sense-experiences and inferences based upon them; but after repeated failures to provide satisfactory analyses, it was gradually realized that the project was actually impossible. For a discussion of these points see Oswald Hanfling's *Logical Positivism* (Oxford: Blackwell, 1981), chapters 4–5.

[3] Of course, tribehood is also a non-observable. There is interpretation at every level!

to provide an adequate methodology for investigating alleged acts of
God. If it were established, for example, that a rapid succession of
extraordinary plagues fell upon the whole of Egypt except where
Israel dwelt, then it might very reasonably be inferred that this was
the doing of a supranatural, purposive agent, even though no-one
had (nor could have) actually observed this agent 'at work'.

In sum, then: Historiography clearly *should* be empirical in the sense
that, if the historian's reconstruction of an event is challenged, then
he or she ought to respond by appealing to appropriate historical
evidence (rather than, say, to intuitions about what would have been
fitting); yet Brett has given us no reason to think that an empirical
historiography (in this sense) would be incapable of investigating alleged acts of God. What excludes this, rather, is Brett's requiring
that historiography be 'empirical' in a strongly positivistic sense; yet
to carry this through consistently would leave the historian unable to
investigate *anything* of historical interest.

A very different approach to these issues has been taken by Robert Morgan and John Barton, who describe the claim that 'acts of
God cannot be spoken of, let alone established, by historical research'
as 'a *presupposition* or *axiom* [which] defines what is meant by historical research'.[4] A historical explanation is 'a rational, . . . non-super-
natural account',[5] which is therefore incapable of dealing with acts
of God (since these, by definition, are supernatural). Morgan and
Barton are careful to add that this does not as such mean that, say,
Jesus did not objectively rise from the dead. The claim that he did,
however, cannot (in their view) be admitted as a *historical* claim; therefore 'believers who . . . wish to speak intelligently of God on the basis
of the biblical witness cannot allow biblical interpretation to be restricted to the task of historical research' (p. 70).

It is well known, of course, that historical-critical studies of biblical
history have in fact strongly favoured naturalistic over supernaturalistic explanations, with events which have hitherto been regarded as
miraculous, divine interventions often being reconstructed as the
product of wholly natural causes. Morgan and Barton's claim (and
they hardly stand alone on this) is that, given that we are to inves-

---

[4] *Biblical Interpretation* (The Oxford Bible Series; Oxford: OUP, 1988), p. 70; italics
added.
[5] Morgan and Barton use this phrase to describe the historical work of Strauss,
Baur and Vatke (p. 68); cf. their fuller account of Baur's views on p. 65, with which
(on this particular issue) they closely align their own.

tigate these matters historically, then they *must* be explained in this way. The important methodological issue which this raises, therefore, is whether the nature of historical investigation is such as *necessarily* to exclude supernatural explanations of that which it investigates. This is the central question that Pannenberg tackles.

## 1. *The Principle of Analogy*

We have seen that, according to Pannenberg, revelation occurs in the events of history, and must therefore be discovered through historical research. Pannenberg is not unaware that hitherto the theological returns of this approach have been meagre; but this, he claims, stems from the basis upon which historical research has been pursued:

> A fundamental antithesis between the world views of historical method and the biblical history of God can be found in the anthropocentricity of the historical-critical procedure, which seems apt to exclude all transcendent reality as a matter of course.[6]

Pannenberg particularly blames this upon the use which scholars such as Ernst Troeltsch have made of the principle of analogy.[7] Pannenberg explains this principle as saying that 'something difficult to understand, comparatively opaque, is to be conceived and understood by the investigator in terms of what lies closer to him' (p. 43), and makes it clear that he is not against the historian's use of analogical argument as such—on the contrary, Pannenberg recognises that it is a legitimate and useful principle, *provided that* each case is nonetheless taken on its own merits. So, for example, there is much to be gained in pursuing as thoroughly as possible the similarities between biblical and extra-biblical religions, because, against this common background, the distinctive aspects of the biblical kerygma stand out more clearly (p. 48). Or again, if positive resemblances are found between certain biblical traditions and extra-biblical literary forms (such as myths and legends) that are generally of little historical value, this can serve as a legitimate critical argument for sifting the biblical material (p. 49).

---

[6] 'REH', p. 39; cf. Childs' complaint against critical studies '[defining] in advance the nature of biblical reality' in ways that prevent its full witness from being heard ('IF', p. 439).

[7] More recently, this has also been discussed at length by William J. Abraham, *Divine Revelation and the Limits of Historical Criticism* (Oxford: OUP, 1982), chapter 5.

Such uses of analogy are acceptable (Pannenberg argues) because the scope and validity of the resemblances are found in and tested by the historical materials themselves. It is not acceptable, however, when analogy is exalted into a universal, *a priori*, principle of criticism; yet this is what happened when Troeltsch spoke of an 'omnipotence of analogy' which includes a 'fundamental homogeneity of all historical events'.[8] The application of this idea to the historian's task is spelt out very clearly by Troeltsch:

> Analogy with what happens before our eyes and what is given within ourselves is the key to criticism. . . . Agreement with normal, ordinary, repeatedly attested modes of occurrence and conditions as we know them is the mark of probability for the occurrences that the critic can either acknowledge really to have happened or leave on one side.[9]

And since virgin births and resurrections of the dead are not among the normal modes of occurrence of the modern scholar, the application of this form of analogy to the Bible would clearly have devastating consequences.

This, then, is a version of analogy which Pannenberg wishes to reject; and he offers three principal reasons for doing so. Firstly, analogy (in this form) gives a one-sided portrayal of what history is really like. Although there clearly are cases where significant analogies can be drawn between one event and another, history is also the realm of the contingent and the unique; and it is precisely the individuality of this or that specific occurrence which particularly engages the historian's attention (pp. 46–47). As an objection to Troeltsch's use of analogy, however, this simply begs the question. Sennacherib's siege of Jerusalem clearly was (as Pannenberg claims) a unique event, in the sense that it arose from a specific set of circumstances, and followed a particular course of its own; and at this level most scholars would probably now agree with Pannenberg that the historian is chiefly interested in this siege for its own particularity, rather than as an instance of sieges-in-general.[10] Yet Troeltsch

---

[8] Troeltsch, 'Historische and dogmatische Methode'; as quoted in 'REH' p. 45. Troeltsch's essay is available in English as 'Historical and Dogmatic Method in Theology', in Troeltsch, *Religion in History* (Edinburgh: T & T Clark, 1991), pp. 11–32.

[9] Troeltsch, as quoted in 'REH' (pp. 43–44).

[10] This would be disputed, of course, by those who still believe in a 'covering law' model of historical explanation, and Pannenberg acknowledges (*ibid.*) that he is utilizing here an argument which was originally developed against that model (which now, in fact, seems to enjoy little support).

could presumably allow this, while still maintaining that the various elements which make up this complex event (e.g., the motives for Sennacherib's attack, the weapons and tactics used, etc.) *are* analogous to what are found in other military engagements—in other words, Troeltsch could explain the uniqueness of this particular siege as consisting in the specific combination of its circumstances, while still insisting that the historicality of each alleged element must be assessed by his principle of analogy. Thus if he were to reject as unhistorical the report in 2 Kgs. 19:35–36 of this siege being brought to an end by the angel of the Lord slaying 185,000 of Sennacherib's army, and were to do so on the grounds that we have no analogous experiences of armies being defeated in this way, then it is difficult to see what Pannenberg's uniqueness argument could say in reply.

Pannenberg's second objection adds a theological twist to the preceding: It is because God in his essence is ultimately free of all cosmic orderings, and is therefore able to bring about that which is genuinely new, that 'theology is interested primarily in the individual, particular, and contingent' (p. 48). This is an interesting theological idea; but as an argument against Troeltsch it is difficult to see how it would cut much ice. Troeltsch, as we have just seen, can account for the individuality of historical events without giving up his version of analogy, and he could presumably argue, therefore, that it is from what we learn in this way about the course of history that we are to understand the freedom of God. Again, then, Pannenberg seems to have largely begged the question against Troeltsch.

Pannenberg's third argument, however, is much stronger: Troeltschian analogy decides by *a priori* decree matters which ought only to be settled by appealing to the relevant historical evidence. Pannenberg cites Jesus' bodily resurrection (which he accepts as a historical fact) as a case in point:

> Does not the postulate of the fundamental homogeneity of all events usually form the chief argument against the historicity of the resurrection of Jesus . . .? But if this is so, does not the opinion . . . that the resurrection of Jesus cannot be a historical event, rest on remarkably weak foundations? Only the particular characteristics of the reports about it make it possible to judge the historicity of the resurrection, not the prejudgement that every event must be fundamentally of the same kind as every other. (p. 49 n. 90)

This, I think, is decisive. Although Troeltsch proposes analogy as a *methodological* principle, it in fact allows one to draw *substantive historical conclusions*—that Jesus was not born of a virgin, did not raise Lazarus from the dead, and did not return to life himself, etc.—without needing to look at a shred of historical evidence; and it allows one, moreover, to hold these conclusions with complete certainty, because Troeltsch's principle ensures that nothing could ever count as evidence against them: If a certain document purports to tell how Jesus was seen alive again after his death, then *by that very fact* it would be discredited as an unreliable historical witness.

Troeltschian analogy, then, is a historiographical version of Catch 22; and this makes it unacceptable as a methodological principle. The purpose of having a sound methodology is to allow the data to be sorted and assessed in such a way that one's conclusions are based upon the relevant evidence, not upon prior convictions about what 'must have been the case'. Of course, the historian makes an active contribution to this in sifting the evidence and trying to fit it into a coherent and convincing reconstruction; yet if this is done within the framework of a proper methodology, the historian's own hypotheses and interpretations will themselves be tested against the available evidence, so that the historian's reconstructions do not degenerate into uncritical expressions of his or her own prejudices. But Troeltschian analogy, on the contrary, *excludes* this sort of self-criticism for a significant range of cases, and ensures in advance that the past cannot possibly be fundamentally different from the present, *whatever* our historical sources may say. It is therefore wholly unacceptable as a methodological principle.

This untenable principle of analogy, then, is the main reason why, in Pannenberg's view, little progress has been made in studying history as the self-revelatory acts of God. To establish his own position, however, Pannenberg needs not only to dispose of this false principle but also to develop an alternative historical methodology; and in fact he makes a number of important suggestions as to how this might be done. Pannenberg strongly endorses R.G. Collingwood's conception of historical method,[11] both in its rejection of the positivists' approach and in its proposing a 'Conjectures and Refutations' method of historical enquiry.[12] Pannenberg believes that the conception of history

---

[11] 'REH', pp. 70–80, *passim*.

[12] R.G. Collingwood, *The Idea of History* (Oxford: OUP, 1961). 'Conjectures and Refutations', of course, is an allusion to Karl Popper, whose philosophy of the natural sciences bears a strikingly resemblance to Collingwood's historical methodology (as Popper himself has observed; *Objective Knowledge* (Oxford: OUP, revised 1979), pp.

as a unified whole is an indispensable presupposition for historical enquiry; therefore one must reject the positivist approach of first gathering together all the 'bare facts', stripped of their historical interrelatedness, and then, as a second stage, bringing them under general laws.[13] Since history is an interconnected whole, one must begin not with artificially isolated particulars but with a conjectural model of the event which displays this interconnectedness. The model must of course be tested by the relevant eye-witness accounts, archaeological discoveries, circumstantial evidence, etc.; and when the evidence requires it, the original conjecture must be modified accordingly. The modified version then provides a new model, to be tested and revised again. Insofar as the model is verified, however, Pannenberg insists that it is to be regarded not as a merely individualistic projection of the historian but as 'a recounting of the event itself in its own context' (p. 71)—i.e., as objectively valid knowledge of what actually happened.[14]

One aspect of historical interconnectedness which Pannenberg particularly stresses is the importance of seeing events within the context of their traditions. This is of some importance for his own discussion of Jesus' resurrection: It was through his return from the dead being understood in the context of the prevailing apocalyptic traditions that it was recognized as the proleptic occurrence of the end of the world.

Pannenberg makes a number of interesting points here, to which

---

186–89). Popper has, however, distanced himself from the more 'psychologistic' aspects of Collingwood (*ibid.*; cf. p. 164), and in this respect Pannenberg's methodology is closer to Popper's than to Collingwood's.

[13] 'REH' pp. 70–71. For a concise summary of positivist historiography see Collingwood's *History*, pp. 126–33; it is very similar (as Collingwood notes) to the Logical Positivists' methodology of the natural sciences, except that it lacks the linguistic orientation of the latter.

[14] Cf. the fifth of Pannenberg's 'Dogmatic Theses on the Concept of Revelation', in Pannenberg (ed.), *Revelation as History* (London: Sheed, 1979), pp. 145–48. Pannenberg ('REH', p. 71), like Popper, is critical of Collingwood for underplaying the objectivity of historical reconstruction. Such a commitment to objectivity assumes that the Smart-Gadamer view of presuppositions can be overturned; I shall argue this in chapter 9 below. In speaking of 'verifiability' Pannenberg is taking a somewhat stronger epistemological stance than Popper, who, rejecting the validity of inductive argument, claims that theories cannot be verified but only 'corroborated'; i.e., that we can only give a report of the critical testing which the theory has already withstood, without drawing any implications about the likelihood of it withstanding further tests (since this would be an inductive argument from past to future). In my view, Pannenberg is to be preferred to Popper on this point, although to discuss this further would take us too far afield.

we shall return presently. Before doing so, however, I wish to look
further at the use of analogy as a critical principle, and especially at
the epistemological issues which this raises. (Part of the motivation
behind the following discussion is to establish a number of methodological principles which will be used elsewhere in this book.) To
open the subject up I turn now to Van Austin Harvey's discussion of
historical methodology, and, in particular, to the question of miracles.

### 2. Harvey's Historical Epistemology

In *The Historian and the Believer*[15] Harvey defends a critical principle
similar to Troeltschian analogy, but incorporates it into a specific
epistemology. For this Harvey draws heavily upon Stephen Toulmin's
analysis of the logic of argument, the main points of which can be
summed up in the following diagram:[16]

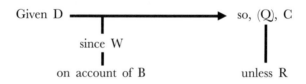

Diagram 1

C represents here the Conclusion for which one is arguing, D is the
Data upon which the argument is based, and W the rule or Warrant
that licences the inference of C from D; for example: (C) Jesus was
judged to have been a political enemy, because (D) he was crucified,
and (W) the Romans only crucified political enemies. Q is a modal
Qualifier that indicates the degree of confidence with which C follows from D and W (e.g., 'necessarily'; 'possibly'). R is a rebuttal, by
which an objector might try to undermine the conclusion of the
argument; for example, 'Your argument would prove that Jesus was
judged to be a political enemy, *unless* (R) the Romans made an exception to their normal practice in this case, to please the Jews'. So
this argument could be represented diagrammatically as follows:[17]

15 London: SCM, 1976.
16 Harvey, p. 54.
17 Harvey, p. 53.

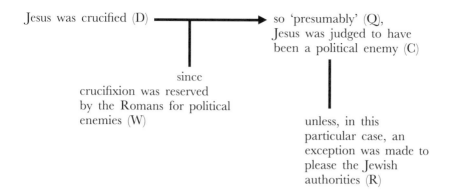

Jesus was crucified (D) ⟶ so 'presumably' (Q), Jesus was judged to have been a political enemy (C)

since crucifixion was reserved by the Romans for political enemies (W)

unless, in this particular case, an exception was made to please the Jewish authorities (R)

Diagram 2

Besides offering a rebuttal, another way in which the argument could be challenged would be to query whether W really was an acceptable warrant. The proponent of the argument would then have to offer some Backing, B, on account of which W was justified (see diagram 1). In practice, of course, an argument would be much more complex than this, with (for example) several different considerations providing Backing; but Harvey sees this diagram as giving the general structure of how argument functions.

Harvey is particularly concerned with how historians seek to justify their conclusions, and hence with the problem of warrants, because

> unless we did tacitly assume some kinds of warrants in any given field, it would be impossible to submit any argument in that field to rational assessment, because the data to which we appeal when challenged depend on just those warrants we are prepared to accept.[18]

By 'field' Harvey (following Toulmin) means a 'logical type' of statement, such as geometrical axioms or legal responsibilities (p. 49). Different fields obviously require different kinds of warrants, which support their conclusions in varying degrees.

Because history is a very diverse subject it draws upon many different fields, and therefore uses a considerable variety of warrants. These include, among other things, the laws of science:

> [History] presupposes physics, for example, insofar as the historian makes judgements about the capabilities of weapons in the battle of

---

[18] P. 52; this is a key principle for Harvey's argument, and in the original is italicized throughout.

Waterloo; . . . and it presupposes biology, insofar as the historian assesses the report about a saint who picked up his head after his execution and marched into a cathedral to sing the *Te Deum*. (p. 81)

Expanding on the last example, Harvey observes that our scientific knowledge about the relationships between vocal chords, brain, and lungs provide warrants that make our reasons for ruling out such an occurrence very strong: Decapitated singing is incompatible with such warrants, which are themselves very firmly established (p. 116). Harvey regards it as one of the major advances in historical studies that such tales are now immediately recognised to be legends—unlike our (relatively recent) forefathers, we are not in the least inclined to believe the stories recorded by the ancients about people born without heads or blood raining from heaven; nor can we envisage them being taken seriously again. The case against their historicity is closed, and firmly sealed by the advance of science.

This argument gains considerable theological relevance, of course, when it is applied to the biblical miracles. Quoting with approval (p. 114) Bultmann's famous dictum that

it is impossible to use electric light and the wireless and to avail ourselves of modern medical and surgical discoveries, and at the same time to believe in the New Testament world of spirits and miracles.

Harvey points out that such uses of modern science are a *de facto* acceptance of its laws and world-view; therefore it is inconsistent not to accept them also as legitimate principles when evaluating the biblical reports of miracles. Harvey charges traditional Christianity in particular of having frequently set aside established scientific warrants simply because they conflict with historical propositions which it prefers to believe. This, he observes, is 'intellectually irresponsible' (p. 118).

Harvey's appeal to scientific law is, of course, a version of Troeltschian analogy; but how, then, might someone who believes that Jesus was raised from the dead go about arguing their position in a way that it intellectually credible? Harvey suggests that there are two possible strategies. Firstly, one might challenge the warrants themselves (p. 87)—in this case, the scientific laws that rule out the possibility of a dead man returning to life. But this (Harvey explains) would be a *scientific* dispute, which the historian, as such, is not equipped to engage in. In Harvey's view, therefore, the only 'live option' is his second strategy: A defender of the resurrection could enter a rebuttal to the effect that the normal warrants do not apply

in this particular case (*ibid.*). Harvey considers this to be methodologically sounder, but thinks there would be insuperable difficulties
in carrying it through. If one does not want to end in scepticism
then some other warrants would have to be found instead; and yet
it is very difficult (Harvey suggests) to see what might be proposed.
Harvey particularly develops this point in connection with claims that
the biblical miracles were a unique kind of occurrences, for this is
simply to say that 'none of our warrants or analogies apply' (p. 122).
But how, then, is it possible even to assess whether the proposed
miracle might be a solution to a historical problem? Some apologists
(he observes) claim that an investigation into allegedly miraculous
occurrences must begin from Christian presuppositions; but if this
means that the uniqueness of the events becomes a presupposition of
the enquiry, then

> there are no more general principles to which one can appeal when
> differences of opinion arise. . . . The Christian apologist is particularly
> vulnerable at this point because the specific presupposition in question
> has to do with an event alleged to be absolutely unique, which is to
> say, an event to which no analogies or warrants grounded in present
> experience can apply. But if such is the case . . . how can any meaningful
> argument concerning that event arise? (p. 225)

Harvey's answer, of course, is that it cannot; and therefore we ought
not to relinquish the warrants that we normally use when discussing
extra-biblical miracles. But then the possibility of establishing the
occurrence of a miracle through historical enquiry is very slim indeed.

In assessing Harvey's position, we can say at once that he is obviously right to demand that an argument for the occurrence of a
miracle must use proper warrants; thus the main questions that need
to be discussed are, What may be used as warrants? and, How are
they to be used? This will lead into a number of epistemological
issues which are relevant not only to Childs' views on historical
referentiality but to a number of other aspects of his programme; so
to explore them more fully I shall consider how an argument between a 'supernaturalist' and an 'atheist' might proceed. (By 'supernaturalist' I refer in what follows to someone who believes that God
raised Jesus from the dead through a miraculous incursion into history; and by 'atheist' to someone who, denying that there is a God,
denies also that there was a resurrection (in this sense)).[19] Harvey's

---

[19] Many other positions, of course, have also been taken on these issues. This

own conception of how such an argument might proceed contains a number of methodological errors, the most obvious of which occur in his comments on uniqueness. It is simply not the case that the supernaturalist holds that *everything* connected with the resurrection was unique, as Harvey implies when he writes as though there could be *no* warrants for assessing a unique event. The supernaturalist does not claim, for example, that the disciples saw the risen Jesus through miraculous visual powers, which enabled them to see things which cannot be observed in the normal way, or that their witness was transmitted through a miraculously preserved tradition. *What* they claimed to see was, in some respects, quite unique; but the claim itself is open to being tested by many of the normal criteria for assessing historical testimony: Were the witnesses in a position to see what they claim to have seen? Are there external motivations which might have led them to give a false account? Does their account agree or clash with the relevant circumstantial evidence? Etc. These considerations alone give sufficient grounds upon which a supernaturalist and an atheist could, in principle, have a rational, historical argument—provided that the atheist does not fall back upon a Troeltschian dogmatism which decides *a priori* that all testimonies to the resurrection *must* be false, because dead men never return to life.[20]

Far more significant for the purposes of this book, however, is the kind of epistemology which Harvey employs. In my view, this is deeply wrongheaded in three, interrelated ways: It is a question-begging version of foundationalism; it is atomistic; and it handles the fact/interpretation issue inadequately. Let us consider each of these points

---

simple dichotomy is adequate for the present discussion, however, since this is concerned with the methodological issues that are raised by an argument between two people who proceed from radically different viewpoints, rather than with the substantive content of the argument for any particular viewpoint. Lest a false impression be given, however, it should perhaps be mentioned that Pannenberg himself is *not* a supernaturalist in the sense defined here; rather, he argues (in my view, unconvincingly) that we do not have sufficient scientific grounds for claiming that Jesus' resurrection is ruled out by the laws of science (see Pannenberg's *Jesus—God and Man* (London: SCM, 1968), p. 98).

[20] Implicit in the preceding is the important methodological point that even with positions as far apart as the supernaturalist's and the atheist's, there must nonetheless still be *some* common ground between them, simply in virtue of them agreeing to have a *certain kind* of argument. In this case they have agreed to have a *historical* argument, and it is therefore common ground that, for example, the eyewitness testimonies of Jesus' associates are potentially relevant data whereas the investigator's dreams about Jesus are not. I shall develop this point more fully when I discuss Stanley Fish's 'community relativism' in section 7.3 below.

in turn. 'Foundationalism' is a generic term for epistemologies which claim that there is a firm 'bedrock' of knowable facts, which can be appealed to in resolving epistemological disputes, and which thereby provides a foundation upon which our knowledge is built up. Thus to take one of Harvey's own examples, two historians who disagree over the capabilities of the weaponry used at Waterloo can, in principle, resolve their dispute through appealing to the relevant laws of science, which provide a sure foundation for the historians' knowledge. This is logically impeccable; and yet disagreements can only be resolved in this way when there does actually exist an established basis which all the relevant parties would accept. This, however, is precisely *not* the case when supernaturalists and atheists discuss the resurrection. The former cannot enter the discussion without bringing in his or her belief in a God who can supernaturally intervene in the course of historical events, and Harvey is quite right to observe both that the atheist will want to dispute this and also that 'there are no more general principles to which one can appeal when differences of opinion arise' (p. 225). He goes badly astray, however, in citing this *as an objection* to the supernaturalist's procedure. What Harvey has overlooked is that he is himself in precisely the same position with regard to his own claim that the laws of science apply *everywhere and always*. This too is an 'ultimate claim' which forms an integral part of the atheist's argument and which the supernaturalist will want to dispute, and yet beyond which there is no *more*-ultimate principle to which the disputants can appeal. Epistemologically, then, the supernaturalist and the atheist are in precisely the same position.

Harvey seems to think that he is actually in a much more advantageous position than someone who believes in miracles, in that his own 'ultimate principle' is well-established, and ought therefore to be used as the epistemological foundation upon which the supernaturalist's claims are adjudicated. This raises questions, however, as to whether the methodology of the natural sciences is in fact capable of establishing the *extremely* high degree of uniformity which Harvey would like to believe that the world possesses, and which it would need to possess if the laws of science are virtually to rule out the possibility of a miracle. There are two aspects of this which can be commented upon here, the first of which concerns the 'inductivist' account of scientific discovery. Although this has now been thoroughly refuted, it is nonetheless useful to review it briefly because (at least among those who are not acquainted with the recent discussions) it still seems to be an important factor in the nebulous but widespread belief that 'science has disproved miracles'. According to inductivism, scientific discovery is made through passing from particular facts to general laws: Various regularities or recurring features are observed among a certain range of phenomena (e.g., concerning the way that planets are observed to traverse the sky), and a law-like generalization[21] is therefore framed which encapsulates these observed regularities and extends them to other related cases. Such generalizations may, at first, be tentatively held; but if they continue to be confirmed by further observations then they gain inductive support and thereby grow in epistemological stature.

It is not difficult to see why this account would pose major difficulties for any belief in miracles: The sheer volume of available evidence would inductively support such generalizations as 'the dead do not return to life' to the point of virtual certainty, and thus reduce the probability of Jesus' resurrection to sub-microscopic proportions. This account of scientific discovery, however, has now been completely discredited. There are a number of reasons for this, but particularly pertinent to the present discussion is the realization that the mature sciences have in fact made progress through a series of 'scientific revolutions', with there characteristically being deep discontinuities between the methods, laws, and concepts of a science before and after a revolution. In consequence of this there was a radical rethinking of how scientific theories are 'established', with it now being realized that anomalous, *dis*confirming events play a crucial role. To discuss this in general terms is far beyond the scope of the present book; but the main points can be sufficiently illustrated from the rise and fall of Newtonian mechanics. For about two hundred years this proved itself time and again to be an immensely successful theory, comprehending within its scope a vast array of celestial and terrestrial phenomena, and explaining them far more accurately than had any previous theory. On an inductivist account, then, Newtonian mechanics was confirmed and established as fully as one could ever expect any theory to be; and yet various 'anomalies' were also discovered—i.e., cases in which there was, *prima facie*, a mismatch

---

[21] By 'law-like' I mean that the generalization goes beyond merely summarizing the observed events, to include (at least) unobserved past events and events which have not yet occurred. The laws of science, of course, are generally held to be 'law-like' in this sense, and it is only if 'The dead do not return to life' is similarly construed that it is relevant to a discussion of miracles.

between what the theory predicted and what was in fact observed. The orbits of neither Uranus nor Mercury, for example, quite agreed with the Newtonian predictions; and for our present purposes it is important to see how these discrepancies were handled. For Uranus the problem was overcome by postulating the existence of a hitherto unknown planet, whose presence was subsequently confirmed by telescopic observations. Recalculating the Newtonian predictions with this extra factor included largely overcame the discrepancies, thus removing the anomaly. And likewise for the anomalous orbit of Mercury, a similar strategy was tried once more—but this time without success. Observation failed to confirm the existence of a further planet that would account for the discrepancies, and no convincing reason could be given as to why, if such a planet did exist, it should remain unseen. Thus 'the precession of the perihelion of Mercury' (as this anomalous motion was called) remained an unresolved discrepancy between Newtonian prediction and astronomical observation; and when an alternative theory emerged (namely, Einstein's General Relativity) which could explain these observations much more accurately, this became an important factor in the downfall of Newton's gravitational theory.

The marked difference of the preceding from an inductivist account of the sciences, and the relevance this has for the 'science and miracles' question, can be brought out in the following two points:

(i) Anomalies cannot be 'overwhelmed' by 'normal' observations— the discrepant motions of Mercury and Uranus could not be resolved by piling up more and more data on the motions of Venus, Mars, and Jupiter which *do* agree with the Newtonian predictions, and then arguing that since this gives such strong inductive support to Newton's theories they *must* be right, and that the discrepancies therefore must be due to errors in observing Uranus and Mercury (even if the errors cannot actually be identified). And similarly, then, one cannot legitimately argue that since we have so many confirming instances, we *must* believe that 'the dead do not return to life', and that the apparently anomalous case of Jesus' resurrection therefore must be due to errors in the reporting of it (even if we cannot actually identify what they are). Such reasoning is *not scientific*; the natural sciences are not inductive in this sense.

(ii) On the other side of the same coin, the discovery of an apparent anomaly characteristically leads, in the natural sciences, to a closer study of the anomaly, in order to see whether it can after all be reconciled with the relevant scientific laws. One aspect of this, of course, will be the critical testing of the relevant observations, to assess whether there are in fact good grounds for accepting the existence of the apparently anomalous occurrences; yet this testing clearly must not appeal as a critical norm to the very laws whose veracity is called into question by the anomaly—to argue, for example, that 'the observed motion of Mercury would contradict Newtonian science; therefore the observations *must* be wrong' would simply ensure *a priori* that the current theories could not in any circumstances be experimentally refuted. Nor, of course, is it necessary to resort to such reasoning, because there will always be other, independent ways of assessing such observations (through appealing, for example, to the optical laws relevant to the design and use of telescopes). And similarly, then, for alleged miracles. The *unscientific* way of responding to Jesus' alleged resurrection would be to argue, 'but we know that the dead do not return to life, therefore the historical sources must be in error', because this simply ensures *a priori* that one's general law remains immune from all possible counterevidence. The scientific response, rather, would be to look more closely at the apparent anomaly, in order to assess whether it really does provide a refutation of the law. It is quite possible, in principle, to do this in a way that does not simply beg the question, because, as we have already seen, there are other ways of assessing historical witnesses than by stipulating that all testimonies to a miracle *must* be in error. In sum, then, once an inductivistic misconception of the natural sciences is replaced by a more accurate account, many of the grounds on which the sciences have supposedly shown that 'miracles cannot happen' simply fall away.

We can now move on to another response to Harvey's claim that it is the laws of science which provide the primary warrants for assessing miracle reports. What in fact the supernaturalist (in the sense defined here) is fundamentally denying is the *applicability* of the laws of science to such events as Jesus' resurrection: Since the resurrection is conceived as being brought about by a direct intervention of God it does not fall under the laws of nature, which are therefore simply irrelevant to an evaluation of whether such an event occurred. Once it is seen, however, that we are concerned with the applicability of scientific laws to particular cases then we can turn to the sciences themselves for some important guidelines.

Scientists apply their laws as a matter of course to the natural world in their quest for a better understanding of it; but in doing so there always has to be an implicit 'other things being equal' clause. If, for example, the scientist is given certain astronomical data at time t, then he or she can, through applying the relevant laws of motion, predict with a very high degree of accuracy the times at which solar eclipses will subsequently occur—*provided that* the system is not disturbed by some kind of external interference (through, for example, the moon being struck by a large meteorite). If these calculations were extrapolated far enough into the future, however, they would go seriously wrong, precisely because the 'other things being equal' condition will not be fulfilled indefinitely—according to current theories, the sun will eventually become a 'red giant' and expand to such a size that it engulfs the Earth. But this gives the supernaturalist a way of answering objections that 'science has disproved the resurrection': Such objections assume that the usual laws are applicable to the death of Jesus, but in fact other things were *not* equal on this occasion—what happened subsequent to his death was not a natural event but a divine intervention. The laws of science are simply inapplicable here.

The methodological point can be conveniently illustrated from Henri Becquerel's discovery of 'uranic rays' (later identified as beta-rays).[22] Shortly after Roentgen's discovery of X-rays emanating from the fluorescent spot of his vacuum tube, it occurred to Becquerel that X-rays might also be produced by other fluorescent sources. To test this hypothesis, Becquerel wrapped a photographic plate in layers of black paper. These could be penetrated by X-rays (which would then darken the plate) but prevented the plate from becoming fogged by exposure to sunlight. The fluorescent substance was then placed on top of this package, and the whole arrangement left in the sun for a few hours, in order to make the substance fluoresce. The plate was then developed and found to be darkened, which Becquerel took as evidence that the fluorescent substance did indeed produce X-rays. On one occasion when it was too cloudy for the experiment to be conducted, however, the apparatus was left in a dark cupboard for several days. For reasons that are unclear Becquerel nonetheless developed the plate, and was astonished to discover that it had fogged

---

[22] The following historical information is drawn from Abraham Pais, *Inward Bound* (Oxford: OUP, 1986), pp. 42–47, 60, and Emilio Segrè, *From X-Rays to Quarks: Modern Physicists and Their Discoveries* (San Francisco: W.H. Freeman, 1980), pp. 26–30.

just as before. The fogging, then, had not been due to the fluores-
cence; Becquerel had discovered (as subsequent experiments confirmed)
a previously unknown form of radiation.

According to the laws of science as they were known when
Becquerel began his experiments, the plate left in the dark cupboard
should not have become fogged. For a Harveyite physicist to have
argued, however, that Becquerel must have been mistaken, or hallu-
cinating, on the grounds that this alleged event contravened (as it
did) our well-established warrants about photographic plates, or for
a Troeltschian physicist to dismiss the fogging because it was
disanalogous to all previous experience (as it was), would be scientific
madness. To specify in advance that all subsequent events *must* con-
form to the world as it is now understood would simply bring all
fundamental research to an immediate halt, because it would amount
to an *a priori* stipulation that nothing new could be discovered.

There are, of course, some obvious differences between Becquerel's
discovery and Jesus' resurrection: Becquerel's results could be repeated
at will, and the newly discovered beta-rays proved to be a well-be-
haved natural phenomenon. This makes no difference, however, to
the methodological principle that emerges here,[23] which is this: Science
is incapable of framing its warrants so tightly, or of comprehending
the world so exhaustively, that it can assure us *a priori* that there are
no further phenomena beyond those covered by its laws as they are
currently framed, and which could produce effects contrary to what
is possible under those laws alone. Science is methodologically incapable of ruling out further 'natural interventions' (such as the beta-
rays made into Becquerel's experiments); much less is it capable of
ruling out divine interventions. In sum, then: Contrary to popular
belief, scientists themselves do not (and, for good methodological
reasons, must not) insist that their laws, as currently framed, apply to
all things at all times, but must be able to recognize situations in
which these laws have proven to be inadequate; and the supernaturalist can therefore defend the possibility of the resurrection by claiming

---

[23] The significance of repeatability, in this connection, is that it enables one to
establish with a high a degree of probability that the anomalous event (in this case
the fogging of the unexposed plates) really has occurred. The methodologically and
epistemologically important point, however, is that one can be reasonably sure about
the occurrence of the anomaly, not that one gains this assurance through repeatability. This is an important distinction for historians, of course, who are interested
in events which are essentially unrepeatable but of whose occurrence they can be
reasonably sure.

that this is just such a situation. Of course, this claim must be supported by appropriate arguments, and to this we shall return below; but the methodological point to note here is that such a claim cannot simply be ruled out of court, because scientists themselves also make the same sort of claim in the course of their scientific work. Or to put it another way: A sound scientific methodology itself requires the investigator to be open to the possibility that there are further factors which science has not hitherto taken into account, and which therefore limit the applicability of scientific law as it is now known. The supernaturalist claims that the resurrection involved one such factor, and therefore cannot be assessed by the normal scientific warrants.

Harvey's foundationalist construal of the dispute between the supernaturalist and the atheist, then, gives his own ultimate principle of scientific uniformity a privileged position to which it is not entitled. The epistemological situation, rather, is that each disputant has their own ultimate principle, in terms of which their own argument is constructed; and some way needs to be found, therefore, of respecting this if one disputant is not simply to beg the question against the other by making their own principle the controlling standard for the whole debate. I shall return to this presently.

The second major flaw in Harvey's epistemology is that it is atomistic. This shows itself in at least two ways. Firstly, Harvey isolates the resurrection from its historical and theological contexts. Someone whose knowledge of the Gospels was based solely upon what can be gleaned from *The Historian and the Believer* would surely conclude that the passion narratives were disconnected appendices about an obscure individual who, for no particular reason, came back to life. Yet this is a travesty of the position defended by the supernaturalist, for whom Jesus did not simply return to life but was raised by God; was not just any Jew but the Son of God; had a unique relationship to his heavenly Father; and whose death and consequent resurrection was intimately related to the three years of remarkable public ministry which immediately preceded it. By isolating the resurrection from these contextual factors Harvey unfairly deprives the supernaturalist of important lines of argument.[24] If, for example, the resurrection were viewed as just an isolated instance of some-

---

[24] Cf. Abraham, *Divine Revelation*, pp. 132–34, 152–54.

one returning to life, then there would be some force in Harvey's charge that

> The orthodox believer . . . is intellectually irresponsible . . . because he continually enters objections to our normal warrants *for no principled reasons.* Consequently, his objections are themselves nonassessible.[25]

The situation is entirely different, however, when the resurrection is discussed in terms of God raising his own Son. God, in Christian theology, is a rational agent with certain plans, intentions, and purposes; and it is therefore perfectly possible, in principle, to discuss why, contrary to his normal practice, he should choose to raise this particular man from the dead. There are well-known warrants for assessing hypotheses about an agent's purposes, several of which are, *prima facie*, applicable to a divine agent; thus we are not forced to choose between the options which Harvey offers us, of either accepting his Troeltschian, supposedly-scientific warrants or letting the argument descend into a morass of unassessable claims and counterclaims. When the supernaturalist's views are not arbitrarily truncated, there are warrants available for assessing them.

Similar considerations also dispose of the other chief bogeyman with which Harvey tries to frighten us into taking refuge under Troeltsch's aegis, namely, that if a suspension of natural law is admitted in Jesus' case, then we may find that we have no principled reason for rejecting tales about decapitated singers and other such nonsense. What, to my mind, makes the decapitation story so implausible, however, is not that it contravenes the laws of science but that it does so for such trivial and arbitrary reasons. The great majority of the miracles in the Gospels have, at the very least, a humane motivation, in that their immediate effect is to relieve suffering and distress.[26] Beyond that, at least some of the miracles have the (further) theological purpose of acting as signs, which call attention to the special identity and mission of the one who performs them. And more specifically, Jesus' resurrection has a profound soteriological purpose, in that his being raised destroys the power of death, and is the firstfruits of the general resurrection of the dead (1 Corinthians 15).

---

[25] P. 118, italics added.

[26] This and the following observations are not, of course, being put forward as simple, knock-down criteria for distinguishing true from false miracle-reports, but to illustrate the methodological point that, even if we reject Troeltschian analogy, there are still ample grounds for reasonable debate.

There are good reasons, then, for the occurrence of such miracles as these. By contrast, the the decapitated singer does nothing more than provide a few minutes of superficial spectacle; thus the story portrays God as making a quite exceptional suspension of the usual course of events for no better reason than to give a little fireworks display. This would be quite out of character for the God portrayed in the New Testament, and therefore gives us very strong reasons to think that he did not act in this way.[27] The supernaturalist, then, is by no means bereft of criteria for assessing other miracle-stories.

The second way in which Harvey's position is unduly atomistic is that it treats the different elements in his diagram as self-contained units—as though (for example) one could try out a number of different warrants without this changing our conception of the data.[28] Again my objection is not to the intrinsic logic, but to the applicability of this kind of reasoning to an argument about miracles. Clearly there are situations in which the different elements *are* independent: It is inconceivable that (given the actual state of these disciplines today) any historical discoveries about the weaponry at Waterloo would refute the laws of physics. That this is not *generally* the case, however, can be illustrated from the second of the two strategies which, as we saw above, Harvey offers the defender of miracles (namely, that the warrants be left unchallenged but that a rebuttal be offered against their applicability in this particular instance). On the one hand, the argument against miracles is decisive only if the warrants are *universal*—something even slightly weaker than this, such as 'In the overwhelming majority of case, the dead do not return to life', concedes that the resurrection *is* a historical possibility, and allows one to enter a rebuttal to the effect that Jesus was one of the (minuscule) minority which this warrant implicitly admits. On the other hand, a universal warrant rules out the very possibility of a rebuttal—'The dead *never* return to life, but Jesus was an exception' is self-contradictory.

Warrants and rebuttals, then, cannot be considered in atomistic isolation from one another; and likewise, neither can warrants and data. For something to serve as data it has to be evaluated and interpreted, which requires an (implicit or explicit) appeal to general

---

[27] Pannenberg's comments (reviewed in section 1 above) on the legitimate use of analogy as a critical principle are relevant here.

[28] Admittedly, this is more an omission on Harvey's part than an assertion of independence; but the oversight is a serious one.

principles; but these in turn may themselves be, or be interrelated with, principles that are used as warrants. If so, then data and warrants are no longer independent—refuting a warrant will also change the evaluation of the data. How one answers the question 'What did the disciples on the Emmaus Road actually experience?', for example, will depend upon one's answers to a host of other questions, such as 'Are hallucinations psychologically possible under those circumstances?', 'Could one countenance a suspension of the laws of nature in Jesus' case?', 'Could Jesus have survived the crucifixion?', and ultimately, of course, 'Is there a God, and is he capable of raising a person from the dead?'. These questions can only be answered as a collective whole—one cannot first decide, as an isolated matter on its own, whether the disciples encountered the risen Jesus and then use this as an established (foundational) fact in deciding whether or not there is a God. Justification cannot be atomistic because the world is not atomistic—it is not just a sequence of discrete particulars but an interconnected whole, and the interconnections are not 'mere interpretations' but (if the interpretations are correct) integral parts of reality. True interpretations state the facts.

The last paragraph also exposes the third major flaw in Harvey's epistemology, namely, its inadequate handling of the fact/interpretation issue; but since this has already been considered at length in section 4.4 it is unnecessary to discuss it further here. Turning instead to what might replace Harvey's epistemology, I return to the Pannenberg-Collingwood-Popper model that was outlined in section 1 above. As we saw there, this model, in recognition of the interconnectedness of reality and the unity of fact and interpretation, proceeds through a series of Conjectures and Refutations towards a progressively more accurate recovery of 'what really happened'. But although this is a major improvement on Harvey's epistemology, one further refinement is needed. The way for the supernaturalist and the atheist to have a fruitful discussion, I would suggest, is not through them arguing directly over the *same* reconstruction, but through them each, in the first instance, giving their own, independent, reconstruction, in accordance with their own 'ultimate principles'.[29] The reason

---

[29] My thinking here has been much influenced by (although in some respects it significantly departs from) Thomas Kuhn's discussion of scientific revolutions in terms of a conflict between competing paradigms (*The Structure of Scientific Revolutions, passim*). Kuhn's work has generated an enormous debate, not least over what his views actually are; but fortunately a major step towards clearing this issue up has recently been

why they should proceed in this way is that each protagonist has fundamentally different ideas about what ought to go into a reconstruction of the 'resurrection-event'; therefore attempting to work together constructively could hardly avoid the sort of question-begging that we identified in Harvey's procedures.

This does not mean, of course, that each simply ignores the other's work. On the contrary, they will also mutually interact, through criticizing each other's reconstructions. So, for example, the supernaturalist will ask that the atheist explains how, if Jesus was not raised, the biblical testimonies to the risen Jesus came about; and if the atheist replies that they stemmed from the disciples' hallucinations, then it will be pointed out that modern psychology has made some important discoveries about the circumstances in which hallucinations can occur, and the supernaturalist will therefore ask for some sort of demonstration that the appropriate conditions pertained for the disciples. If the atheist offers a reconstruction of this then it too can be challenged and critically tested; and if a plausible response is not forthcoming, then the supernaturalist can rightly object that the atheist has ultimately fallen back upon unproven dogmatism. But if, on the other hand, the atheist is able to give satisfactory responses in terms of his or her own ultimate principles, then this strengthens the claims for the soundness of a naturalistic reconstruction.

So then, it *is* possible for two people with fundamentally opposed principles to have a rational debate, without them having to find some common foundation, and without them begging the question against each other. The way to proceed is for each disputant (i) To construct, in accordance with *their own* principles, a comprehensive and coherent account of the phenomena under debate; and (ii) To criticize, in accordance with the opponent's principles, the opponent's attempt to complete the constructive task—i.e., to argue that *the opponent's* reconstruction is incoherent. Both these tasks, undertaken by both protagonists, are an essential part of the argument. The ultimate winner is (ideally) the one who shows that their own ultimate

---

taken with the publication of Paul Hoyningen-Heune's excellent study, *Reconstructing Scientific Revolutions: Thomas S. Kuhn's Philosophy of Science* (Chicago: University of Chicago Press, 1993). To review these debates is beyond the scope of the present book; however, I have discussed some relevant aspects of Kuhn's work in 'Hermeneutics and Postmodernism: Can We Have a Radical Reader-Response Theory? Part II', *RelStud* 31 (1995), section iii. For a very perceptive application of Kuhnian ideas to theological disputes, see Basil Mitchell's *The Justification of Religious Belief* (New York: OUP, 1981)

principles, but not their opponent's, make sense of the whole puzzle in a natural and coherent way—or at least, who shows that they get much closer to this ideal than the opponent does. (How far one is able to get with any particular case will depend, of course, upon the quantity and the quality of the available evidence.) Thus the putative occurence of a miracle *can* be rationally debated by historians.

The discussions in this chapter, then, have generally been favourable to Pannenberg's idea that a new historical methodology should be developed, based on a non-Troeltschian principle of analogy. It still needs to be asked, however, how beneficial this might be to Pannenberg's broader programme of the historian uncovering 'revelation in history'; and here there are two points to make. Firstly, although the discussion has largely centred around the issues which would arise from a historical investigation of Jesus' allegedly miraculous resurrection from the dead, it should be recalled that Pannenberg himself is not a supernaturalist (in the sense we have defined). Nonetheless, the methodology developed here is not exclusively tied to debates between supernaturalists and atheists, and much of the discussion would also be applicable to other attempts at defending a non-supernaturalistic defence of the resurrection as a literal historical event (albeit one that does not involve a direct incursion of God into history).

Secondly, however, we have seen that in Pannenberg's view it is *history as a whole* which is revelatory of God; and similarly, Childs' claims that God has revealed himself through the history of Israel are clearly intended to apply to more than just its overtly miraculous/supranatural moments. The next question to be tackled, therefore, is whether the methodology which has thus far been formulated in relation to miraculous events can be extended into a broader programme of 'revelation in (canonically interpreted) history'.

### 3. *Faith, History, and Objectivity*

We saw in section 2.2 that in response to Stendahl's dichotomy Childs relativizes the distinction between the descriptive and the normative/constructive tasks—the first, when properly conceived, is not a neutral undertaking; rather, *both* tasks, according to Childs, must proceed from a faith-commitment. This chapter, I think, has vindicated certain aspects of Childs' response, although care must be taken not to overstate what has been achieved. Although the role of faith in textual interpretation has not yet been discussed,[30] I will now suggest that the following is intuitively plausible: For such texts as those relevant to Jesus' resurrection, there *is*, as Stendahl claims, a faith-neutral, descriptive/exegetical task, insofar as one's aim is simply to recount the story—the supernaturalist and the atheist can both agree, for example, that in the Emmaus Road narrative (taken just as a story) Jesus was recognized as being alive again after the crucifixion. Things get more complicated, however, when the text's significance for the modern believer is considered. This raises two broad questions: Is the text's principal claim *true*?; and, What implications does this have for today's church? To give a positive response to the second question is, as Stendahl recognized, to make a faith-commitment; but the discussions in this chapter have shown that substantive issues of faith-commitment are also raised by the first question. An atheist is not, of course, excluded from the rational discussion of this question; but nonetheless, (i) *How* the atheist discusses it will be heavily affected by his lack of faith (i.e., he will use different fundamental principles in assessing the evidence); and (ii) If the atheist is committed to following the discussion through to the end, then she has to reckon with the possibility that she might no longer be an atheist when the final conclusion is reached—the supernaturalists's faith-committed position may prove to be the better explanation of the evidence. In both these senses, then, discussing whether Jesus was raised from the dead is not a faith-neutral task; and yet it *is* a descriptive task. Thus Stendahl's aligning of the distinction between the descriptive and the constructive aspects of theology with, respectively, a faith-neutral and a faith-involving approach by the scholar, breaks down in the case of allegedly miraculous occurrences.

The reasons for this breakdown are of considerable methodological significance for Childs' project. In both 'BTCon' and 'Method' Stendahl is clearly motivated by a strong conviction that Biblical Theology should be an *objective* discipline. This has some obvious attractions—many scholars would be deeply unhappy with a situation in which every denomination and sect could, to its own satisfaction, find in the Scriptures confirmation of its own distinctive beliefs, and yet could rarely agree on a common interpretation with those outside

---

[30] This will be considered in section 12.4 below.

its own communion.[31] Yet in his commendable desire for objectivity, Stendahl seems to have assumed that Biblical Theology must therefore be pursued in a way that is *faith-neutral*. Such a correlating of objectivity with neutrality is certainly plausible; for if the approach of each particular scholar were 'slanted' in ways that depend upon his or her own faith-stance, then surely each would get idiosyncratic results which they themselves find to be subjectively plausible but which are unlikely to be acceptable to anyone outside their own 'faith-circle'. The present discussion, however, has shown this 'argument for neutrality' to be wrong in two ways. First, it is wrong in thinking that starting from a particular faith-stance necessarily undermines the objectivity of the descriptive task, because in fact there *can* be rational argument between those with fundamentally different faith-commitments, without either party having to compromise their integrity, and without the argument becoming circular or question-begging. The decisive factor, epistemologically, is not the point from which one begins but the way in which one subsequently has to move as that starting-point is subjected to the scrutiny of a properly-critical methodology. And secondly, the 'argument for neutrality' is wrong in thinking that to start from a neutral position when trying to resolve such descriptive questions as 'Was Jesus raised from the dead?' is even a possible option. This impossibility is methodological: An investigation such as this has to make an evaluation of the various claims to have seen Jesus alive, of the various explanations that have been offered for Jesus' tomb being empty, etc.; and this is impossible unless the investigator begins with some prior beliefs that are 'strong enough'[32] to interact critically with the pertinent data. Someone with no particular views about whether there is a god, whether nature is lawlike, and whether its laws could be broken, would be completely out of their depth in such a debate. Far from a neutral investigator being the ideally objective historian, they would be unable even to enter the discussion![33]

---

[31] Childs himself, it will be recalled, has always been sensitive to the charge that 'interpretation in faith' is essentially fideistic, and clearly accepts that, if this could be sustained, it would constitute a very serious objection to his programme.

[32] In the sense of having a significant degree of substantive content; not necessarily in the sense of the investigator having a strong subjective commitment to them being true.

[33] Although, then, this book will defend the possibility of objective knowledge, it does *not* defend but rejects the traditional, *tabula rasa* strategy for achieving objectivity, in which the scholar is supposed to reach an unbiased conception of the subject

Having said this, however, it is also important to note the inherent limitations of the previous discussion. This has argued that (i) *some* sort of prior faith-commitment is necessary; and that (ii) Harvey cannot insist that this *must* be his own favoured commitment to naturalistic uniformity. Yet by the same token, Childs cannot insist that we *must* start from *his* favoured commitment to Christian belief. I cannot see that Childs has any telling objections against the resurrection being investigated from an atheistic standpoint; and there seems to be no reason, therefore, to insist that scholars must have a certain faith-commitment before they can be accepted as '*real* theologians'. All that matters is that one be genuinely willing to enter the debate, with the risk which this entails of possibly having one's own starting-point refuted.

Childs is on much stronger ground, however, in his polemics against the supposed neutrality of critical historiography. We have just seen that some issues *cannot* be debated from a neutral standpoint, and Childs is therefore right to suspect that a 'hidden principle' is implicitly guiding such research (albeit, perhaps, unwittingly) when it claims to be following a neutral[34] methodology. Scholars who, for example, authomatically put a red line through every miracle-narrative, just because it *is* a miracle-narrative, cannot justify this by claiming that they are only following the dictates of a neutral historiography; and similarly for those who classify as *ex eventu* every prophecy which claims to foretell the future solely on the grounds that it gives an accurate portrayal of the events to which it refers. Such a historiography is *not* neutral, but is implicitly assuming some fairly rigid version of natural uniformity. It is to the general benefit of scholarship, therefore, that this be explicitly recognized, so that the assumption can be brought out into the open and its strengths and weaknesses explicitly evaluated. Simply to accept that critical historiography is unable—as a matter of principle—to investigate the miraculous accounts in the Bible is far too complacent. A sound methodology must be capable of handling the full range of its subject matter, yet without prejudging the sub-stantive issues; therefore insofar as the standard critical approach fails to do this it needs to be revised.

Since Childs has been very reluctant to engage in critical investigations

---

under investigation through clearing his or her mind of all preconceptions about it. This will be discussed more fully in sections 8.4 and 9.6 below.

[34] Or 'scientific', as it is sometimes (inappropriately) called.

of 'referentiality in the text', he does not directly benefit from this conclusion. We saw in section 4.2, however, that Childs' own theological concerns ought to make him more attentive to 'what really happened', and that he therefore needs to engage much more fully with the current debates about, for example, the historical reconstruction of Israel's true origins, or the historical Jesus. The thesis of this chapter is that in doing so one is entitled to start from a Christian faith-stance—one need not become a methodological atheist in order to be a genuine historian.

I shall return to Childs presently; but first it is necessary to make a fuller assessment of Pannenberg's position. The discussion so far has, on the whole, endorsed his methodological points, although he seems not to have adequately grasped the dynamics of how an argument between historians who are working from different fundamental convictions should be conducted. But granted that his historical methodology is basically sound, there is still the question of what can be discovered through it. Can even this revised methodology investigate the 'revelation as history' which Pannenberg envisages? It seems to me that some major problems are raised here by James Barr's well-known argument against the *Heilsgeschichte* theologians, concerning the inseparability of divine acts and divine words:

> A God who acted in history would be a mysterious and supra-personal fate if the action was not linked with . . . verbal conversation. It is in the verbal conversation that the anthropomorphic aspect of the God of Israel is most profoundly retained and most creative. . . . In his *speech* with man . . . God really meets man on his own level and directly. . . . All assertions of the personal nature of the God who deals in history make hidden borrowings from the account of this verbal conversation.[35]

This somewhat overstates the case: If the ten plagues did 'coincidentally' keep striking the Egyptians but missing the Israelites then it would be difficult *not* to infer that a personal God who specially favoured Israel was revealing himself.[36] But Barr's basic point is surely

---

[35] *Old and New in Interpretation* (London: SCM, second edition 1982), p. 78; Barr's italics. G.G. O'Collins, quoting a similar passage from elsewhere in Barr, raises this as a decisive objection against Pannenberg ('Revelation as History', *HeyJ* 7 (1966), p. 402).

[36] Strictly speaking this would not be a revelation, in Pannenberg's sense, but only a manifestation, since it would not (he claims) disclose God in his *essence* (see his 'Introduction' to *RaH* and the first two of his 'Theses'). Although this distinction is very important for Pannenberg's overall programme, it is unnecessary to consider it here.

correct. It is exceedingly difficult to see how the mere *events* of the exodus—even if the full historicity of the miraculous elements is allowed—are supposed to reveal that the God who is now intervening is the same God who revealed himself to the Patriarchs, that he intends to form a covenant with Israel (involving her in a mass of precise legal obligations), and that he will give her a land of her own. The problem becomes all the more acute when we consider non-miraculous spans of history. Even using Pannenberg's historical methodology, the amount we would learn about 'the personal nature of God' from a modern reconstruction of the monarchic period, apart from the 'set-piece' speeches and overt theological commentary that has been incorporated into the account in Kings is surely very small indeed.[37] Pannenberg's revised methodology still seems to be the wrong tool for this job.

Pannenberg would probably reply that I have begged the question against him with my reference to 'mere events', since his position is that events are revelatory when interpreted as interconnected wholes, and *within the context of their traditions*. Unfortunately Pannenberg never analyses this idea with any precision; but there is one event for which he at least sets out his views quite fully, namely, for Jesus' resurrection. In this event God completely revealed himself,[38] but only indirectly. As the power who determines all reality God can ultimately be revealed only at the *end* of history, since only then is the final meaning of an event given. (Prior to that the meaning of an event can be changed by further occurrences—the meaning of Israel's settlement in Canaan was changed by the subsequent exile, then further modified by the return from exile.) Jesus, however, has fully revealed God, because in his resurrection the end of the world has already occurred proleptically. This can be established (Pannenberg claims) through a historical reconstruction of Jesus' resurrection within the context of the prevailing traditions:

> The resurrection of Jesus first assumed the meaning of being the anticipation of the end in connection with the understanding of history in the apocalyptic literature. It was only within the horizons of the apocalyptic expectation that the disciples of Jesus would designate as 'resurrection' all experiences of the Living One who is distinct from

---

[37] This appears to be the objection that Childs is raising against Pannenberg in *OTTCC*, p. 16.

[38] This in fact is the only event that counts as a 'revelation' in Pannenberg's strict sense, because this alone discloses God's essence.

the earthly life on the other side of death. . . . In the sphere of this
expectation, the appearance of the risen Jesus had its own language. . . .
It . . . means the end has broken in with the fate of Jesus and that God
is manifest in him.[39]

This is certainly a very bold and imaginative argument; and yet I
think it is unsatisfactory[40] because, despite Pannenberg's intentions,
event and interpretation are not held together in a genuine unity. In
fact, the main objection which Pannenberg levelled against the
kerygma theologians also poses a serious difficulty for his own position:
If Jesus' resurrection was not, intrinsically, a proleptic occurrence of
the Eschaton then its happening in a context of high apocalyptic
expectation does not make it so; and if it *was* a prolepsis, then the
apocalyptic traditions do not 'add' anything to it. Unfortunately it is
difficult to develop this argument as precisely as one would wish
because Pannenberg's notion of 'the proleptic occurrence of the end
of the world in the resurrection of Jesus' is itself very obscure. For
the sake of illustration, however, let us suppose that it includes the
claim that, on the basis of Jesus' resurrection, God's relationship to
the world has fundamentally changed—the resurrection has inaugu-
rated a 'New Age'. Then Pannenberg faces the following dilemma:
If such a change has been effected then this is in virtue of the relationships *actually pertaining* between God, the world, and Jesus' resurrection, not through the latter having occurred in the context of
apocalyptic expectations; and conversely, if in the absence of these
expectations the pertaining relationships do not amount to the inauguration of a New Age, then it is very difficult to see how 'adding
on' the apocalyptic traditions makes it into such an inauguration. Or
in other words, the traditions may help us to *recognize* certain aspects
of God's relationship to the world, if such relationships do in fact
pertain; but they cannot make it to be the case that they do pertain.
Yet the meaning of the resurrection is primarily determined by the
relationships which set it within the eschatological purposes of God,
rather than by its interconnectedness with other events within the
world; and with this we are surely moving into realms of meaning
that are beyond the historian's range of investigations.

The problems in Pannenberg's position may be further explored

---

[39] 'Theses', p. 146. See also his fourth and fifth theses; cf. 'REH' pp. 35–38,
66–8; *Jesus—God and Man*, especially ch. 3.
[40] O'Collins also senses that there is a problem here (p. 405), but does not really
put his finger on it.

by looking at Gerhard von Rad's very different handling of these issues. As is well known, von Rad's version of *Heilsgeschichte* centres on the progressive development and reinterpretation of Israel's traditions as testimonies to God's saving interventions in her history. So, for example, Yahwism absorbed into itself the traditions from the pre-Mosaic worship of the patriarchs, because it recognized 'in the promise of a land made to the ancestors . . . the voice of its own God'.[41] And yet (von Rad observes, pp. 322–23), the earlier traditions could only be reused through being sifted and thoroughly reinterpreted. The promise of a land was projected forward to the time of Joshua, with the patriarchs' wanderings being interpreted as a sojourning which still awaited the true fulfilment; and elements which were 'incompatible' with Yahwism had to be 'quietly discarded', or else the latter would have lost its distinctive character. Similarly, the prophets showed a remarkable freedom in their use of Israel's election traditions, on the one hand denying Israel the right to appeal to the salvation they promised, and on the other hand reinterpreting them as typologically foreshadowing a new exodus and a new covenant (p. 323). The prophets had no fixed procedures for handling the traditions, but adopted, adapted, and discarded as needs required (p. 325); and this leads von Rad to the following very significant characterization of their work:

> The whole way by which old traditions are actualized in the prophets' predictions, these men's close attachment to the old, their habit of carrying over the old into the new, and their contrasting but connected habit of ignoring some aspects of the old which they believed to be superseded, can only be understood as [a] *fundamentally charismatic procedure*, or, to put it more exactly, as an eclective process based on *charisma*.[42]

This, in my view, makes a very important point, and shows that Pannenberg has left something vital out of his own account. Faced with a mass of ancient traditions it is far from clear how, within the methodological framework that Pannenberg proposes, they are to be shaped into Holy Scripture. Were the tradents correct, for example,

---

[41] *Old Testament Theology* II, p. 322.

[42] P. 324, italics added; cf. pp. 400, 402, 407. 'Charismatic' is also used by von Rad of the New Testament's interpretation of the Old (pp. 331, 386, 407, 409), and of how the post-biblical age ought to interpret the Old Testament (p. 409). Von Rad compares these three uses in ways which suggest that they are essentially the same (pp. 407, 409); but although there are clearly significant similarities between them, the latter two also raise problems different from those being considered here.

in thinking that they heard the voice of Yahweh in the promise of a land to the patriarchs, or in accepting the prophetic reinterpretation of the exodus? Have these shapings of the tradition given us something that is theologically insightful? It is difficult to see how one could give a positive answer with any confidence if the redactors had used a Pannenbergian historical methodology, because although this allows for a divine dimension in the reconstruction, it is far from clear how, in practice, one would be able to 'get a grip' on just where and how the divine purpose had truly disclosed itself if one were confined to working solely in terms of the historical traditions. What is needed, rather, is (in Barr's terms) a 'conversation' which can give us insight into what, theologically, these traditions really signify; or (in von Rad's terms) a 'charismatic' shaping of the traditions is necessary, to bring out their true theological import. In other words, one needs some kind of doctrine of 'inspiration'.

With these thoughts in mind, I return to Childs' views on facts and interpretations. According to Childs,

> The manner in which the reader [of Kings] is constantly referred back to the writer's sources indicates that he did not envision his composition to be in contradiction with his sources. He was not ... writing a 'theological history' which operated on its own principles apart from the history found in the official records. *Event and interpretation belonged together* and he needed only a selection from a larger historical sequence to demonstrate his thesis.[43]

The point Childs is developing here (cf. pp. 288–89) is that, beyond a mere citing of the relevant sources, there is a deeper, more theological purpose to the standard formula with which Kings closes its account of each successive king of Judah and Israel (viz., 'Now the rest of the deeds of ____, and how he . . ., are they not written in the Book of the Chronicles of the kings of Judah/Israel?'). By repeatedly calling our attention, in this very obtrusive way, both to the fact that he had excellent sources and that he could therefore have told us about many important events which he has actually chosen to omit, the writer is inviting us to ask ourselves what led him to recount just those events which he did include. Childs' answer, of course, is that his motives were primarily theological; and in fact Childs' own messianic interpretation of David provides a good illustration of how this 'interpretation through selection' can work. As we saw in

---

[43] *IOTS* p. 289; italics added.

section 3.2, this claims that certain events have been selected from David's career and arranged in such a way that the tensions between them point beyond David to a greater king.

This has the very important corollary, however, that we will recognise David as a messianic prefiguration *only* if we respect the shape that has been given to the story by the canonical text. An independent historical reconstruction of David's career—i.e., in Childs' terminology, the seeking of a 'positivity behind the text'—will not disclose a *messianic* figure. To understand the theological significance of his kingship we must respect the canonical text.

To this Pannenberg would perhaps object that if we accept a messianic depiction of David which cannot be verified by the historian then we are opening the door to arbitrariness: As with the kerygma theologians, events and interpretations are coming apart once more, leaving the theologian with historical events which are largely irrelevant and with theological interpretations that lack objective controls. It seems to me, however, that what Childs' example illustrates is not the kerygmatic bifurcation of fact and interpretation, but that there are some crucial differences between the modern concept of history and the biblical histories; and that once these differences are appreciated, they show that the positive contribution which the historian can make to theology is much more limited than Pannenberg has realized. An essential element in the modern concept is the idea of intrinsic interconnectedness—we expect a historian to show us not simply 'what happened next' but how the course of history developed, with one event giving rise to another. By contrast, the biblical narratives are usually highly episodic and disconnected, briefly recounting a small number of related incidents but then passing over several years or decades in silence. What holds these accounts together is often not historical interconnectedness (the Succession Narrative and passion stories are quite atypical in this respect) but the author's own overarching themes and purposes; but these generally have a theological rather than a historical orientation. The messianic presentation of David is a good illustration of this. The *secular* meaning of kingship is an intra-historical matter, concerning the role of the king in relation to the army, judiciary, and priesthood, etc.; but its *theological* meaning is not primarily to be found in these relationships. To identify David as a messianic figure, rather, is to 'place' him within the larger scale purposes of God—it is to claim that God has given him a kingship of such a kind that it

provides a pattern for another figure, whom God intends to crown
as king in a more exalted sense. It is a question, in other words, of
'divine interconnectedness', with the significant connections between
David and Jesus being established through the divine will.

It is difficult to imagine what a historian, as such, can do with this
kind of interpretation. Although the discussion of Jesus' resurrection
has shown that there *are* instances where the historian can, in principle,
make a significant positive contribution to the theological discussion,
there are special factors involved in such cases. Firstly, in the passion
and resurrection narratives a multitude of events are concentrated
into a relatively brief timespan, thus making these accounts potentially
rich in the kinds of intrahistorical connectedness which the historian
is well-equipped to handle. And secondly, if the biblical portrayals
are even broadly accurate, the central events were overtly miraculous,
and thus displayed the divine involvement and intentions in an unusually direct way. These factors are not true of biblical events
generally, however; and I can therefore see no reason for according
historical studies the foundational role which Pannenberg claims for
them. If we are to perceive David as a messianic figure, it will only
be through viewing him from the perspective of the canonical text
which, through being 'charismatically shaped' or 'divinely inspired',
provides the commentary necessary for a theological understanding
of the historical events.[44]

In bringing this discussion of historical methodology to a close, some
of its main themes can be drawn together by returning to Childs'
distinction between 'source' and 'witness', and asking how well this
can deal with such cases as the life of David. Can it hold together
the legitimate demands of both history and kerygma, while also recognizing the proper limitations of each? On the one hand, 2 Samuel
purports to tell us *about David*; therefore questions as to what the
historical David was really like are entirely legitimate, and must be
taken seriously by the theologian. One cannot kerygmatically proclaim
David to be a messianic figure while also accepting that, historically,
he never existed, or was a zealous worshipper of Baal, or spent his
entire life as a shepherd. Although we have seen that Childs is right
to claim that the relationship between theological value and historical

---

[44] The David example also suggests that this commentary need not take the form
of direct or overt interpretation, but could function through the literary shape of the
text which recounts the events in question.

veracity is highly variable, the connection rarely falls away completely. The kerygma cannot detach itself from the history without undermining its own theological value; and it is for this reason that I would doubt the consistency of Childs criticizing von Rad both for his professed inability to relate Israel's 'confessional history' to the modern reconstructions of her history and for basing his interpretations of Israel's witness upon the critical reconstructions. Theological claims are *truth* claims, which therefore cannot ignore the pertinent historical truths without undermining their own status; and the proper way to investigate historical truth-claims is through a critical, historical methodology. Theology must take account of the results this produces—it *must* be based upon the critically reconstructed history—and one cannot specify in advance how this might affect the interpretation of Israel's kerygma.

Questions of historical interconnectedness, then, are both legitimate and important, and must therefore be thoroughly investigated. Insofar as this involves the biblical text being regarded as a source of information for historical reconstructions this is entirely legitimate (although one must be careful not to distort or mis-evaluate one's source through interpreting it by means of a question-begging methodology). In view of this, I would suggest that Childs needs to be a little more discriminating in the suspicions he sometimes expresses about the 'alleged objectivity' of the historical-critical approach. This, we can now say, is primarily oriented towards investigating one particular kind of interconnectedness, namely, the immanent/intra-historical (the occasions when there is any likelihood of it identifying divine interventions being very few); and *within this domain* there seems no reason to doubt that it can, in principle, yield objectively valid reconstructions of 'what really happened'. Where Childs *would* have reason to protest, however, is if historical reconstruction were to claim a privileged access to 'the *really* real', as though the objects of its investigations were somehow 'more factual' than the theologian's. As we have now seen, the world is not made up of historical 'hard facts' plus 'mere theological interpretations', and there is therefore no intrinsic reason for believing that the one is telling us something intrinsically 'more real' than the other. 'David committed adultery' and 'David sinned against God' are *both* factual statements about 'what really happened'; where they differ is in which aspects of reality they focus upon. To undertake a historical reconstruction is to choose to make one particular aspect of the real the focus of one's studies, namely, that which views events through their intra-wordly connections;

and this entails that its ability to make a constructive contribution to theology is limited to those rare occasions when the divine becomes more-or-less overtly manifest in the events of history. Of course, this is not a criticism of historiography as such, but a recognition of the appropriate domain for the methods it uses. But for the theologian the intra-worldly domain is not the whole of reality; and therefore historiography cannot be the whole of theological method.

Childs, then, is justified in fearing that where history is given a dominant role then theological concerns will tend to disappear, although again care must be taken about how one applies this observation to the contemporary situation. We have seen that Childs charges Cross' reading of the Old Testament with being reductionistic, and this is clearly correct insofar as Childs is pointing out that things which the Old Testament portrays as being the work of God are regarded by Cross as being explicable without remainder as the product of natural, intra-worldly factors. This can only be cited as an *objection* to Cross, however, if such a reduction actually leaves out something important. To revert to a previous example, the supernaturalist cannot refute the atheist's interpretations of the resurrection merely by pointing out that the latter's construals of the Gospels are reductionistic—on the contrary, the atheist fully intends them to be. To refute the atheist, therefore, it further needs to be shown that this reduction cannot in fact be carried through satisfactorily. And similarly, then, Childs' accusations of reductionism need to be backed up with a much fuller investigation of the historical issues than he generally undertakes, in order to show that the proposed naturalistic reconstructions of, say, the development of Israel's cultic worship is historically untenable. But granted this, Childs is nonetheless right to insist that attempting to read the text not only as a source but also as a witness to those dimensions of reality which necessarily escape the historian's tools is perfectly legitimate—an antisupernaturalistic reductionism is not the only viable methodology. Of course, in allowing the text to function as a witness one must be cautious about *uncritically* accepting messianic interpretations of David; one cannot simply assume that everything which claims to be a revelatory commentary really is so, and some kind of critical control is therefore needed if theology is not to lapse into credulity. But the critical controls must be appropriate to their subject-matter. It is of little help to have a methodology which guards against theological waywardness by simply eliminating the theology.

# CHAPTER SIX

# TRADITIONS AND THE FINAL FORM

I suggested in section 4.1 that Childs' thoughts on referentiality can be divided into two parts, concerning 'referentiality *in* the text' and 'referentiality *behind* the text'. The previous two chapters have discussed the former in some detail, so this chapter will primarily be concerned with the latter—i.e., with things that are *not* explicitly referred to in the final form of the text, such as the underlying sources, and the streams of tradition, which scholars critically reconstruct. Childs, of course, accepts that such things lie behind the text as we now have it, but stresses that in drawing upon this material the authors of the canonical scriptures reworked it in such a way as to 'hide their own footprints'. Nonetheless, Childs clearly does *not* believe that underlying sources and pre-canonical traditions can simply be ignored—on the contrary, his own work deals with them at some length. The contribution which Childs considers this to make to his canonical programme therefore needs to be discussed more fully.

The principal issues to be considered in this chapter, then, are: (1) How does Childs conceive the traditions that lie behind the canonical form of the text?; (2) What significance does he give to their critical reconstruction?; and (3) How are historical-critical studies related to understanding the meaning the final form?

## 1. *Critical Illumination of the Final Form*

We saw in section 3.2 that one of Childs' principal aims in *IOTS* was to re-orientate the critical study of the Old Testament in such a way that it would make a more positive contribution to the semantic—and, in particular, to the theological—understanding of the canonical text. In the present section, therefore, I shall consider more fully how Childs envisages this happening, and whether this attempted redeployment of the critical tools is successful. As is well known, each chapter in Parts Two to Five of *IOTS* begins by reviewing the historical-critical discussion of the book in question; but unfortunately

Childs' critics have not always grasped the significance of these sections, nor of them invariably being followed by a discussion of the book's canonical shape. Particularly wide of the mark is the following explanation by James Barr:

> [*IOTS*] offers us very little in the way of reasons [for accepting Childs' idea of the canon].... The logic of the book is one of exhortation ('take the canon seriously'), or pressure upon the reader to accept the canonical reading, rather than one of reasoning.... Now it is precisely because of the lack of reasoned argument in other respects ... that the demonstration of the case comes to be excessively dependent on one particular element, namely the contrast between the weaknesses and antinomies of historical criticism on the one hand and the virtues of the canonical reading on the other. The necessity of this contrast for demonstration is the reason why historical criticism is depicted in rather dark colours.[1]

A more careful reading of *IOTS* soon discloses, however, that this is not at all how Childs proceeds. Although Childs' reviews of the critical discussion (which generally occur in sections headed 'Historical Critical *Problems*') characteristically focus upon the inconclusive nature of the debate and the 'impasses' into which it has run, they do so for a much more constructive purpose than Barr has discerned. Childs makes it clear on page after page of *IOTS* both that he accepts many of the results of critical studies,[2] and that any alternative to the standard approach must take these results fully into account.[3] Moreover, he is also well aware that the unresolved critical problems cannot be cited as an 'indictment' of the critical approach (pp. 323–24). Childs' point, rather, is that the success which the critical approach has achieved *in some respects* (such as the recovery of the literary prehistory behind the canonical text) has often been accompanied by an *inability* to bring about a corresponding advancement in our understanding of the meaning of these books, and in particular, of their meaning as the Scriptures of the church. The canonical approach, then, is put forward after a review of the critical debate because it

---

[1] 'Childs' *Introduction*', p. 14.

[2] 'Historical critical research has demonstrated convincingly, in my opinion, that the present form of the book of Amos has been reached only after a lengthy history of development which has shaped the material both in its oral and literary stages' (p. 399); etc.

[3] 'Any attempt to offer a different approach to the study of the Pentateuch which does not take into account the achievements of historical critical scholarship over the last two hundred years is both naive and arrogant' (p. 127); etc.

is being advanced as a way of tackling a particular group of problems which the critical approach has repeatedly failed to solve, and is to do so in a way that takes account of the results which critical studies *have* achieved.

By proceeding in this way Childs is offering an argument for the canonical approach which is not unlike that which is commonly advanced for, say, the Graf-Wellhausen hypothesis. Reviewing the various inconcinities and anachronisms in the Pentateuch has a threefold purpose: It shows why a theory of Mosaic authorship is inadequate, motivates the development of an alternative theory, and collects the 'raw data' which a successful alternative would have to account for. Likewise, Childs' 'Historical Critical Problems' sections perform a similar function for the canonical approach: They show the inadequacy of the standard critical handling of these problems, motivate the development of an alternative approach, and collect the critical results which a successful alternative must take into account. *Contra* Barr, this is both a reasoned and a reasonable way of proceeding.

The next matter to consider is *how* Childs envisages the critical tools as contributing to the understanding of the final form. We saw in section 3.2 that in *IOTS* Childs' main point was that the critical tools had uncovered various problematic features of the text which the canonical approach was to consider in relation to their contribution to its meaning. In his most recent book Childs has discussed the rationale for this at some length;[4] and yet in my view, the case which he makes out is far from convincing. There are a number of reasons for this, but much of the problem turns on the inability of the historical-critical tools to further the *particular kind* of understanding which is important for Childs' programme; or more precisely, insofar as they do contribute to such understanding of the final form, this is not in virtue of anything about them that is distinctively *critical*.

This criticism can be substantiated by noting how Childs' own discussions of the text's prehistory typically make no distinctively critical contribution to his canonical readings.[5] A particularly instructive example to consider is Childs' discussion in *BTONT* of the Genesis creation stories, since in this case the same theological themes and

---

[4] See especially *BTONT* pp. 104–106, 216–17, 262–65, 534–37.
[5] We saw in section 2.4 above that Childs himself acknowledges that this is often the case for his Exodus commentary. Too much should not be made of this, however, since *EC* probably comes in part from a time before Childs' thought on these matters had fully developed.

the same texts are central both to the diachronic 'Discrete Witness' section and to the synchronic 'Biblical Reflection'. If the critical tools are capable of contributing to the semantic-theological understanding of the final form, it should be particularly evident here.

In the section of 'The Discrete Witness of the Old Testament' which deals with creation, Childs begins by affirming the usual analysis of Genesis 1–2 into J and P material and briefly rehearses the critical consensus concerning their origins: P is of post-exilic date, and developed from Babylonian and Sumerian traditions; J, by contrast, originated in a Syro-Palestinian setting.[6] But granted that Israel appropriated much of its creation material from its ancient Near Eastern environment, Childs suggests that the 'the basic issue turns on establishing the oldest levels in which Israel's own tradition functioned as a witness to God as creator' (p. 109). Essentially following von Rad, Childs argues that, even though some of the creation material is very old, it entered Israel's faith as secondary to the confession of Yahweh as delivering the nation from its Egytian bondage (p. 110). Noetically, then, creation was subordinated to redemption.

This discussion, which has mainly been concerned with the pre-literary traditions, is followed by two sub-sections which are headed, respectively, 'The Priestly Account' and 'The Yahwist Account' (pp. 110–13). These include a rather mixed bag of observations on the final form of these passages,[7] various critical issues,[8] and connections between these passages and other parts of the Old Testament.[9] This part of the discussion is then concluded by Childs arguing that the joining of the two creation accounts through the redactional (Priestly) formula in 2:4a has been largely successful in changing the semantic level of the J account, so that it now functions 'not as a duplicate creation account . . . [but] on the level of figurative language'.

Turning now to the chapter in the 'Theological Reflection on the Christian Bible' which deals with 'God, the Creator', Childs begins

---

[6] *BTONT*, pp. 107–108.

[7] E.g., concerning the interpretation of Gen. 1:1; the culmination of P's account with rest on the seventh day; and the subordination in J of the creation account to 'the theme of harmonious order'.

[8] E.g., the tension between the six creative days and the eight creative acts as a possible clue to the prehistory of P; the aridity of the world prior to its creation as showing the Syro-Palestinian background to J.

[9] E.g., between P's six days of world creation and the building of Israel's sanctuary, and between Genesis 2 and 3 in J.

the section on 'The Old Testament Witness' by referring back to the discussions we have just reviewed, and explaining that

> [their] concern was to establish, as far as possible, the origins, age, and provenance of these [creation] traditions, and to determine the direction of these traditio-historical trajectories leading up to the book's final structuring within the Hebrew canon.[10]

This was presumably intended to prepare the way for the present section, whose purpose is 'to explore the theological dimension of the Old Testament's witness' (*ibid.*); but in fact the connection between them is highly problematic. Childs begins his theological exploration of the Genesis creation material with the following comments:

> From a theological perspective it is significant to note that the present canonical shape has subordinated the noetic sequence of Israel's experience of God in her redemptive history to the ontic reality of God as creator. This is to say, although Israel undoubtedly first came to know Yahweh in historical acts of redemption from Egypt, the final form of the tradition gave precedence to God's initial activity of creating the heavens and earth. (p. 385)

But given that it is the final form which is theologically normative, what is the significance of von Rad's recovery of the historically correct noetic sequence from Israel's preliterary traditions? Unfortunately Childs does not discuss this; in fact, the noetic sequence receives no further attention. The impression is left, however, that the critically reconstructed sequence ultimately counts for nothing, because the canonical form finally decided that it was ontic rather than noetic issues that were theologically significant. In practice, this critical discussion seems to make no contribution at all to the kind of understanding that matters for Childs' programme.

Childs next makes a number of interesting observations on the effect of the J account being subordinated to that of P, on creation as the beginning of history, the possible eschatological and redemptive connotations of the creation story, the clear distinction it draws between God and the world, and the echoes of Genesis 1–2 that can be heard in other parts of the Old Testament and elsewhere (pp. 385–89). Insofar as this draws upon his discussions in the 'Discrete Witness' section, however, it utilizes his comments on the final form of Genesis 1 and 2, and/or their connections with other parts of the

---

[10] *BTONT*, p. 384.

Old Testament; and conversely, the distinctively critical strands in these earlier discussions, such as his identifying the Babylonian [Syro-Palestinian] provenance of the traditions behind the P [J] creation story, are not taken up in the subsequent 'Old Testament Witness' section.[11] Contrary, then, to Childs' programmatic claims, the critical tools do not in fact make a substantive contribution to his theological understanding of the final form.

There are a number of more general comments which can now be made. Firstly, the preceding discussion is not intended to imply that Childs' studies of the canonical text derive no benefits at all from critical scholarship. As is well known, many of the differences between Genesis 1 and 2, and the peculiar features of each chapter, were first recognized through a quest for underlying sources; therefore when Childs tries to integrate these features into his own canonical readings, there is an important sense in which his interpretations of the final form are in fact based upon the results of critical study. This connection, however, is accidental rather than essential, because *these* results of critical study could equally have been discovered in some other, non-critical way—they could have been recognized simply through a literary 'close reading' of Genesis, precisely because they lie *in* the text rather than *behind* it.

If this is so, then Childs is perhaps further from his critical colleagues than he has realized—sufficiently far, in fact, that it might be better for him not to use critical terminology when discussing the final form but to adopt instead a more 'phenomenological' vocabulary, which would confine itself to pointing out (for example) 'language akin to that in Deuteronomy', rather than using such phrases as 'deuteronomistic redaction'. The latter implies a particular historical explanation of this kinship which, though Childs may accept it, has no role to play in the kind of understanding of the text which he is trying to achieve. Childs' point about the normativity of the final form is precisely that one does *not* interpret, say, certain passages in Joshua as the insertions of a late-monarchic reforming school, with a distinctive theologico-political programme of its own, but seeks, rather, to discover the theological significance of Joshua using the concepts and phraseology of Deuteronomy to characterize the Conquest. I cannot see how the critical tools, as such, are able to contribute to this.

---

[11] Similar comments also apply to the section entitled 'Biblical Theological Reflection on Creation', *BTONT* pp. 396–402.

Secondly, however, the discussion in this section does not support the charge that Childs' programme is essentially anti-critical or neo-fundamentalist. Although I have argued that Childs is wrong in claiming that the critical tools help one to understand the meaning of the final form, we have already seen in previous chapters that there are other respects in which critical studies *do* have an essential contribution to make. Further aspects of this will be discussed in the remainder of the present chapter. And thirdly, I have not argued that Childs' studies of the final form are (or could be, or should be) essentially 'ahistorical', in the sense that someone who is interested in the meaning of the final form has little or no use for *any* kind of historical enquiry. On the contrary, the text was produced in a particular historical-cultural situation, and knowledge of this situation is therefore indispensable for a sensitive reading of the final form.[12] Thus (to borrow some of Sternberg's examples), we cannot appreciate the metaphorical import of a certain passage unless we know the literal meaning(s) of its vocabulary, and whether this metaphor is dead or newly coined (pp. 11–12); or to gauge the significance of the biblical narrator assuming an omniscient standpoint we must know whether this was simply the conventional way of writing such narratives in the ancient Near East or whether it was an innovation of the biblical authors (pp. 12–13). Or again, it is foolish to give a canonical, 'synchronic', interpretation of features that have an obvious historical, 'diachronic', explanation—a commitment to canonical interpretation must not be pressed to the extremes of resting content with the Masoretic Text's claim that 'Saul was one year old when he began to reign' (1 Sam. 13:1) and declining to explain it as a textual corruption (p. 14).

Many other examples could be added of the historical knowledge that is needed for a semantic understanding of the canonical text— including, of course, a detailed knowledge of ancient Hebrew. Yet accepting this is quite different from admitting that such understanding is aided by a critical reconstruction of the text's prehistory. I cannot see that Childs' arguments for the value of this 'depth dimension' are at all persuasive.

---

[12] This has been argued very fully and clearly by Meir Sternberg, *The Poetics of Biblical Narrative: Ideological Literature and the Drama of Reading* (Indiana Studies in Biblical Literature; Bloomington: Indiana University Press, 1985), pp. 7 23. It also seems to be the point of Childs' comments on Hosea in *BTONT*, p. 105.

## 2. *The Shaping of the Traditions*

The next subject to consider is Childs' account of how the traditions
which lie behind the canon developed.[13] The broad outlines of his
views are set out clearly in the 'Preface to the Second Edition' of *IOTS*:

> I am suggesting that a religious reading of Israel's traditions arose early
> in its history and extended in different ways through the oral, literary,
> and redactional stages of the growth of the material until it reached a
> fixed form of relative stability. This religious interpretation . . . involved
> a peculiar construal which sought to give the material a shape which
> could be appropriated by successive generations within Israel. The
> process did not happen all at once; there was no overarching herme-
> neutic to realise the goals; some attempts were more successful than
> others. (pp. 16–17)

Childs subsequently explains this more fully by distinguishing between
Literary and Canonical histories. By the former he means the development of the traditions in accordance with the laws of literary form,
social influences, changing scribal techniques, etc., which are the
normal fare of Old Testament scholarship; whereas the latter refers
to their development as the authoritative Scriptures of the believing
community.[14] Childs' point here—and it is of cardinal importance
for his programme—is that the whole development involved a substantial *religious* component virtually from the beginning. Although
Childs sees the religious component as becoming increasingly important
in the exilic and post-exilic stages, decisions taken in the earlier periods
'were not qualitatively different from the later' (p. 59). The literary
and canonical histories, then, are not[15] chronologically distinct stages;
on the contrary, Childs' intention is particularly to oppose the idea
that the development of Israel's literature was a mainly secular process,
with religious considerations entering only at the end, when it was
decided which writings were to be 'canonized'.[16] Instead, Childs

---

[13] I shall concentrate almost exclusively upon the Old Testament; Childs' views
on the New Testament traditions (summarized in *NTCI*, ch. 2) are too similar to
need much additional comment.

[14] See especially pp. 57–62; for some helpful clarifications of Childs' views see
Bonnie Kittel, 'Brevard Childs' Development of the Canonical Approach', pp. 3–5.

[15] *Contra* Douglas A. Knight, 'Canon and the History of Tradition: A Critique of
Brevard S. Childs' *Introduction to the Old Testament as Scripture*', *HBT* 2 (1980), pp.
144–45. Cf. Childs' reply to Knight; 'A Response', pp. 209–10.

[16] This, in various forms, seems to be his chief objection to the alternative canonical theories of J.A. Sanders, G. Hölscher, and D.N. Freedman (although Childs'
comments are sometimes rather obscure): Childs is 'critical of Sanders' existentialist

envisages a unitary process in which the traditions were shaped both by non-religious factors and by their growing acceptance and refinement as the theologically normative Scriptures of Israel.

At this point, however, a serious problem arises. It is clear from the preceding account that Childs is making some significant *historical* claims about the processes through which the writings were formed, and it therefore comes as something of a jolt when he next tells us that

> because of *the lack of historical evidence* it is extremely difficult to determine the motivations involved in the canonical process.... For example, it remains exceedingly difficult to determine to what extent a canonical force was at work in the uniting of the J and E sources of the Pentateuch or how a consciousness of the canon exerted itself in the process.[17]

In other words, Childs is apparently claiming that although we can (often) recover the course of the text's prehistory, little can be known about what motivated it. But how, then, can he justifiably claim that it *was* the religious motivations which predominated?

Childs is aware of the problem (pp. 67–68), and in the next stage of his argument he offers a 'transcendental' solution which would allow him, on very general, theological, grounds, to make this historical affirmation without needing to consider the (largely inaccessible) historical details. This is done through appealing to a particular conception of the final form of the text. Childs' point is that all the theological gains that were made through the religious shaping have been 'fixed' in the text which this produced:

> The shape of the biblical text reflects a history of encounter between God and Israel. The canon serves to describe this peculiar relationship and to define the scope of this history by establishing a beginning and an end to the process.... The significance of the final form of the biblical text is that it alone bears witness to the full history of revelation. (pp. 75–76)

Childs admits that earlier stages of the text were also regarded as canonical at one time; yet they are not to be so regarded today,

---

categories' (p. 57) because they '[turn] the canonical process on its head by couching a basically theological move in anthropological terms' (p. 59); Hölscher is faulted for failing to reckon with the religious factors that influenced the pre-rabbinic shaping of the writings (pp. 54–55); and Freedman is criticised for reductionistically explicating 'canonization' in purely historical-literary terms (p. 55).

[17] P. 62; italics added.

precisely because the canonical process moved on past that stage. Therefore to recover J and E as separate documents is to prescind from the full witness to God's revelation in favour of a partial witness that has long since been superseded (p. 76).

This is certainly a bold argument; and yet it is open to a number of serious objections. Firstly, far from Childs' transcendental argument solving the problem posed by our lack of knowledge, it only repeats it on a higher plane: If, due to an absence of historical evidence, there is doubt as to whether J and E were combined for predominantly religious reasons, then there is surely at least as much uncertainty as to whether the resultant text really was a true witness to the history of revelation or a confused falling away from its earlier, purer forms. It is exceedingly difficult to see how Childs' claim that 'The significance of the final form of the biblical text is that it alone bears witness to the full history of revelation' could itself be justified; therefore appealing to this principle as vindicating Childs' particular conception of the tradition-process at best only moves the need for justification back to a realm where it cannot be met. And secondly, most scholars believe that the motivations behind a particular development often *can* be reconstructed with a fair degree of certainty, and that in some cases at least, they are damaging to Childs' position. Thus the Succession Narrative (according to many scholars) was a politically-motivated *apologia* for Solomon's unexpected and bloody accession to the throne; the visions of Zechariah 1–8 were propaganda for the Zadokite restoration programme; etc. In other words, many scholars would hold that, for some parts of the Old Testament at least, we can be reasonably confident that the motivations which shaped the traditions were *not* predominantly religious or theological but political or sociological. If this is so, however, then Childs' central claims about the tradition-process are simply wrong on historical-critical grounds.[18]

Childs, of course, is not unaware of this challenge to his position; and despite his claims about the lack of historical evidence, there is a strand of argument (albeit somewhat muted) running through Childs' work from at least the publication of *IOTS* in which he has attempted to surmount this sort of problem through involving himself in historical

---

[18] Childs appears to be on much safer ground when discussing the formation of the New Testament writings, for which predominantly literary/sociological/political explanations have gained less acceptance than for the Old Testament.

arguments about what happened 'behind' the canonical text. Thus in *IOTS* itself Childs implicitly concedes that if the author of Daniel 7–12 (for which Childs accepts the usual critical dating in the Maccabean period) were fraudulently passing off his own words as those of the sixth century prophet then this would 'call into question the validity of [their] message' (p. 616); and Childs therefore argues at some length that the Maccabean author was in fact motivated by a legitimate desire to show how the prophecies of Daniel 2 applied to his own age. Similarly, in his response to Barr's review of *IOTS*, Childs explicitly recognizes that if Deuteronomy were a 'pious fraud created . . . to support the political aspirations of the Jerusalem priesthood' then this would undermine his canonical interpretation, and points out that it is for this reason that he has argued that such an interpretation does not do justice to the text.[19] Or again, we have already noted[20] that in *OTTCC* Childs deals with similar problems in relation to the priestly traditions by endorsing a critical reconstruction of their development which sees the process as being primarily motivated by theological concerns; and likewise he takes issue with Gottwald's sociological reconstruction of Israel's origins on historical grounds (pp. 176–77). Similarly in Childs' most recent book, the same point can be illustrated from his discussion of P.D. Hanson's theory that a major factor shaping the growth of apocalypticism was the political tensions between rival religious parties in the post-exilic period.[21] Childs, then, is by no means as vulnerable to criticism on this point as some of his detractors imagine.

To this it must nonetheless be added, however, that since these discussions invariably occur in the course of Childs' pursuit of larger goals, they are generally too brief and incomplete to carry full conviction as historical studies. Thus although Childs is aware of these problems, it remains an open question as to whether his programme can deal adequately with them. I shall return to this in section 5 below; but first there are some further aspects of the tradition-process that need to be considered.

---

[19] 'Response to Reviewers', p. 56.
[20] See section 3.2 above.
[21] See *BTONT* pp. 182–83.

### 3. *The Rationality of the Religious Tradents*

Whatever doubts one might have about Childs' general characterization of the tradition-process, there are nonetheless *some* parts of the Bible (particularly in the New Testament) for which most scholars would accept that religious motivations played a dominant role in (at least the latter stages of) their formation; yet even here thing are not as straightforwardly favourable to Childs' position as they might at first appear. A careful examination of Childs' reconstructions of the tradition-process shows that he has grouped together some highly diverse factors under the general rubric of 'religious motivations', and it is therefore necessary to ask more specifically about *what kind* of religious concerns shaped the traditions, and whether this affects the viability of Childs' adherence to the normativity of the final form.

To illustrate this point I shall consider two contrasted examples from *IOTS*, beginning with Childs' reconstruction of the prehistory of Jonah. Reviewing the critical discussion of this book, Childs notes that, according to many scholars, its original message has been obscured by the insertion of chapter 2. Previously, the two commissions to visit Nineveh (1:1; 3:1) had been parallel, with 'the focus of the story' falling in both cases 'on the heathen reaction, the threat of judgement, the prayer for deliverance, and the ensuing rescue' (p. 422). Following this, chapter 4 shifts our attention to Jonah, with the point of the story finally being given in the speech by God. In this reconstructed version of the story Jonah's concern is not to be a false prophet; but God responds by defending his right to allow his mercy to override the prophet's word. So then,

> By the removal of ch. 2 the sharp lines of the original story emerge, thus confirming the interpretation which related the purpose of the book to the issue of unfulfilled prophecy. (p. 423)

In assessing the value of this reconstruction, Childs accepts that chapter 2 was a later interpolation but claims (appealing to Landes' studies) that chapter 2 is a parallel to chapter 4. The former passage is a psalm of thanksgiving for a deliverance already received; but in the latter Jonah reacts negatively to Nineveh being included in the divine mercy that had previously been reserved for Israel. Thus the insertion of chapter 2 has refocused the issue from concern over the fulfilment of prophecy to the proper recipients of divine mercy; yet Childs sees this as an extension of its original point:

In the 'first edition' the theological point turned on God's right as Creator to override his prophetic word for the sake of his entire creation. The 'second edition' merely amplified the point respecting the whole creation in terms of the nations, but it did not alter the basic creation theology by substituting one of election.[22]

In my view, Childs' discussion of Jonah is one of the more successful critical sections of *IOTS*, because he can plausibly argue that this book was formed through a process of rational development—chapter 2 is not a disparate fragment that was inserted awkwardly, but a thoughtful supplementation; the 'second edition' did not ride roughshod over the intentions of the 'first edition' but developed them more fully; etc. In other words, Childs shows that there are *good reasons* why the final form should be preferred, in that it is an improvement on the pre-canonical version of the book.

Very different, however, is his study of Chronicles, which includes an extended discussion of the Chronicler as an exegete. Modern studies have established that 'the Chronicler sought to interpret Israel's history in relation to a body of *authoritative scripture*',[23] and Childs claims that much of his exegetical technique stemmed directly from this conception of Israel's writings. In particular, Childs discusses the Chronicler's use of harmonization (which resulted from the Chronicler '[viewing] his sources all on the same plane with no regard for historical development', p. 648), of supplementation (i.e., the addition of further material into a basic account in order to bring out an event's full significance), and of typology (which Childs characterizes as 'a non-historical ordering of material according to patterns which arise from a similarity of content', p. 650). It is unnecessary to rehearse the details, but Childs sums up his study as

> [having] sought to demonstrate that the Chronicler in the process of giving his material its canonical shape has made use of a variety of exegetical methods many of which are akin to later Jewish midrash and all of which are looked upon with askance [*sic*] by modern historical critical methodology. (p. 654)

This raises a number of important questions. Firstly, does the Chronicler's midrashic methodology provide canonical warrant for a

---

[22] P. 425. Childs' reconstruction has been criticised by George M. Landes ('The Canonical Approach to Introducing the Old Testament', *JSOT* 16 (1980), pp. 38–39); but whether or not the details of this particular example can be sustained, it serves as a good illustration of the methodological issues being discussed here.

[23] P. 647; italics added.

modern exegete to do likewise? Childs' answer is a flat No; and even without going into his reasons (which seem to me very weak)[24] it is obvious why he wants to answer this question negatively: If modern scholars *were* permitted such exegetical license, then biblical studies would quickly degenerate into subjectivism. But secondly, given that Chronicles *was* largely shaped by such methods, how does this affect our estimate of its status as Scripture? Childs' answer is that it makes no difference—all that apparently matters, in his view, is that the final form was the outcome of a theologically motivated process of development. It is far from clear, however, how this reply could be justified. If a modern application of such methods would lead only to subjective interpretations which were of little or no theological value, then why did they not produce similarly deficient interpretations when the Chronicler used them? In cases such as this[25] it seems that Childs has not fully grasped what the problem is.

In summary then, although Childs has correctly recognized both that the question of the tradents' motivations is an important issue and that this needs to be explored through a critical reconstruction of the text's prehistory, he has not been sufficiently discriminating about the *kind* of reconstruction that would vindicate an adherence to the final form of the text. *Prima facie*, the theological value of the final form *is* called into question if it were predominantly shaped by various unsound influences, even if they were religiously motivated. Where historical-critical reconstructions show this to have been the case, it needs to be seriously asked whether the final form of the text can still be accorded hermeneutical priority.[26]

---

[24] The pertinent issues here are very similar to those raised by the New Testament's interpretations of the Old Testament. I shall discuss Childs' views on this at some length in section 11.1 below.

[25] Similar comments also apply to Childs' discussion of Daniel. We have seen that Childs has responded to the charge that the author of Dan. 7–12 was fraudulent by arguing that he was offering an interpretation of the earlier chapters which was intended to bring out their true, contemporary significance (*IOTS*, p. 616); yet although, if correct, this would show that chapters 7–12 were shaped by predominantly religious concerns, the exegetical manoeuvres which Childs has to postulate are so extraordinarily eccentric that if these chapters really were put together through the irrational techniques and numerous exegetical blunders that Childs reconstructs, then it is extremely difficult to see how they could be taken seriously today as Holy Scripture.

[26] It may appear that the preceding discussion has led to the more definite conclusion that, in the circumstances envisaged, the final form *cannot* be accorded priority; but since I have not yet considered Childs' anti-intentionalist strategy for dealing with these problems, this conclusion would be premature. I shall discuss author's intention in the next chapter.

## 4. *The Synchronic and the Diachronic*

So far, then, it has been argued that (i) critical reconstruction of the traditions behind the canonical text *do* make an essential contribution to Childs' programme, insofar as the theological viability of the final form is dependent upon the motivations that shaped it; but that (ii) the critical tools are incapable of performing the further task of aiding our semantic/theological understanding of the final form. With these points in mind, I now wish to consider more generally how the 'diachronic' study of the text's development is related to the 'synchronic' study of the meaning of its canonical form. What bearing do these two very different orientations have upon each other, and how might each influence the applicability of the other to any particular text?[27]

There are many possible answers to these questions, but most of them can be grouped into the following categories: The synchronic and diachronic approaches are either (1) Mutually unrelated, so that each can be pursued without reference to the other; or (2) Mutually complementary or supportive, so that the results of each may aid the other; or (3) Mutually antagonistic or destructive, so that success in one is obtained at the expense of the other.[28] Of the three, the first two are apparently the more attractive options, insofar as they allow scholars with different interests (e.g., 'literary' rather than 'historical') still to further each other's work (category 2), or at least to get along without treading on each other's toes (category 1). In practice most biblical scholars appear to hold some version of these alternatives. The third option, however, has been cogently defended by R.W.L. Moberly, who argues that the synchronic and diachronic approaches will (sometimes) find themselves pitched against each other, because each offers a *rival* explanation of the *same* features in the text. Since the underlying sources of the Pentateuch have not survived as independent documents, their recovery is entirely dependent (Moberly

---

[27] The remainder of this section closely follows the central sections of my article, 'Synchronic and Diachronic Approaches to Biblical Interpretation', *JLT* 7 (1993), pp. 131–48.

[28] These categories roughly correspond, respectively, to L. Alonso Schökel's alternatives of (1) 'courteous non-communication', (2) division of labour', and (3) 'mutual condemnation'; see his 'Of Methods and Models', *VTSup* 36 (1985), pp. 7–8. Schökel himself is particularly concerned that there should be constructive dialogue between those who subscribe to different methods.

observes)[29] upon them being reconstructed from the text into which
they have been incorporated. This, of course, proceeds through using the various infelicities of the final form as evidence for its composite nature; but a perennial problem for such work is deciding
when a certain feature really is infelicitous, rather than just appearing so to us because (say) we are reading the text with inappropriate
preconceptions of what 'good narrative style' is.

Moberly thinks that this problem should be solved through making
a careful synchronic exegesis of the final form *before* diachronic reconstructions are attempted, because only when we have made every
effort to understand the text on its own terms can we see which
aspects really are infelicitous.[30] Moberly makes the important observation that insofar as the synchronic reading of a text 'works', this
undermines our ability to reconstruct its prehistory: A text which
reads satisfactorily as a coherent, well-integrated whole is one which,
*ipso facto*, is largely free from the infelicities which provide the evidence
for a diachronic reconstruction. Moberly persuasively illustrates his
point by comparing an early source-critical analysis of Gen. 7:17–20
with a more recent study. Observing that in this short passage we
are told four times that the waters prevailed upon the earth, Richard
Simon rhetorically asks, 'Is it not reasonable to suppose that if one
and the same writer had been describing that event, he would have
done so in far fewer words, especially in a history?'.[31] In other words,
Simon is suggesting that the text is far more repetitious than we
would expect if it were the work of a single writer, and is offering
this as evidence for composite authorship. B.W. Anderson, on the
other hand, suggests that there are good literary reasons for this
repetitiveness: It creates an 'ascending effect' which vividly portrays
the mounting-up of the waters. Accepting Anderson's explanation,
Moberly comments:

> Although the present literary unity [of this passage] is not incompat-
> ible with composite authorship, one cannot take this one factor in the
> text, that is the fourfold repetition, and argue that it shows both unity
> and disunity. If the literary assessment of the repetition as a unity is
> sound, then the fact of repetition in itself provides no evidence of
> composite authorship. (p. 30)

---

[29] *At the Mountain of God*, p. 23.
[30] Pp. 23–24; I have reservations about this proposal, which I shall return to
presently.
[31] Quoted by Moberly, p. 29.

Moberly is duly cautious about drawing over-general conclusions from this example. The bulk of his book is a careful exegetical study of Exodus 32–34, which (he argues) shows a high degree of literary unity; other passages, however, might disclose a far more composite character. Yet where synchronic studies are as successful as they appear to be for Exodus 32–34, this has significant implications (Moberly claims) for the diachronic study of that text. Noting that his book offers few positive proposals about the text's prehistory, Moberly explains that this

> [largely] results from a growing unease as to the ability of our modern critical tools to perform the task they are employed for. That is, the prolonged study of the contents of Ex. 32–34 has left this reader at least with a growing sense of their impenetrability. This is not to say that the chapters constitute a kind of seamless robe for they do not. . . . But it is to wonder whether the text really affords sufficient evidence for the kind of thoroughgoing critical analysis that is customarily attempted. This is not to deny that diverse sources and traditions may underlie the text, but it is to ask whether we are still in a position to recover them. (pp. 43–44)

In other words, a successful synchronic reading of a certain passage precludes one from also making a source-critical analysis of that same passage.[32]

This, in my view, is a very important argument, with implications even more radical than Moberly himself has realized. To show this, I will first clarify his position slightly by distinguishing two distinct points within it, and shall then add a further point of my own. Firstly, then, a successful synchronic study undermines the diachronic study of that text in two distinct ways: (i) It removes the *evidence* by which a diachronic study would proceed, through explaining the requisite textual features synchronically instead; and (ii) It removes the *motivation* for attempting to reconstruct the text's prehistory. It is not altogether clear whether Moberly has fully appreciated this second point, although it seems to be implicit in his comment that

> the weakness in Simon's approach [to the source-analysis of Genesis] is not simply that of literary insensitivity, but the fact that his insensitivity seems to be based upon an anachronistic application of the notion of literary coherence and appropriate style. (p. 30)

---

[32] A similar argument for a 'disappearing redactor' has been considered but rejected by John Barton (*Reading*, pp. 56–58). I have discussed this in 'Synchronic', pp. 145–46.

In other words, if Simon's assessment had used more appropriate criteria then he would have discovered far fewer anomalies in this text, which is to say that there would have been much less which *needed* to be accounted for by positing a multiplicity of authors. Or more generally, a prehistory such as the Documentary Hypothesis was developed as the solution to a perceived problem; but if this problem turns out to be a misperception then the proposed solution becomes superfluous.

The substance of these two points can be summed up by saying that a diachronic reconstruction is predicated not simply upon repetitions, tensions, etc. in the text, but upon it displaying *redundant* repetitions and *unfruitful* tensions.[33] In other words, it is built upon the observation of features in the text which lack sufficient *intrinsic* motivation, such as repetitions that go beyond what is needed for the text's information-conveying purposes, and yet make no other positive contribution (through, for example, adding appropriate emphasis, or conveying a sense of stagnation, or providing a refrain that binds the narrative together, etc.). When there is insufficient intrinsic motivation then it is natural and proper to seek an extrinsic cause (e.g., that the repetitiveness stems from a conflation of sources); yet the whole point about a successful synchronic study is that it explains (virtually) all the text's features *intrinsically*, and thus leaves (virtually) nothing to be explained extrinsically. Of course, this does not show that the text lacked a prehistory; but it does (i) remove one of the principal motivations for trying to recover it,[34] and (ii) show that, whether we wish to recover it or not, we are in no position to do so.

To these points I wish to add a third: Certain kinds of source-analysis, including most of those which have featured in Old Testament studies, are actually *incompatible* with a successful synchronic reading of the final form; so that if (for example) such a reading of Genesis 1–11 could be sustained then this would provide very strong

---

[33] Even a patent self-contradiction *can* be fruitful—that in Prov. 26:4–5, for example, reminds one that wise behaviour cannot be reduced to a set of universally applicable rules, to be followed mechanically, but requires discernment as to which of the alternative courses of action is actually wise in this or that specific set of circumstances.

[34] There can, of course, be other motivations too—someone interested in the historical veracity of the patriarchal narratives may want to recover the underlying sources so that the reliability of each can be individually assessed.

reasons for believing not only that (as Moberly claims) the prehistory of these chapters is now irrecoverable, but also that the Graf-Wellhausen account of that prehistory is almost certainly wrong. To develop this point, I shall first distinguish between two different kinds of source-analyses: Quotation- and Resource-Theories.[35] By the former I mean a theory of composition in which the final text has been formed through (parts of) the original documents being incorporated into it verbatim; thus the Graf-Wellhausen hypothesis is an almost-pure example of a Quotation-theory. By a Resource-theory, on the other hand, I mean a theory of composition in which the author has used the available source(s) as a resource from which ideas about plot, character, themes, etc., can be freely drawn, without being tied at all closely by the treatment they receive in the sources. Some parts of the Chronicler's use of the Deuteronomistic History are perhaps moving in this direction, although a purer example would be the use that Shakespeare's *Coriolanus* makes of Plutarch's *Lives*.

My claim, then, is that there is a fundamental incompatibility between a successful synchronic interpretation of a text and a Quotation-theoretic account of its prehistory; indeed, the more successful the synchronic reading, then the further one has to move towards postulating a Resource-theoretic prehistory. Yet the further one moves in this direction the more difficult the recovery of the prehistory becomes,[36] because the connection between the sources and the final form becomes more indirect and tenuous. At this end of the spectrum the author plays a very substantial *creative* role, and thus opens up a considerable gulf between the final text and its underlying sources.

This argument can be illustrated by considering the relationship between Genesis 38 and the Joseph narrative. According to the virtually unanimous critical consensus there is 'no connection at all'[37] between these passages; and if this is correct, they are a good illustration of a Quotation-theoretic method of composition: The Judah-Tamar pericope developed orally into 'a self-contained individual narrative';[38] this was found in the tradition by a redactor who, wishing to preserve

---

[35] These are not sharply distinct types, but opposite ends of a continuous spectrum. Examining the limiting cases, however, is the clearest way of developing the methodological issues.

[36] At least, if the prehistory has to be reconstructed solely from the final text, as is generally the case in biblical studies.

[37] Gerhard von Rad, *Genesis: A Commentary* pp. 356–57.

[38] Claus Westermann, *Genesis 37–50* (London: SPCK, 1987), p. 49.

it (because it deals with one of Jacob's sons),[39] inserted it *en bloc* into
his composition, with virtually no editorial reshaping. Not surprisingly, it therefore displays very little interconnectedness with its new
literary context.

Despite the impressive critical consensus, however, it seems to me
that this explanation is quite wrong, both in its synchronic and in its
diachronic claims—or, more precisely, in its synchronic and therefore also in its diachronic claims. Far from Genesis 38 having 'no
connection at all' with the Joseph story, I would suggest that they
are intimately interrelated at a deep, structural level—so much so, in
fact, that they are variant forms of essentially the same story, with
Joseph and his brothers playing the same roles in one as Tamar and
Judah, respectively, play in the other. I shall now try to demonstrate
this by reviewing the main points of correspondence.

The Joseph story begins (ch. 37) with an expansive *account of the
unhappy relationship* between Joseph and his brothers, detailing the
reasons for their hatred of him and telling how they took their re-
venge. Initially intending to kill him, the brothers eventually decide
instead to sell him as a slave. Thus the *wrong* which they commit
against Joseph *leads to a lengthy separation between the main protagonists.*
(The brothers no doubt expect the separation to be permanent, but
things do not in fact work out that way.) Likewise the Tamar story
begins with an *account* (this time in a much more matter-of-fact, summarizing style) *of the unhappy relationship* between Tamar and Judah.
Each of Judah's eldest two sons in turn become Tamar's husband,
and each dies. By the custom of levirate marriage Tamar should
now be given the third son as her husband, but instead Judah sends
her back to her father's house. Judah's explanation to Tamar is that
she should wait there until the third son comes of age, but the insight which the narrator gives us at this point into Judah's thoughts
(v. 11) shows that in fact he is deceiving her—his true intention is to
withhold his son, lest he suffers the same fate as his brothers. Tamar
duly returns to her father's house; thus (in parallel with the Joseph
story) the *wrong* that Judah commits against Tamar *leads to a lengthy
separation between the main protagonists.*

The Joseph story continues with an extended account of Joseph's
*transformation* from Hebrew slave to viceroy of Egypt (via Potipher's
house and the royal prisons), and of the measures he takes to miti-

---

[39] Westermann, *ibid.*

gate the effects of the famine. This latter development then leads the story back to Joseph's brothers. The famine means that they too are in need of food; and at the prompting of their father, they eventually travel down to Egypt to buy grain. This, of course, is distributed by Joseph; thus the brothers are brought into the peculiar position of *unwittingly seeking the satisfaction of their need from the very one whom they wronged.* Joseph's transformation, however, means that *they do not recognize him*, although he recognizes them.

The Tamar story has a very similar continuation. Judah's wife has died; so when Tamar (who by now has realized that Judah has no intention of giving her his surviving son) hears that Judah is coming up to Timnah, she 'can plausibly infer that Judah is in a state of sexual *neediness*'.[40] Tamar therefore *transforms* herself, putting off her widow's garments and adopting the guise of a prostitute. Positioning herself, face covered, in the gateway, Judah encounters her and *seeks the satisfaction of his* (sexual) *need from the very one whom he had wronged.* Tamar's veil ensures that *he does not recognize her*, although she recognizes him.

The *price* that Tamar and Judah agree for their transaction is a kid, which Judah, having *received* what he sought, *attempts to pay* (through the mediation of his friend, Hirah). He is *prevented* from doing so, however, *by Tamar herself* (i.e., by the very person to whom the payment is due), who disappears before the kid can be sent. Likewise, the brothers attempt to pay the price due for the grain they have received, but are prevented from doing so by Joseph himself, who (through the mediation of his steward) has their money returned to them.[41]

The Joseph story shows its greater complexity at this point (among others) by now having the brothers seek grain a second time.[42] Again Joseph returns their money to them, but this time adds his own silver goblet—which he then promptly uses as a pretext for having the brothers arrested and brought back to him. The 'non-payment' motif is thus further developed, through the one who prevented the payment now using this *to provoke a final confrontation* with those who originally

---

[40] Robert Alter, *Narrative*, p. 7 (italics added).

[41] The parallelism between Hirah and the steward, however, is somewhat qualified: Both act as intermediaries in the 'non-payment' episode, but whereas Hirah acts (unsuccessfully) for the one *making* the payment, the steward is the (successful) agent of the one to whom the payment is due.

[42] This, of course, is connected with Joseph testing the attitude of the brothers towards Benjamin—a theme that has no parallel in the Tamar story. I shall say more about the differences between the stories in a moment.

wronged him; and again this is paralleled in the Tamar story. By disappearing before Judah could send the payment, Tamar was able to keep Judah's seal, cord, and staff. When it is discovered that Tamar is pregnant Judah summarily sentences her to death, apparently without even interviewing her;[43] but Tamar *provokes a final confrontation* with the man who originally wronged her by producing his identifying marks and asking him to recognize them. Judah, now *made aware of the identity* of the 'prostitute' he had consorted with, confesses that 'she is more righteous than I, inasmuch as I did not give her my son Shelah' (38:26)—i.e., he *admits the wrongfulness* of his original action, seeing this as 'justifying' the course that Tamar had taken. Similarly in Joseph's final confrontation with his brothers, they are *made aware of the identity* of the Egyptian viceroy with whom they have been trading (through Joseph disclosing who he really is), and *confess the wrongfulness* of what they originally did to him.

Finally, each story has a parallel 'coda' concerning the dual offspring of (respectively) Joseph and Tamar. In both cases this coda is concerned with the theme of 'the reversal of primogeniture': Zerah is the first to show from Tamar's womb, and his hand is duly marked with a scarlet thread; but he then withdraws his hand, and his brother is actually born before him. With Joseph's two sons, Manasseh was the firstborn and Joseph expects Jacob to give him the principal blessing; but Jacob (against Joseph's protests) crosses his hands so that Ephraim, the younger son, receives the blessing from his right hand.

Before discussing the methodological significance of this reading, something should first be said about the differences between the Joseph and Tamar stories. Despite the parallel roles of Tamar and Joseph, and of Judah and the brothers, they (and the other major characters) are not mere cyphers but well-developed individuals in their own right. Moreover, there are several important characters in the Joseph story (e.g., Jacob; Potiphar's wife; Pharaoh) who have no counterparts in the Tamar narrative, and who are linked to central thematic developments that are unique to the Joseph story: Joseph's repeated ascent from the lowest position to become the master of, in turn, Potiphar's house, the royal prison, and Pharaoh's kingdom;[44] Joseph's ability to interpret dreams; the brothers' changing relationship to their

---

[43] He may even have been secretly relieved that her (seeming) infidelity gave him a way of finally settling the problem of her marriage.

[44] In each case Joseph is, technically, the second in command; but each of his masters places matters so completely in his hands that, for all practical purposes,

father, and to his favourite sons (Benjamin being a parallel character to Joseph in this respect); the eclipse of the ineffectual firstborn son, Reuben, and the ascendancy of Judah; etc.[45] Again, there is a marked contrast between the expansive style of the Joseph story, with its relative abundance of circumstantial detail and several extensive, near-verbatim repetitions, and the much sparser style of the Tamar story. Or again, the Tamar narrative is much the more secular tale: God is mentioned only twice here (and both times very cryptically, 38:7, 10), whereas in the Joseph story the narrator repeatedly tells us that it was God who made to prosper everything which the hero touched, and Joseph himself insists that it is not he who interprets dreams but God, that God meant the brothers' evil act for good, and that to yield to the solicitations of Potiphar's wife would be a sin against God.

These very significant contrasts make it quite clear that one story is not, in any simple sense, a mere variant of the other—each has a style and a content of its own. This makes the parallels between them all the more significant, however, especially when it is also borne in mind that (i) they cover *all* the main incidents in the Tamar story, including its somewhat disconnected coda; and (ii) they relate not just to isolated episodes but between them add up to a quite comprehensive *structural* parallelism: One incident motivates and leads on to the next in much the same way in one story as do its parallels in the other, so that (despite the Joseph story including a lot of material that has no counterpart in the Tamar narrative) each has a remarkably similar plot development.

Now if this synchronic reading is basically correct,[46] then a Quotation-theoretic account of its prehistory must surely be wrong—to suppose that its author found the Tamar story in the tradition as an independent, ready-made narrative which, despite its many important

---

Joseph is effectively the ruler. Joseph, in turn, is completely loyal in exercising his power in the best interests of his master. Did the apostle Paul perhaps have this in mind when he wrote 1 Cor. 15:23–28?

[45] Most of these themes are discussed in Alter (*Narrative*, pp. 159–76); Sternberg (*Poetics*, pp. 285–308); and James S. Ackerman, 'Joseph, Judah, and Jacob' (in Kenneth R.R. Gros Louis with James S. Ackerman (eds.), *Literary Interpretations of Biblical Narratives II* (Nashville: Abingdon, 1982), pp. 85–113).

[46] Alter (*Narrative*, pp. 3–12) also argues for a considerable degree of literary unity between these stories on the grounds of them having a number of shared features. These considerations certainly carry some weight; and yet the somewhat piecemeal nature of Alter's list makes it difficult to decide how much of this is simply coincidental. The parallels pointed out in the present discussion, however, cover a *comprehensive* series of *interconnected* features, which makes coincidence a much less likely explanation.

differences from the Joseph story, 'just happened' to parallel it at so many significant points, is to stretch coincidence well beyond the bounds of plausibility. By far the most natural explanation for the extensive parallelism is common authorship, with the accent on authorship as a creative activity in which the author is not constrained by the 'raw material' but is its master. Of course, this does not necessarily imply that these chapters are simply a free composition; and yet if their author did use sources then he must have allowed himself considerable freedom to rewrite them in accordance with his own purposes[47]—in other words, only a theory of composition close to the Resource end of the Quotation/Resource spectrum seems adequately to account for the final form. Yet because sources and final text are then connected only quite indirectly, there seems little likelihood of reconstructing the former from the latter. To produce this degree of parallelism the author has clearly not proceeded in a mechanical, 'block-by-block' manner, but has worked flexibly—sometimes, perhaps, just changing a word or two in the sources, but perhaps in other places substantially rewriting major portions of the text. Thus one could imagine, for example, that Tamar was actually executed in the original version, without Judah's involvement with her ever coming to light (the story functioning as a grim, cautionary tale against trying to outwit the *paterfamilias*). Or perhaps Tamar originally had a sister-confidant who tried to dissuade her from such a risky plan, but who was deleted by the author to heighten the parallelism with Joseph. Or did the author, for similar reasons, simply invent Judah's original wronging of Tamar? (Perhaps the original was a bawdy comedy, in which a young widow plays the harlot but is crafty enough to get away with it.) Of course, these alternatives are not being seriously offered as possible prehistories for the present story; my point, rather, is that, for all we can discover, these or any number of other highly diverse 'originals' may have lain behind the final narrative, because the connection between the (re)sources and the final form must have been very loose. Once it is accepted that the final text is not a scissors-and-paste compilation, and that 'what stands written' in it, therefore, cannot provide evidence in any direct way for what the sources contained, then the recovery of those sources becomes exceedingly

---

[47] Cf. the similar, but more cautious, views of Alter, 'Introduction [to *The Literary Guide*]', in Robert Alter and Frank Kermode (eds.), *The Literary Guide to the Bible* (London: Collins, 1987), pp. 24–26.

difficult—as difficult, in fact, as reconstructing Plutarch's *Life of Coriolanus* solely from Shakespeare's play.

The main point is that a Quotation-theoretic method of composition not only can but almost certainly will produce a rough, somewhat incoherent final text. In a Quotation-theoretic composition the redactor significantly curtails the extent of his or her control over the final text—whereas a genuine author can freely add or delete characters, modify the plot, etc., in order to shape the materials into a well-integrated whole, the redactor is largely constrained by the sources. It is therefore highly unlikely that the final text will display much literary subtlety at any level which transcends the source boundaries, because the redactor has very few ways of producing meanings at such levels. Worse still, if the sources have divergent styles or viewpoints, there is little that can be done to moderate the disparities when combining the texts. In summary then, a Quotation-theoretic method of composition is virtually certain to produce a final narrative which is, at best, lacking in literary subtlety, and in all probability will also be somewhat rough and incoherent; therefore if the final text is in fact a subtle and well-integrated whole then one can be very confident that it did not have a Quotation-theoretic prehistory. Success in one's synchronic studies is incompatible with this kind of diachronic reconstruction.

So far I have only considered idealized cases from close to the endpoints of the Quotation/Resource spectrum, and resulting from only a single stage of redaction/authorship. In practice, of course, few texts have been found to exhibit such extremes of coherence or incoherence, and would therefore have to be placed at some intermediate point. Thus for example, even if we accept that Moberly has demonstrated that Exodus 32–34 is sufficiently coherent that (as he claims) its sources are irrecoverable, and that (as I would then infer) it was not composed through anything remotely resembling a Quotation-theoretic approach, Moberly himself nonetheless admits that there are still *some* (though few) infelicities in the final form; and it may be that (as with the accession of the infant Saul) these ultimately have to be accounted for extrinsically. Perhaps for this kind of case (although not necessarily for this specific text) one might postulate a prehistory in which the bulk of the passage is the Resource-theoretic product of a single author, but which has subsequently been slightly marred through interpolations by a clumsy redactor, or by textual corruptions, etc. Or to consider a contrasted example, the

Flood narrative is *so* repetitious that a Quotation-theoretic conflation of sources is, *prima facie*, a plausible description of its basic mode of composition; yet the narrative is not completely without signs of literary skill, and this also has to be accounted for at some point in its postulated prehistory.

For most texts, then,[48] it may well be that, as Sternberg claims, a mixture of synchronic and diachronic considerations are needed to account for all their features; and this is why I have reservations about Moberly's proposal that a close synchronic study should be undertaken before a diachronic reconstruction is attempted. Of course, Moberly's reason for this (namely, that unless one has made a thorough attempt to understand a text on its own terms one's diachronic reconstructions are liable to be based upon 'infelicities' that are not really infelicitous) makes, at one level, a sound point; but so too does the argument of someone who would give priority to the diachronic over the synchronic: Unless one has first made a thorough source-analysis of the text one's synchronic studies are liable to find unwarranted meanings in merely accidental features of the text. The point is that priority can be given to neither the synchronic nor the diachronic, but that one will advance towards a fuller understanding of the whole text by tacking between the two, in the ways that Sternberg describes so well (pp. 17–23). In this respect I think that Sternberg is right to see the synchronic and the diachronic approaches as complementary; and yet Moberly has the deeper insight when he sees that they are mutually antagonistic.

## 5. *Pluralism, Theology, and Sociological Criticism*

With the relationship between certain kinds of synchronic and diachronic approaches to biblical interpretation now clarified, this is an appropriate point at which to discuss Mark Brett's views on 'hermeneutical pluralism'. As he initially presents it, Brett's thesis is that since there are a plurality of legitimate yet distinct hermeneutical goals one might pursue, different scholars should be content to investigate the particular kind of question that interests them without, on the one hand, being critical of those who pursue other kinds of

---

[48] At least as we currently perceive them; although this could change through further detailed studies like Moberly's.

issues, and without, on the other hand, allowing themselves to be inhibited from developing their own field of research to its full extent by the fact that others are engaged in fields of research which are logically distinct from their own:

> On the pluralist view, synchronic interpretation of the final form can be performed without chronological scruples; it could make use of connections made by historical critics as well as connections prohibited by them. Hermeneutical monism, on the other hand, would suggest that all biblical interpreters are doing basically the same kind of thing only with different emphases.... On the monistic view, final form readings cannot conflict with the findings of historical critics, and conversely, historical critics cannot transgress the findings of final form critics.[49]

In Brett's view, hermeneutical pluralism is a 'coherent attitude', whereas monism is 'incoherent' (*ibid.*).

Especially in the earlier chapters of *Crisis?*, this distinction is used as a standard by which Childs' programme is assessed. Although, in Brett's estimation, Childs is sometimes a healthy pluralist, on other occasions his work becomes monistic. Brett sees one instance of this monistic tendency in Childs' alleged unwillingness to allow his final form interpretations of certain texts in Exodus to take account of other texts which, according to the Graf-Wellhausen hypothesis, come from a later period. Brett is critical of Childs for allowing himself to be held back by these 'chronological scruples', and suggests that unless Childs can overcome them it is difficult to see how the canonical approach can establish itself as a 'style of research' distinct from, say, redaction criticism.[50]

Brett also sees Childs' monism as making him unnecessarily hostile towards scholars who are engaged in studies of a kind different from his own. Brett particularly develops this point in relation to the

---

[49] *Crisis?*, pp. 41–42//*CAOTS* p. 116.

[50] See *Crisis?*, pp. 39–41; whether Childs is in fact chronologically inhibited in this way seems to me a very moot point. There are numerous instances in *IOTS* where his interpretations span across what Childs himself clearly recognizes as source-critical boundaries—as Brett himself points out, 'Although Childs reviews [in *IOTS*] the historical critical problems pertinent to each biblical book, he does not allow historical reconstruction to constrain his exegesis. A long list of scholars are criticized in the *Introduction* for allowing their work to be so constrained' (*Crisis?* p. 66//*CAOTS* p. 147). The same point can also be made from *OTTCC* and *BTONT*, where Childs can hardly have been unaware that he was drawing together material from very different periods.

exchanges between Childs and Norman Gottwald. Childs has faulted
Gottwald's sociological approach to the Hebrew Bible for '[destroy-
ing] the need for closely hearing the text on its verbal level', while
Gottwald has in turn criticized Childs for failing to take account of
the sociological factors which shaped the text.[51] According to Brett,
however, both these arguments are only near-tautologous restatements
of each scholar's respective interpretative concerns:[52] Childs' emic-
like interests in the final form mean that he accords high value to
'closely hearing the text on its verbal level', whereas Gottwald's interests in etic interpretation mean that for him sociological factors
are of primary concern. Although Brett does not deny that the validity of an interpretative aim can be debated, his pluralistic orientation strongly inclines him towards allowing each scholar to go his
own way. His advice to Childs, therefore, is that

> [T]he canonical approach should not be tied to any attacks on critical,
> historical reconstructions. . . . It would be far better simply to articulate
> the distinctive goals of the canonical approach and allow other inter-
> preters to pursue their own interests in relative isolation. (p. 13)

Given that (as Brett points out, p. 11) biblical studies currently
embraces a wide diversity of interpretative interests, this 'live and let
live' policy can seem very attractive. In my view, however, it is
methodologically unsound, with Brett being confused both in his
arguments for (this version of) pluralism and in the use he makes of
it in criticizing Childs. To begin with the latter point, 'closely hearing the text on its verbal level' cannot be fenced off as an interpretative interest which is distinctive of the canonical approach, and
which others need not pursue; rather, it is a criterion which *all* must
meet as a minimum standard for qualifying as a legitimate approach.
The aim of *all* interpretation (albeit in very different ways) is to
understand the final text, whether this is then explicated as understanding it as a subtle literary structure, or as a theological discourse,
or as a complex intersplicing of sources, or as the product of certain
social conditions, etc. Whichever of these (or other) interpretative
interests someone might pursue, they are nonetheless offering an
interpretation *of the final text*—paying attention to, and accounting
for, its fine details is as much a part of the (diachronic) work of the

---

[51] See *Crisis?*, pp. 11–12; the quotation is from Childs' *OTTCC*, p. 25.
[52] P. 12; cf. p. 52.

source critic as of the (synchronic) work of the literary critic.[53] Some-one, therefore, who professed to have no interest in closely hearing the text would simply be opting out of *all* legitimate forms of inter-pretation. Or to put it another way: If my reading of Genesis were characterized by airy generalizations about its religious symbolism which made little contact with what the text actually said, or if it switched about arbitrarily between literal, symbolic, and allegorical interpretations, or showed a cavalier disregard for the syntax, or assigned unattested meanings to many of the words, then it would be a simple matter to 'prove' that this text was the product of a skilful literary artist, or of a mechanical, 'scissors-and-paste' redactor, or of a workers' revolution against their oppressive overlords, or of a repressed Oedipal complex, or of almost anything else one might care to imagine. In other words, it is 'closely hearing the text on its verbal level' which prevents *all* forms of interpretation, whether synchronic or diachronic, from descending into a trivial and point-less game. That Gottwald's brand of interpretation 'destroys the need' for such hearing, therefore, is a perfectly legitimate kind of objection for Childs to raise,[54] which cannot be brushed aside as Childs monistically imposing his own interpretative interests upon others.

That this is also a highly pertinent objection for Childs to raise soon becomes clear when we consider more closely what his own interpretative interests are. If they had to be summarized in a brief sentence one might say that Childs' aim is to interpret the canonical writings as the normative Scriptures of the church; but as one begins to unpack what this means it soon becomes evident that it entails having specific interests in the whole range of biblical and theological disciplines: '*Canonical* . . . Scriptures' implies an interest in the final form, and hence in the various 'synchronic' approaches that are appropriate to the reading of literature at the level of chapter, book, and canon; 'Scriptures *of the church*' implies an interest in theological interpretation, and hence in such matters as the theological signifi-cance of the text's literary shape (recall Childs' messianic interpretation of David), and in the relationship between biblical and dogmatic theology; '*normative* Scripture' implies an interest in questions of

---

[53] Brett himself comes close to recognizing this on p. 42, but has not grasped how this rules out some of his objections to Childs.

[54] Whether or not Gottwald's programme really *is* destructive in this way is, of course, another question, which could only be answered through a detailed study of Gottwald's own work. This, however, lies outside the scope of the present book.

authority and truth, and hence in such questions as the divine reality to which the Scriptures bear witness, and (for reasons we have already discussed at some length) to the questions of historical veracity which the 'diachronic', critical tools are designed to handle. All these issues are integral to Childs' own interests, and it is therefore entirely appropriate for him to discuss the alternative views which other scholars might hold about each and every one of them.

The canonical approach, then, is *not* an 'approach' in the narrow sense of a particular technique or circumscribed field of interests—it is not the latest addition to the family of 'criticisms' (as the unfortunate designation of Childs' work as 'canon(ical) criticism' tends to imply), which takes up roughly where redaction criticism leaves off. Rather, it is a comprehensive vision whose interest is in tackling ultimate theological questions, and which therefore orders and arranges all the sub-disciplines within this field towards the answering of such questions. One major weakness of *Crisis?* is that it fails to capture the breadth of this vision. Instead, one narrowly conceived interpretative interest is distinguished from another and each put in a distinct compartment. Childs is assigned to the compartment which studies the canonical text synchronically, with his 'proper' task thus being defined as the production of such studies. As a representative of this particular interest, however, it is deemed improper for him to venture an opinion on some other compartment. When he does so he is castigated for being a hermeneutical monist, and his work is charged with displaying an unhealthy 'totalitarian tendency' (p. 11). Setting the discussion up in these terms, however, simply ensures *a priori* that Childs' programme is never given a chance to present itself fairly on its own terms.

A good example of how this seriously distorts the discussion of Childs' work is provided by Brett's comments on the chapter in *IOTS* on Daniel.[55] Noting that Childs has gone to some trouble here to reconstruct the midrashic methodology of the Maccabean author of chapters 7–12, Brett quotes Childs' remark that because '[this writer's] own identity had no theological significance . . . [he] therefore concealed it', and then comments:

> [T]his [reconstruction] is not a description of the final form as such . . .
> [but] diachronic emic description—a legitimate part of . . . historical

---

[55] *Crisis?* pp. 68–70//*CAOTS* pp. 149–52. The following page numbers refer to *Crisis?*.

criticism. . . . The *distinctive* aspect of the canonical approach appears in Childs' attitude towards this self-effacing Maccabean author. Rather than providing an interpretation of Daniel based on a reconstructed Maccabean situation, he focuses on the communicative intention of the *text itself*.[56]

Childs is therefore charged with 'exegetical schizophrenia' (p. 68), on the grounds that he haphazardly intersperses his comments on what Brett considers to be the proper concern of the canonical approach (namely, a '[focusing] on the communicative intention of the text itself') with extraneous discussions of a historical-critical nature. In fact, however, Childs has himself explained very cogently why he addresses *this particular historical issue*: As we saw in section 2 above, Childs is refuting an alternative historical reconstruction which, if correct, would undermine the status of Daniel 7–12 as normative Scripture; and since this way of understanding the Bible is a central element in Childs' canonical approach, historical reconstructions such as this are integral to his work, and cannot be lopped off without leaving his programme seriously maimed. Contrary, then, to Brett's claim that 'the canonical approach should not be tied to any attacks on critical, historical interpretation' (p. 13), there are some historical interpretations which, if *not* successfully attacked, would seriously undermine the value of the canonical approach. In sum, then, Brett's compartmentalizing of interpretative interests leads to an over-hasty dismembering of Childs' work which obscures its true intent.

The reason why Brett divides up theology into discrete compartments is that '[i]n this situation of pluralism [sc., in which biblical scholars are in fact pursuing 'a whole range of interpretative interests', p. 11] we should take care not to conflate interpretative interests that are logically separable' (pp. 5–6). There are two comments to be made on this. Firstly, the claim of logical separability is only correct if interpretative interests are construed very narrowly—as we have seen, far from Childs' interpretative interests being logically separable from those of the 'pure' source critic or literary critic, they logically entail that he *must* have a particular interest in these disciplines. And generalizing this point, we might wonder how many scholars *are* 'pure' source (or whatever) critics, who simply pursue their own narrow goal for its own sake, without any thought as to how it contributes to the broader theological enterprise. In other words,

---

[56] P. 69, Brett's italics.

it is questionable whether Brett's analysis makes much contact with the sort of interpretative interests that real scholars actually have. And secondly, even when we allow that there is a *certain* degree of logical separability between interpretative interests, it is questionable as to whether this has any significant methodological implications. If 'interests' is construed narrowly enough then one clearly can identify interpretative interests which are logically separable from one another, if one means by this that their aims are conceptually distinct from one another: 'What is the meaning of this text as we now have it?' and 'How did it come to be in this form?' are two logically separable questions which can both be asked of one and the same text. It would be something else entirely, however, to claim that two such questions can (or should) each be answered without regard to the answers which are given to the other,[57] or without considering how one might go about answering the other.[58] Even if these claims were correct they would not follow simply from the logical separability of the interpretative interests, because all this says is that one does not bear upon the other *as a matter of purely logical or conceptual necessity.* This leaves it completely open, however, as to whether there in some *other* connection between them, and whether this would rule out the possibility of each being (sensibly) pursued without reference to the other. The point can easily be illustrated with the predicates 'has a father' and 'has a mother'. Clearly these are logically/conceptually separable—whatever other objections might be raised against the virgin birth, it cannot be dismissed out of hand as a logical contradiction. The nature of our world is such, however, that, miracles apart, there are certain causal connections between fathers, mothers, and offspring which allow inferences to be made from one to the other. Thus if, in interpreting a fragmentary text, one discovers that an otherwise unknown entity called 'X' had a mother, then one can infer with a very high degree of plausibility that X also had a father. Thus even though 'Did X have a father?' and 'Did X have a mother?' are *logically* separable research interests, it would normally make no

---

[57] As Brett thinks that Childs should have answered his questions about the meaning of passages from Exodus in their canonical context without being inhibited by the answers which source critics have given to questions about the dating of this material; see above.

[58] As Brett advises when he suggests that 'It would be far better simply to articulate the distinctive goal of the canonical approach and allow other interpreters to pursue their own interests in relative isolation' (p. 13).

methodological sense at all to investigate one without reference to the answer that is given to the other.

Separability, then, is not a matter of logic alone; other possible interconnections also have to be taken into account. In particular, I argued in section 4 that certain kinds of synchronic and diachronic investigation are methodologically interdependent—someone proposing a Quotation-theoretic account of a text's prehistory cannot proceed 'in relative isolation' from synchronic studies of that text, because certain discoveries about the latter could prove that the former is quite untenable.

Brett himself shows some awareness of this in his interesting discussion of the 'Bridegroom of Blood' pericope (Exod. 4:24–26).[59] Brett introduces this with the comment that the case he has made out thus far for hermeneutical pluralism 'does not . . . imply that diachronic and synchronic methods cannot mutually influence one another' (p. 47). To illustrate this, Brett begins with a final form reading of Exod. 4:24–26 which argues that the averting of Yahweh's attack through the bloody circumcision of Moses' firstborn anticipates the passover narrative in Exodus 12,[60] and then considers whether his new reading might have any implications for historical-critical studies. Although, in view of the obscurity of the text and the complexity of the historical issues, Brett is rightly cautious in his conclusions, he does suggest that his reading may establish a connection between firstborn and passover which would count against some reconstructions of how the Exodus traditions have developed.[61] This, however, is essentially the same kind of conclusion that was drawn above when discussing the Joseph and Tamar narratives; and it is difficult to see, therefore, how Brett's discovery of important interconnections between synchronic and diachronic approaches can be reconciled with the pluralism he espouses when criticizing Childs' alleged monism. In sum, then, there seem to be three strands in Brett's discussion of pluralism which do not sit together at all comfortably: (i) His advocating an innocuous form of pluralism which rightly[62] but inconsequentially

---

[59] *Crisis?* pp. 47–52//*CAOTS* pp. 121–128. The following page numbers refer to *Crisis?*.

[60] See pp. 48–49. Brett also considers several other aspects of the meaning of the final form, but this one point is sufficient for the methodological issues which need to be discussed here.

[61] See p. 51; again Brett also discusses a number of other historical issues which need not be considered here.

[62] Provided that, in the following quotation, 'final form interpretation' is under-

points out that 'the goal of final form interpretation is not to be confused with the various goals of historical criticism' (p. 52); (ii) The methodological advice (which Brett incorrectly believes to be entailed by this innocuous pluralism) that 'It would be far better simply to articulate the distinctive goal of the canonical approach and allow other interpreters to pursue their own interests in relative isolation' (p. 13); and (iii) the conclusion he draws from his Bridegroom of Blood study, that 'a final form reading might well turn out to have significance for historical reconstruction' (p. 52), which at the very least seems to strongly imply that, contrary to the methodological advice I have just quoted, scholars with final form and with historical interests should *not* develop them 'in relative isolation' from one another, as this could leave them in ignorance of factors that are relevant to their own pursuits.

Brett confuses the situation still further when he returns to the debate between Childs and Gottwald.[63] We have already seen that, in the earlier part of his book, Brett's pluralistic instincts lead him to suggest that the objections which these scholars level against each other are really near-tautologous restatements of their own hermeneutical priorities, and that each should therefore be more tolerant in allowing the other to develop their respective interests. In the light of his further discussions of synchronic and diachronic approaches,[64] however, Brett seems to realize that their projects are not so readily separable after all. Childs is now severely criticized because

> [He] wants both to emphasize the truth value of canonical Old Testament theology *and at the same time* to reject etic biblical studies which reformulate biblical theologies and reconstruct Israelite history using modern analytical concepts.[65]

This rejection, however, leaves him with 'no adequate way of re-

---

stood in the minimal sense of simply understanding the meaning of the canonical text, without raising any Childsian questions about its normativity or theological truth. Construed in this way, Brett is calling attention to an example of logical separability.

[63] *Crisis?* pp. 149–53//*CAOTS* pp. 253–58. The following page numbers refer to *Crisis?*.

[64] In addition to the material reviewed above, Brett also has a section entitled 'What is Synchronic Interpretation?' (pp. 104–15). This argues that 'Childs's' approach to exegesis is formalist rather than strictly synchronic' (p. 115), and suggests that the kind of New Critical principles put forward by Wimsatt and Beardsley offer certain advantages to biblical interpretation. I shall discuss this in sections 7.1–2 below; it does not contribute to the points being considered here.

[65] P. 149; Brett's italics.

sponding' to 'charges of fideism or dogmatic classicism',[66] and thus makes him particularly vulnerable to such critics as Gottwald. Quoting Childs' assertion that those who shaped the canonical writings 'did their best to obscure their own identity', Brett sees this as playing straight into Gottwald's hands: As the latter has pointed out, one of the primary reasons why a writer or redactor may obscure their own identity is to make what are really their own, socially conditioned judgements appear to be timeless truths, emanating from heaven.

The fundamental difference between Childs and Gottwald, then, lies (as Brett rightly observes) in 'their different hypotheses as to the *motives* of [the] canonical editors'[67]—Childs' main reason for giving hermeneutical priority to the final form is that he believes it to be the outcome of *theological* reflections, whereas Gottwald thinks that political and economic factors played a major part. What the editors' motives *really* were, however, cannot be decided simply by citing what the editors themselves tell us about them in their final text—the purpose of such declarations might be precisely to hide their true motives. To discover whether this is so one would also have to consider whatever relevant evidence can be found *outside* the canon; and at this point Brett finds himself 'forced to conclude' that

> [T]he canonical approach *cannot itself provide the kind of evidence necessary to support one of Childs's key arguments for reading the final form.* Canonical exegesis can tell us very little about the motives of the canonical editors, yet it is precisely Childs' theological understanding of the canonical editors which legitimates his focus on the received text. He recommends that we need not recover original socio-historical differences since these have been subordinated to theological concerns. . . . But he cannot draw this conclusion by simply reading the final form.[68]

Brett suggests, therefore, that Childs should perhaps move closer to J.A. Sanders' version of 'canonical criticism', since this 'seeks to reconstruct the canonical process' (p. 153).

There are a number of things to comment on here. Firstly, it should by now be obvious that a 'canonical approach' which is unable to discuss the motives of the canonical editors is certainly not the programme advocated in *IOTS*, *NTCI*, *OTTCC*, or *BTONT*, where

---

[66] *Ibid.*; by the second charge Brett is suggesting that Childs' valuing of the Old Testament as (in Gadamer's sense) a 'classic' text has become an unreasoned 'dogma'. I shall discuss this more fully in chapters 8 and 9 below.

[67] P. 151; Brett's italics.

[68] Pp. 152–53; Brett's italics.

the critical reconstruction of the redactors' true motives is a recurrent theme. That Brett should finally be forced to the conclusion I have just summarized is a good index of how confused his discussion has been. This began, it will be recalled, by 'saving' Childs' programme from hermeneutical monism by lopping off its historical-critical components—these, we were told, are not what the canonical approach is *really* about; rather, they are symptoms of an 'exegetical schizophrenia' in which Childs oscillates between being a 'canonical interpreter' and a 'part-time . . . historical critic' (p. 68). Since this diagnosis is made without considering Childs' views on what Brett aptly calls 'the truth value of canonical Old Testament theology' (p. 149), the impression is easily created that Childs' critical discussions are merely loose cogs which could be discarded without loss. This done, Childs and Gottwald are counselled each to pursue their own programme without treading on the other's toes. In the latter part of his book, however, Brett himself shows that this is impossible, since Childs and Gottwald are *both* essentially concerned with questions of motivation, and hence with questions of historical reconstruction. Brett is therefore forced to conclude that Childs *should* investigate the very issues which Brett himself had previously argued that, as a *canonical* interpreter, are outside his remit. What Brett finally establishes, then, is that both synchronic and diachronic investigations are integral to Childs' work, and that the hermeneutical pluralism which Brett advocated in criticizing Childs' supposed schizophrenic and totalitarian tendencies is itself methodologically untenable.[69]

Secondly, Brett's claim that 'Childs . . . wants . . . to reject etic biblical studies which reformulate biblical theologies and reconstruct Israelite history using modern analytical concepts' (p. 149) needs to be discussed more fully. There are in fact two claims being made here, which are best considered separately:

(i) The claim about the reformulating of biblical theologies, though not incorrect, is misleading insofar as it gives the impression that Childs' intention is to formulate the biblical theologies solely in terms

---

[69] Lest the preceding discussion has given a misleading impression, I should perhaps add that my rejection of Brett's pluralism does not mean that I am arguing in favour of hermeneutical monism. My point, rather, is that Brett's monism/pluralism distinction is unilluminating because *both* terms are confused and confusing: Each makes a *blanket* statement (whether of affirmation or denial) about the interrelatedness of interests, whereas what is needed is a discussion of the particular kind(s) of interrelatedness that may (or must, or cannot) pertain between this and that specific interest.

that are drawn from the canonical writings themselves. Childs in fact
has no objection, in principle, to extra-biblical categories being used
for this; on the contrary, he intentionally uses concepts drawn from
Dogmatics throughout *OTTCC* and *BTONT*. His criterion for deciding which categories to use is not whether they are 'modern analytic
concepts' (or medieval Aristotelian concepts, or whatever), but whether
they do justice to the subject matter. Thus even when 'the canonical
approach' is reduced to no more than the describing of the biblical
writings in their canonical form, it is still some distance removed
from the kind of emic enterprise which Brett's comment might lead
one to envisage.

(ii) The claim about the reconstructing of Israelite history needs
to be nuanced more carefully. We saw in section 5.3 that even a
Pannenbergian historical methodology would generally be able to do
little with the kind of interconnectedness which is theologically significant; therefore insofar as Childs is rejecting the substitution of a
critically reconstructed history for the canonically recounted history
as the basic 'datum' from which one's theological reflections must
proceed, he is making a good point. Nonetheless, we have also seen
that the canonically recounted history often cannot be detached from
'what really happened' without undermining its own theological value;
therefore Brett makes a valid point insofar as he is arguing that Childs'
reluctance to address such questions *as* questions of historical reconstruction leaves his theology vulnerable to charges of fideism.

Thirdly, a synchronic study of the final form can sometimes give
much more definite information about the motives which produced
it than Brett has realized. The point can again be illustrated from
my discussion of the Joseph and Tamar stories. In outlining the critical consensus on these narratives, I quoted from Claus Westermann's
claim that

> A redactor has inserted [the Tamar narrative] into the Jacob story so
> as to preserve it like other individual narratives about the sons of
> Jacob. . . . [It] has been appended because it deals with a son of Jacob.[70]

This is a statement about the redactor's motives, claiming that these
were primarily concerned with the preservation of a narrative about
a son of Jacob (presumably because the redactor judged that his
audience would, or should, be interested in hearing about his exploits).

---

[70] *Genesis 37–50*, p. 49.

If my synchronic reading of Genesis is correct, however, then Wester-mann's claim, though not necessarily wrong, is surely inadequate: Preservation may have been *part* of the motive, but something more than this is needed to explain why the 'redactor' subtly paralleled the Tamar and Joseph stories. In other words, there is more to be explained than Westermann has realized, and a correspondingly more complex account of the underlying motives is therefore needed.

This synchronic reading of Genesis also allows certain inferences to be drawn about the author's intended readership. Although at one level these are very readable, entertaining stories which could appeal to a wide audience, their fuller 'literary dimension' is unlikely to have been perceived by many of their readers. Assuming that the author was not unaware of this, an adequate account of his motives would have to explain why he wrote in this way. Whatever 'point' the author was making through the parallelism, it was clearly of some importance to him (since he took the trouble to develop it in detail and at length), and yet it was intended for the eyes of a few rather than for a wide audience.

Similar considerations are also relevant to arguments about theo-logical *versus* sociological motivation. A sociological critic who was persuaded by Childs that 2 Samuel portrays David as a messianic figure might be tempted to explain this literature as political propa-ganda which tries to inculcate loyalty to the Davidic dynasty by portraying its founder as a divinely appointed prefigurement of what its future rulers would be. Against this, however, it could be pointed out that since the relevant theological point is made through a subtle literary device, most readers of Samuel were probably unaware that David *was* being portrayed in this way.[71] Yet this would render the propaganda hypothesis highly implausible, because such literature has failed in its very *raison d'être* if its message is not clearly perceived by the majority of its readership.[72]

---

[71] In order to keep the methodological discussion straightforward I am consider-ing just this one element in the depiction of David. A sociological critic might well argue that there are other, much more overt, evaluations of the Davidic dynasty which *do* support a political analysis of the motivations behind Samuel; yet be this as it may, an adequate reconstruction of the author's motivations would still have to account for him also using subtle literary techniques in order to make important theological points in unobvious ways. Where such an argument might lead would clearly depend upon one making a close literary study of the book as a whole.

[72] Cf. David Gunn's astute argument against the Succession Narrative being political propaganda: Noting that scholars who so classify this narrative disagree among them-

That the author of Samuel has taken the trouble to write in such a way that some of his finer theological points will be grasped only by his more perceptive readers suggests that a primary factor in his motivation was to write theology for those who were sufficiently attuned to theological nuances as to search them out in the less obvious aspects of his work. Theological *subtlety* in the final form of a book provides good *prima facie* (though not, of course, incontrovertible) reasons for believing that it was written from primarily theological motives. It seems, then, that Childs is broadly correct in thinking that a 'transcendental' argument for the priority of the text's final form can be based upon the final form itself—this can itself provide grounds (i) for believing that, even when we lack the requisite historical evidence to reconstruct the detailed process behind it, the underlying motivations were predominantly religious; or (ii) for refuting a critical reconstruction which claims that the motivations were mainly non-religious.

Having said this, however, it should also be pointed out that there is an important difference between Childs' transcendental argument and the one developed here. Childs' version was based upon a theological conception of the canon which, if it could be affirmed, would vindicate the priority of the final form in its full extent. The present version, however, is premised upon the theological sophistication of the final form, and is therefore only applicable to those texts where this quality can be demonstrated exegetically. Furthermore, it would clearly be wrong to see this transcendental argument as a 'trump card' which automatically overrules all historical-critical or sociological attempts to reconstruct the redactors' motives. What it does show, however, is that there are factors relevant to such reconstructions which have not so far been given their due weight, and which may prove very useful to Childs. His adherence to the final form may therefore yet prove to have a much greater inbuilt resistance to traditio-critical attempts at undermining it than has generally been recognized.

---

selves as to what political position it espouses, Gunn rightly argues that this strongly suggests that, '[even] if there is a particular political *Tendenz* in the narrative *it is by no means obvious what it is*' (*The Story of King David: Genre and Interpretation* (JSOTS 6; Sheffield: JSOT Press, 1978), p. 23, Gunn's italics; cf. pp. 25, 26). As Gunn points out, this undermines the hypothesis that it is political *propaganda*, since the whole point of such literature is to advocate a definite political position, which therefore needs to be clearly conveyed.

## 6. *Canon and Community*

The final topic to consider in this chapter is the role of the believing
community in the shaping of the canonical traditions. Although Childs
naturally accepts that much of the actual collecting and editing was
done by particular redactors and/or redactional 'schools', he is nonetheless at pains to emphasize that the material with which they worked
was the sacred traditions of the community as a whole, and that the
development of the traditions was an integral part of its ongoing life
as the people of God.

Childs' main reason for attaching such importance to this 'all Israel'
perspective is a desire to rebut any potential accusations that the
resultant Scriptures express (merely!) the views of one particular interest
group. This comes out especially clearly in Childs' discussion of the
the Deuteronomistic History, for which he suggests that we should

> assume [*sic!*] that the material which the final redactor gathered and
> shaped had already exerted such an 'official' force on the community
> by its use that he was unable or unwilling to attempt a change. *Far
> from being an idiosyncratic opinion of one author*, the shaping of the Former
> Prophets reflects a long process within the community of Israel which
> incorporated the witness of many previous generations.[73]

Unfortunately, however, Childs' 'all Israel' perspective is a historical
hypothesis which seems to be open to a number of serious objections. Firstly, the pre-exilic and even the post-exilic community (the
latter being, in Childs' view, chiefly responsible for the canonical
shaping) was often quite heterogeneous in its religious composition,
with views which would finally be accepted as 'true Yahwism' sometimes being kept alive by no more than a small minority. This makes
it questionable whether the final form would have been so decisively
pro-Yahwistic and anti-syncretistic if it had been put together in the
way Childs envisages. Even if full allowance is made for the diversity
to be found within the canon, the normative Yahwism which it now
advocates is much narrower than the range of religious options that
often found living expression in Israelite society.

Secondly, to the extent that studies of the final form have shown
that many of the biblical books are skilful literary creations, this would
argue against them being community products in anything more than

---

[73] *IOTS* p. 236, italics added; cf. pp. 223, 291, 300, etc.

their broad outlines. This becomes particularly important when we recall that Childs sees the main theological thrust of some passages being made through a subtle literary shaping of the final form (his interpretation of 2 Samuel as offering a messianic portrayal of David being a case in point). Although one might envisage the individual pericopae being developed by the community as a whole, and allow that the general course of the story was fixed by the common usage of these traditions, it seems much more difficult to give any sub-stance to the idea that the community as a whole was somehow involved in the careful selecting and editing process through which (according to Childs' interpretation) the messianic portrayal was con-veyed. One would expect a community to produce a much more mundane literature than Childs himself finds the canonical texts to be—it is hard to imagine *King Lear* being written even by a committee, much less by a whole community. Where the final form displays a fair degree of subtlety it seems quite unrealistic to envisage a large number of people being involved in its detailed shaping; and in the context of Childs' discussions this implies that the community had little part in shaping the text's main theological motifs.

Thirdly, Childs' hypothesis runs directly counter to those critical reconstructions which find *rival* 'schools' within the community. If Childs' view is to prevail, therefore, it needs to be defended much more fully as a historical reconstruction against alternatives. And fourthly, Childs seems to be making a curious 'safety in numbers' assumption that does not bear closer scrutiny. While there obviously is a sense in which the literature of a closely-knit school is likely to be much more 'individual' than that which condenses out of the community as a whole, at another level this itself becomes relativized. Israel's 'official' religion, as it is presented in the canonical writings, was also highly 'idiosyncratic' in comparison with other ancient Near Eastern religions; yet Childs presumably does not regret this, or believe that the Scriptures would have benefitted from stronger Canaanite and Babylonian influences. Nor need individualism necessarily be a weakness—the Pauline epistles are very individual writings, but that does not detract from their status as Scripture. Of course, Paul did not write as an *isolated* individual, but from within a generally accepted framework of ideas and practices; and likewise more recent Old Testament studies have undermined the 'romantic' image of the prophet as a poet who spoke out of his or her own individual experience of God, by showing their dependence upon the inherited traditions. Yet nonetheless, we are indebted to Paul's 'personal genius' for the penetrating insights he has given into these generally accepted ideas; and similarly, many of the insights embodied in the Old Testament could perhaps be more plausibly explained as the work of gifted individuals or schools who refined the common traditions, rather than as a community products *per se*.

So then, giving a productive role to the community as a whole is highly problematic; but fortunately Childs does not really need this hypothesis. What is significant for Childs' programme is that the Scriptures were shaped by (appropriate) religious concerns; and although 'the community as a whole' is one way of explicating this, it is not the only possible way, and in many cases is far from being the most plausible alternative. It seems, therefore, that Childs could save himself from some unnecessary problems here by being more flexible in his account of the tradition-process.

# CHAPTER SEVEN

# AUTHOR, READER, AND CONTEXT

Although the issues discussed in the previous chapter did not raise any serious methodological problems for Childs' programme, they nonetheless show that, if he were to engage more fully with contemporary debates about the traditions behind the canonical text, then he would have a daunting historical-critical mountain to climb: Contrary to Childs' frequent assertions that the traditions were primarily shaped by religious motives, there are actually many cases in which currently respected critical theories claim to have detected, at the very least, a considerable admixture of social and political influences as having left their mark on the final form. For Childs to overturn these alternative reconstructions piecemeal, through arguing out the critical issues in each individual case, would be a herculean labour.

We saw in section 3.2, however, that Childs has also toyed with a more philosophical way of not so much solving as circumventing this problem, namely, through separating textual meaning from author's intention. In *IOTS* the main use of this idea is apologetic, with canonical intentionality being appealed to in cases where it is unclear or even doubtful, on historical grounds, that the traditions were primarily shaped by religious motives.[1] Of no less importance for Childs' broader programme, however, is his more positive use of the same principle in *NTCI* to justify canonical 'meanings that no-one meant'. Thus in discussing the Matthean and Lukan infancy narratives Childs finds a 'linkage' between them that 'is not derived from any individual author's intentionality, nor from a subsequent redactional editing of the collection', but from their inclusion in 'the one literary corpus' of the New Testament canon. Yet even though the relationship between them is not intentional, it can still be the subject of 'theological reflection'.[2]

One application of this idea that would seem to be particularly

---

[1] See especially the programmatic statement in *IOTS* pp. 78–79; cf. pp. 258f., 485f.

[2] See *NTCI* pp. 161–63; cf. pp. 185–86, 291–95, etc.

helpful to Childs is in justifying a christological reading of the Old Testament. A standard critical objection to such a reading, of course, is that the Old Testament writers and redactors did not *intend* to refer to Christ, and their work should therefore not be read as so referring.[3] Separating meaning from author's intention, however, would answer this in a way that naturally developed ideas which have already proved useful to Childs in the *Introductions*. It is surprising, therefore, to find that very little is made of canonical intentionality in either *OTTCC* or *BTONT*. The intentionalist objection remains to be answered, however, and if a satisfactory solution cannot be found then suspicions arise as to whether Childs' conception of Biblical Theology is methodologically untenable.

Author's intention is also closely related to the question of original context, and both intentionality and original context are central concerns of the historical-critical approach—one of its primary reasons for recovering the original form of, say, a prophetic oracle is that it can only be interpreted accurately (so it is claimed) when it is heard in its original setting, because it is this context that determines the meanings which the words had when the author wrote his text.[4] Now this, of course, is a version of 'referentiality' that Childs vehemently opposes; yet we have seen that the tension between original and canonical contexts is a significant problem for his programme. Looking at intentionality is a helpful way of throwing some further light on these matters.

There are a number of reasons, then, why the relationship between meaning and author's intention is an important issue for Childs' programme; and the present chapter will therefore try to shed some light on these issues.

## 1. *Aspects of Author's Intention*

Although we have seen that regarding Childs' canonical hermeneutics as a sort of theological structuralism is too simplistic, one might nonetheless still ask whether there are arguments for the separation of meaning from author's intention that Childs might take over from

---

[3] This has been raised as a major criticism specifically of Childs by Sean McEvenue, 'The Old Testament, Scripture or Theology?' pp. 238–40. I shall discuss McEvenue's article in section 1 below.

[4] Cf. James Barr, *HS* pp. 85–87.

literary studies. 'The death of the author' has been a recurrent theme in several modern schools of literary theory, as criticism has switched its attention away from the author (who was the focus of study in Romantic criticism) towards 'the text itself' (New Criticism; Structuralism), or towards the reader (Reader-Response Theory; Reception Theory; Ideological Criticism).[5] The potential value for Childs of such a reorientation is well illustrated by the claim of W.M. Wimsatt and Monroe C. Beardsley, in their highly influential article on 'The Intentional Fallacy', that

> A poem can *be* only through its *meaning*—since its medium is words— yet it *is*, simply *is*, in the sense that WE HAVE NO EXCUSE FOR INQUIRING WHAT PART IS INTENDED OR MEANT;[6]

to which they add the similar but more specific contention that

> The history of words *after* a poem is written may contribute meanings which if relevant to the original pattern should not be ruled out by a scruple about intention.[7]

If this form of anti-intentionalism could be sustained, it would allow Childs to find specifically Christian meanings in an Old Testament text without having to heed the objection, 'But its author could not have intended it to mean that!'. In fact something like this has already been proposed by John F.A. Sawyer, who distinguishes between 'what is the meaning of Isa. 7:14 in the context of eighth-century B.C. Jerusalem' and what this text means in the context of the Christian canon. In answering the latter question Sawyer claims that full account must be taken of the relationship between Isa. 7:14 and Matt. 1:23, and dismisses 'the historical questions as to whether Isaiah actually and miraculously foretold the virgin birth eight centuries before Christ' as 'irrelevant'.[8]

---

[5] For a classification of literary criticisms in these terms see M.H. Abrams, *The Mirror and the Lamp: Romantic Theory and the Critical Tradition* (Oxford: OUP, 1953) 3–29; Abrams' scheme has been adapted for Biblical Studies by Barton, *Reading* 198–207. For thumbnail sketches of the latest versions of literary criticism to find their way into Biblical Studies see David J.A. Clines and J. Cheryl Exum, 'The New Literary Criticism', in Exum and Clines (eds.), *The New Literary Criticism and the Hebrew Bible* (JSOTS 143; Sheffield: Sheffield Academic Press, 1993), pp. 16–20.

[6] In David Newton-De Molina (ed.), *On Literary Intention* (Edinburgh: Edinburgh University Press, 1976), p. 2; italics original, capitals added.

[7] Note 7; italics original. Why '*original* patterns' are given this privileged position over patterns that later readers find (or create) in the poem is not explained. There appears to be an unexpurgated remnant of intentionalism here.

[8] 'A Change in Emphasis in the Study of the Prophets', in Richard Coggins *et al.*

Anti-intentionalist theories of meaning have been strongly contested, however, both by literary theorists and biblical scholars. Among the former, one of the most vigorous defenders of author's intention has been E.D. Hirsch.[9] What particularly concerns Hirsch is that the 'banishment of the author'[10] removes the only viable criterion of valid interpretation, and thus opens the floodgate to all sorts of fanciful subjectivisms (p. 3). To prevent this, Hirsch introduces his distinction between Meaning and Significance. We discussed this in section 4.2 above in relation to Stendahl's dichotomy between 'what it meant' and 'what it means', but now we need to look at its connection with author's intention. Significance, being defined in relational terms, is intended to siphon off the reader-oriented, subjectivistic aspect of interpretation, and thus to uncover an underlying, determinate meaning of the text. Meaning, in Hirsch's sense, is defined to be 'that which is represented by a text; it is what the author meant by his use of a particular sign sequence; it is what the signs represent' (p. 8); or again,

> Verbal meaning is whatever someone has willed to convey by a particular sequence of linguistic signs and which can be conveyed (shared) by means of those linguistic signs. (p. 30)

The way in which meaning is related to author's intention will have to be considered presently;[11] but these quotations at least make it clear that intention undergirds Hirsch's belief in the *objectivity* of meaning.

On the theological front, a similar conception of meaning has been developed by Sean McEvenue into an argument against canonical interpretation. It is McEvenue's view that

> for exegesis (i.e., exact interpretation of a text in its original meanings) the wholeness of the canon is meaningless. It is simply not true that

---

(eds.), *Israel's Prophetic Tradition* (Cambridge: CUP, 1982), p. 246.

[9] See especially his two books, *Validity in Interpretation* and *The Aims of Interpretation* (Chicago: Chicago University Press, 1976). It should be added, however, that over the years Hirsch has become increasingly isolated, and in 'Meaning and Significance Reinterpreted' (*Critical Inquiry* 2 (1986), pp. 627–30) he substantially modifies his original position. For extended criticism of Hirsch see David Hoy, *The Critical Circle* (Berkley: University of California, 1978), pp. 11–40; Frank Lentricchia, *After the New Criticism* (London: Methuen, 1983), pp. 256–80; William Ray, *Literary Meaning: From Phenomenology to Deconstruction* (Oxford: Blackwell, 1984), pp. 90–103.

[10] *Validity*, p. 1.

[11] To forestall possible misunderstandings, however, I would mention that although I am sympathetic to Hirsch's distinction between meaning and significance, my account of *how* meaning is related to author's intention is very different from his.

the proper context for understanding one text of the Bible is every text of the Bible.[12]

This, of course, is indisputably true, since it is a tautology: If one first defines exegesis as 'interpretation of a text in its *original* meanings' then it follows ineluctably that exegesis cannot possibly discover new, canonical meanings. As a refutation of Childs, however, this completely begs the question: Childs would simply reject such a definition of 'exegesis' as unacceptably narrow. To transform the tautology into a telling argument, therefore, some reason is needed for restricting 'exegesis properly so-called' to *original* meanings; and it is here that McEvenue appeals to author's intention and to the closely related idea of original context:

1. Nothing will be considered as a biblical teaching, or a biblical meaning, unless a biblical author intended that meaning.
2. Biblical meanings are illuminated by their historical context *and* defined or limited by their historical context.[13]

Although McEvenue is aware that literary critics have largely discounted 'author's meaning', he sees this as having little bearing upon the historical-critical work of the biblical scholar:

If one says that the literary work has its own meaning apart from authorial intention, and if this means that the Bible should be interpreted on the basis of textual data rather than on the basis of hypotheses about an author's interests as known from independent sources, then I will agree. If it means that the text may have resonances that go beyond what the author himself fully grasped, then I will assent to that view cautiously. . . . If it means that a published text becomes community property and may be given new meanings by the community as it is used in different contexts, I will agree only on the understanding that the new meanings will not be of the text but rather of the community. (pp. 237–38)

Thus McEvenue is willing (p. 238) to accept the meanings of the J and P sources as meanings of Scripture, and likewise accepts the meanings of the redactor who combined them. What he will not countenance, however, is new meanings emerging simply from the collection of texts into an 'anthology' (*ibid.*), without anyone having intended such meanings. 'Canonical meanings', therefore, are completely unacceptable to him (p. 237).

---

[12] 'The Old Testament, Scripture or Theology?', p. 237.
[13] P. 239; McEvenue's italics.

Unfortunately this reads much better as autobiography than as a contribution to biblical methodology—McEvenue tells us quite fully and clearly what he would and would not call 'a meaning of the text' but offers no supporting argument as to *why* author's intention should be accorded this all-controlling role. Insofar as his views have a plausible ring to them (at least in some corners of biblical studies) this is due to their highly traditional character—McEvenue is simply telling us that we ought to do what (until quite recently) the great majority of biblical scholars have in fact been doing. Thus I cannot see that McEvenue's refutation of canonical interpretation amounts to anything more than a complaint that Childs is not doing things in the good, old-fashioned way—an observation which is unlikely either to surprise Childs or to persuade him to abandon his programme.

One major reason for McEvenue's complacency seems to be his failure to grasp what the anti-intentionalism of modern literary criticism really entails. McEvenue claims that 'I do not intend to criticize this approach . . . but rather to warn about possible abuses' (p. 237); yet his own appeal to author's intention in ruling out canonical meanings clearly *is* an instance of the intentional fallacy, according to Wimsatt and Beardsley's definition—it is Sawyer's christological interpretation of Isaiah 7 rather than McEvenue's strictures against canonical meanings that accord with the passages I quoted from 'IFal' above. Or again, it is difficult to imagine H-G Gadamer or Roland Barthes endorsing McEvenue's view that 'Nothing will be considered a meaning of a text unless the author of the text intended that meaning', or T.S. Eliot echoing McEvenue's anti-canonical sentiments.[14] Despite his nod towards modern literary theory, McEvenue has entirely missed the direction in which (with a few exceptions, such as Hirsch) its major theorists have been heading.

Of course, McEvenue's failure to give adequate reasons for his views does not show that they are wrong. I end this section, however, by pointing out an uncomfortable dilemma for the pro-intentionalist. It is generally recognized by pro- and anti-intentionalists alike that an author's indications of his or her intentions that occur *outside* the work in question (e.g., statements in the author's autobiography) cannot be of more than heuristic value for the interpretation of that work—one can always, in principle, appeal to the work itself to refute even

---

[14] Cf. Barton's discussion of Eliot in *Reading*, pp. 151–53.

its own author's explanation of its meaning. It seems, therefore, that an argument for intentionality will have to be a defence of author's intention insofar as it manifests itself *within* the work itself. But once this much has been granted, author's intention seems to have been reduced to a hermeneutically-superfluous concept. If a text's meaning is, as Hirsch claims, 'what the author meant [i.e., intended] by his use of a particular sign-sequence', and yet this intention is only relevant insofar as it is manifested in the sign sequence itself, does not interpretation come down after all *just* to studying the signs, without any further scruples about what the author intended? Or as Wimsatt and Beardsley crisply argue:

> How is [the critic] to find out what the poet [intended] to do? If the poet succeeded in doing it, then the poem itself shows what he was trying to do. And if the poet did not succeed, then the poem is not adequate evidence, and the critic must go outside the poem—for evidence of an intention that did not become effective in the poem.[15]

It is not difficult to illustrate this point from the writings of intentionalists such as Hirsch, because once the discussion gets beyond matters of general principle and starts to consider the concrete details of what the interpreter is actually to do with the text, it soon has to be allowed that, as Hirsch explains, statements about author's intentions must 'be recast in terms of sharable conventions, since we have no direct access to the author's mind'.[16] But once it is admitted that the interpretative procedure must ultimately be explained in terms of 'sharable conventions', everything that the anti-intentionalist wishes seems to have been conceded—interpretation has become entirely a matter of studying 'the text itself', with its author nowhere in view.

The fundamental problem, then, which the pro-intentionalist has to solve is to show that there is a relationship between meaning and intention which, on the one hand, avoids those versions of intentionalism that are now generally recognized to be fallacious, and yet, on the other hand, does not achieve this by giving such a 'thin' account of intentions as to become anti-intentionalist in all but name. It is to this problem that the next section is addressed.

---

[15] 'IFal', p. 2.
[16] *Validity*, p. 99.

## 2. *Meaning and Context*

We have already noted that the relationship between the meaning of
a text and its author's intentions[17] is a recurrent theme in several
schools of modern criticism. If this were followed up in detail it would
take us into many diverse aspects of literary theory and linguistics;
but unfortunately this is not possible within the scope of the present
work. Instead I shall explore the essentials of this subject, insofar as
it impinges upon Childs' work, by first considering two specific examples of the dependence of meaning upon context which apparently
lead to quite different (and incompatible) conclusions, and by then
showing why one of these examples is in fact misleading.

The first example, then, is provided by Caiaphas' statement[18] in
John 11:50 that 'It is expedient for you that one man should die for
the people, and that the whole nation should not perish'. This is
presented in John's Gospel in such a way that two quite different
meanings can be found in it. On the one hand, enough of the original context is recorded to enable us to discern what Caiaphas himself intended by it: Addressed to a council of chief priests and Phari-
sees, its meaning can be paraphrased as, 'It is expedient that Jesus
should die, because then we, the Jewish nation, will retain the advantages of the present status-quo; whereas otherwise the Romans
will very likely destroy Jerusalem'. By Caiaphas' utterance being
described as a 'prophecy', however, we are invited to find a Christian meaning in it; and following the text's own hints (11:51f.), we
see that it can also be paraphrased as, '. . . because through Jesus'
death we who believe gain eternal life, whereas otherwise we would
be eternally lost'. Obviously this is *not* a meaning that Caiaphas himself intended; and yet it seems difficult to deny that, in its present
literary context, this *is* (part of) what his utterance means. That it
had originally been authored without any such thoughts in mind makes
no difference; its meaning was not tied to Caiaphas' intentions. Or
as Wimsatt and Beardsley put it:

> The poem is not the critic's own and not the author's (it is detached
> from the author at birth and goes about the world beyond his power

---

[17] More precisely, I am concerned here with what Brett calls 'communicative
intentions'.

[18] To keep the example straightforward, I shall discuss this as though John has
accurately reported a real, historical event. Whether this is really the case makes no
difference to the methodological issues being considered here.

to intend about it or control it). The poem belongs to the public. It is embodied in language, the peculiar possession of the public. . . .[19]

Having given his utterance to 'the public', through expressing it in the public language, Caiaphas could not prevent it from acquiring new meanings.

My second, contrary, example is drawn from Thomas Kuhn. In the Preface to *The Essential Tension*, Kuhn gives an illuminating account of his struggles to understand Aristotle's *Physics*. Being already well acquainted with the Newtonian revolution, Kuhn was not surprised to find that much of what Aristotle had written was wrong. What did puzzle him, however, was that it often seemed patently absurd, in a way that was quite uncharactcristic of his other work:

> When dealing with subjects other than physics, Aristotle had been an acute and naturalistic observer. In such fields as biology or political behaviour, his interpretations of phenomena had often been, in addition, both penetrating and deep. How could his characteristic talents have failed him so when applied to motion? How could he have said about it so many apparently absurd things? And, above all, why had his views been taken so seriously for so long a time by so many of his successors?[20]

Kuhn found the solution to these puzzles when he realized that Aristotle's subject was not motion as such but change-of-state in general—including changes as diverse as the fall of a stone and the growth of a child. Within this broad field motion, as change of position, 'was at best a still-not-quite-isolable special case' (*ibid.*). Rereading Aristotle from this new perspective transformed Kuhn's understanding:

> Strained metaphors often became naturalistic reports, and much apparent absurdity vanished. . . . Thereafter I had few problems understanding why Aristotle had said what he did about motion or why his statements had been taken so seriously. I still recognised difficulties in his physics, but they were not blatant and few of them could properly be characterised as mere mistakes. (p. xii)

In my view this example graphically illustrates what will happen, in general, when a text is read in a linguistic or conceptual context that is significantly different from that which its author intended. This is how Kuhn at first tried to read Aristotle, in so far as he imposed upon the text a concept of 'motion' that was quite different from

---

[19] 'IFal', p. 3.
[20] *The Essential Tension* (Chicago: Chicago University Press, 1970), p. xi.

Aristotle's. The result was that the meanings which Kuhn then found were hardly worth discovering; and it is not difficult to see why. Linguistic communication is only possible if author and reader have *shared conventions* about the meaning of words and about how they may be combined. When Aristotle made his customarily-astute observations on change-of-state in general, he was able to write a book that accurately expressed his thoughts by choosing words with the correct semantic values, arranging them in grammatically correct sequences, etc.;[21] and since his contemporaries were familiar with these same linguistic conventions they were able to understand him correctly, and therefore recognized his *Physics* as a serious contribution to the subject. By contrast, when Kuhn (inadvertently) imported his modern concept of motion into this same text he introduced into Aristotle's carefully-orchestrated linguistic performance disruptions that were quite arbitrary, in that they made semantic changes which Aristotle could have in no way anticipated or allowed for. More precisely, Kuhn changed the referent of certain key terms, so that what in the writing of the *Physics* had been astute observations about change-of-state in general became in the reading of it similar observations about a neo-Newtonian concept of motion. But remarks that are insightful and illuminating observations about the former may well be completely misguided as comments upon the latter. Thus it is entirely to be expected that Kuhn's recontextualising of Aristotle produced not just different meanings but *degraded* meanings, with insights being reduced to absurdities.

With this mind, it is easy to see that the first example discussed above does not in fact support an anti-intentionalist position after all. The reason why Caiaphas' saying yields two intelligent meanings is because each meaning had its own author. John *intentionally* authored a second meaning through placing the saying in an *appropriate* context—that is, one in which its comments on dying and perishing cohered with the themes of its new setting, and which provided suitable referents for its noun phrases ('one man', 'the people'), etc. If, on the contrary, it had fallen at random into, say, a scientific textbook, or a telephone directory, then its meaning would have been

---

[21] Semantics and grammar, of course, are not the only means through which a text can communicate. A full account would also have to reckon with the contributions made by genre, rhythm, figures of speech, etc.; but this is unnecessary for my present purposes, since the added complications would not introduce any new principles.

degraded in just the same way as the second example illustrated. Very few contexts can supply just what this sentence needs in order to make good sense, and they therefore have to be deliberately, intentionally, chosen.

What I am arguing, then, is that author's intention is a 'Regulative Principle' for correct interpretation. A text is an instantiation of some particular language-system, with reference to which the author made certain choices in producing his or her text—the author selects from among the options that are available in that language, arranging its components in such a way as to express the desired meaning.[22] It will therefore be through interpreting a text in relation to the milieu of its production that the most worthwhile meanings will be found in it—alternative contexts are inherently inferior because they will yield inferior meanings.

The preceding discussion can be summed up and generalized a little by introducing the idea of a text's 'intentional context'—i.e., the linguistic, social, and cultural context in relation to which the author's intentions were exercised in producing that text. Scholars who believe that author's intention must be taken into account in interpreting a text often speak of reading it 'in its original context'; but in fact some further complications can arise here. If, for example, a modern author were to write a play in Elizabethan English, then it would have to be read in accordance with the conventions of *that* era, rather than the author's, in order to appreciate it full meaning, because these are the conventions in relation to which the author's intentions were exercised. So then, the case we have argued here can be summed up by saying that a text's intentional context is hermeneutically privileged, because it is through being interpreted in relation to this context that it yields its maximal meaning.[23]

Yet although the preceding discussion has argued that meaning cannot be separated from author's intention, its conclusions are

---

[22] I am of course aware that, without further qualification, this would be an unduly 'mechanical' account of writing—an author is not, for example, *completely* restricted to using words in their 'dictionary definition' sense, but can use language creatively to extend its range or add more subtle nuances. I shall say more about this in section 8.2 below, where it will become clear that these additional complications do not affect the point that is being made here.

[23] In practice, of course, the intentional context will often be the original context, and I will therefore use the more familiar terminology when no confusion can arise. The importance of the more precise concept will nonetheless become clear as the discussion proceeds.

significantly different from certain other well-known intentionalist proposals. In particular, I am *not* suggesting that the aim of interpretation is to recreate the author's inner life or thought processes;[24] nor am I claiming that the meaning of a text is decided by appealing to what may be known about the author's intentions from sources outside the text. Both these latter positions are forms of what might be called 'the (auto)biographical fallacy', in that they misconstrue the relationship between (auto)biographical information about the author's intentions as they stand *apart* from the text and the intentions that come to expression *in* the text.[25] On the one hand, although an author may *sometimes* pour his inner life into his work, so that the text becomes a mirror of his soul, he may also adopt a highly stylized form of presentation that hides his individuality behind the conventions of the genre, or may present his work through an 'implied author' whose personality is quite different from his own. To define the aim of interpretation, therefore, as the reading of a text as a fragment from the author's autobiography is to saddle hermeneutics with a task which, in many cases, cannot be performed. And on the other hand, although it may be of considerable heuristic value when interpreting a certain novel to learn from the author's diary that she intended her leading character to display a certain kind of quiet fortitude in the face of life's troubles, this can only be accepted as part of the novel's meaning insofar as the text itself succeeds in portraying such fortitude (rather than conveying an attitude of fatalistic resignation or suppressed resentment), and is accepted precisely *because* it is 'there in the text', not because the author had said elsewhere that this is what she intended it to mean. But in contrast to these fallacies, the point of author's intention as a Regulative Principle is that since meanings are expressed through an intentional ordering of the available linguistic and historical resources, a satisfactory explication of a text's meaning must be compatible with its author *intending* it to have that meaning—

---

[24] *Contra* Emilio Betti: 'What occurs [in interpretation], then, is an inversion of the creative process: in the hermeneutical process the interpreter retraces the steps from the opposite direction by re-thinking them in his inner self. . . . [T]he interpreter is called upon to reconstruct a thought and recreate it from within himself, making it his own. . . .' ('Hermeneutics as the General Methodology of the *Geisteswissenschaften*', in Joseph Bleicher (ed.), *Contemporary Hermeneutics: Hermeneutics as Method, Philosophy, and Critique* (London: Routledge, 1980), p. 57).

[25] This, in part, is also what Wimsatt and Beardsley argue in 'The Intentional Fallacy'. I accept these conclusions but think that their title is unfortunate, because it suggests that *every* kind of appeal to author's intention is fallacious.

in particular, it must cohere with what can be known about the author's linguistic competence and historical situatedness.[26] It follows, therefore that 'the author cannot have intended that!' *is* a methodologically legitimate objection to a proposed interpretation.

A further point which follows on directly from this is that the relationship between meaning and intention permits inferences to be made in both directions; that is, both from intention to meaning *and* vice versa. Thus if, for example, a pair of disparate documents were simply set next to each other then it would make little sense to attempt to read them 'canonically' in the hope or expectation of finding a higher level of meaning in their juxtaposition, because, *ex hypothesi*, no-one *intended* (i.e., authored) further meanings at this level. But conversely, if a careful exegesis shows that there *are* meanings at the canonical level then this is of itself strong evidence that, whatever prehistory may lie behind its various parts, its present shape has been intentionally produced, and produced, moreover, by an author who *intended* its final form to have these meanings—a few happy accidents aside, there is no other rational explanation as to how it *could* have such meanings.[27] As we shall see presently, this line of argument may have significant implications for Childs' programme.

I shall now make a preliminary assessment of how these considerations relate to Wimsatt and Beardsley, to Childs, and to McEvenue. Firstly, then, Wimsatt and Beardsley's claim that, if the history of a word *after* a poem is written makes a relevant contribution to its meaning, then it 'should not be ruled out by a scruple about intention' envisages a situation which in practice will almost never arise. Meanings which the words of a poem acquired only subsequently to its composition cannot have been encompassed within its author's intentions, and are therefore far more likely to cut across and disrupt the original patterns, and hence degrade the meaning, than to make

---

[26] As this reference to linguistic competence implies, I am including in 'author's intention' not only things that are *consciously* intended but also subconscious and unconscious intentions—anyone writing in their native tongue does not *consciously* think out, for example, many of the grammatical details of their sentences. For the argument being developed in this section the salient notion is of the author as productive agent, as this is what explains why the author's text has just these particular characteristics. Whether the author produced them consciously or unconsciously is of no consequence here.

[27] These principles, it will now be recognized, were implicit in my discussion of the Joseph and Tamar stories in section 6.4 above, which therefore provides an illustration of the case I have argued here.

a positive contribution. This is illustrated very clearly by the Kuhn-Aristotle example.

Secondly, Childs' anti-intentionalist defence of the final form does not seem to be viable.[28] If he is right in claiming that, for some parts of the Old Testament, 'the canonical shaping depends largely upon what appear to be unintentional factors which subsequently were incorporated within a canonical context',[29] then this is a very strong reason for expecting there to be little worthwhile meaning at the canonical level, and therefore for adopting a 'behind the text' policy (in these instances) that tries to recover a level where intentional factors *were* prevalent.

There are in fact signs in Childs' more recent writings that he is becoming less inclined to appeal to unintended meanings. Thus although in *BTONT* Childs repeats from *NTCI* his view that, 'in spite of the lack of a single editorial intentionality', the juxtaposition of the four Gospels within the one canonical context is hermeneutically significant (p. 75), very little further use is made of this idea (although *prima facie* it would have been particularly pertinent to his Biblical Theology). And on the other side of this coin, it is in his *Theologies* that Childs most clearly recognizes that it would be very damaging to the canonical approach if 'the present form of the text is merely a cover for the real political forces which lie behind it',[30] and in which he correspondingly seems more willing than before to engage in historical-critical argument with alternative reconstructions of the underlying traditions.[31] Yet even if Childs does prove to be largely successful in these critical debates, we saw at the beginning of this chapter that there are a number of other important problems—in particular, the legitimacy of interpreting the Old Testament christologically—which cannot be solved in this way. If, as I have now argued, they also cannot be solved by separating meaning from author's intention, either the aims of Childs' programme will have to

---

[28] We saw in section 3.2 that Childs' anti-intentionalism apparently denies the relevance of both communicative intentions and motivations. This chapter has only been concerned with the former; yet since it has argued against the kind of formalism with which, in this strand of his thought, Childs apparently wishes to displace questions about the author's motivations, this second aspect of his anti-intentionalism is also called into question.
[29] *IOTS* p. 79.
[30] *OTTCC*, p. 148.
[31] E.g., *OTTCC* pp. 145–49, 176–77; *BTONT* pp. 182–83, 413–20.

be significantly curtailed or some other way of achieving them will have to be found.

Thirdly, McEvenue is basically correct, in my view, to claim that

> Where an editor has simply collected texts side by side without meaning anything further, then no further meaning can be said to be biblical. . . . One must *show* that a unit is not just an anthology, but is an intended structure with meaning.[32]

This goes a bit too far in that, if a certain meaning can be demonstrated at the 'anthological' level by sound exegetical arguments then, even if it did arise as an unintended consequence of certain texts being collected together, it is still a biblical meaning (i.e., a meaning that can be shown to be present in the Bible as we now have it). In the light of the preceding discussion, however, the point to make is that such meanings are highly improbable, and will therefore only occur very rarely, if at all. Thus a scholar who devoted his or her career to finding meanings at the anthological level would be largely wasting their time; and to propose 'the anthology' as the basic hermeneutical principle for a new Biblical Theology would be a grave methodological error—as McEvenue more or less realizes, there would be very little worthwhile meaning at that level.

But granting this, it still has to be asked how damaging McEvenue's argument is to Childs' programme. In the first place, the biblical canon is not a mere anthology. The New Testament, quite consciously, makes extensive use of the Old, drawing teaching and examples from it, and offering its own interpretations of it. Thus far from the collecting together of the New Testament writings with the Old Testament being a mere anthologizing, it would be more accurate to describe the New Testament, from the point of view of its literary relationship, as a reflective supplementing of the Old;[33] and it is therefore by no means as strange as McEvenue suggests that the two Testaments be read together as a single canon. Of course, one also has to consider how adequate was the New Testament's use of the Old, and how this might affect the sense in which *we* can read both Testaments as a single canon—one might ask, for example, whether Hebrews sufficiently respects the integrity of the Old Testament witness, and whether we might, in some respects, have to part company from it. These

---

[32] P. 238, McEvenue's italics.

[33] This, of course, by no means covers all aspects of the relationship between the Testaments. These issues will have to be discussed more fully in subsequent chapters.

questions will be taken up in subsequent chapters; but the point to make here is that canonical meanings cannot be ruled out by dismissing the canon as a mere anthology.

Secondly, it is questionable whether Childs is as dependent upon new meanings emerging at the canonical level as McEvenue assumes. Childs' messianic interpretation of David, for example, *does* respect the meanings of the words in their original contexts, and of the source documents into which (Childs accepts) 2 Samuel should be analysed; the messianic meaning emerges (as we saw in section 3.2 above) from the tensions that arise when these sources are juxtaposed. Now in the light of the preceding discussion I would argue that, if we are persuaded by Childs' messianic exegesis of the final form, then whoever put the final text together in this way must have *intended* it to have such a meaning; but this argument does not seem to raise any particular difficulties for Childs. His messianic interpretation of David does not depend upon claiming that there are 'meanings that no-one meant' at the canonical level.

It is not altogether clear what McEvenue himself would say about this particular example, although the second of his three exegetical principles does seem to be intended to at least curtail the scope for making such interpretations. This principle, it will be recalled, claims that 'Biblical meanings are illuminated by their historical context *and* defined or limited by their historical context';[34] and in illustrating what he means by this McEvenue suggests that if the intended meaning of the ark narrative is that God was radically free in his choice of David then this must not be further interpreted as God being free in his choice of Solomon, or of Josiah, or Jesus (pp. 239–40). Unfortunately, however, there are significant ambiguities as to what McEvenue's principle is claiming and what its status is. From his initial *statement* of the principle, it can most naturally be taken as a linguistic rule which claims that, for example, the words of 2 Samuel must be understood with the senses they had in the situation in which they were written (rather than having nuances from modern Hebrew imported into them), that allusions to kingship must be interpreted in relation to ancient Near Eastern (rather than medieval or Renaissance) monarchies, etc. This of course is true; but Childs *does* observe these constraints, and yet he is still able to interpret David as a messianic prefigurement. McEvenue's *illustration* of his principle, how-

---

[34] P. 239; McEvenue's italics.

ever, suggests that it is not only meanings that, in his view, are 'defined or limited by their historical contexts', but references also—a preexilic story about one of Israel's early kings cannot be referring to Jesus.

But even if we allow McEvenue to extend his principle into a restriction of both meaning *and* reference to 'the original context', would it even then cause methodological problems for Childs' messianic interpretation of the Old Testament? The answer would seem to depend, on the one hand, upon how specific a messianic anticipation Childs would want to find in such passages as 2 Samuel and Isaiah 53, and on the other hand, how restrictively McEvenue would construe his second principle. Unfortunately neither scholar analyses these issues as fully or as clearly as one might wish; but in order to advance the methodological discussion, I shall suggest (at the risk of making some rather broad generalizations) what the main alternatives might be. On the one hand, most scholars would presumably have little difficulty, in principle, with accepting a messianic interpretation of the Davidic narratives if this were understood as no more than an expression of hope, expectation, or belief by the narrator that at some future time a king similar in kind to David but far greater than he would rule over Israel. There appears to be no reason why this need be incompatible with McEvenue's strictures about meanings being 'defined or limited by their historical contexts', or with the limitations that historical context sets upon reference—no-one would want to construe these limitations so restrictively as to deny that Hebrew is capable of expressing future-oriented hopes and beliefs. This, in fact, seems adequate to account for Childs' messianic interpretation of David in *OTTCC*.

This sort of broad messianic expectation, however, is hardly adequate for Childs' full conception of *Biblical* Theology, the distinctive claim of which is that 'both Old Testament and New Testament bear truthful witness *to Jesus Christ*', albeit 'in different ways'.[35] We have already seen that this raises a number of complex problems, which will have to be discussed in later chapters; but for the specific issue we are considering here, enough can be gleaned from Childs' comments on Isaiah 53. Discussing how a biblical text may be interpreted in the light of a fuller understanding of God gained from the whole Bible, Childs is careful to point out that the distinctively Old Testament voice of Isaiah 53 cannot be heard if its witness 'is directly

---

[35] *BTONT* p. 477; italics added.

identified with the passion of Jesus Christ' (p. 382); and yet

> to know the will of God in Jesus Christ opens up a profoundly new
> vista on this prophetic testimony to God who 'laid on him (the ser-
> vant) the iniquity of us all... whose will it was to bruise him and to
> put him to grief'. For those who confess the Lordship of Jesus Christ
> there is an immediate morphological fit.[36]

Childs' idea seems to be that there is a correspondence between the
pattern or structure of the suffering servant's afflictions and Jesus'
passion; and although to describe Isaiah 53 as a *prediction* of Christ's
sufferings would impose more upon Childs than he would himself
claim, he does seem to find here a strong presentiment of them which,
in terms of the specificity of its referent and its fullness of detail, goes
considerably further than the messianic expectations we considered
above. The question that has to be asked, therefore, is whether there
are methodological reasons for ruling out such interpretations of the
Old Testament.

According to Childs' interpretation of Isaiah 53, this passage gives
an accurate delineation of events which, at the time it was written,
were still in the distant future. In other words, it displays a measure
of foreknowledge that exceeds the capacities of normal human knowing; and without in any way trying to judge whether this helped to
motivate McEvenue's reinterpretation of his second principle from a
restriction upon meaning to a restriction upon reference, it is of
methodological interest to ask whether the reinterpreted version of
his principle offers a sound objection to Childs' 'prophetic' interpretation of Isaiah 53.

In this connection there are two comments to make. First, as a
restriction upon meaning McEvenue's second principle is, as we have
seen, linguistically well motivated; but when it is reinterpreted as a
restriction upon reference it would, if construed restrictively enough
to rule out foreknowledge, cease to be a *linguistic* principle—there is
nothing about the Hebrew language as such which prevents one from
making true statements about the future. At the very least, then, this
leaves the principle in need of a justification quite different in kind
from the issues discussed in McEvenue's article. But secondly, if the
reinterpreted principle is used this restrictively then it seems very
dubious anyway—it then looks suspiciously like a version of Troeltschean analogy, which stipulates in advance that the Old Testament

---

[36] *Ibid.*; the parentheses and ellipses are Childs'.

writings, 'like any other book', cannot display genuine foreknowledge. This, however, is open to the same objection that we raised in section 5.1 above: Used in this way analogy is not a legitimate methodological principle, because it decides substantive issues of interpretation (in this case, of textual meaning) *a priori*, without needing to look at the linguistic or exegetical arguments that might be offered in any particular case. In other words, it completely begs the question.

To sum up this part of the argument, then: The main points to emerge from our discussion of McEvenue's second principle are (i) that the meaning of a text must be sought, in the first instance,[37] from the meanings of its words in their original context; and (ii) that McEvenue's principle offers no sound reason why a text should not be interpreted as showing genuine foreknowledge of the future. Of course, a text which is plainly about David should not be *arbitrarily* taken as referring to Josiah or Jesus as well,[38] and the onus therefore lies upon anyone who claims such references to give supporting arguments; but I can see nothing here which, as a matter of methodological principle, would cause any problems for Childs.

Turning now to a different line of argument, it might be suggested that Childs' interpretation of Isaiah 53 is nonetheless ruled out by McEvenue's *first* principle: Since 'a satisfactory explication of a text's meaning must be compatible with its author *intending* it to have that meaning', and since the author of Isaiah 53 had no knowledge of Jesus's passion, he could not have intended to write about that event; therefore his text cannot be interpreted as referring to it. This argument is logically impeccable; but as I pointed out above, the connection between intention and meaning permits inferences in both directions, and this allows a defender of Childs to make the following reply: A thorough exegetical study of Isaiah 53 shows that in fact it *does* display accurate foreknowledge of Jesus' passion; this would be impossible if the text was produced by merely *human* authorship; therefore we have strong exegetical reason to believe that it was not so produced—there must also have been a divine element in its authorship.

---

[37] 'In the first instance' is included to cover the special cases that will be discussed in chapter 11 below. This does not materially affect the argument of the present section.

[38] Perhaps, after all, McEvenue intended nothing more than this by the reinterpreted version of his principle; although it is difficult to imagine who, among the likely readership of his article, would need to have this pointed out to them.

Which of these arguments is the more persuasive need not be discussed here, since we are concerned with methodological principles rather than with the actual interpretation of Isaiah 53. The methodological point to emerge from this discussion is that if Childs' belief that the Old Testament bears witness to Christ is to be filled out into something more specific than a general presentiment of a coming Messiah—and both the New Testament and the christian church, for most of its history, has found a much more specific witness in the Old Testament than that—then Childs will need to develop quite a 'strong' doctrine of biblical inspiration. Only *divine* authorship could account for the meanings that Childs wishes to find in the Bible.

Childs has said very little about biblical inspiration, although there is one significant comment in his 'Critical Reflections on James Barr's Understanding of the Literal and the Allegorical'. Contrasting the pre- and post-Enlightenment views of the Bible, Childs illustrates the former position from the work of Origen, for whom

> The biblical text possessed ... different levels of meaning by which divine truth was reached. These levels stemmed intentionally from the divine author who had so formed Scripture as to provide a multiple entry into the mysteries of the faith. (p. 4)

Childs further adds that 'Origen remains a classic example of an exegete who held to a theory of verbal inspiration' (*ibid.*); and although this does not go so far as to commit Childs himself to such a doctrine, it is certainly suggestive of the direction in which he may need to move in order to hear the Old Testament as a witness to Christ. In the present section we have seen that there are strong methodological reasons why this is in fact the case.

### 3. *Reader-Centred Hermeneutics*[39]

The final subject to discuss in this chapter is reader-response theory. We have already seen in section 3.3 that, *prima facie*, this has much to offer Childs: If 'interpretation in faith' can be explained as a kind of reading strategy, then Stendahl's dichotomy is finally overcome and yet fideism is avoided.

There are many different forms of reader-response theory,[40] but I

---

[39] I am grateful to Dr. Mark G. Brett for his comments upon an earlier version of this section.

[40] For a general survey, see S.R. Suleiman, 'Varieties of Audience-Oriented

shall concentrate exclusively upon Stanley Fish's version,[41] which appears particularly promising for Childs. In *Is There a Text in the Class?*[42] Fish argues that

> the identification of what was real and normative occurred within interpretive communities and what was normative for members of one community would be seen as strange . . . by the members of another. In other words, there is no single way of reading that is correct or natural, only 'ways of reading' that are extensions of community perspectives.[43]

This sounds remarkably similar to Childs' claim that, although there are many different ways in which the biblical documents *can* be read, theologians *ought* to read them 'in faith', from the perspective of the Christian community.

Fish's primary argument focuses upon one particular example, which, according to his analysis, shows the non-objective, reader-dependence of the meaning of a text. Fish recalls (p. 322) how he used to teach two successive courses in the same classroom. The first was on the relationship between linguistics and literary criticism, and in one such class he wrote the following on the board:

Jacobs-Rosenbaum

Levin

Thorne

Hayes

Ohman (?)

---

Criticism', in Suleiman and I. Crosman (eds.), *The Reader in the Text: Essays on Audience and Interpretation* (Princeton: Princeton University Press, 1981), pp. 3–45. Many different approaches are represented by the articles in the Suleiman and Crosan volume, and also in Jane P. Tompkins (ed.), *Reader-Response Criticism: From Formalism to Post-Structuralism* (Baltimore: Johns Hopkins University Press, 1980). For a survey oriented towards Biblical Studies see Mark G. Brett, 'The Future of Reader Criticisms?', in Francis Watson (ed.), *The Open Text: New Directions for Biblical Studies?* (London: SCM, 1993), pp. 13–31.

[41] I have discussed this much more fully in 'Hermeneutics and Postmodernism: Can We Have a Radical Reader-Response Theory?', Parts I and II. In addition to any relevance Fish's theories may have for Childs' programme, they also merit discussion because a number of New Testament scholars have recently suggested that they are of value to Biblical Studies more generally; see 'Hermeneutics (I)', p. 420 nn. 4–5 for further details. In *BTONT* Childs himself refers, non-committally, to Fish as '[having] developed a sophisticated analysis of "reader-response"' (p. 202).

[42] *Is There a Text in This Class?: The Authority of Interpretive Communities* (Cambridge, MA: Harvard University Press, 1980); cf. Fish's *Doing What Comes Naturally: Change, Rhetoric, and the Practice of Theory in Literary and Legal Studies* (Oxford: Clarendon, 1989).

[43] *Text*, pp. 15–16.

These were the authors or editors of various textbooks on linguistics, which Fish set his students to read as an assignment. ('Jacobs' and 'Rosenbaum' were in fact two such scholars who had jointly written and edited a number of books. The question-mark after 'Ohman' reflects Fish's uncertainty about its spelling, which should in fact have been 'Ohmann'.) The second course was on religious poetry; so Fish told this class that the assignment was a religious poem, and invited their interpretations. These the students provided both readily and abundantly; and since they are important for the point I shall make, I will quote Fish's description of them at length:

> The first line of the poem . . . received the most attention: Jacobs was explicated as a reference to Jacob's ladder, traditionally allegorized as a figure for the Christian ascent to heaven. In this poem, however, . . . the means of ascent was not a ladder but a tree, a rose tree or rosenbaum. This was seen to be an obvious reference to the Virgin Mary who was often characterised as a rose without thorns. . . . At this point the poem appeared to the students to be operating as an icono-graphic riddle. It at once posed the question, 'How is it that a man can climb to heaven by means of a rosetree?' and directed the reader to the inevitable answer: by the fruit of that tree, the fruit of Mary's womb, Jesus. Once this interpretation was established it received support from, and conferred significance on, the word 'thorne', which could only be an allusion to the crown of thorns. (p. 324)

In other words, the students were easily able to read this assignment as a poem, once they were convinced (through Fish priming them) that this was how it ought to be read.

From this example Fish develops a strong polemic against the reader-independence of meaning. One widely believed account of how one knows that a certain text is a literary work is that one recognizes in it various characteristics which distinguish poems from other kinds of writing. This, Fish claims, is completely undermined by his example, which shows that 'poetic features' are not objectively 'in the text itself', but are *created* through the prior expectations which the reader brings to the text; therefore (Fish concludes) 'Interpreters do not decode poems: they make them' (p. 327). And by parity of reasoning, this text is not objectively an assignment either, but becomes one through being interpreted by means of the appropriate prior beliefs.

One obvious objection to Fish's position is that it leads to an unacceptable form of relativism that would undermine serious liter-ary debate: Each interpreter simply reads in his or her own way, and 'how it seems to me' is not open to inter-personal criticism.

Fish, however, strenuously denies that his position entails this, because

> the means by which [objects] are made are social and conventional. That is, the 'you' who does the interpretive work that puts poems and assignments and lists into the world is a communal you and not an isolated individual. (p. 331)

So, readers who are members of the same literary community will use quite similar interpretative strategies; therefore each will constitute essentially the text, about which there can then be rational argument. An important corollary of this, however, is that although Fish rejects a relativism with respect to individuals, he does so only by embracing a thoroughgoing community-relativism.

To many biblical scholars this last step in the argument will perhaps seem unduly paradoxical; yet even here we are still traversing ground where plausible analogies can be found between Fish and Childs. We have seen that a recurrent theme in the latter's work is his respect for Jewish interpretations of the Hebrew Bible, which does not 'naturally' unfold into the New Testament but is read by both Jews and Christians in the context of their respective traditions.[44] Translating this into a Fishian idiom, one would say that the Jewish and Christian interpretative communities each come to the Hebrew Scriptures with their own distinct reading-strategies, and therefore each constitutes its meaning in their own way. Neither can claim, in some transcendental sense, to be '*the* correct interpretation' (the writings do not lean towards one or the other); but insofar as each makes a serious attempt, within its own terms of reference, to wrestle with the meaning of these Scriptures, it can be respected as a valid response to the text.

This would perhaps sound attractive to Childs; yet if he were to accept this much help from Fish it would be very difficult for him then to avoid being led on to some much more unpalatable conclusions. From a Fishian perspective the Jewish and Christian interpretative communities cannot claim to be hermeneutically privileged in their readings of the Hebrew scriptures in any way that would set them apart from, say, the Qumranite, Buddhist, Humanist, or Marxist communities—provided that each is self-consistent in carrying out the interpretative task, in the terms in which they conceive it, then each of their readings is equally valid. The question of which reading

---

[44] See section 3.4 above.

is 'really correct' cannot be raised, because this would be tantamount to asking what the Scriptures mean when considered apart from how any particular community reads them; and in reader-response terms this is not a coherent request. Therefore as regards the correctness of the various community interpretations, there is nothing more ultimate to be said than that each is 'right' in its own terms.[45] This, however, would be an extreme version of the very fideism which Childs has always vehemently repudiated, a fideism of 'the pre-Gabler days when preconceived theological systems silenced the literal meaning of the text'.[46] Fish's hermeneutics implies that Gabler and his critical successors were fundamentally mistaken in thinking that there is a literal (or any other kind of) meaning of 'the text itself'—as the 'Jacobs-Rosenbaum . . .' example graphically illustrates, one cannot *but* read a text through a 'preconceived system' of some kind, which thereby *makes* it into a text of that kind. But for Childs to accept this would fundamentally change the character of his programme.

The consequences of Fish's hermeneutics for Biblical Studies[47] have recently been explored by Anthony Thiselton, who sees them as a prime example of a 'socio-pragmatic' (as opposed to a 'socio-critical') theory—i.e., it is a hermeneutics in which the text, being read in the light of an individual's or a community's beliefs, reflects and affirms them (as opposed to a hermeneutics which allows the text to offer a critique of those beliefs 'from outside').[48] Fish's socio-pragmatism (Thiselton argues) would make '[p]rophetic address as that which comes "from beyond"' a virtual impossibility, since it is ultimately 'the community itself [which] has created the word'. Similarly, there could be no revelation as a 'given' that stands over against the community; and since interpretation is not a search for 'authentic meanings of biblical texts', disagreements between different religious communities,

---

[45] See especially Fish's succinct statement of this point in *Text*, p. 174.

[46] 'IF', p. 438; cf. *NTCI*, p. 37.

[47] Fish himself has repeatedly argued that his hermeneutical theories cannot have any consequences for critical practice (*Text*, pp. 318–21; *Doing*, pp. 14–15, 26–29, 153–57, 322–25, 347–51, etc.). This conclusion is endorsed by Brett ('Future', pp. 16–17), but I have argued elsewhere that Fish is wrong on this point ('Hermeneutics (I)', section i).

[48] For Thiselton's explanation of the 'socio-pragmatic'/'socio-critical' distinction (which appears to be an interesting development of the traditional distinction between eisegesis and exegesis) see *NHH* pp. 6, 7, 27–28, 379; on Fish see especially pp. 515–16, 537–50.

such as occurred during the Reformation, become 'a dispute over alternative community life-styles'.[49]

Thiselton considers these to be 'disastrous entailments for Christian theology' (*ibid.*); but without casting our net as wide as this, we can certainly say that they would be disastrous for Childs' belief in a normative Bible which '[bears] truthful witness to Jesus Christ' as an independent reality. On Fish's theory the Church is necessarily its own ultimate authority, whatever doctrine of biblical authority it may profess—the Bible can only mean what the Church interprets it to mean, and it does indeed have that meaning through the church interpreting it in that way. This is not at all the sort of normativity that Childs advocates.

So then, far from Fish's reader-centred hermeneutics saving Childs' programme from its tensions between Faith and Reason, it is something that Childs needs to be saved from. This I shall now try to do, by arguing (i) that Fish's hermeneutics have solipsistic consequences which virtually all scholars, including Fish, would find totally unacceptable; and (ii) that a more careful analysis of Fish's own example shows that there are ways of deciding which interpretation is objectively correct.

I begin, then, with the problem of solipsism.[50] We saw above that it was to avoid this that Fish introduced his notion of the interpretative community; but in my view this solution does not work, because a consistent application of Fish's own hermeneutical principles to the interpretive community itself raises precisely the same difficulty again at a more fundamental level. This problem is in fact half glimpsed by Fish himself when he asks the seemingly innocuous question, 'how can any one of us know whether or not he is a member of the same interpretive community as any other of us?'. To this he gives the extraordinary response,

> The answer is that he can't, since *any evidence brought forward to support the claim would itself be an interpretation.* . . . The only 'proof' of membership is fellowship, the nod of recognition from someone in the same community, someone who says to you what neither of us could ever prove to a third party: 'we know'.[51]

Resorting in this way to mystical 'nods of recognition' and empathetic

---

[49] See *NHH* p. 549; I have removed Thiselton's italics from some of these quotations.
[50] Cf. my 'Hermeneutics (I)', section vi.
[51] *Text* p. 173, italics added; cf. pp. 178–79.

acknowledgements is, of course, totally illegitimate, since it violates Fish's own fundamental principle that there is *nothing* that we perceive or apprehend as an uninterpreted 'given'. (If Fish allows unmediated, intuitive recognition of community members, then how could he exclude similarly ineffable apprehensions of a text's true genre or meaning?) Yet if these mystical intuitions are ruled out, then we are forced to conclude that the interpretative community is itself *produced by the individual*: Whatever Professor X may write or do to show that he belongs to the same interpretative community as me only *is* so for me because, in interpreting it thus, I *make* it thus. An interpretative community, however, which is brought into existence through the individual's interpretations, far from being a safeguard against solipsism, leads straight to a thoroughgoing form of solipsism—if the constraints upon interpretation are themselves created by the individual then all interpretation necessarily becomes extremely individualistic.

What this *reductio ad absurdum* of Fish's hermeneutics shows, I believe, is that there is something fundamentally wrong with his notion of interpretation bringing meanings (and facts generally) into existence. Since, however, it would add little to the purposes of this book to analyse these problems further,[52] I shall instead move to my second line of attack against Fish. What I now wish to argue, then, is that contrary to Fish's own analysis of his 'Jacobs-Rosenbaum . . .' example, there *are* ways of deciding which interpretation is objectively correct.[53] As a preliminary step, however, I shall first make a small correction to Fish's account. Fish repeatedly calls the text that he wrote in the first class 'an assignment',[54] but this is inaccurate. To qualify as an assignment it would have to give not only the authors' names but also the titles of the particular pieces that Fish wanted his students to consult, together with some indication of what was to be done with them. What Fish originally wrote, then, was simply a list of names. In this case it was used to set an assignment, but on another occasion the same text could have functioned as, say, a list of scholars invited to submit papers for a colloquium.

Granted this small correction, then, what I am going to argue is that there are overwhelmingly strong reasons for declaring Fish's text

---

[52] I have discussed them at length in 'Hermeneutics (II)', *passim*.

[53] For a much fuller analysis, which raises a number of additional objections to Fish's position that space does not allow me to discuss here, see my 'Hermeneutics (I)', sections ii–iv.

[54] E.g., *Text*, pp. 322, 327, 329.

to be, objectively, not a poem but a list of names, with my 'objectively' implying that *all* reasonable scholars ought to accept my arguments (if I have formulated them correctly) as 'strong reasons'. Before turning to Fish's text, however, I shall first make some methodological comments about how I am going to proceed, because when arguing against a relativist one has to be particularly careful not to beg the question. I have just spoken of there being 'overwhelmingly strong reasons'; but Fish's obvious rejoinder would be that what counts as a strong reason is itself community-relative. Thus for me to appeal to 'strong reasons' as though there were universally binding standards appears to proceed from an assumption which Fish rejects.

In response to this I would make two points. Firstly, since Fish is ostensibly addressing a certain set of reasonably well defined issues in the current debate, he has thereby committed himself to a number of general principles and ideas; therefore to avoid self-contradiction, Fish is obliged to accept them as pertinent considerations when others also appeal to them. More specifically, in advancing a theory about *interpreting* texts Fish must presumably be discussing a notion that is not altogether discontinuous with what other scholars would also recognise as interpretation—otherwise he is simply talking at cross-purposes to the rest of the academic world. Thus he could not have supported his thesis by recalling how he once put *King Lear* through a paper-shredder and discovered that, taking full advantage of the licence for textual rearrangement that this afforded him, he was able to read it as a very persuasive comedy. Processing a text in this way is not *interpreting* it.

Fish himself gives a pertinent example of the constraints an interpreter works under when he tells us that 'Readers of poetry know that no part of a poem can be slighted (the rule is "everything counts") and they do not rest until every part has been given significance' (p. 330). Although Fish offers this as a rule for interpreting poetry it is clearly a canon that must be observed quite generally. It would be a simple matter to 'interpret' *King Lear* or *Is There a Text in This Class?* as a religious poem (or as almost anything else) if whatever obstructed one's chosen reading could be 'slighted'. Such readings, however, would be rejected out of hand by one's professional colleagues precisely because they had 'broken the rules' that constrain and define legitimate interpretation. My first point, then, is that there are certain general constraints that we *all* put ourselves under simply in virtue of offering an *interpretation*; and similarly, if we try to persuade others that a certain text can be interpreted as, say, a religious poem, then we put ourselves under the further constraints of our shared notions of what a religious poem is.

My second methodological comment is that a number of the issues raised by Fish's work are very similar to matters we discussed in chapter 5 above. Fish's case rests on the claim that there is interpretation at *every* level. We have already seen that, according to Fish, literary features do not subsist in the text as 'brute facts', but are produced by the reader's interpretative strategies. Moreover, this cannot be circumvented (Fish claims) by appealing to the actual words of the text, or the marks on the page, as things that are 'just there', because these are also the product of interpretation; and so on right down to the level of atoms.[55] Now I have myself argued in section 4.4 that there is interpretation at every level (although it will be recalled that in my account interpretation *states* facts rather than creating them).[56] Moreover, there is also some measure of truth in Fish's claim that readers who come to the text with different expectations will generally interpret it in different ways. (This can be illustrated by numerous disputes in Biblical Studies.) Where I differ from Fish, however, is that in my view there can be objective argument as to which interpretation is the correct one, which ought to persuade both the disputants. In fact, I developed a methodology for resolving just this sort of dispute in section 5.2 above, where I argued that even scholars who proceed from different fundamental premises can still argue about which of them is objectively correct. In what follows, therefore, I shall apply this methodology to Fish's own example, and thus establish that it (really, objectively) is a list of names, not a poem.

The first step, then, is to show that, *by Fish's own standards of interpretation* (and in particular by his 'everything counts' rule, quoted above), his reading of 'Jacobs-Rosenbaum . . .' is untenable—in other words, that his argument for it being a poem is internally inconsistent. This in fact is easily done, since his interpretation is full of

---

[55] *Text*, p. 331. In his more recent writings Fish has identified this line of argument as the application of anti-foundationalist epistemology to literary theory; see *Doing*, pp. 143–44, 344–45, etc.

[56] The argument I gave for this in section 4.4 would not cut much ice with Fish; at that point I was refuting those who would make a sharp separation between fact and interpretation, rather than those who, like Fish, recognize that they are inseparable but give an incorrect account of *how* they are related. I have, however, shown how my account of fact and interpretation can be turned against Fish in 'Hermeneutics (II)', section iv.

exegetical fallacies. Thus his interpretation of 'Jacobs-Rosenbaum', for example, does not reckon seriously enough with the features that I have underlined. It could perhaps be accepted as an allusion to Jacob's ladder if it had said 'Jacob's Rosenbaum', but unfortunately it does not. Fish simply reads 'Jacobs-' as though it were the genitive of 'Jacob'; but in the absence of any supporting argument this arbitrarily 'slights' what is actually there in the text. Moreover, Fish gives no reason why the German 'Rosenbaum', rather than 'rose-tree', should appear in a poem which he otherwise interprets as being in English. Similarly, no reason is forthcoming as to why the third line, if an allusion to the crown of thorns, is spelt 'Thorne', or why a singular rather than a plural is used; and no interpretation is even attempted of the religiously unpromising 'Hayes'. Nor is the striking '(?)' accounted for; and if it were suggested that this is related to 'Ohman' being triply ambiguous, then the further question arises as to why the doubly ambiguous 'Levin' is not similarly flagged.

But moving on from these important points of detail to some more general considerations of the poem's meaning and structure, the christological allusion that Fish finds in the first line, and which has an important structural role in thematically linking this to the succeeding lines, is simply read into it without textual warrant—'Jacobs-Rosenbaum' makes absolutely no reference to the *fruit* of the rosenbaum. And despite the quite unwarranted exegetical licence that Fish has allowed himself, the poem which emerges is still little more than a loose jumble of vaguely-related ideas. Again this evaluation is based upon Fish's own standards of what a poem ought to be, in that he himself calls attention to supposed conceptual/thematic connections between its parts. Yet the poem is in fact a conceptual/thematic mess, with succeeding lines neither (to any significant degree) cogently developing the ideas of the preceding lines, nor introducing thoughts that are interestingly contrasted or counterpoised, nor shedding further light on the same substance from a different angle, nor forming a progressive narrative, nor doing anything else at all intelligent, insightful, or noteworthy. In short, Fish's attempt at reading 'Jacobs-Rosenbaum . . .' as a religious poem is an exegetical disaster.

The second step in the argument is to show that the alternative interpretation of this text *is* exegetically defensible. Consulting a large collection of names (such as a telephone directory or a library catalogue) would easily establish the viability of taking each item as a proper name; moreover, the physical arrangement of the words on the page is consistent with it being a list. Since, however, it is only a very simple list, without even a heading or title, there is little more that can said about it. Lists *can* have interesting structures (alphabetical ordering being one simple example); but this is not an essential characteristic, so its absence from this text does not militate against it being a list. Neither does the '(?)' against 'Ohman', which is consistent with the sort of cryptic annotations that are sometimes added to a list in order to remind its user of something connected with a particular item (e.g., 'But would Ohman be free on that date?'). What that might be in this case could not be deduced from the text; but this again is quite typical of a list.

Interpreted as a list, then, this is quite a dull text. However, the interpretation *can* be followed through coherently—every feature is easily accounted for in ways that are consistent with it being a list, and even its dullness is of the kind one would expect of a brief, unstructured, untitled list of names. In view of the spectacular failure of the alternative interpretation to follow through, this is not a trivial discovery.

What emerges from this discussion, then, is that, even without appealing to universal or intercommunity standards of literary judgement in ways that would beg the question, it is still possible to give good reasons why this text is, objectively, a list of names rather than a poem: Read as the former it makes coherent and illuminating sense, according to the standards that are appropriate for such lists, whereas trying to read it as a poem is, by its own standards, a chronic failure.

This brings me back, finally, to some further comments on author's intention. Although Fish believes that meaning cannot be separated from author's intention, he further maintains that (in line with his general anti-foundationalist epistemology) authors' intentions, like all other facts, are *created* by interpretation.[57] One consequence of this is that author's intention imposes no independent constraints upon interpretation, as Fish's 'Jacobs-Rosenbaum . . .' example well illustrates: To argue that it is a poem (that is, to constitute it as a poem) *is* to argue that its author intended it to be a poem; but this cannot then be cited as a reason why this same text cannot be interpreted as an assignment (or a novel, or whatever). On the contrary, interpreting

---

[57] See *Text*, pp. 161, 163–64; *Doing*, pp. 98–100, 116–19, 295–96, 299.

it as an assignment thereby constitutes it as an assignment, and in one and the same act also brings into existence an appropriate assignment-intending author.

Since we have now seen that texts are not capable of being reinterpreted in the way Fish claims, it follows that his account of author's intention is oriented towards the wrong issues. The real question is not 'How can author's intention be made compatible with radical textual reinterpretability?', but 'Why does one particular way of reading a given text work far better than another?'. This in fact is easily accounted for by the preceding discussion of author's intention. When Fish wrote his text he intended it to be a reading-list, and therefore shaped it accordingly—whether a particular item appeared on the list was determined by whether it named the author of something which Fish thought it appropriate for his students to read; names were separated or conjoined according to whether the authors had written separate pieces or a joint article; etc. Therefore when it is read *as* a reading-list it makes good sense, because its details were put together precisely with the intention that, when read in this way, they would impart 'reading-list meanings'. But language is inherently rich, and words generally have further meanings and connotations beyond those for which they are being used on any particular occasion. Now of course, a competent author takes account of this when writing his or her text; therefore when it is read in a way which is appropriate for that kind of text, only the relevant meanings are 'actualised'. If, however, the text is read in some other way, then other connotations may be brought out instead—if Fish's text is read as a religious poem then it will be the religious associations of 'Jacobs' that are significant, and the fact that this is also the name of a contemporary linguist will count for nothing. Yet it should also be clear by now why very little coherent sense will emerge when a text is read against the author's intention. Fish did not have the religious connotations of the words in mind when he originally wrote his list; thus the religious dimension that Fish, as author, wove into his text was an entirely random affair. When, therefore, his text is read in such a way as to actualize its religious dimension, what is in fact being actualized is a set of randomly collocated meanings. It is therefore entirely to be expected that, as we have seen, they add up to a minimal amount of cogent religious sense. Random assemblages of words will not yield religious insight; on the contrary, what is needed if a text is to convey worthwhile meanings is that its parts have been carefully ordered so as to embody a meaning;[58] and the only way to get worthwhile meanings out of it, therefore, is to read it in such a way as to respect the ordering that the author gave it—meaning is conveyed through linguistic ordering. This is the *only* way that good sense will be elicited from the text, because it is the only way in which good sense is embodied in it.

Let us summarize, then, the implications of this chapter for Childs' programme. Negatively, we have seen that two apparently promising literary-theoretical ways of justifying Childs' procedures are in fact untenable: (1) The canonical meanings that Childs finds in the juxtaposition of the four Gospels, and his (restrained) christological interpretations of the Old Testament, cannot be defended by separating meaning from author's intention; and (2) Faith-interpretation cannot be explicated as a Fishian reading-strategy. But on the positive side, we have also seen that (1) There is a determinate 'hardness' about texts, such that they resist attempts at misinterpreting them. Although we have not considered here the implications of this for Childs' work, it will emerge subsequently that it may be used in developing an exegetical methodology which *is* faith-informed but is *not* fideistic. (2) It may still be possible to defend Childs' canonical and christological meanings if they can be attributed to *divine* intentionality—if, that is, an appropriate doctrine of biblical inspiration can be developed. I shall return to these subjects in subsequent chapters.

---

[58] Cf. the discussion of the Kuhn-Aristotle example in section 2 above.

# CHAPTER EIGHT

# PHILOSOPHICAL AND CANONICAL HERMENEUTICS

## 1. *Childs and Philosophical Hermeneutics*

The first scholar to have highlighted the affinities between Childs' work and the philosophical hermeneutics emanating from Germany appears to have been James Barr, who sees a significant similarity between 'the wave of interest in hermeneutics which was felt in the United States in the earlier sixties', and 'canonical criticism':[1] Both are particularly concerned with the present-day relevance of the biblical material and, concomitantly, tend to play down the question of what it meant to the author and his original audience. Barr sees this sort of hermeneutics as being 'anti-objectivist and anti-historicist' (*ibid.*), adding that the use which American theology made of it was deeply confused and largely unfruitful (pp. 143–45). The fact, therefore, that 'canonical criticism' has a similar hermeneutical orientation is not to its credit.

Unfortunately Barr's discussion is too brief and polemical to be particularly illuminating, and Childs' response does little to clarify the issues either. Acknowledging his indebtedness to Gerald Sheppard, Childs insists that an adequate hermeneutics must take account both of the 'givenness' of the text—we cannot construe it however we please—and of the modern situation of the interpreter—it is *we* who construe the text, not an abstract, atemporal, ideal reader.[2] In neglecting or denying this second aspect, Barr

> seems strangely out of touch with much of the serious hermeneutical debate both in America and on the continent. . . . When Barr seeks to establish as the sole criterion of exegesis 'what the text actually says', his appeal rings unusually hollow in the light of the last two hundred years of critical exegesis. Is it not at last obvious that what 'the text actually says' cannot be separated from the context from which it is read and into which it is directed?[3]

---

[1] *HS* p. 142; Childs is not explicitly mentioned. This is anticipated in his Preface to the Second Edition of *Old and New in Interpretation*, pp. 13–14.

[2] 'Review of *HS*', p. 69; cf. *OTTCC* pp. 12–15.

[3] 'Review of *HS*', p. 70. There are clear affinities here, of course, with Childs'

Yet although this indicates in a general, programmatic way what Childs' hermeneutical goal is, it gives little indication as to how he might achieve it. Nonetheless, the issues raised here are of central importance, being closely related to the tensions between Faith and Reason that we discussed in chapters 2 and 3: Is it possible to read the Bible from a pre-given faith-commitment without falling into fideism? Can the interpreter fully meet the demand that he proceed in a reasonable way without his own faith-commitment thereby being marginalized? One of the main questions to be tackled in this and the next chapter, then, is whether the reader-oriented stance of modern philosophical hermeneutics, which is nonetheless as concerned as Childs not to fall into mere subjectivism, might help him to resolve these tensions.

Whether Childs can in fact be helped in this way will clearly depend upon (1) where the similarities between his own programme and philosophical hermeneutics actually lie; and (2) whether the (relevant aspects of the) latter are themselves well-founded. An important step towards answering the first question has been taken by Stephen Fowl in his brief but insightful article, 'The Canonical Approach of Brevard Childs'. Fowl notes three interesting similarities between Childs' methodology and the hermeneutics of Hans-Georg Gadamer. Firstly, both are contending against what they consider to be a 'false objectivism' which imagines 'that the critic can extract himself from his historically conditioned state' (p. 173). According to Gadamer, this kind of objectivism is an ideal of the natural sciences which the *Geisteswissenschaften* cannot achieve; and similarly Fowl sees Childs as being dissatisfied with the historical-critical methodology because it claims an unattainable objectivity for itself.[4] Secondly, Fowl points to the positive significance that both Childs and Gadamer see in an interpreter working from within a tradition. Reason, Gadamer insists, necessarily start from *some* kind of 'preunderstanding', which is shaped by the tradition within which one works. As Fowl observes, Childs adopts essentially the same position in claiming that the Bible should

---

rejection of Stendahl's conception of 'what it meant', which aimed for a reader-independent, objective understanding of the text.

[4] As Childs comments at one point, 'One of the disastrous legacies of the Enlightenment was the new confidence of standing outside the stream of time and with clear rationality being able to distinguish truth from error, light from darkness' (*OTTCC*, p. 14). More recently Childs has himself called attention to this aspect of Gadamer's thought (*BTONT*, p. 201).

be interpreted as the Scriptures of the church: The church's confession of faith is the 'preunderstanding' from which the Scriptures can be rightly understood.[5] And thirdly (though less significantly) Fowl also finds a parallel between Gadamer's views on effective-history and Childs' interest in the history of interpretation, in that 'An understanding of how others have handled a text influences and aids Childs in his own interpretation'.[6]

A further interesting point of contact between Childs and Gadamer has been suggested by Scalise and Brett, in their discussions of Gadamer's views on classic, or eminent, texts. These are texts which, rising above the fluctuations of taste and criticism, have continually shown their worth throughout their history. Scalise and Brett point out that there are similarites here to how Childs views canonical texts.[7]

In addition to these connections, there are at least two further points to investigate. Firstly, Childs and Gadamer both see the interpreter's task as involving him or her, through their interaction with the text, in wrestling with the subject-matter itself.[8] We have seen that this idea is already present in 'Interpretation in Faith', where Childs links it with the normativity of Scripture;[9] in *BTONT* it has become a central plank in his programme. And secondly, Gadamer's views on application appear to be helpful to Childs. According to Gadamer, the application of a text to the present is not a 'second stage' that is undertaken once the text has been interpreted, but, in the very nature of the case, is necessarily an integral element in all interpretation.[10] This has clear affinities with Childs' insistence that

---

[5] Pp. 173–74; cf. Charles Scalise, *Hermeneutics* pp. 167–74. Anthony Thiselton has drawn upon similar ideas from Gadamer in discussing the relationship between exegesis and systematic theology; see *The Two Horizons: New Testament Hermeneutics and Philosophical Description with Special Reference to Heidegger, Bultmann, Gadamer, and Wittgenstein* (Exeter: Paternoster, 1980), pp. 306–307, 314–19).

[6] P. 175; cf. Scalise, pp. 163–67. Again Childs has recently noted Gadamer's work on this subject (*BTONT*, pp. 202–203). Both Fowl and Scalise also suggest parallels between Gadamer's discussion of 'effective-history' and Childs' views on the traditions behind the canonical text; but in my view this is dubious.

[7] Brett, *Crisis?* pp. 134–48, 154–56, etc.; cf. *CAOTS*, pp. 236–52, 258–60, etc. Scalise, pp. 174–78.

[8] *Truth and Method* (London: Sheed and Ward, Second, Revised Edition 1989), pp. 362–69 and passim.

[9] 'IF', pp. 443–44.

[10] *TM* pp. 307–11. Gadamer appeals to theological hermeneutics, when conceived as having as its goal the proclamation of the Scriptures in the church's preaching, as a particularly clear example in this respect of the character of general hermeneutics, although he also recognises that recent theology has separated application from

the Bible must be read as addressing the modern church; it also recalls his attempts to break down the sharp dichotomy between 'what it meant' and what it means'.

Besides these possible connections between Childs and Gadamer, there are two further reasons for considering the latter's work in some detail. Firstly, Gadamer's thought has had a broad influence upon theological studies in recent years, both through important theologians (in various fields) drawing explicitly upon Gadamer's work,[11] and also through the influence upon biblical hermeneutics of ideas which, if not derived directly from Gadamer, are closely related to central motifs in his thought. And secondly, this study of Gadamer will supplement the discussion of author's intention and objectivism begun in the previous chapter. From the standpoint of a Gadamerian understanding of historical situatedness, the role of the interpreter's own preunderstanding, and the hermeneutical circle, various objections might be raised against the position for which I have argued thus far; therefore in the following sections these will be duly considered and refuted.

This preliminary orientation, then, has suggested that there are a number of ways in which a study of Gadamer's thought might be illuminating. It should, however, be stressed at the outset that Gadamer's hermeneutics is a closely integrated philosophical whole, and must therefore be assessed as such, rather than as a source from which parallels useful to Childs might be drawn piecemeal; and although this does not necessarily mean that Childs could only make an 'all or nothing' appropriation of Gadamer's hermeneutics, it *does* imply that he could not draw upon, say, Gadamer's views on application without also carefully considering the viability of his notions of 'prejudices', the hermeneutical circle, and the nature of under-

---

'objectivistic' exegesis. Cf. his 'On the Problem of Self-Understanding', in Gadamer, *Philosophical Hermeneutics* (Berkley: California University Press, 1977), pp. 57–58.

[11] Among New Testament specialists Thiselton especially has discussed the relevance of Gadamer's hermeneutics for Biblical Studies at some length, both in *Two Horizons* and in *NHH*; in systematics, David Tracy has drawn extensively upon Gadamer in *The Analogical Imagination* (New York: Crossroads, 1981). In the Old Testament field, parallels between Gadamer and Gerhard von Rad have been explored by Manfred Oeming (*Gesamtbiblische Theologien der Gegenwart*), who also makes a number of comparisons between Gadamer and Childs (pp. 202–203 n. 49). For further bibliography see Bernd Jochen Hilberath, *Theologie zwischen Tradition und Kritik: Die Philosophische Hermeneutik Hans-Georg Gadamers als Herausforderung des Theologischen Selbstverständnisses* (Düsseldorf: Patmos, 1978).

standing, because it is from his distinctive conception of these ideas that Gadamer develops his views on application.

Before turning to Gadamer, however, there are two other hermeneutical theorists whom I wish to discuss. The first is F.D.E. Schleiermacher, whose views are in *some* respects very similar to the objectivist hermeneutics that I am developing in this book. Schleiermacher is extensively criticized by Gadamer, who holds him primarily responsible for leading hermeneutics into the 'wrong turn' which Gadamer is trying to reverse. The success or failure of Gadamer's various arguments against Schleiermacher will be of particular importance for the case I am building.

The second theorist to consider here is Rudolph Bultmann. Bultmann's views on the impossibility of presuppositionless exegesis are well known in Biblical Studies, and (as we shall discover in subsequent sections) raise a number of issues that are of relevance to our discussion of Gadamer's work. It is to these predecessors of Gadamer, therefore, that I now turn.

## 2. *Schleiermacher's Convergent Circle*

According to Schleiermacher,[12] a text is a 'point of intersection' between the language-system through which the author expressed him- or herself, and the thoughts which its author wished to express; so correspondingly, hermeneutics consists of two 'moments' which between them exhaust its entire task: Grammatical and psychological (or technical) interpretation.[13] In the former, the individuality of the author recedes into the background, so that he or she is regarded as an occasion for the language to manifest itself; thus the purpose of grammatical interpretation is the study of the text 'as language',[14] so

---

[12] For a detailed exposition of Schleiermacher's hermeneutics which brings out particularly well the many-sided character of his thought, see Anthony Thiselton, *NHH* pp. 204–36; see also Richard L. Corliss, 'Schleiermacher's Hermeneutic and Its Critics', *RelStud* 29 (1993), pp. 363–79.

[13] See 'Hermeneutics: The Compendium of 1819 and the Marginal Notes of 1828', in Schleiermacher, *Hermeneutics: The Handwritten Manuscripts* (Atlanta: Scholars, 1986), pp. 97–98; 'The Separate Exposition of the Second Part', in Schleiermacher, *Hermeneutics*, pp. 161–65. In 'The Marginal Notes of 1832–33' Schleiermacher makes a 'relative distinction between psychological and technical interpretation' (in Schleiermacher, *Hermeneutics*, p. 222), but this refinement need not be considered here.

[14] 'The Separate Exposition', p. 161.

as both to understand it as a part of the 'language system' in which it was written and to grasp the linguistic individuality of that particular text.[15] And conversely for psychological interpretation, the language is now regarded as the background 'given', and the focus is upon the individuality of the author who communicates his or her thoughts through this linguistic medium.[16]

At a number of points Schleiermacher is careful to explain that grammatical and psychological interpretation are complementary: 'Understanding takes place only in the coinherence of these two moments'.[17] In seeking a fuller understanding of the text the interpreter tacks back and forth between them, the ideal limit being reached when 'either side could be replaced by the other',[18] that is, when the results of each are not modified by the findings of the other.

Both grammatical and psychological interpretation proceed through a combination of 'divination' (or 'intuition') and 'comparison'.[19] For psychological interpretation, Schleiermacher describes divination as the interpreter transforming himself into the author, so that he can 'gain an immediate comprehension of the author as an individual';[20] yet this must be rigorously checked by the comparative method, through first subsuming the author under a general type and then trying to account for any distinctive traits through comparing him or her to others within the type. Similarly for grammatical interpretation: Faced with a novel construction, the interpreter may first give an intuitive explanation, based on his or her experience of and 'feel' for the language, but this interpretation must then be justified through linguistic comparison with other, (near) parallel passages.[21] In practice,

---

[15] P. 162; Thiselton, following J. Duke and J. Forstman, suggests that this is similar to Ferdinand de Saussure's distinction between *la langue* and *la parole* (*NHH*, p. 217).

[16] 'The Separate Exposition', p. 161.

[17] 'Compendium', p. 98. Cf. *ibid.* pp. 100, 116; 'The First Draft of 1809–10', in Schleiermacher, *Hermeneutics*, pp. 68–69, 70; and 'The Separate Exposition' p. 161.

[18] 'Compendium', p. 100; cf. pp. 116–17, 146–47.

[19] See especially 'The Academy Addresses of 1829', in Schleiermacher, *Hermeneutics*, pp. 190–95; also 'A Loose Page from 1810–11', in Schleiermacher, *Hermeneutics*, p. 93; 'The Separate Exposition' pp. 171–72; 'Compendium' pp. 150–51.

[20] 'Compendium', p. 150.

[21] 'Addresses', pp. 191–92; I shall set out Schleiermacher's views on parallel passages more fully below. Although one must be careful not to over-intellectualize Schleiermacher's notion of divination (which is predominantly intuitive), there appears to be an important analogy between Schleiermacher's views on divination and comparison, and the Popperian methodology of making conjectures and then testing them (cf. section 5.1 above).

there will often be much alternation between divination and comparison as the interpreter advances towards a better understanding.

Central to both grammatical and psychological interpretation is the hermeneutical circle, which, according to Schleiermacher's conception of it, expresses the mutual interdependence of part and whole: A particular utterance is but one part of the whole language, which is itself the sum-total of all such utterances; and likewise the writing of a certain text is but one moment in the author's life, which is the totality of all its moments. I shall consider here only the grammatical circle, which (as Schleiermacher points out) works at a number of different levels: Between the individual words in a sentence and the sentence as a whole; between the sentence and the whole passage; between the passage and the whole book.[22] More specifically, many words have a range of possible meanings, and so the meaning of any particular instance can only be determined by evaluating the contribution that it makes to the sentence in which it occurs; yet to do so one has to have grasped the sense of the whole, which cannot be attained without understanding its individual words. Or again, the meaning of a word depends upon its place within the language as a whole, and yet to understand the language one has to understand its individual words. There is a circular movement from part to whole and back again.

This undoubtedly has a somewhat paradoxical air about it, which has led some scholars to wonder whether the hermeneutical circle involves making a self-contradiction. According to Richard Palmer and to Gadamer it does; thus Palmer writes,

> Of course, the concept of the hermeneutical circle involves a logical contradiction; for, if we must grasp the whole before we can understand the parts, then we shall never understand anything. Yet we have asserted that the part derives its meaning from the whole. And surely, on the other hand, we cannot start with a whole, undifferentiated into parts.[23]

This naturally prompts Palmer to ask whether the hermeneutical circle is an invalid concept, to which he gives the optimistic answer,

---

[22] 'Addresses', pp. 195–98.

[23] *Hermeneutics: Interpretation Theory in Schleiermacher, Dilthey, Heidegger, and Gadamer* (Evanston: Northwestern University Press, 1969), p. 87; similarly Gadamer, who claims that 'It has always been known that this is a logically circular argument' (*TM* p. 190). Both Palmer and Gadamer are specifically discussing Schleiermacher's version of the hermeneutical circle in these passages.

> No; rather we must say that logic cannot fully account for the work-
> ings of understanding. Somehow, a kind of 'leap' into the hermeneutical
> circle occurs and we understand the whole and the parts together. (*ibid.*)

This is far from satisfactory, however, because the problem raised by
the first passage is not whether we can account for 'the workings of
understanding' by logic alone, but whether one of the central concepts
that we introduce into our account is self-contradictory. If (as Palmer
claims) it is, then this is a very serious flaw, because the purpose of
hermeneutical theory is to give us insight into how understanding
'works'; yet if the hermeneutical circle really is self-contradictory—if
it is basically saying that we already understand what we cannot yet
understand—then it is offering no insight at all. A self-contradictory
concept simply takes back with one hand what it gave with the other,
leaving us no wiser than when we started; therefore if the hermeneutical circle is to be understood as Palmer and Gadamer construe
it, then it would indeed be an invalid concept. For Palmer to appeal
to 'a kind of "leap"' is to abandon explanation for mysticism.

Fortunately, however, Schleiermacher's version of the circle cir-
cumvents the logical problem; for, having pointed out the part-whole
nature of the text,[24] he then adds:

> Here, too, there seems to be a circle. [But] this provisional under-
> standing requires only that knowledge of the particulars which comes
> from *a general knowledge of the language.*[25]

Schleiermacher's point is that the purpose of the circle is not to
produce knowledge out of nothing but to improve upon the preliminary understanding that comes from reading a text with at least an
elementary grasp of its language (p. 116)—Schleiermacher is careful
to point out in a number of places that hermeneutics assumes that
the interpreter is *already* familiar with the language in which the text
is written.[26] Thus although Palmer's problem has theoretical interest
for the philosophy of language, it is pitched at the wrong level to
affect biblical hermeneutics. Implicit in his argument is the assumption that the interpreter begins by knowing virtually nothing about
his text, as though he or she is in much the same position as an
anthropologist who, for the very first time, is trying to understand

---

[24] 'Compendium', p. 115.
[25] P. 116; italics added.
[26] 'Compendium', pp. 96, 101, 108, 113; 'Addresses', pp. 181–82. Cf. Corliss'
reply to Palmer, p. 375.

the language of a newly-discovered tribe. Now in this situation there presumably would have to be some kind of divinatory/intuitive 'leap' into the language, as Palmer proposes—to make any sense of their utterances, the anthropologist would have to postulate simultaneously not only the meanings of the natives' words but also the basics of their theory of reference and 'ontology'.[27]

This is not at all the situation, however, of the biblical scholar, who comes to the text already armed with detailed lexica and grammars. No-one seriously doubts that these give us at least a basic understanding of the language; and this, in Schleiermacher's view, provides a sufficient starting point for the hermeneutical circle to get started. The circle can then *progressively refine* this preliminary understanding into a more precise comprehension of the text's meaning, in ways which Schleiermacher discusses at some length in connection with his First and Second Canons.[28] Between them these canons 'comprise the whole of grammatical interpretation', which also includes Schleiermacher's important views on parallel passages. Schleiermacher's basic idea is that although every word, when 'considered in isolation', has 'a certain range of usages',[29] by their co-occurrence in the same (or a closely similar) context they impose mutual restrictions upon each other which thus determine the meaning of the text.[30] Therefore by some intelligent trial-and-error one can progressively improve one's understanding of the text, through adjusting its parts

---

[27] These issues have been much discussed in recent philosophy in connection with W.V.O. Quine's thesis of the indeterminacy of translation; see his *Word and Object* (Mass.: MIT, 1960), ch. 2. Quine's argument, very briefly, is that an indefinite number of incompatible translations of a native's utterance can all be justified if we make corresponding adjustments to the ontological commitments that we ascribe to him. Thus, for example, if the native responds affirmatively to 'gavagai' in the presence of rabbits we could translate 'gavagai' as 'rabbit', *if* we also assume that the native conceives of his world as made of concrete particulars, such as tables and rabbits; or it could be translated 'rabbithood', if we assume that the native thinks primarily in terms of abstract universals; or as 'temporal rabbit stage' if the native thinks of material objects as four-dimensional spatio-temporal wholes; etc. Unfortunately space does not allow me to discuss Quine's thesis in any detail, although I believe that it can be overcome through much the same sort of considerations that Schleiermacher advances in explaining how the hermeneutical circle converges upon a determinate meaning (see below). For a tortuous but telling refutation of Quine which uses essentially this strategy, see Gareth Evans, 'Identity and Predication', *JPhil* 72 (1975), pp. 343–63.

[28] 'Compendium', pp. 117–46.

[29] 'Compendium', p. 117.

[30] 'Every modifier excludes a certain number of otherwise possible meanings, and the determination of the word emerges by a process of elimination' (p. 128).

in such a way that, without doing violence to their natural meanings, they add up to an intelligible, coherent whole.[31]

There are two points in Schleiermacher's account that are of particular importance if this is to be a workable procedure. Firstly, a good lexicon can give considerable practical help by showing the range of possible meanings that a certain word may have. This means that instead of being in the impossible position of having to try out a virtually limitless range of possibilities, the interpreter starts from a manageable number of options. If the word is then used in some particular sentence, its specific nuances in that context will usually be quite clear, because only a part of its semantic range will be appropriate for that setting. Any residual ambiguities will in turn be restricted by the other components in the sentence, which will itself be constrained by its place within the larger context, etc. Of course, this broadening out into successively wider contexts will add considerably to the material which the interpreter needs to weigh up; but Schleiermacher has again safeguarded the workability of his hermeneutical circle through the second of the two points I want to highlight here, namely, his discussion of what counts as *relevant* contexts and parallels.[32] The specific meaning of a word is much more strongly influenced by a *few* other words to which it is especially related in various ways: A parallel passages must be 'near' to the passage being considered, in that it continues the same thought sequence or is separated only by a transitional sentence; passages with a very similar construction are particularly relevant parallels; those from the same work generally more so than those from a different one; those from a work of the same genre, or the same school of thought, rather than from another; etc. Once again, then, the hermeneutical circle is viable because the interpreter has only a relatively restricted range of alternatives to consider.

Of course, no competent scholar—and certainly not Schleiermacher—imagines that interpretation can restrict itself to the meanings recorded in the lexicon, or to the rules given by the standard grammar

---

[31] See especially 'Compendium' pp. 127–28, 134–35; 'Addresses', pp. 196–8, 202–203. Evans, in his reply to Quine, similarly argues that although there may be considerable scope for alternative translations of 'gavagai' *when it is considered only as a one-word sentence*, the fact that the translator also has to account for its use within complex sentences introduces very significant restrictions.

[32] See especially 'The First Draft', pp. 84–86, 88; 'Compendium', pp. 128–29, 140–42.

book. These are themselves based upon someone's interpretations of various texts, which may need correcting; so the competent interpreter will 'go behind' the standard reference tools and work directly with the primary sources.[33] These complications can again be dealt with, however, by means of the principles that have already been discussed—the interpreter turns to the primary sources in search of passages that provide relevant parallels to the one currently being discussed, and assesses them through a circular movement between part and whole. Schleiermacher's methodology, then, while taking the standard reference tools as its starting point, is sufficiently powerful to pass beyond them.

This latter point has an important corollary. Schleiermacher is fully aware that a creative author can endow words with novel meanings, and he is able to take account of this in terms of his basic hermeneutical principles. So, for example, in Rom. 7:18 *sarx* is clearly being used in a sense which differs from its standard, first-century meanings, so that even Paul's original readers could not have understood this passage directly from their native knowledge of the language. Rather, they would have had to interpret it through the Schleiermacherian procedures of (1) considering *sarx* in the context first of its own sentence and then in relation to the wider argument that Paul is developing, and (2) comparing it with the similar occurrences in 6:19 and 7:25. The main point to make here, however, is that these are viable procedures only because the other words in these contexts *are* generally being used in their standard senses. If Paul had given all his words special senses of his own then the Schleiermacherian methodology could not have been employed, because his readers would have had no basic understanding from which to start—Paul would no longer have been writing in Greek but in a private language of his own invention, which even his original readers would have had no way of interpreting.[34] Therefore even though language can be used in novel ways, the standard usage remains the more fundamental because, unless this is sufficiently respected, the text simply lapses into unintelligibility.

Granted, then, that we have at least a basic grasp of the language, Schleiermacher claims that we can then progress towards a more

---

[33] 'Compendium', pp. 113–14, 121–22, 140–41.
[34] They would, in effect, have been in the Palmer-like position of having already to understand what cannot yet be understood.

refined understanding of any particular part through, on the one hand, making intelligent comparisons between related passages, and, on the other hand, relating the part to the successively wider wholes within which it stands:

> When we consider the task of interpretation with this principle [of whole and part] in mind, we have to say that our increased understanding of each sentence and of each section, an understanding which we achieve by starting at the beginning and moving forward slowly, is always provisional. It becomes more complete as we are able to see each larger section as a coherent unity . . . until suddenly at the end every part is clear and the whole work is visible in sharp and definite contours.[35]

Schleiermacher's hermeneutical circle is therefore better characterised as a spiral, which advances asymptotically towards the objective, determinate meaning of 'the text itself'.

### 3. Bultmann on 'Presuppositionless Exegesis'

The hermeneutical circle is also of fundamental importance for Gadamer's work; yet his conception of it is quite different from Schleiermacher's.[36] Whereas Schleiermacher's 'circle' spirals towards a reader-independent understanding of the text, Gadamer argues that understanding is always historically conditioned. Rejecting, therefore, Schleiermacher's conception of the circle as an intra-linguistic movement between part and whole, Gadamer instead adopts Martin Heidegger's account,[37] in which the movement is between the text and its *historically situated* reader.

Unfortunately it is beyond the scope of this book to discuss Heidegger's philosophy; however, the salient points can be introduced through considering the hermeneutics of Rudolph Bultmann. Although Bultmann has little to say about the hermeneutical circle as such, similar issues are raised by his influential views on presuppositions. In 'Is Exegesis Without Presuppositions Possible?',[38] Bultmann begins

---

[35] 'Addresses', p. 198.

[36] Again I am primarily considering *grammatical* interpretation, although we can add in passing that Gadamer is also highly critical of Schleiermacher's views on psychological interpretation. Gadamer's objections will be discussed at length in section 9.3 below.

[37] *TM* pp. 259, 265–70.

[38] In Kurt Mueller-Vollmer (ed.), *The Hermeneutics Reader* (Oxford: Basil Blackwell, 1986); see pp. 242–43.

by distinguishing presuppositions from prejudices. Exegesis must certainly be without prejudices, in that it must not decide in advance what the results of exegesis should be (as has happened, in Bultmann's view, with some allegorical interpretations of the Bible). Likewise, every interpreter should seek to free his exegesis from the influences of his own individual biases and habits. Yet no-one can come to a text or a historical event with a mind that is free from all assumptions. The interpreter must, in the first place, presuppose the historical-critical method, and this brings with it certain assumptions about the interconnected nature of history (pp. 243–44). But this in turn means that, secondly, the interpreter must already have some preunderstanding of the 'forces' that connect the individual events together—e.g., economic needs, political ambitions, human passions and ideals, etc. (p. 244). And furthermore, one must also understand the historical subject matter which these forces interconnect:

> For can one understand political history without having a concept of state and justice, which by their very nature are not historical products but ideas? Can one understand economic history without having a concept of what economy and society in general mean? (p. 245)

Thus the demand that the interpreter should come to the subject matter without any presuppositions is a false ideal, because if the mind was somehow transformed into a *tabula rasa* this would destroy the very conditions that make understanding possible. There can only be interpretation if there is already a 'life-relation' between the interpreter and the subject matter, for only then can it 'speak' to him or her:

> The 'life-relation' is a genuine one . . . only when it is vital, i.e., when the subject matter with which the text is concerned also concerns us and is a problem for us. If we approach history alive with our own problems, then it really begins to speak to us. . . . To understand history is possible only for one who does not stand over against it as a neutral, nonparticipating spectator, but himself stands in history and shares responsibility for it. (pp. 245–46)

With this last sentence the more radical side of Bultmann's thought appears: Presuppositions are indispensable for interpretation, yet are themselves shaped by the interpreter's own place in history. In Bultmann's view, therefore, the subject/object schema of the natural sciences is inapplicable to the *Geisteswissenschaften*: Whereas the natural scientist stands over against the object of his study as something that is quite distinct from him and by which he is not affected, the historian can only interpret history from inside history itself (*ibid.*). Therefore the meaning of a text or historical event is not definitively fixed, 'once-and-for-all'; rather, its meaning can only be known through the interpreter questioning it, and yet this questioning grows out of 'the claim of the now' (p. 246).

This conclusion, as we shall see, is close to Gadamer's views on the historical situatedness of understanding, and is also at odds with the case for objective interpretation that I have developed thus far; yet a careful reading of Bultmann's argument shows that it turns on an important *non sequitur*. The main question that his article tackles is, as its title announces, whether 'exegesis without presuppositions [is] possible'; and good reasons can indeed be given for answering this, with Bultmann, in the negative: If someone tried to read, say, a graduate level text on the economics of the Roman Empire without already knowing something about economic theory and the relevant history then it would make little sense to them, either because they were unacquainted with the meanings of some of its terms, or because they were unable to supply the missing premises that connect together the author's thoughts into a cogent argument. In this sense, then, Bultmann is clearly right in claiming that a pre-understanding of the subject matter is necessary.

These observations, however, in no way justify Bultmann's radical conclusions about the historicality of understanding. What they show is that someone who approached the text 'without presuppositions' would simply fail to understand it *at all*, either in a historically conditioned way or in any other. The real starting-point for Bultmann's radicalism, then, is not 'Are presuppositions necessary?', but the quite different question, '*Which* presuppositions are hermeneutically viable?'. Can a text be read equally well from *different* preunderstandings— e.g., by people versed in either Capitalist or Marxist economic theory, in either Mommsen's or Gibbon's history of Rome, or in the philosophy of history of either Heidegger or Popper? What Bultmann's argument implicitly assumes is that the very different presuppositions which arise from the 'now' of, say, an ancient Greek and a modern American will *both* provide a viable basis for textual interpretation; or to put the point more generally, it assumes that any given text can be interpreted in terms of an indefinitely broad plurality of alternative presuppositions, arising from the correspondingly broad plurality of historical situations from which the interpreter might work.

This principle, however, (which I shall hereafter refer to as 'Bultmann's plurality principle') by no means follows from the (in itself correct) claim that presuppositionless exegesis is impossible; neither does Bultmann offer any independent arguments for it. It is simply an unstated assumption in his argument.

If, however, Bultmann's argument is essentially dependent upon his plurality principle, then it appears to be vulnerable to the 'objectivist' arguments that emerged from my discussions of the Kuhn-Aristotle example and of Fish's 'Jacobs-Rosenbaum . . .', because, *prima facie*, these are striking counter-examples to the plurality principle. Kuhn, it will be recalled, began his interpretation from a historically conditioned (post-Newtonian) preunderstanding of the subject matter of Aristotle's text, and it was *precisely for this reason* that his initial reading was largely nonsensical—the text simply could not be understood in those terms. Progress was made towards a better understanding only when Kuhn *overcame* his historically conditioned starting-point. This, of course, does not mean that he now proceeded without presuppositions; rather, he succeeded through adopting a preunderstanding which accorded with Aristotle's own understanding of the subject matter, and which showed its accord through making sense of numerous passages which had hitherto been problematic.[39] In other words, Kuhn greatly improved his understanding of Aristotle's text by adopting an Aristotelian preunderstanding; and his final interpretation was therefore *not* distinctively Kuhnian or coloured by his twentieth-century standpoint, but an objective, reader- and history-independent rendering of what the text itself meant. What this example apparently shows, then, is that we are not trapped in the preunderstanding from which we begin, because Bultmann's plurality principle is wrong; therefore one's starting point can be critically transcended by trying out alternative presuppositions and seeing whether this makes the text more intelligible.[40]

What I have argued for, then, is the correctability of one's starting point; and since Bultmann himself clearly does not think that we are

---

[39] The same point is also demonstrated by my discussion of Fish's list-poem in section 7.3 above.

[40] A similar point was implicit in my discussion of historical methodology in section 5.2 above, where I argued that (1) a historian who had no presuppositions at all would be unable to contribute to the discussion; but (2) even if each historian starts from different presuppositions, there can nonetheless be rational debate as to which of them is objectively correct.

merely the helpless victims of whatever presuppositions our historical situation has foisted upon us, it is not surprising to find him occasionally making a similar point himself. As we noted above, Bultmann himself insists that the interpreter must overcome his or her own biases; and in explaining why 'the historical method' must be used in interpreting a text he even recalls a case, strongly reminiscent of the Kuhn-Aristotle example, in which the (historically conditioned) translation of *pneuma* as 'Geist' by many nineteenth century idealists was refuted by Gunkel's demonstration that this did not fit the New Testament's usage (p. 243). But once this much has been conceded, it is far from clear why the same methodology could not be applied right across the board, so that *all* the relevant presuppositions are purged of whatever is personal or historically conditioned.[41] Bultmann, in fact, seems to be faced with an awkward dilemma. To avoid individualism one must, as he notes, allow one's presuppositions to be criticized and corrected by the text; but how can one then prevent the same critical methodology from successively eliminating *all* that is distinctively 'mine' (insofar as it pertains to the text's meaning), so that one is left with a reader-independent interpretation of what the text itself means? The Schleiermacherian methodology does not appear to be tied to a particular kind of preunderstanding—on the contrary, any presupposition that can be identified as affecting one's understanding of a text could presumably be replaced (at least as a working hypothesis) by a contrary presupposition, to see whether or not this improves the interpretation. It appears, then, that once Bultmann has allowed that our initial presuppositions can and must be corrected by the text, he then has no way of establishing a stable, non-arbitrary 'stopping-point' that would prevent the hermeneutical circle from spiralling down to a Schleiermacherian objectivism. In other words, the concession that he makes to criticism in avoiding individualism seems to have consequences that are much more far-reaching than Bultmann has realized.

Bultmann's failure to reckon with these consequences appears in part to stem from him glossing 'having a preunderstanding of the subject matter' as having a 'life-relation' to it, with this being something of vital concern to the interpreter.[42] Now in *this* sense, of course,

---

[41] The one example of an unrevisable presupposition that Bultmann gives—namely, a somewhat Troeltschian historical methodology (p. 244)—is hardly persuasive.

[42] Lurking behind this is a rejection of Hirsch's distinction between meaning and significance.

our life-relations are not easily changed—for someone like Kuhn, who has appreciated the enormous insight that Newtonian mechanics has given us into (certain aspects of) nature, it is not a live option to take up again the Aristotelian conception of change-in-general as something about which he can have a vital concern as an insight into the physical world. Yet however alien or untenable it may have struck him as a scientific concept, he was still able to adopt it as an interpretative hypothesis when trying to understand Aristotle's text, and this is all that was needed to break free from his own historical standpoint. Of course, if he does have a vital concern for some contrary outlook, this hypothetical reorientation may be difficult to achieve; but this does not affect the basic 'logic' of the hermeneutical situation.

In rounding off this discussion of Bultmann, two clarifications should be added. Firstly, the points that I have made against Bultmann concerning criticism and convergence are not 'assured results' that can now be quoted as knock-down arguments to refute Gadamer—on the contrary, even if it is agreed that Bultmann has no resources for preventing the hermeneutical circle from converging, it still has to be asked whether Gadamer's much fuller and more subtle discussions of such topics as historical situatedness, the fusion of horizons, and the dialogical nature of interpretation provides him with just the resources that Bultmann lacks. This will be one of the major concerns of the following sections; but approaching these questions via Bultmann helps to clarify what is at issue. And secondly, in rejecting Bultmann's plurality principle, I am not suggesting that there is one, single, way in which a particular text can be interpreted, which all interpreters must therefore adopt. On the contrary, I shall myself be arguing for a version of plurality. This, however, will be an objectivist version, because the nature and scope of this plurality will ultimately be determined by the text, not by the interpreter's historical situatedness. Again, this will be clarified in the following sections.

## 4. *Gadamer's Anti-Objectivism*

I have already explained in section 1 why, for the purposes of this book, objectivism is an issue that particularly needs to be discussed. In the present section I shall further clarify the form of objectivism I wish to defend and the alternative that Gadamer is proposing, and will also look at how the argument between these positions is to be conducted. (It is particularly important to clarify these issues before turning to the details of Gadamer's position because, as I shall argue subsequently, several of his arguments do not touch the points that are really at issue.) As we have already noted, Gadamer wants to free the *Geisteswissenschaften* from the objectivism that is characteristic of the natural sciences.[43] According to Gadamer, the fundamental difference stems from the fact that, for the natural sciences,

> research ... derives the law of its development not from these circumstances [sc. the historical situation in which the research is undertaken] but from the law of the object it is investigating',[44]

whereas the very nature of the *Geisteswissenschaften* is such that this situatedness cannot be overcome. The former study 'an "object in itself"' (p. 285); 'research penetrates more and more deeply' into the object (p. 284) as it strives towards 'the perfect knowledge of nature' (p. 285). For the human sciences, however, there is no such thing as an 'object in itself' for them to study, because

> the particular research questions ... that we are interested in pursuing are motivated in a special way by the present and its interests. The theme and object of research are actually constituted by the motivation of the inquiry. (p. 284)

To claim, therefore, that 'scientific', objective knowledge of, say, the meaning of Genesis is possible is tantamount to arguing that one can, in principle, 'methodically [eliminate] the influence of the interpreter and his time on understanding' (p. 333); and this, in Gadamer's view, is impossible.

The central point, then, at which I wish to take issue with Gadamer

---

[43] To anyone familiar with the natural sciences it will be immediately apparent that Gadamer's conception of them is seriously aberrant, particularly in him seeing them as proceeding from a will to control and dominate nature (an idea which is extremely difficult to apply to one of the oldest and most precise of the sciences, planetary astronomy), and as achieving certainty through a Cartesian methodology of systematic doubt (see *TM*, pp. 238–39, 450–56, 459–60, etc.). It should also be mentioned that the traditional conception of the natural sciences as sources of objective knowledge is currently a much-disputed issue within the philosophy of science. Fortunately it is not necessary to untangle these complex questions here, because the important point for the present discussion is the kind of objectivity that Gadamer is opposing to the *Geisteswissenschaften*, not whether that standard is actually exemplified by the natural sciences, or whether it is achieved by a Cartesian methodology or by some other means.

[44] P. 283; cf. p. 314, where Gadamer explains 'objective knowledge' as 'the knower ... standing over against a situation that he merely observes'.

concerns *the reader-dependence or independence of meaning*, with reader-dependence referring not to the idiosyncrasies of this or that particular reader but to his or her reading being essentially conditioned by the reader's historical situatedness within a particular tradition. What I am going to argue, then, is that there is a (centrally important) sense of 'the meaning of the text'[45] of which the following is true: As the natural sciences give us knowledge[46] of what the world is like 'in itself', independently of the historical situatedness of the investigator, or of the scientific community, so likewise it is possible to attain (or approximate more and more closely to) a reader-independent knowledge of the meaning of a text.[47] To clarify this thesis, however, there are two distinctions that need to be drawn. The first is between textual *indeterminacy* and textual *ambiguity*. Indeterminacy is well illustrated by Stanley Fish's reader-centred hermeneutics: Since different interpretative communities will approach any particular text with an indefinitely broad range of reading strategies ('read it as an assignment'/ 'read it as a religious poem') the text will, according to this theory, yield a correspondingly broad range of meanings. Quite different from this, however, is the ambiguity of such sentences as 'Flying planes can be dangerous', or 'The policemen were ordered to stop drinking at midnight'. Indeterminacy is clearly incompatible with the objectivism for which I am arguing, but ambiguity is not—that a certain text has two (or more) determinate meanings is no less of an objective (i.e., reader-independent) fact about the text itself than that it has a single, determinate meaning.[48] To refute objectivism, therefore, one needs to argue for indeterminacy (though not necessarily for Fish's version of it); pointing out examples of ambiguity is not sufficient.[49]

---

[45] The sense I have in mind, of course, is that which Hirsch identifies as the text's meaning, in contrast to its significance (although with the caveat that my account of the relationship between meaning and author's intention is very different to Hirsch's).

[46] Or more precisely, 'move towards an increasingly accurate knowledge'.

[47] I also recognize, of course, that there are other senses of 'the meaning of a text' (namely, those which fall under Hirsch's definition of the text's significance) of which this may not be true.

[48] In the visual realm the same point can be made with reference to the well-known Gestalt diagrams (e.g., Necker's cube, the wine glass and two faces, etc.). What these cunningly constructed pictures illustrate is not indeterminacy but ambiguity, because the only option that they give the viewer is to chose between the determinate alternatives that the diagram itself offers.

[49] Fish himself is thoroughly confused on this issue; see, for example, his discussions of the ambiguities (they are no more than this!) of 'This stuff is light enough

The second distinction that needs to be made is between *indeterminacy* and *selectivity*. Someone who comes to Genesis with questions about syntax and grammar will obviously produce a different kind of study from someone who asks about character and plot development. This, of course, poses no problem for the objectivist, who will see these scholars as having selected to study different aspects of what is objectively there in the text. The objectivist could rightly point out that textual interpretation is in fact no different from the natural sciences in this respect. No scientist makes 'the world as such' the object of study, but selects a certain aspect of it (electromagnetic phenomena; planetary orbits) for investigation. And similarly even in pure mathematics: No-one simply studies, say, the natural numbers 'as such', but investigates some particular problem pertaining to them (e.g., the distribution of the primes, or the solutions of Diophantine equations).[50] Now in each of these cases there is a sense in which one could say that the answers one gets depends upon the questions one asks, but this raises no difficulties for the objectivist, since it is clearly calling attention to nothing more than a selectivity among the different aspects of nature (or the number system) that are there to be studied.

As with the first distinction, the primary reason for distinguishing between indeterminacy and selectivity is to close off certain tempting but inadequate lines of argument that are sometimes used against objectivism.[51] Thus it is insufficient merely to point out that different interpreters, beginning from the different 'claims of the now' that their respective historical situations make upon them, each come to the text with their own distinctive questions, because the objectivist can readily accept this as saying no more than that different ages characteristically study different aspects of a problem[52]—Wellhausen came to Genesis with questions about its written sources, Gunkel

---

to carry', and 'Is there a text in this class?' (*Text*, pp. 281–83, 305–307). Even if Fish were right to claim that all language is ambiguous (p. 281)—a highly dubious contention, in my view, which Fish promotes by discussing only short, very simple sentences that are entirely unrepresentative of texts generally—this is still quite different from claiming that all language is indeterminate.

[50] I.e., equations with integer coefficients, and for which integer solutions are to be found.

[51] As we shall see presently, Gadamer is not altogether clear on these issues.

[52] Cf. Emilio Betti's rejoinder to Bultmann's rejection of historical objectivism ('Hermeneutics as the General Methodology of the *Geisteswissenschaften*', pp. 65, 67–68). This in part, however, rests on a misunderstanding of Bultmann's position; see the next footnote.

asked about the prewritten, oral traditions, and Alter is interested in its literary features; yet the fact that each has produced very different studies of the same text is far from sufficient reason, of itself, for denying the objectivity of what each has done. For this the crucial issue is not 'What questions do the interpreters ask?' but 'What questions will the text answer?',[53] because it is the latter rather than the former question that distinguishes between selectivity (i.e., choosing which from among the range of questions that *the text itself* is willing to answer one will actually investigate) and indeterminacy (i.e., denying that the text has a sufficient measure of independent 'thereness' for it to give reader-independent answers to the questions that are put to it). So, for example, Fish's hermeneutics entails that there is *no* question that a sufficiently ingenious interpretative community could not get a given text to answer, because, as Fish himself explains,

> [W]hile there are always mechanisms for ruling out readings, their source is not the text but the presently recognized interpretive strategies for producing the text. It follows, then, that no reading, however outlandish it might appear, is inherently an impossible one.[54]

In other words, claiming that a text can be made to answer any question that is put to it is equivalent to an extreme form of indeterminacy, which stands at the opposite pole to the objectivism that I am defending—meaning is strongly reader-dependent because (recalling my argument in section 7.3 above that a consistent application of Fish's principles leads to unbridled individualism) each interpreter makes the text in his or her own image. Or to take a less radical example, most scholars would presumably agree that anyone who comes to Genesis with questions about, say, quantum field theory or the life of Julius Caesar will not receive any sensible answers; but to admit even this much already makes some concessions to objectivism— namely, that the text has sufficient independent 'thereness' to refute at least these attempted interpretations. Or to put it another way,

---

[53] As we saw in the previous section, Bultmann's argument against historical objectivism turns upon him implicitly assuming this question is answered by his plurality principle. This is what makes his position a form of anti-objectivism rather than the objectivistic selectionism that Betti's critique of Bultmann (see the previous note) attributes to him.

[54] *Text*, p. 347. I have discussed this aspect of Fish's thought in 'Hermeneutics (I)' section iv; most scholars, I suspect, more in touch with the realities of textual interpretation than is Fish at this point, would probably regard Fish's reasoning here as a *reductio ad absurdum* of his own hermeneutics.

such a concession admits that it is a reader-independent fact about the text that, whatever else it may be, it is not a treatise on *those* subjects. Or to consider a more conservative example, in putting forward the Kuhn-Aristotle example as an illustration of objective interpretation, I argued that this 'worked' through the text having a sufficient measure of reader-independence for it to refuse (sensibly) to answer the questions that Kuhn initially put to it—in other words, that it was the text rather than the interpreter that ultimately set the agenda. To refute this claim it would not be sufficient to show that the *Physics* also gives informative answers to questions about subjects other than motion (such as Aristotle's views on politics or biology) because this would simply illustrate selectivity. Rather, the (in) determinacy issue would have to be tackled, through showing (for example) that, *contra* Kuhn, a sufficiently ingenious interpreter *could* read the *Physics* equally well as an answer to questions about either change of position or change in general.

Summing up, then, this part of our discussion: To show that a certain text yields sensible answers to a range of different but *logically compatible* questions cuts no ice with the objectivist, because this establishes nothing more radical than a selectivity that is fully compatible with objectivism. To refute objectivism one would have to argue for some form of interpretative indeterminacy, which, in terms of the 'questions' metaphor, would mean showing that a certain text will yield sensible answers to a range of questions that are both different and *logically incompatible* (as Fish attempts to show that 'Jacobs-Rosenbaum . . .' will satisfactorily answer both 'assignment questions' and 'religious poem questions'). To argue for less than this would refute only simplistic and outdated versions of objectivism, which no-one should wish to defend anyway.

This is also an appropriate place to say something about the widely used—but, in my view, deeply misleading—metaphor of interpretation as a 'seeing from a certain perspective' or 'point of view'. All (visual) observation, it is pointed out, is perspectival, so that what one sees (when observing, say, a table) depends upon where one stands—i.e., it is 'viewer relative'. Moreover, this is an *essential* feature of observation, which cannot be circumvented—there is simply no such thing as seeing 'the table itself', apart from any perspective (or 'from a God's eye point of view', as it is sometimes put). Nor is there a specially privileged perspective that shows 'the table as it really is'; rather, different points of view are just that—different, but equally viable, points of view, none of which, therefore, reveal '*the* truth' about the table.

There are a number of comments that an objectivist can make in reply. Firstly, if one takes the realities of visual perception seriously then what it most obviously displays is not indeterminacy but selectivity. Of course if I stand in front of a table I will see something different from what I would see if I stood behind it; yet it is also true that if anyone else stands in front of the table then they will see the same as I saw from that perspective—in other words, if two observers agree to 'ask the same question' then they will get the same, viewer-independent, 'answer'. As we have seen, very similar comments can be made about mathematics and the natural sciences, and they call attention to nothing more than a form of selectivity that is perfectly compatible with objectivism.

Secondly, in visual observation it is the object viewed that fundamentally 'sets the agenda', not the viewer; the viewer's 'perspectivity' is limited to choosing between the options that the object itself puts on offer. Again, this is characteristic of selectivity rather than indeterminacy.

Thirdly, the impossibility of aperspectival viewing refutes only simplistic and outdated versions of objectivism. 'Viewing from a perspective' is a metaphor for approaching that which is to be interpreted with certain questions, beliefs, and assumptions already 'in place'; thus the impossibility of aperspectival viewing, when construed as an objection to objectivism, translates into the claim that objective knowledge cannot be attained through making one's mind a *tabula rasa*. This of course is true;[55] but it makes no inroads against the kind of objectivism defended in this book, which claims that objective knowledge can be attained by some means *other than* the *tabula rasa* strategy (namely, through a critical testing and revising of one's presuppositions).

In addition to the preceding points, there is another, more fundamental, objection to the perspectives metaphor that needs to be considered. Understanding a text and observing an object are, of course, quite different things; and one can only act as an illuminating model or metaphor for the other insofar as there is a genuine

---

[55] *Contra* Gadamer, who has claimed that the objectivity of the natural sciences is due to them being 'presuppositionless' ('Semantics and Hermeneutics', p. 72). This, of course, is now widely recognized as a complete misconception of the natural sciences.

analogy between the relevant aspects of each. In fact, however, there is a centrally important *disanalogy* between them which makes this metaphor entirely inappropriate as an argument against objectivism. For seeing a table, *all* perspectives are observationally tenable—whatever angle of vision is selected, one experiences a coherent visual field. It is fundamental to the objectivist's position, however, that not all interpretative perspectives are hermeneutically tenable—on the contrary, the argument for Fish's 'Jacobs-Rosenbaum . . .' being objectively a list turned on precisely the claim that *only* this interpretation was viable, because attempts to interpret it as a poem proved to be incoherent and thus self-refuting. To appeal to visual perspectivism as a refutation of textual objectivism is therefore entirely question-begging, because it posits a hermeneutical model that simply omits the very point which is of central importance for the objectivist's position. The objectivist is therefore entitled to set this metaphor aside as woefully inadequate, and not consider himself bound by any conclusions that may be drawn from it.

The only hermeneutical position, in fact, for which the perspectives metaphor provides an adequate model is a Fishian relativism in which 'no reading, however outlandish it might appear, is inherently an impossible one'.[56] Very few scholars would wish to defend as extreme a view as this, however; and since we have in any case seen that, once it is put to the test of concrete exegesis, Fish's hermeneutics soon runs into severe problems, the perspectives metaphor can now be set aside as having nothing relevant to contribute.

With these points now clarified, I shall next look more closely at Gadamer's anti-objectivism. This, as we have seen, is based on the idea that, for the *Geisteswissenschaften*, the scholar's historical situatedness cannot be overcome; therefore 'Every age has to understand a transmitted text in its own way',[57] because

> The real meaning of a text, as it speaks to an interpreter, does not depend on the contingencies of the author and his original audience. It certainly is not identical with them, for it is always co-determined also by the historical situation of the interpreter. . . . [U]nderstanding is not merely a reproductive but always a productive activity as well. (*ibid.*)

---

[56] Fish himself often uses the perspectives metaphor, both in setting out his own views and in answering his critics (e.g., *Text*, pp. 16, 335–36, 360, 365–66; *Doing*, pp. 78, 141–42, 185, 187–88, 190, 291, 347).
[57] *TM*, p. 296.

Therefore, Gadamer concludes, 'we understand in a *different* way, *if we understand at all*.'[58]

Gadamer's arguments for this will be examined in the following sections. What I wish to do here, however, is to look at a particular example which (with a few minor variations) Gadamer has used on a number of occasions to illustrate his own position and to provide (what he takes to be) a counter-example to the objectivist. It concerns the ease with which we can recognize the work of scholars from past generations as being conditioned by their own historical circumstances:

> [W]hen you read a classic essay by Mommsen you immediately know its era, the only era when it could have been written. Even a master of the historical method is not able to keep himself entirely free from the prejudices of his time, his social environment, and his national situation, etc.[59]

In other words, the historical scholarship of even the most careful and erudite historians is itself historically conditioned.

But granting Gadamer's historical claims about Mommsen, it is somewhat less than clear, in my view, how this is supposed to show that objectivism is seriously flawed. There are perhaps two ways in which Gadamer's argument might be construed. First, he may be calling attention to the fact that *what a historian studies* is conditioned by the historian's own historical situatedness—scholars living through a period of intense and prolonged constitutional crisis may become preoccupied with the legal and constitutional affairs of the peoples they study; a school dominated by Marxist philosophy will naturally gravitate towards studies of social unrest and class conflict; etc. It should be clear from the preceding discussion, however, that the objectivist can accept this as illustrating no more than selectivity. Construed in this way Gadamer's argument would simply be saying that the questions one asks depend upon one's own historical circumstances, and that if one asks different questions then one will generally get different answers. Both of these points, however, can be fully accepted by the objectivist, who could therefore only be refuted

---

[58] P. 297; Gadamer's italics.

[59] *TM* p. 512. In 'The Universality of the Hermeneutical Problem' (in Gadamer, *Philosophical Hermeneutics*) essentially the same example is cited in arguing that 'the last one hundred years have taught us most emphatically that there are serious difficulties involved in its claim to historical objectivity' (p. 6; cf. 'On the Scope and Function of Hermeneutical Reflection', in Gadamer, *Philosophical Hermeneutics*, pp. 28–29).

by arguing that the interpreter is historically conditioned in a stronger
sense than has been considered so far (e.g., by showing that our
situatedness is such that scholars in different situations cannot even
ask the same questions). This, however, could hardly be established
merely by pointing out the historically conditioned character of this
or that particular scholar's work.

A second way of construing Gadamer's argument, however, is that
it calls attention to the fact that *how a historian studies* his or her chosen
subject is historically conditioned, with each scholar drawing upon
the moral concepts, political beliefs, and philosophical ideas of their
own particular age. Again, however, it seems that the objectivist can
accept this as a statement of historical fact without it raising any
hermeneutical problems, because the objectivist would further maintain that the beliefs from which one starts can be critically tested
and revised in such a way that the conditionedness of one's starting
point may be overcome. (This was the point of the Kuhn-Aristotle
example.) Gadamer, of course, would not be entirely happy with this
reply, because (for reasons that will be discussed more fully in section
9.3 below) he rejects the idea that the hermeneutical circle may
converge upon a determinate, correct reading. The point to make
here, however, is that even if this were so, it cannot be established
merely by calling attention to examples of historically conditioned
scholarship. In sum, then, as an argument against the objectivist
Gadamer's example carries no weight, because the objectivist can
easily account for these facts in terms that are compatible with his or
her own beliefs.

Gadamer, of course, has several other reasons besides the Mommsen
example for rejecting objectivism, and these will be fully discussed in
the next chapter. To keep a balanced picture, however, it is perhaps
worth reiterating at this point that I also recognize that, in addition
to discovering the text's objective meaning, there are other activities
which readers can (and do) engage in. A reader may, for example,
criticize a character whom the author presents as the faultless hero
of the story, or criticize the author for so presenting him, or explain
why he or she (sc. the reader) feels particularly drawn towards (or
repelled by) the story's principal villain, etc. I do not wish to deny
that these may indeed be legitimate and valuable things to do; nor
would I necessarily argue that these are objective matters.[60] My point,

---

[60] How these various issues are to be resolve would naturally depend, in each

rather, is simply that these are different things from studying the meaning of the text, and must not be confused with it: The Deuteronomist's evaluation of David, made in terms of his (sc. the Deuteronomist's) particular theology, and the evaluation that a modern reader may make of David (or of the Deuteronomist) in terms of his or her own, twentieth century, standards, are two quite different things, which should (and can) be kept quite distinct from one another.

This, of course, is essentially Hirsch's distinction; and in the next chapter I shall argue at some length (i) That this is indeed a legitimate distinction; and (ii) That Gadamer's blurring of it (particularly in his views on the fusion of horizons, and on the unity of understanding and application) leads him into serious difficulties. Some care is required, however, to ensure that the argument is conducted in the right way. To invoke Hirsch's distinction *as a criticism of Gadamer* would beg the question, because, as Georgia Warnke has rightly observed,

> Gadamer's position does not merely overlook a [Hirschian] distinction between understanding meaning and understanding significance; it *denies* one. On his view, we understand the meaning of a text, work of art or historical event *only in relation to our own situation* and therefore only in light of our own concerns. In other words we understand it only in light of its significance.[61]

The argument between Gadamer and objectivism, in fact, is another example of a dispute between positions that proceed from fundamentally different principles, and will consequently be tackled in the way I discussed in section 5.2. The following chapter will therefore be particularly concerned with showing the internal incoherence of Gadamer's hermeneutics. To prepare the ground for this, however, I shall conclude the present chapter by setting out those aspects of *Truth and Method* which are relevant to this book, and exploring more fully how they relate to Childs' hermeneutics.

---

case, on how and why a particular line of research was being pursued. This, however, raises matters that are quite different from those I am considering here, and to which the conclusions about meaning for which I am presently arguing cannot be straightforwardly applied (if, indeed, they can be applied at all).

[61] *Gadamer: Hermeneutics, Tradition, and Reason* (Cambridge: Polity, 1987), p. 68; Warnke's italics.

## 5. *Some Themes from* Truth and Method

One of the principal aims of Gadamer's *magnum opus* is to reverse (what he considers to be) the drastic wrong turn that hermeneutics took with Schleiermacher. Referring particularly to Spinoza and Chladenius, Gadamer observes[62] that pre-romantic interpreters needed to resort to hermeneutics only on a few, special occasions, because understanding was assumed, for the most part, to occur quite naturally, without the help of any special arts. The truth-claims of the Bible and of classical literature upon the reader were generally direct and clear; thus it was only for problematic passages—in particular, for those dealing with supernatural occurrences—that Spinoza turned to hermeneutics. Since miracles, in Spinoza's view, contradicted reason, the truth-content of these passages was not immediately evident, and they therefore had to be understood 'historically', i.e., as the culturally conditioned opinions of an author who lived in a less enlightened age than our own.[63]

Although, then, historical-genetic understanding did have a certain place in pre-romantic scholarship, it was generally a minor one. With Schleiermacher, however, Gadamer sees it becoming the norm. Describing 'the assumption that understanding occurs as a matter of course' as 'a less rigorous' form of hermeneutics, Schleiermacher continues:

> There is a more rigorous practice of the art of interpretation that is based on the assumption that misunderstanding occurs as a matter of course, and so understanding must be willed and sought at every point.[64]

This meant, however, that hermeneutics could no longer be regarded as an occasional practice for resolving special problems, but would henceforth be the habitual way of dealing with a text, in order to guard against the ever-present dangers of misunderstanding. With Schleiermacher, therefore, there was a fundamental reorientation of interpretative interests, from the truth-content of the text to the life and circumstances of its author:

> What is for Spinoza a limiting case of intelligibility, and hence requires a detour via the historical, is for Schleiermacher the norm and the presupposition from which he develops his theory of understanding.[65]

---

[62] See *TM*, pp. 181–84.
[63] Cf. Childs' brief comment on Spinoza in *IOTS*, p. 34.
[64] 'Compendium', pp. 109–10; cf. *TM*, p. 185.
[65] *TM*, p. 186.

This, then, is the Schleiermacherian 'wrong turn' which Gadamer is trying to reverse, through reintroducing an updated version of the pre-romantic conception of understanding as 'agreement'.

'Agreement concerning the subject-matter' is a central concept in *Truth and Method*; moreover, it is an idea which, as we have seen, could be extremely useful to Childs. Unfortunately, however, it is also one of the most problematic aspects of Gadamer's thought, with it being far from clear even what kind of 'agreement' he is proposing. Thus at one point Gadamer claims that

> When we try to understand a text ... we try to transpose ourselves into the perspective within which [the author] has formed his views. But this simply means that we try to understand how what he is saying could be right. . . . This happens even in conversation . . .; (p. 292)

and in filling out his notion of conversation as a model for interpretation, Gadamer suggests that

> Reaching an understanding in conversation presupposes that both partners are ready for it and are trying to recognize the full value of what is alien and opposed to them. If this happens mutually, and each of the partners, while simultaneously holding on to his own arguments, weighs the counterarguments, it is finally possible to achieve ... a common diction and a common dictum. (p. 387)

These are broad claims, but, for that reason, appear to be relatively uncontentious, because their breadth enables them to cover the many different kinds of 'understanding relationships' that can arise. Two people of very different political persuasions, for example, who engage one another in a genuine discussion of their views, will each 'try to understand how what [the other] is saying could be right', giving their opponent's 'counterarguments' due weight and yet not surrendering their own 'arguments' without good reason; and even if the conversation ends (as such discussions often do) with their substantive political beliefs still poles apart, they may still have come to an understanding with respect to the subject-matter in the sense which Gadamer apparently envisages here—namely, that they more fully comprehend and respect the other's 'perspective'.

What Gadamer seems to propose here, then, is understanding as a *quest* for agreement—it is the understanding that emerges in the course of such a quest.[66] As Gadamer sets out his hermeneutics more

---

[66] This is closely related to the 'Hegelian' sense of the fusion of horizons that Warnke finds in *TM*. I shall discuss this more fully in the next chapter.

fully, however, this quite modest claim soon develops into something much stronger. A few lines on from the passage on p. 292 that I have just quoted, Gadamer rephrases it as 'We have seen that the goal of all attempts to reach an understanding is agreement concerning the subject matter' (*ibid.*); and although this could also be understood in the same, moderate sense if this 'goal' was conceived as an ideal which we *hope* to achieve, while also recognising that there are some people and texts with which we simply cannot agree, Gadamer shows that he has something more radical in mind when he immediately continues, 'Hence the task of hermeneutics has always been to *establish agreement* where there was none or where it had been disturbed in some way' and cites as an example Augustine's attempt to 'mediate the Gospel with the Old Testament'.[67] In a similar vein it is now claimed that in a 'true conversation'

> each person . . . truly accepts [the other's] viewpoint as valid and transposes himself into the other to such an extent that he understands not the particular individual but what he says. What is to be grasped is *the substantive rightness* of his opinion, so that *we can be at one with each other on the subject.*[68]

In other words, understanding a text is now conceived as reaching a substantive agreement with it concerning its contents. The task of hermeneutics is to bring this about.[69]

In passages such as these, then, Gadamer seems to be advocating a much stronger sense of agreement than the 'quest for agreement' that we looked at above. *Prima facie*, this stronger version would have problems accommodating the 'political conversation' example I outlined above; and more generally, appears to be open to numerous counter-examples of cases where we do understand a text perfectly well but reach little or no substantive agreement with it. Whether this stronger version is defensible, then, will depend very much upon the account that Gadamer gives of 'understanding a text'. For this he draws heavily upon Heidegger's notions of understanding as 'thrown projection',[70] but adds a new twist by explicating thrownness in terms of tradition and 'prejudice'. These concepts, Gadamer observes, were heavily attacked by the Enlightenment: Tradition was seen as a source

---

[67] *Ibid.*, italics added.
[68] *TM* p. 385, italics added; cf. p. 180.
[69] On the role of hermeneutics see *TM* pp. 294–95.
[70] For a lucid account of this see Warnke, pp. 37–40.

of prejudices which, because of the authority of the tradition, tended to be accepted uncritically. Thus the Enlightenment set tradition and reason over against each other, with the former being denigrated in the name of the latter (pp. 271–72), but Gadamer argues that in fact this is a false antithesis. On the one hand, reason is itself historically conditioned—things that appear perfectly reasonable to one age or culture can seem absurd or barbaric to another. And on the other hand, tradition is not *necessarily* unreasonable, but may be a source of insight and understanding.

So then, accepting Heidegger's analysis of understanding as proceeding from a historically-situated 'fore-conception' of (or, in Bultmann's terms, from a 'life-relation' to) that which is to be understood, Gadamer argues for the positive value of prejudice as the precondition that makes understanding possible. Tradition is not something 'outside' of ourselves; rather,

> we are always situated within traditions, and this is no objectifying process—i.e., we do not conceive of what tradition says as something other, something alien. It is always part of us. (p. 282)

Our family background, education, and social life fill us with the beliefs and opinions that are integral to us being what we are; and it is these preconceptions which both direct us to the problems we try to solve and give us the wherewithal to do so. '[B]elonging to tradition' is 'one of the conditions for understanding in the human sciences' (p. 328); if (though it is impossible) someone could free themselves from tradition they would not then understand in a true, 'unprejudiced' way but would be incapable of understanding anything at all.

Of course, Gadamer is also well aware that tradition is not uniformly commendable. There are some prejudices that hinder rather than help our understanding, and these should clearly be rejected. Yet Gadamer makes the further, interesting point that this cannot be done in advance of coming to understand but only through trying to do so. We cannot first purify our minds and only then, armed with the 'right' prejudices, set about interpreting the Bible; rather, 'this separation must take place in the process of understanding itself' (p. 296). Thus understanding emerges from a 'dialogue' between text and interpreter, in which, on the one hand, our prejudices are the preconditions that make the text meaningful to us, and yet, on the other hand, the text sifts and refines our prejudices.

Guided by a concern for the subject matter, the dialogue issues in agreement concerning the text's truth-claims, which elsewhere Gadamer calls a 'fusion of horizons'. 'Horizon' is Gadamer's metaphor for a life-perspective, conveying an awareness of how one's values and beliefs are structured and interrelated: 'A person who has an horizon knows the relative significance of everything within this horizon, whether it is near or far, great or small' (p. 302). The interpreter has his or her own, historically situated, horizon; but so too does the text, and the interpreter must respect this by not riding roughshod over its perspective but placing him or herself within it. Yet this does not mean, as the objectivist thinks, reconstructing it as something independent of oneself; rather, in understanding the text through our own prejudices a merger occurs between its outlook and ours:

> When our historical consciousness transposes itself into historical horizons, this does not entail passing into alien worlds unconnected in any way with our own; instead they together constitute the one great horizon that moves from within and that, beyond the frontiers of the present, embraces the historical depths of our self-consciousness. Everything contained in historical consciousness is in fact embraced by a single horizon. Our own past and that other past toward which our historical consciousness is directed help to shape this moving horizon out of which human life always lives and which determines it as heritage and tradition.[71]

This is why Gadamer insists that application is an integral part of interpretation: To interpret a text is a reciprocal process of understanding the text as part of our ongoing life, and understanding our life in terms of the text, and being shaped by it.

---

[71] *TM*, p. 304. There appears to be a significant misunderstanding at this point in Thiselton's exposition of Gadamer, according to which Gadamer believes that 'each [horizon] is *first* to be respected *before* a fusion of these two horizons can take place' (*NHH* p. 516, in Thiselton the whole quote is italicized; cf. pp. 8, 412, 610). If this were so then Gadamer would have reverted to something close to Hirsch's distinction, with the reading of the text within its own cultural-linguistic horizon giving its (Hirschian) meaning and the fusion of this with our own horizon yielding its significance. Gadamer in fact initially explains the fusion of horizons as though this *was* his view (see *TM*, pp. 302–304); but in the immediately following passage (pp. 304–307) he makes it clear that each horizon can only be formed through and in terms of the other, so that neither can first be reconstructed 'on its own terms' and only then fused with the other. (Cf. his very clear restatement of this in the 'Afterword' added to the third German edition; see *TM*, pp. 576–77.) Thiselton is nonetheless correct to point out (p. 412) that for Gadamer there is a 'tension' between the two horizons—it is not Gadamer's intention to allow the present to simply take over the past entirely in its own terms.

It seems clear, then, that there is much in *Truth and Method* which is potentially of great value to Childs: A hermeneutics which accomplished a fusion between the faith-stance of the modern church and the ancient Scriptures such that, while doing justice to each, a substantive agreement between them emerged concerning the truth-claim that the Bible makes upon our lives, would fulfil virtually all the major goals of Childs' programme. Thus Gadamer's significance for Childs extends far beyond the individual points that Fowl, Brett, and Scalise identify, to offer a general philosophy of understanding of which canonical hermeneutics would be one specific instantiation.[72] If Gadamer's hermeneutics is defensible then most of Childs' methodological problems would be solved.

I shall consider the tenability of Gadamer's hermeneutics at some length in the next chapter; but before turning to this, it is already possible to identify one point from Gadamer's book that is of some benefit to Childs. This is Gadamer's insistence that there is more to hermeneutics than is recognized by a 'hermeneutics of suspicion' which largely bypasses the substantive content of a text in its quest for the psychological or social situation from which it sprang. Since this is of some importance for both Childs and Gadamer, I shall enlarge upon it further by considering, as a concrete example, A.P. Rossiter's 'historical' reading of Shakespeare's *Coriolanus*. Believing Coriolanus' 'anti-democratic' speeches to express Shakespeare's own sentiments, Rossiter explains this drama's political stance genetically, as stemming from Shakespeare's fear—fuelled, perhaps, by the recent corn-riots—of the disorder that would ensue upon the common people interfering in the affairs of State.[73] This may be distasteful to a modern believer in democracy; but if we are to 'grasp' the play and appreciate its exploration of political forces and feelings, then (Rossiter claims) 'we must swallow our democracy, and . . . accept that the political convictions of Marcius are *right*' (p. 153).

---

[72] Although since Childs has generally been quite wary of theology accepting 'outside help' from such philosophies as Hegelianism and existentialism, he might not be overenthusiastic about this suggestion. I shall discuss the relationship between canonical hermeneutics and general philosophy in section 12.6 below.

[73] 'In considering what Shakespeare gave [Marcius] Coriolanus to think right, we cannot overlook the fact that in May 1607 there was . . . a peasant insurrection; and partly about corn . . . [T]hese risings . . . kept happening in Elizabethan times; and if you ask what is [Shakespeare's] fear of the mob and disorder, it is answered at once in Marcius's mouth . . .' ('Political Tragedy', in B.A. Brockman (ed.), *Shakespeare: Coriolanus* (Basingstoke: Macmillan, 1977), p. 152).

As we have seen, Gadamer would strongly object to our political convictions being guarded in this *a priori* way against any possible critique by the play; and in this he is surely correct. For even if (as Rossiter claims) Shakespeare's politics *were* coloured by contemporary events, his reaction to them (to judge from *Coriolanus* itself) was nonetheless an intelligent one; therefore in according the politics of this play a merely genetic interpretation, Rossiter misses a major strand in the argument of Shakespeare's play. For there *is* an argument here (although it is conducted in a style appropriate to a drama rather than a political tract): Through having the events unfold in a politically and psychologically plausible way, and thus showing us what the consequences of certain political options might be, Shakespeare is arguing that there are many inherent defects in (at least some forms of) democratic government: Crowds are short-sighted and fickle, tending to approve whatever is to their own, immediate benefit, but giving less consideration to the longer-term consequences for the State as a whole; they can easily be exploited by a clever rabble-rouser; the need to win the approval of the masses can be a strong temptation to dissimulate; etc. In other words, one has missed much of the value of *Coriolanus* if it has not been allowed to subject one's own views to its searching critique—which it cannot do if we bracket ourselves out in the way that Rossiter recommends. And even if, having read *Coriolanus* and weighed its arguments, we still believe that democracy is the best form of government, we should at least have gained from it a deeper perception of democracy's inherent weaknesses and limitations. To this extent at least there has been a fusion of our horizon with the text's.

This has important affinities with Childs' critique of the standard critical approach to the Bible, which he likewise accuses of being so concerned with understanding the text genetically that understanding its content is neglected—i.e., scholars fail to interact seriously with *die Sache*.[74] This, in part, is the point of Childs' polemics against historical referentiality,[75] and is also implicit in the way he contrasts his canonical approach with redaction criticism:

---

[74] Of course, Childs is by no means the first to be concerned about this, although he goes much further than most in the extent to which he blames the critical approach for 'the strange silence of the Bible in the modern church'.

[75] E.g., *IOTS* p. 41; cf. pp. 408, 485–86; similarly in his critique of Gottwald: 'To claim that these [biblical] confessions [of God bringing something new into being] are simply symbolic expressions of common social phenomena not only renders the

Canonical analysis focuses its attention on the effect which the different layers have had on the final form of the text, rather than using the text as a source for other information ... such as the editor's self-understanding.[76]

Although Childs assumes too readily that the formation of the biblical traditions was dominated by primarily religious concerns, he nonetheless makes a valid point, similar to Gadamer's: We are liable to miss the main purpose and value of a text if our efforts are directed primarily to explaining it as the product of its historical milieu. Even if our historical-critical investigations do enable us to identify a certain text as having its origins in, say, the official court polemic against the high places, and as being written to promote the king's centralization programme, we must still (*contra* Rossiter) wrestle seriously with the text's subject-matter. Of course, it *may* be that the text in question is nothing more than an insincere declaration of what the king would like his subjects to accept as religiously proper, though actually promulgated for no other reason than the king's belief that this will help him achieve his own political ends. On the other hand, it may be that the king's centralization programme was itself (in part) prompted by genuine religious insights into the shortcomings of the high places, which will simply be missed if one adopts a purely genetic approach. Insofar as Childs' criticisms of historical referentiality are directed against critical scholarship being overly genetic in its orientation, he is making a methodologically valid point.

---

uniquely biblical witness mute, but destroys the need for closely hearing the text on its verbal level' (*OTTCC*, p. 25).

[76] 'Significance', p. 68.

# CHAPTER NINE

# HERMENEUTICS AND OBJECTIVISM

With the previous chapter having clarified the basic hermeneutical issues and set out the relevant aspects of *Truth and Method*, it is now time to assess Gadamer's contribution to the hermeneutical debate and to discuss the implications of this for Childs' work.

## 1. *Gadamer's 'Oscillation'*

We saw at the end of the previous chapter that Gadamer and Childs are united in their belief in the reasonableness of tradition, and have made very similar diagnoses of the shortcomings of a 'historicist' hermeneutics. But granted that a historicist approach is untenable, things become more problematic when we ask how 'strong' a replacement is (a) desirable and (b) defensible. We have seen Gadamer making some striking claims about reaching substantive agreement with a text; and yet the fact that he also retains a number of weaker formulations may be a recognition that agreement is not universally attainable. For Childs, however, the weaker version would not be adequate—if (in the manner of the political conversation I envisaged in the previous section) we can finally say of a substantial part of the the Old Testament no more than that we understand its perspective and respect its views but nonetheless think that, for the most part, they are substantively wrong, this would be tantamount to rejecting Childs' centrally important claim that both Testaments bear witness to the one true God. It seems then that it is Gadamer's stronger claims about substantive agreement concerning the subject matter that are of relevance to Childs' work, and I shall therefore primarily consider Gadamer's defence of this.

In reaching a substantive agreement, there are two obviously-wrong approaches to be avoided—namely, that the interpreter's views are imposed upon the text in a way that rides roughshod over its own concerns; or that the interpreter's ideas are subordinated to the text's so passively as to commit a *sacrificium intellectus*. Nor, of course, is

Gadamer unaware of these pitfalls; and yet his attempts to steer a course between them often look suspiciously like an alternate stumbling first into the one declivity and then into the other. As Warnke observes:

> [Gadamer's] hermeneutics appears to founder on a dilemma: on the one hand it can avoid opportunism in interpretation only by becoming what one might call 'conservative' and accepting the truth of the object; conversely it can avoid this conservatism only by becoming opportunistic and failing to provide any criteria for discriminating between understanding and misunderstanding.[1]

Since, in my view, this points to some fundamental problems in Gadamer's hermeneutics, it is worth looking more closely at how this 'oscillation' (as Warnke calls it, *ibid.*) manifests itself in *Truth and Method*,[2] before considering the underlying causes. For Gadamer, application is one aspect of the fusion of horizons, which (as we have seen) must be understood in terms of the inescapable 'thrownness' of interpretation and the necessarily situated character, therefore, of understanding ('we understand differently if we understand at all'). But how, then, is application—which, we recall, involves coming to a substantive agreement with the text—how is such application to be distinguished from an opportunistic twisting of the text by each interpretative community or individual, who thereby impose their own preconceived 'prejudices' upon it? Gadamer's answer is that the text makes normative claims upon us, which cannot be capriciously set aside:

> We have the ability to open ourselves to the superior claim the text makes and to respond to what it has to tell us. Hermeneutics in the sphere of philology and the historical sciences is not 'knowledge as domination'—i.e., an appropriation as taking possession; rather, it consists in subordinating ourselves to the text's claim to dominate our minds.[3]

The obvious objection to this extreme conservatism, however, is that there are some texts, such as Nazi literature that depicts Jews as rats, to which we should certainly not subordinate our minds. Again Gadamer is aware of the problem, and insists (as we have seen) that

---

[1] *Gadamer*, p. 99. Warnke in fact believes (incorrectly, in my view) that this is only an *apparent* problem, which can for the most part be resolved by her 'Hegelian' interpretation of the fusion of horizons. I shall discuss this fully in section 2 below.

[2] Warnke's main discussions of this, to which the following is indebted, are on pp. 63–72, 74–75, 88–91, 98–99, and 134–38.

[3] P. 311; as Warnke points out (pp. 79, 105), this normativity is exemplified by Gadamer's views on the classical.

what tradition passes down to us (including the texts it preserves) must be tested and sifted; but in evaluating this reply it must be borne in mind that, according to Gadamer's own views on understanding, this testing and sifting will be done by historically situated human beings, who cannot but proceed on the basis of their own 'prejudices', and who will each understand, sift, and apply these texts in their own, culturally conditioned, way. With this, however, we seem to have returned once more to precisely the difficulty we started with. Thus far from resolving either the opportunistic or the conservative problems, Gadamer simply oscillates between them.

Although, in one sense, opportunism and conservatism are opposite errors, they nonetheless stem from the same basic fault of being insufficiently critical: Opportunism (in Warnke's sense) means failing adequately to submit our preconceptions to the criticism of the text, whereas conservatism means that we are insufficiently critical of what the text is claiming. The crucial issue in assessing Gadamer's hermeneutics, then, is whether it can accommodate sufficiently strong critical principles to avoid falling into these twin dangers.

Gadamer himself affirms the need to be self-critical when he appropriates Heidegger's notion of preunderstanding. Quoting with approval Heidegger's claim that

> our first, last and constant task in interpreting is never to allow our fore-having, fore-sight, and fore-conception to be presented to us by fancies and popular conceptions, but rather to make the scientific theme secure by working out these fore-structures in terms of the things themselves,[4]

Gadamer explains that the literary critic must understand 'the things themselves' in a twofold sense: Of the text that is being interpreted, and of the objects with which the text is concerned (p. 267). Criticism is guided by the 'fore-conception of completeness' (pp. 293–94), which Gadamer describes as 'a formal condition of all understanding' (p. 294). Its point is that interpretation proceeds on the assumption of a unity of meaning,[5] and again Gadamer explicates this with

---

[4] Martin Heidegger, *Being and Time* (Oxford: Blackwell, 1962), p. 195; as quoted in *TM* p. 266.

[5] Although Gadamer admits that this assumption may not always be fulfilled—a certain text may, for example, be self-contradictory. His point, though, is that we should strive to interpret the text as a unified whole until the text itself proves to be intractable. Only then should we give up our attempt to understand its truth-claim, and content ourselves with a historical explanation. As Gadamer recognizes, this is the basis for critical work on a text (p. 294).

respect to both texts and their objects: The reader both assumes that there is 'an immanent unity of meaning' in the text, and also 'is . . . guided by the constant transcendent expectations of meaning that proceed from the relation to the truth of what is said' (p. 294).

Gadamer's intention, then, is to use certain conceptions of unity and completeness as critical principles which, while not being 'tight' enough to lead to Schleiermacherian convergence, provide sufficient hermeneutical control to make interpretation a viable and worthwhile procedure. In evaluating Gadamer's hermeneutics, therefore, the main issue that needs to be addressed is whether these critical principles can in fact save him from either the 'conservative' or the 'opportunistic' tendencies that Warnke finds in some of his work. It is to these questions that I now turn.

## 2. *Agreement Concerning Truth-Claims*

We have seen that one aspect of Gadamer's hermeneutics which has particularly important affinities with Childs' work concerns his stronger claims about achieving substantive agreement; so in the present section I shall discuss this in some detail. With this I take up the conservative side of Warnke's oscillation; or, to put the issue in terms of the critical capacities of Gadamer's work: Does Gadamer achieve agreement through being insufficiently critical of the text?

We saw in section 8.5 that Gadamer likens understanding to a conversation, in which both participants (or 'partners', as Gadamer sometimes calls them) are genuinely seeking the truth about the subject-matter. Ideally the conversation issues in 'agreement concerning the subject-matter', although no-one knows in advance what this will consist in. Rather, in the course of reaching agreement the initial position of each participant is likely to have been substantially modified.

At first sight this may seem a curious model for understanding a text, in that a text cannot 'answer back' to its interpreter as an independent contributor to the dialogue. Gadamer is aware of this potential objection, and his response to it takes us to the central issues in his hermeneutics. Gadamer admits that the text can speak only through 'the written marks [being] changed back into meaning' by the interpreter (p. 387), but he then transforms this apparent problem into an advantage:

[T]his means that the interpreter's own thoughts too have gone into re-awakening the text's meaning. In this the interpreter's own horizon is decisive, yet not as a personal standpoint that he maintains or enforces, but more as an opinion and as a possibility that one brings into play and puts at risk, and that helps one truly to make one's own what the text says. . . . [T]his is what takes place in conversation, in which something is expressed that is not only mine or my author's, but common. (p. 388)

In other words, the fact that the text must be given its voice from within the interpreter's horizon, and yet cannot have the interpreter's own opinions simply thrust upon it, already brings text and reader into mutual conversation. Or as Gadamer explains a few pages later:

To think historically always involves mediating between those ideas [of the past] and one's own thinking. To try to escape from one's own concepts in interpretation is not only impossible but manifestly absurd. To interpret means precisely to bring one's own preconceptions into play so that the text's meaning can really be made to speak for us. (p. 397)

There is an obvious objection, however, to Gadamer's claims about agreement, which must now be discussed: Even when we have fully heeded Gadamer's strictures about the qualities of a genuine conversation and the possibility of our own views being revised, it is surely still the case that there are some texts with which we simply cannot and must not come to agreement concerning *die Sache*—it is logically impossible to agree with the geocentric astronomy of Ptolemy's *Almagest* without committing a *sacrificium intellectus*; and it would be morally reprehensible to agree with the racist politics of *Mein Kampf*.[6] In such cases we must surely insist that the text is *wrong* in its opinions about the subject-matter—we know better than it does.

*Prima facie*, then, such texts seem to pose a major problem for Gadamer's hermeneutics; but before they can be accepted as decisive refutations, we must first consider whether there is a notion of 'agreement' that can accommodate them. A survey of the numerous interpretative examples in *TM* soon reveals that the degree of substantive agreement which Gadamer himself establishes with the various texts he discusses is in fact extremely variable. As Warnke has pointed

---

[6] This is Warnke's example (p. 90), although she thinks that it does not furnish a decisive objection to the kind of agreement that Gadamer is proposing (at least in some parts of *TM*). We shall consider this below.

out (p. 90), there are some authors (such as Plato and Hegel) with whom Gadamer does reach a significant measure of agreement, finding in their writings important insights which he is able to take up and integrate into his own work. In contrast, his discussions of, say, Schleiermacher and Dilthey are 'an example of the insights to be won through critical distance'[7]—their contribution to the contemporary debate consists largely in having shown (albeit inadvertently) that their own paths of enquiry were in fact false trails. In view of this, Warnke makes the interesting suggestion that 'agreement' for Gadamer consists in a 'Hegelian' fusion of horizons, which

> involves appropriating [the tradition], integrating it within our own understanding of the subject-matter at issue in the sense that we can see strands of agreement and disagreement and use these to come to a 'better' position.[8]

In Warnke's view, it is this Hegelian construal of the fusion of horizons that saves Gadamer's hermeneutics from being shaken apart by its oscillation between conservatism and opportunism. Gadamer's conservatism (on this interpretation) expresses his expectation that the text will have something of value to say; and his opportunism claims that what it says is to be 'fused' with our views. According to Warnke's Hegelian construal, however, this fusion does *not necessarily* involve a substantive agreement between text and interpreter;[9] rather, the basic idea is simply that we integrate the text's views into our own outlook.[10] This, however, may come about through either agreement *or* disagreement with the text's truth-claims, and how it does so will vary from one case to another. Hegelian fusion can still occur, therefore, even with a text whose opinions we find totally unacceptable— 'we simply agree to disagree' (p. 103).

There are a number of comments to make on this. Warnke's

---

[7] Warnke, *ibid.*

[8] P. 103; Warnke's main discussions of this are on pp. 103–104, 107–108, and 169–70.

[9] Warnke is very clear about this: 'Such fusion . . . does not entail any concrete agreement', p. 107. What one is then to make of the numerous passages in which it is just such a 'concrete agreement' that Gadamer seems to be advocating will be considered in a moment.

[10] Thus for understanding the (scientifically outdated) concept of perpetual motion, Gadamer explains that 'We understand how certain questions came to be asked in particular historical circumstances. Understanding such questions means, then, understanding the particular presuppositions whose demise makes such questions "dead"' (p. 375). Presumably Gadamer would deal with the *Almagest* in the same way.

Hegelian construal of fusion is certainly helpful in clarifying an important strand in Gadamer's discussion of 'agreement'; however, it is the *weaker* of the two versions that we outlined in section 8.5 above, namely, understanding as a *quest* for substantive agreement which may or may not succeed. We identified this from Gadamer's methodological comments, whereas Warnke has persuasively argued that it is the mode of agreement actually exemplified by Gadamer's interpretative work. This is of no help, however, in defending the stronger version of 'agreement', which, because it explicates understanding as the *actual achieving* of substantive agreement, seems particularly vulnerable to the *Almagest* and *Mein Kampf* counterexamples.

Warnke is fully aware of this stronger version of agreement, but thinks that it is not supported by 'Gadamer's analysis of the conditions of understanding' (p. 106). In my view, however, this is highly debatable. On the one hand, some of Gadamer's discussions of tradition, and some versions of his conversation model, do indeed support the weaker version. On the other hand, however, when one looks at how Gadamer develops his fundamental principles of understanding, one finds them leading quite directly to the *strong* version of the fusion of horizons and substantive agreement. The basic line of argument is in fact quite straightforward. To understand is to understand through our (historically and culturally given) prejudices; therefore if we have understood at all then we have *necessarily* understood in this 'prejudiced' way. Of course, this does not mean that we simply wrest the text to fit our pregiven prejudices; rather, there must be a critical distancing that respects the text's horizon. Thus when we read the Succession Narrative, for example, we recognize it as an *ancient Israelite* story about (among other things) kingship, and therefore try to understand it in terms of *ancient Israelite* concepts of monarchy. Yet the Gadamerian analysis of understanding tells us that this is an unattainable ideal: Insofar as we understand this story at all, we do so through our modern prejudices—including *our modern conception* of ancient monarchy. But this means that as soon as understanding has occurred there has *already* been a fusion between the text's horizon and our own. In other words—and this is crucial for grasping the fundamental character of Gadamer's hermeneutics—the fusion of horizons is not a 'second step' that one takes after the text has been understood, but necessarily occurs with it, because this fusion is itself a part of what it is to understand.[11] This, however, seems to

---

[11] Cf. note 71 and the text preceding it in section 8.5 above. As Gadamer ob-

undermine the weaker, Hegelian, construal of the fusion of horizons, because it eliminates the 'critical distance' necessary for distinguishing between (i) understanding that *Mein Kampf* advocates racist policies and (ii) deciding that fusion with its horizons can only occur as a distancing of ourselves from it. Or to put it another way, the weaker version requires one to make a distinction (not unlike Hirsch's!) between 'what it means' and 'how we evaluate it', whereas the fundamental logic of Gadamer's views undermine this distinction.

The same can also be said about the application of a text to the interpreter, because for Gadamer application just is the fusion of the interpreter's horizon with the text's.[12] According to Gadamer, application became problematic when romanticism fused together understanding and interpretation in such a way as wholly to exclude application from hermeneutics. By contrast, Gadamer himself '[considers] application to be just as integral a part of the hermeneutical process as are understanding and interpretation',[13] and his definitions in fact ensure that they are logically inseparable: To understand a text is to understand it through our prejudices, which is to fuse its horizon with our own, which is the same thing as applying the text to ourselves—application *is* the understanding of it through *our own* prejudices; therefore 'application is neither a subsequent nor merely an occasional part of the phenomenon of understanding, but codetermines it as a whole from the beginning'.[14] Once again, then, we see Gadamer achieving his theoretical goals in a way that unfolds naturally into his 'strong programme'. The basic logic of his position allows for no exceptions, and thereby excludes the critical, reflective distancing that is needed for his 'weak programme'.

Precisely the same thing occurs once more with the subject of 'agreement', where it is again clear that Gadamer considers the stronger version to be entailed by his analysis of understanding. Particularly instructive in this respect is the following passage, which, in view of the central importance of this subject, is worth quoting at length. Reminding us that his discussion of play has shown that 'it is the game itself that plays, for it draws the players into itself' (p. 490), Gadamer then applies this to understanding:

---

serves at one point, the Heideggerian analysis of understanding as thrown projection still applies 'even if the intention of the knower is simply to read "what is there" and to discover from his sources "how it really was"' (*TM*, p. 262).

[12] See *TM*, p. 307.
[13] *TM*, p. 308.
[14] P. 324; cf. pp. 340, 341.

Thus, understanding is not playing, in the sense that the person understanding playfully holds himself back and refuses to take a stand with
respect to the claim made on him. *The freedom of self-possession necessary
for one to withhold oneself is not given here.* . . . Someone who understands is
*always already* drawn into an event through which meaning asserts itself. . . . When we understand a text, what is meaningful in it captivates us just as the beautiful captivates us. It has asserted itself and
captivated us *before we can come to ourselves and . . . test the claim to meaning
that it makes.* . . . In understanding we are drawn into an event of truth
and arrive, as it were, too late, if we want to know what we are supposed
to believe.[15]

Unfortunately the logic by which one gets from understanding to
substantive agreement is not as clear as one might wish, but the
important point is that Gadamer evidently believes that the two
necessarily go together. Once again the critical distance between
understanding what a text says and deciding whether it is true, which
is crucial for the weaker version of agreement, is completely excluded.

It seems, then, that the strong and the weak versions of agreement
must be assessed very differently. On the one hand, the weak version—especially as this is elaborated by Warnke—offers a plausible
description of how scholars do in fact interact with the texts they
interpret. In doing so, however, it implicitly assumes that a fairly
rigid distinction can be drawn between the meaning of the text and
the interpreter's evaluation of it; yet this is precisely the distinction
which Gadamer's fundamental principles must necessarily reject. The
strong version, on the other hand, follows very naturally from
Gadamer's fundamental principles but runs into numerous counter-
examples which seem quite irrefutable: As examples such as *Mein
Kampf* make clear, reaching substantive agreement with a text is *not*
integral to understanding it.[16] Or to put it another way, disagreeable

---

[15] *Ibid.*, italics added; this passage gains particular significance from occuring in
the penultimate paragraph of *TM*, where Gadamer is synthesizing and summing up
the diverse strands in his argument. Warnke (p. 105) rightly quotes from this passage to show that Gadamer sometimes advocates a (problematic) strong version of
agreement, but seems not to have noticed that Gadamer—quite correctly—regards
this as necessarily following from his views on understanding. As Thiselton has aptly
remarked, Gadamer's views on play imply that 'Consciousness takes a secondary
place, and reflection is replaced by reflexivity' (*NHH*, p. 320).

[16] One could, of course, formally overcome this problem by redefining 'understanding properly so called' in such a way that a text has not been 'properly understood' unless one has grasped something of its application to the present. (Warnke's
defence of Gadamer sometimes slides towards this; see pp. 95–97, and cf. David
Hoy, *The Critical Circle* p. 54.) The problem with this, however, is that one then loses

or controversial texts forcibly remind us that their application to ourselves (whether individually or collectively) is, in general, inherently debatable, and therefore needs the critical distance which only the weaker version allows.

The conclusion to which this discussion points, then, is that because Gadamer denies Hirsch's distinction between meaning and significance he runs together things which, *prima facie*, examples such as *Mein Kampf* show us can and should be kept apart. The next issue to look at, therefore, is whether Gadamer in fact has any good arguments against Hirsch's distinction. More specifically, do Gadamer's views on tradition and prejudice really undermine the possibility of objective, reader-independent understanding of a text's meaning?

## 3. *Criticism and Convergence*

We have already seen that Gadamer himself recognizes the necessity of self-criticism in order that our initial preconceptions can be corrected by 'the things themselves'. In the present section I shall consider more fully how Gadamer develops this when 'the things themselves' are construed as the texts one is interpreting; and in particular, I will consider the linguistic aspects of this problem.

As interpreters, 'we regard our task as deriving our understanding of the text from the linguistic usage of the time or of the author';[17] yet we are hampered in this by an unconscious tendency to impose our own linguistic usage upon the text. Nonetheless, this can be corrected. Gadamer calls our attention to 'the experience of being pulled up short by the text' (p. 268), i.e., of finding that the text is meaningless, or that its meaning is incompatible with our expectations. When this happens it warns us that our usage may be different from

---

touch with the issues which motivated hermeneutical reflection in the first place. There is an important sense in which someone who has no idea about how, for example, Leviticus applies to the modern world but who can accurately summarize its contents in their own words, can answer questions about how and when the various sacrifices were offered, and can discuss the theories of atonement which informed them clearly *does* 'understand' this book quite well. It is a sense of 'understanding Leviticus' which is central to writing a commentary, and which one would hope that hermeneutical theory might illuminate; therefore redefining 'to understand' so that this does not even count as 'real understanding' hardly seems to be a helpful step.

[17] *TM*, p. 267.

the text's. Likewise when Gadamer discusses preunderstanding under the metaphor of the questions we put to a text, he points out that some questions are 'slanted' in that they move away from the right direction; therefore although they genuinely intend to ask a question, they cannot in fact be answered (p. 364).

Gadamer, then, fully accepts that our initial prejudices can be corrected through seeing whether they 'work out' in interpreting the text—this, in fact, is fundamental to his hermeneutics. But how, then, can he avoid having the hermeneutical circle turn into a spiral, which objectively converges upon a determinate, reader-independent meaning? Gadamer recognises that this is how Schleiermacher viewed interpretation; but against this he raises three main objections. His first objection is that the dialectic between whole and part is not (or not always) a sufficiently strong constraint to force convergence. As Warnke puts it,

> If one begins to understand the individual parts of a text in light of an assumption as to the meaning of its whole, it is not clear how these parts, so understood, can lead one to revise one's understanding of the whole. . . . Why, in other words, is the hermeneutic circle not simply a vicious one in which one's understanding of the individual parts of a text confirm one's assumption as to the meaning of the whole and vice versa?[18]

Warnke illustrates the problem from Wordsworth's 'A Slumber Did My Spirit Seal'. Cleanth Brooks reads the poem as an expression of inconsolable grief at Lucy's death, interpreting the final lines,

> She neither hears nor sees;
> Rolled round in earth's diurnal course,
> With rocks, and stones, and trees.

as portraying her utter lifelessness. F.W. Bateson, on the other hand, reads it as a pantheistic expression of hope, with these same references to rocks and trees now interpreted as affirming that Lucy has been taken up into the life of Nature.[19] Hirsch thinks that the second

---

[18] P. 84, following *TM* p. 268 (the reference in Warnke on p. 187 n. 18 is a misprint). This passage is actually part of Gadamer's discussion of 'the things themselves' in the sense of the objects referred to by the text; nonetheless, it is appropriate to discuss it here because (as Warnke explains, p. 86) its purpose is apparently to show that interpretation which is confined to 'the text itself' (i.e., which does not consider the truth-claims of its objects) is too indeterminate. If this were so, it would constitute a major objection to Schleiermacher's grammatical circle.

[19] The arguments are reviewed by E.D. Hirsch in *Validity*, pp. 227–30.

interpretation is more probable because we know from various sources other than this poem that Wordsworth *was* a pantheist at this time;[20] but Warnke objects that

> [Hirsch's] solution fails to clarify how the kind of extra-textual evidence to which he appeals is supposed to aid purely textual interpretation since one also needs an interpretation of this evidence and its relation to the text. (p. 85)

Warnke therefore concludes that 'the viciousness of the hermeneutic circle may not always be avoided by relying on criteria of coherence alone' (p. 86).

In my view, Warnke's analysis of this example is faulty. Her objection to Hirsch raises two separate points: Firstly, How does the external evidence bear upon the interpretation of the poem? An adequate answer, however, is that knowing Wordsworth to have been a pantheist alerts us to the connotations that rocks and stones had for him, and what might therefore be conveyed through associating Lucy with them. Even Wimsatt and Beardsley allow that one can look to sources outside the text (including private letters and diaries) to discover the particular nuances of an author's vocabulary, although they rightly caution that it is another question again as to whether the meanings discovered in this way are also present in the text.[21] There does not seem, then, to be anything problematic with this aspect of Hirsch's position.

Secondly, however, Warnke raises the spectre of an infinite regress, moving back from the text to the external evidence to whatever aids are used in interpreting that evidence, etc. But this is a pseudo-problem that stems from Warnke's unrealistic description of the situation. Warnke writes as though little can be done about the uncertainties of the text until, as a prior, self-contained step, the external evidence has been interpreted, which in turn cannot be done until, as another discrete step prior to that, the aids by which this is to be done have themselves been interpreted; but this is too atomistic. The situation, rather, is that (i) The text and the external evidence, together with numerous other writings, are all parts of a linguistic whole; and (ii) much is already known about this whole.[22] For the most part, therefore, the external evidence will be straightforwardly

---

[20] *Validity*, pp. 238–41.
[21] See 'IFal', section IV.
[22] As we saw in section 8.2, Schleiermacher's circle is intended to *improve* our

comprehensible in terms of the linguistic knowledge one already has; and where residual difficulties remain, these can be dealt with by the methods of whole and part (including the use of parallel passages). As we saw when reviewing Schleiermacher's discussion of these methods, they are workable because one is dealing with a relatively limited range of unknowns within an area where much is already known. One is simply not in the situation that Warnke envisages, where virtually everything is uncertain—or if (like the pioneer anthropologist) one *is* in such a situation, then Schleiermacher's circle was never intended to deal with it, and it cannot, therefore, be cited against him. Once this is realized, I cannot see that Warnke has raised any new problems.

The most important methodological point to emerge from the Wordsworth example, however, is the importance of distinguishing between indeterminacy and ambiguity: Showing that there are two viable interpretations of a certain text establishes no more than that this particular text is ambiguous. This is in fact the main point that Hirsch makes, going on to observe that

> Ambiguity . . . is not the same as indeterminateness. . . . To say that verbal meaning is determinate is not to exclude complexities of meaning but only to insist that a text's meaning is what it is and not a hundred other things. (p. 230)

In other words, this poem is not amenable to just any fore-conception of the whole, nor even to a limited range (e.g., those concerned with bereavement)—anyone trying to read it as an affirmation of the resurrection of the dead or of a Platonic doctrine of the soul would quickly be 'pulled up short' by the text. If, then, both Brooks' and Bateson's interpretations can be sustained exegetically, the conclusion to draw is not that the circle is sometimes vicious, but that for this particular text there are two ways of bringing it to a satisfactory conclusion—i.e., that the text objectively has two determinate meanings.

This naturally leads on to Gadamer's second objection to Schleiermacher, which concerns the true character of the hermeneutical circle. For Schleiermacher this was a *methodological* circle, understood as a formal relationship between part and whole;[23] but Heidegger recon-

---

understanding of a passage that is in a language for which we *already* have at least a basic lexicon and grammar.

[23] P. 293; Gadamer has at this point 'set aside Schleiermacher's ideas on subjective interpretation' (p. 292) and is considering only his views on grammatical interpretation.

ceived the circle as an analysis of the necessarily circular character of understanding. This moves between the tradition (of which the text is a part) and the interpreter, both of which evolve under the influence of the other: Tradition is the source of the 'anticipations of meaning' through which we interpret a text; and yet

> Tradition is not simply a permanent precondition; rather, we produce it ourselves inasmuch as we understand, participate in the evolution of tradition, and hence further determine it ourselves. (p. 261)

From the developing tradition, however, there arise new anticipations of meaning and hence new interpretations; thus far from the circular movement finally tapering out as perfect understanding is achieved, it is constantly reaffirmed.[24]

This raises two issues which need to be discussed here, the first of which concerns the viability of Heidegger's circle as an account of textual interpretation. Heidegger's analysis, of course, is intended as a general account of what it is to understand, and *a fortiori*, therefore, of what it is to understand a text. If, then, it *is* an accurate analysis, it should be possible to use it in giving an illuminating account of various specific examples of understanding a text—or, with respect to the particular issue being considered here, of those aspects of understanding in which it is supposed to be superior to Schleiermacher's analysis. One of the major strengths of Schleiermacher's hermeneutics, in fact, is that his accounts of parallel passages and the hermeneutical circle do seem to match up very well with the realities of biblical interpretation. It therefore needs to be asked whether the Heidegger/Gadamer theory can also provide insight into (some relevant aspect(s) of) our hermeneutical endeavours.

Unfortunately Gadamer gives us very little help in deciding this, because he leaves it desperately unclear how the abstract, Heideggerian analysis is supposed to 'cash out' in terms of what real-life interpreters actually *do* with their texts. As Stephen Fowl has aptly observed,

> Gadamer talks about concepts such as 'judgement', 'tact', the '*Sensus Communis*', *et al.* as guiding principles in determining what is and is not justifiable in one's preunderstanding. ... When it comes to discussing how one might exercise these principles in certain situations, however, Gadamer is painfully silent.[25]

---

[24] *Ibid.*; cf. Gadamer's fuller discussion of Heidegger's circle on pp. 266–67.
[25] 'The Canonical Approach of Brevard Childs', p. 176.

Anyone interested in evaluating Gadamer's hermeneutics is therefore largely left on their own in finding plausible illustrations of how it is all supposed to work; and in fact it seems extremely difficult to find a realistic example which both fits Gadamer's account *and* provides a counterexample to Schleiermacher.[26] Thus if, for example, one considers Gadamer's analysis in relation to the developing history of scholarship, then insofar as it makes a valid point it is one that Schleiermacher could accept. There clearly is an evolving, non-convergent tradition of Shakespeare studies, with one generation focusing on character and plot, another on language and imagery, etc.; and in *this* sense it is therefore true to say that there is no single, correct set of presuppositions with which to read Shakespeare. There is no reason why this should trouble the objectivist, however, who could rightly point out that what this illustrates is a version of historical *selectivity*, and that this is perfectly compatible with a belief in objective meaning—the Schleiermacherian circle never claimed convergence in the sense of showing that, say, the one objectively correct way of interpreting *Coriolanus* is to analyse the character of its leading protagonists (rather than its political arguments, or its imagery); so pointing out that scholarship has not in fact converged in this way would be entirely beside the point.[27]

To carry weight as an argument against Schleiermacher, then, the Heideggerian analysis would have to be applied to the same kind of interpretative problem as the Schleiermacherian circle is intended to tackle (such as the Kuhn-Aristotle example, or 'Jacobs-Rosenbaum . . .'). But here the Heideggerian circle looks much more questionable, because, *prima facie*, the history of scholarship provides numerous examples where interpretation *does* converge—there are many cases in which it seems quite correct to say that we can now give better (fuller, more accurate) answers to questions about the meaning of Genesis or of John's Gospel than were given to these same questions two or five or fifteen centuries ago. When put to the test, then, of which circle deals best with the realities of interpretation, it looks as

---

[26] The question at this stage, it will be recalled, is whether a Heideggerian analysis of the circle refutes Schleiermacher's claim that it converges upon determinate meanings. Whether one should instead construe the Heideggerian and Schleiermacherian circles as *complementary* analyses of different aspects of the hermeneutical problem will be considered below.

[27] These are essentially the same issues that were discussed in section 8.4, particularly in connection with Gadamer's Mommsen example.

if a strong case can be made in Schleiermacher's favour.

The second issue to arise from Gadamer using Heidegger's circle to refute Schleiermacher's version is whether they are really discussing the same *kind* of circle. Gadamer himself apparently believes that there are fundamental differences: Schleiermacher's circle is 'methodological', seeking to guide the interpreter through the practicalities of textual interpretation, whereas Heidegger's is an 'ontological' circle, which explores understanding as a dimension of being human. But if this is correct, does Gadamer's appeal to Heidegger really constitute an *objection* to the project that Schleiermacher is pursuing, or has Gadamer (as Richard Corliss argues)[28] simply proposed a different, but compatible, project of his own?

Corliss' suggestion is an interesting one; yet in my view it is inadequate, because it fails to recognize the substantive similarity between Gadamer's project and Schleiermacher's which is implicit in them both being concerned with how we *understand* texts. Now within the broad field of hermeneutics there are (as Corliss rightly perceives) many different problems to be tackled, including both the 'methodological' and the 'ontological' questions we have just outlined. Unless, however, this diverse work remains oriented to the understanding that emerges when real-life readers read, interpret, discuss, re-read, and argue about real-life texts, then it simply puts itself outside the hermeneutical debate.

Both Schleiermacher and Gadamer, on the whole, are well aware of this; and their respective projects therefore have much more in common than Corliss realizes. The dispute between them (insofar as it pertains to matters of grammatical interpretation) can be summed up by saying that Schleiermacher, on the one hand, believes that (through following his methodology of the hermeneutical circle and parallel passages) it is possible to arrive at a determinate, reader-independent, understanding of a text; whereas Gadamer, on the other hand, while not himself interested in questions of methodology, believes that the nature of understanding is such as to be necessarily reader-dependent. There is more than enough common ground here for it to make sense to ask which of these scholars gives the better account of understanding; and the principal way of deciding this is to test the alternatives against some concrete exegetical examples.

In my view, a truer assessment of the Gadamer-Schleiermacher

---

[28] 'Hermeneutics', pp. 363–64, 376–78.

debate may be found in a direction precisely opposite to that which Corliss suggests: The Heideggerian and Schleiermacherian circles are actually much more *similar* than Gadamer realizes. Although Schleiermacher describes his circle in abstract terms, it is obviously not 'the whole' and 'the part' which somehow interact of themselves, but rather the interpreter's fore-conception of the whole which interacts with his or her preunderstanding of the text's language and subject matter as the interpreter strives to read the text as a unified whole. Going beyond this, Gadamer makes a valuable contribution in calling attention to the indispensable role of tradition, culture, and historical milieu in 'giving' the interpreter his or her language and fore-conceptions, and in doing so not in an 'external' way but in virtue of them being integral to human life. I can see no reason, however, why Schleiermacher could not accept this as a further development of his own position; and given that Gadamer also believes, with Schleiermacher, that our initial preconceptions must be revised and refined as we try to understand the text through them, it becomes difficult to see how Schleiermacher's circle differs substantially from Heidegger's contention that our fore-conceptions must be 'worked out' in terms of the things themselves (bearing in mind that, at this stage, we are considering 'the things themselves' as just the texts, not the objects with which the texts are concerned). Of course, there *would* be a substantial difference if, to achieve objectivity, the Schleiermacherian circle was supposed to progressively eliminate the interpreter's presuppositions in a quest for the mythical *tabula rasa*. In that case Gadamer would be justified in finding Schleiermacher's circle to be 'ontologically' deficient; but in fact its concern is not with *eliminating* presuppositions but with moving towards better ones.

In a third line of argument against Schleiermacher, Gadamer rejects author's intention as a criterion of meaning:

> It sounds at first like a sensible hermeneutical rule ... that nothing should be put into a text that the writer or the reader [*sic*] could not have intended. But this rule can be applied only in extreme cases. For texts do not ask to be understood as a living expression of the subjectivity of their writers. This, then, cannot define the limits of a text's meaning. (p. 395)

In the light of our previous discussions of author's intention, this argument is easily answered. Insofar as Gadamer is making a valid point he is calling attention to the '(auto)biographical fallacy'; but as we saw in section 7.2, even when this has been set aside there is still

an important role for author's intention as a constraint upon interpretation[29] which has nothing to do with understanding texts as 'a
living expression of the subjectivity of their writers' in the psychologistic
and/or genetic senses that Gadamer finds objectionable.

To sum up, then, this section has argued that Gadamer is unable
to prevent the convergence of the grammatical circle, and has no
defence, therefore, against such counterexamples as Kuhn-Aristotle
and 'Jacobs-Rosenbaum . . .'. *Contra* Gadamer, then, it seems as though
texts *do* have determinate, reader-independent meanings, and that
Hirsch's distinction between meaning and significance *is* valid.

## 4. *The Significance of the Author*

It is appropriate at this point to discuss more fully the role of psychological interpretation in Schleiermacher's hermeneutics. This completely dominates Gadamer's account of Schleiermacher, who is discussed almost entirely as the scholar primarily responsible for leading
hermeneutics into the psychologistic 'wrong turn' from which Gadamer
wants to rescue it. A very different picture of Schleiermacher's
hermeneutics, however, is presented by Anthony Thiselton. While
recognizing that one of Schleiermacher's major concerns was with
'"getting inside" the author's thoughts and feelings', Thiselton nonetheless claims that 'Schleiermacher's emphasis on "sharing the form
of *life*" *prohibits a merely psychologistic interpretation of this principle*',[30] and
further explains that

> Schleiermacher's close attention to language as both system . . . and as
> temporal speech-act or event . . ., together with complex and careful
> qualifications which are very often overlooked, does not compel us to
> tie Schleiermacher's hermeneutics with psychologizing notions of in-
> tentionality.[31]

---

[29] It should also be clear from this why Gadamer's attempted *reductio ad absurdum*
of 'the original reader' (*ibid.*) is misguided. The hermeneutical significance of the
original readers is that they share a common language with the author (cf.
Schleiermacher, 'The First Draft' p. 70; 'Compendium' pp. 113, 117; 'The Marginal Notes of 1832–33', p. 216), and it is clearly inappropriate to define this sort
of 'contemporaneity' by drawing a precise 'line'. It is a matter, rather, of degree—
or more precisely, of varying degrees, depending upon which aspect of the problem
one is discussing.

[30] *NHH* p. 223, Thiselton's italics.

[31] P. 559; cf. p. 560. In his exposition of Schleiermacher's thought, Thiselton is
careful to explain that for Schleiermacher grammatical and psychological interpretation

And yet despite this, Thiselton also quotes Palmer's 'apt' characterization of Schleiermacher's hermeneutics as 'the reverse of composition, for it starts with the fixed and finished expression and goes
back to the mental life from which it arose',[32] and himself draws
attention to Schleiermacher's interest in the spirit that lay behind the
text, and in the thoughts and events from which it sprang (pp. 225–
28; 232). Although Thiselton plays down these aspects, they appear
to go a considerable way towards reviving the psychologistic interpretation of Schleiermacher that Thiselton would like to overcome.
To what extent, then, is Gadamer's negative evaluation of Schleiermacher's hermeneutics really justified?

In my view, considerable light has been shed on this issue by Heinz
Kimmerle's detection of a development in Schleiermacher's thought.
There are a number of aspects to this, but the most important for
the present discussion is Schleiermacher's change of focus from (what
we might call) 'the author *in* the text' to 'the author *behind* the text'.
As Kimmerle notes, there is a significant shift between Schleiermacher's
earlier and later writings in his conception of the relationship between thought and language. In his earlier work Schleiermacher held
that 'thought and expression are essentially and internally entirely
the same',[33] and that psychological interpretation is therefore concerned with the personality and individuality of the author insofar as
these come to expression in the text. Thus in the 'Compendium'
Schleiermacher states that 'The goal of technical interpretation . . .
[is] the complete understanding of style' (p. 148), which he explains
as grasping the author's distinctive way of handling both language
and thought. This naturally requires historical knowledge of such things
as 'the state of a given genre when the author began to write' (p. 149),
but this is only to provide the background against which the 'distinctiveness' of the author can be discerned. The central point is to grasp
this distinctiveness from '[an] overview of the [author's] work' (p. 150),
and the acid test of whether psychological interpretation has been
successful is the ability to write in the same style oneself (p. 149).

In Schleiermacher's later thought, however, thinking and speaking
were more clearly distinguished, and the aim of hermeneutics was

---

were closely interrelated, with neither being intrinsically the 'higher' task (see *NHH*
pp. 216–33 *passim*).
   [32] Quoted in *NHH*, p. 224.
   [33] Quoted from Schleiermacher's *Sämmtliche Werke* by Kimmerle ('Editor's Introduction', in Schleiermacher, *Hermeneutics*, p. 36).

reconceived as '[grasping] the thinking that *underlies* a given state-ment'.[34] This is worked out more fully in the 'Addresses', where Schleiermacher defends the thesis that '[T]he task of hermeneutics is to reproduce the whole internal process of an author's way of com-bining thoughts' (p. 188), further explaining that ideally this would trace out the complete process of composition, from the initial 'mo-ments of creativity' to the final text (p. 204). The extent to which Schleiermacher's attention is now upon the author apart from the text is brought out by his regretting that, due to our paucity of in-formation, we cannot accomplish this nearly so well for the classical authors as could their 'original readers' (p. 207).

Looking back from the perspective of Schleiermacher's later thought, Kimmerle draws this very significant contrast: 'The object of inter-pretation [for Schleiermacher] is no longer the given content. It is now the process of movement from the internality of thought to language' (p. 39). Kimmerle's second sentence reminds us of Gadamer's psychologistic Schleiermacher, who was guilty of the (auto)biographical fallacy; his first sentence, however, brings into view a kind of under-standing that Gadamer never really considers. According to Gadamer's history of hermeneutics, there has been a shifting about between just two options: Understanding as agreement or understanding genetically. Schleiermacher's supposed crime is that he turned hermeneutics into an exclusive quest for the latter; but there are two things that need to be said in reply: (i) Schleiermacher was *never*, at any stage in his career, remotely as one-sided a geneticist as Gadamer portrays—gram-matical (linguistic) interpretation remains a central strand even in Schleiermacher's last notes on hermeneutics, and psychological inter-pretation remains firmly tied to it.[35] (ii) Schleiermacher's earlier work points to another conception of hermeneutics from those considered by Gadamer (and which, due to the continued importance for

---

[34] 'Compendium' p. 97, italics added; although as Kimmerle points out (p. 38), the new conception that is here expressed in the *Introduction* to the 'Compendium' is not worked out in the section on psychological interpretation, which still reflects Schleiermacher's earlier thought.

[35] 'Each side [sc. the linguistic and the personal] is carried to such an extent that at the end the result is the same as that reached by the other. . . . Neither task is higher or lower.—Both require a linguistic talent and knowledge of human nature' ('The Marginal Notes of 1832–33', p. 215). In the 'Afterword' to the third German edition of *Truth and Method* Gadamer admits that 'Perhaps I overemphasized Schleiermacher's tendency towards psychological (technical) interpretation rather than grammatical-linguistic interpretation' (see *TM* p. 565).

Schleiermacher of grammatical interpretation, is by no means sub-
merged in his later work), namely, that (as Kimmerle puts it) 'The
object of interpretation is . . . the given content' (p. 39), not (necessarily) as something one agrees (or disagrees) with, or whose underlying sources one is (necessarily) interested in, but simply as what the
text says. This, of course, is a sense of 'understanding' that is closely
related to the convergence of the grammatical circle.

At this point, however, a possible objection might be raised: If, in
order to avoid the (auto)biographical fallacy, questions of author's
psychology and the like are excluded, it may appear that we have
after all fallen back into the sort of New Critical position that was
previously rejected. Or to put it another way: Of what positive value
for the interpreter is a *text immanent* author? Does this not still come
down, in the end, to nothing more than a formalist reading of 'the
text itself'?

That this is not in fact the case has been ably demonstrated, in
my view, by Thiselton's illuminating applications of Schleiermacher's
hermeneutics to the New Testament. Discussing the anonymous Epistle
to the Hebrews, Thiselton comments:

> [W]hat is important is not our knowledge of the *name and biography* of
> an author, but that the text which the author produces is understood . . .
> as a *wholeness which represents the vision of a human mind and which belongs to
> some larger context or life-world.*[36]

As one reads and re-reads a text such as Hebrews or 1 Corinthians
one gains a lively sense of its author as a living, feeling, thinking
human being, with a distinctive personality of his or her own, and
who addresses the matters at hand in his or her own particular way;
and this is hermeneutically significant, because further sentences are
then read and re-read as (say) *Pauline* sentences, that is, in the light
of certain fore-conceptions about Paul's characteristic ideas, modes
of thought, and ways of expressing himself—i.e., in terms of what
Schleiermacher would call his 'style'.

Of course, this style has itself been discerned from numerous other
Pauline sentences, and our conception of it must in turn be cor-
rected by close and detailed study of particular passages within the
Pauline corpus.[37] The question then arises once more, however, given

---

[36] *NHH* p. 261; Thiselton's italics.
[37] As Thiselton is careful to point out, pp. 237, 238–39, 257, 261, etc.

that (to avoid the (auto)biographical fallacy) we are concerned with the author only insofar as he or she can be discerned in the text, whether the concept of authorship, even if heuristically useful, is nonetheless hermeneutically redundant. What is the difference between reading a text as the work of a text-immanent author and simply reading the text?

To my mind, this question makes the same sort of empiricistic mistake as that which asks what more do we 'actually see' than certain patches of various colours. According to our discussion in section 4.4 there is nothing 'more' in the sense of a 'something' that one can point to as an additional 'bit'; rather, it is the very structuring and organizing that makes our perceptions a coherent visual field rather than a mere kaleidascope of tumbling colours. If, in a misguided quest for certainty, this interpretative structuring is discarded then one will never re-integrate the coloured fragments; and similarly, I would suggest, it is the interpretative structuring of the immanent author concept which enables one to discern and comprehend a text's unity and coherence.

This argument can be clarified by considering the inadequacy of what Gadamer puts in the author's place, namely, his principle of the fore-conception of completeness. This states that 'only what really constitutes a unity of meaning is intelligible',[38] and interpretation therefore proceeds on the assumption of the text's completeness. There are two major problems with this principle, however, the first of which concerns its 'status'. Gadamer correctly describes it as a 'formal' principle (*ibid.*), but for this reason it encounters the same problem that I noted when discussing Childs' notion of the canon as a formal principle:[39] it lacks justification. *Why should* we strive to understand the text as a coherent whole? The obvious answer is that the author very likely *intended* the text to have a unified meaning;[40] but this reply admits that our hermeneutical procedures only make sense if we read the text as the product of an author.

Secondly, there is a problem with the *applicability* of Gadamer's principle, which stems from it stating an abstract, ideal, standard.

---

[38] *TM*, p. 294.
[39] See section 2.3 above.
[40] Alternatively, one might answer pragmatically that interpretation 'works well' if one adopts completion as a formal principle; but then essentially the same question of justification recurs again in the form, 'Why does *this particular* principle work well, when so many others do not?'.

There are in fact relatively few texts that meet this standard; most writings (at least, if they are of any length or complexity) will display *some* degree of irregularity, variability, or contradictoriness. Gadamer is not unaware of this, and rightly points out (*ibid.*) that the detection of such irresoluble inconsistencies is the starting point for textual criticism. This, however, is just one, relatively straightforward, example of the innumerable cases in which Gadamer's principle cannot be applied in its pure form. Not uncommonly one meets a certain unevenness in a text which is not of such a kind or degree as to warrant textual emendations or source-critical analysis, but has to be accounted for in terms of the author's 'style'. Some authors, for example, have a much tauter style of exposition and argument than others, so that an apparent minor inconsistency or digressiveness that would not trouble us in one text might in another lead us to suspect that we have not fully understood the author's argument. Or again, an author who is generally a clear and reasonable thinker may have a characteristic blind spot when dealing with a certain kind of subject matter; or the same author might display quite different standards when writing a personal letter rather than an academic article; and so on. These broad distinctions, and the innumerable finer ones that have to be made when dealing with the individual style of this or that particular author, cannot be summed up under a Gadamer-like formal principle (or catalogue of such principles) for the exegete to learn and apply, because texts and authors cannot be categorized into a finite set of discrete and determinate pigeon-holes. The interpreter, rather, is guided through these issues by his or her 'tacit knowledge' of, broadly speaking, the sorts of things that authors do, and more particularly, of what this particular author might characteristically (though not invariably) do. Without this non-formalizable knowledge, concepts such as 'completeness', 'unity', or 'intelligibility' are far too vague and undifferentiated to be of any practical value.[41] Thus it is *only* through reading the text as the work of an author that one will succeed in reading it at all, because the fundamental interpretative concepts of intelligibility, coherence, and the like, are essentially grounded in our tacit knowledge of how authors produce texts.

In sum, then, interpretation cannot be *equated* with grammatical interpretation as a formal movement between part and whole; rather, it must also take account of the text as the work of an author, be-

---

[41] Cf. Stanley Fish's illuminating discussion in *Doing*, pp. 120–32.

cause this is what infuses the formal concepts with the material content which transforms them into a working methodology.

## 5. *Elijah and the* Qôl Děmāmâ Daqâ

To consolidate the discussion thus far, and to prepare for the next
stage in the analysis, I wish to look briefly at a concrete exegetical
example. It concerns what Elijah heard after the wind, earthquake,
and fire had passed, namely, a *qôl děmāmâ daqâ* (1 Kgs. 19:12), for
which Stephen Prickett offers the very literal but mysterious translation, 'a voice of thin silence'.[42] He notes, however, that most modern
versions do not translate it in this way. Instead, the *Good News Bible*
renders it as 'the soft whisper of a voice', and the *NEB* as 'a low
murmuring sound'; while the *Jerusalem Bible* 'outdoes the nascent
naturalism of its Protestant rivals by eliminating all suggestion of speech
with its "sound of a gentle breeze"' (p. 8).

What particularly strikes Prickett about these renderings is the extent
to which they minimise the mysteriousness and ambiguity of the
original Hebrew—a fact which he explains as the effect of modern
cultural presuppositions upon the translators' work. According to
Prickett,

> A noticeable feature of modern English . . . is an intolerance of ambi-
> guity. We have come to expect that narrative will convey its own frame
> of reference so that we know, almost at once, for instance, whether we
> are reading what purports to be 'fact' or 'fiction' and adjust our mental
> sets accordingly. Writers who mix their genres are apt to leave us uneasy;
> (p. 8)

and this, he suggests, is why the translators of 1 Kings 19 have not
done very well here—the story does not give us the indications which,
as modern readers, we expect to receive. Did Elijah experience something external to himself, or was it in his own mind? The passage
does not really opt for either alternative. Were these 'natural' or
'supernatural' phenomena? We are told that God was *not* in the wind,
earthquake, or fire; yet their suddenness and violence suggests that
they *were* caused by God. Unfortunately the translators were culturally
ill-equipped to handle these ambiguities, and therefore tended to

---

[42] *Words and* The Word (Cambridge: CUP, 1987), p. 7; Prickett acknowledges his
indebtedness to Sten Stenson for this translation.

smooth them out through offering translations that are rather more
clear-cut than the Hebrew warrants.

Prickett finds this diagnosis confirmed by the statement of policy
in the Preface to the *Good News Bible*:

> The primary concern of the translators has been to provide a faithful
> translation of the Hebrew, Aramaic, and Greek texts. Their first task
> was to understand correctly the meaning of the original ... the trans-
> lators' next task was to express that meaning in a manner and form
> easily understood by the readers ... Every effort has been made to use
> language that is natural, clear, and unambiguous.[43]

The problem with this policy, however, is that sometimes the original
Hebrew is *not* 'natural, clear, and unambiguous'; the outcome, therefore, is that modern ideals are being imposed upon the original.

Prickett sums up the moral of his tale, somewhat sharply, in this way:

> Not one of these three major modern translations manages to suggest
> an inherent peculiarity about the event that might indicate a quite *new*
> kind of experience. Indeed, it is precisely that oddity or paradox in the
> original text that the modern translators, themselves responding to the
> unstated assumptions of the scientific revolution, found either untrans-
> latable, or, more probably, unacceptable. Since our distinctions between
> 'inner' and 'outer' are un-biblical categories (so the argument appears
> to run) we can only be 'modern' by treating the whole story at one
> level: it must be made *either* miraculous *or* natural. ... Yet such ratio-
> nalism would seem to strike right at the heart of the original story.[44]

Without wishing to endorse Prickett's apparent suggestion of a more-
or-less wilful perversity on the part of these translators, they have
nonetheless provided a good example of Gadamer's claim that our
cultural 'prejudices' can significantly affect our perception of a text's
meaning—there is, as Prickett points out, a striking congruence between their stated policy of providing a translation that is 'clear and
unambiguous' and their failure to capture the ambiguity of the Hebrew
text. The main point to emerge from this example, however, is that
the initial prejudices do not make any difference, *in the long term*, to
our ability to arrive at an objectively correct understanding of its
meaning, because, as Prickett demonstrates, these presuppositions can
be detected and, when found to be inappropriate, amended. The
fundamental point is that over against any interpretative, pre-

---

[43] Quoted by Prickett, p. 4; excisions by Prickett.
[44] P. 9; Prickett's italics.

suppositionally-influenced translation, such as 'a low murmuring sound' or 'sound of a gentle breeze', one can appeal back to the established facts of the Hebrew language—is 'sound' within the established semantic range of *qôl*, or 'murmuring' of *děmāmâ*? (And which Hebrew word is supposed to support 'breeze'?) Of course, these linguistic facts have themselves been established by interpreting other passages; but seeing each 'part' in relation to a variety of *different* 'wholes' provides a number of cross-checks that together determine the semantic ranges more accurately.[45]

Of course, once the meaning of the passage has been determined[46] there are still many other questions that one might want to ask. What are *we* to make of this story? Does its ambiguity remind us of a genuine 'depth dimension' to reality, which cannot be captured in straightforward either/or categories; or does it speak of a nature-mysticism which the strong, clear light of modern science has now rendered obsolete? Clearly these are an entirely different *kind* of question from those we discussed in the preceding paragraphs. There we were considering Stendahl's 'what it meant', trying to grasp the passage on its own terms, and arguing that this can be done objectively; now the focus has turned to evaluating it in terms that are external to the passage itself—to asking whether *we* should assess its 'message' as insightful or misguided. Such questions are clearly an aspect of Stendahl's 'what it means', or Hirsch's 'significance'; and, granted that an objective answer can be given to 'what it meant', 'what it means' is then a distinct question of its own. Gadamer and Smart, then, are right insofar as they point out the tendency to read back 'what it means' into our exposition of 'what it meant'; but this tendency can be counteracted—critical, self-correcting exegesis enables us to understand the passage on its own terms, as distinct from its 'meaning for us'. To this extent, then, Stendahl's dichotomy is vindicated.

### 6. *Preunderstanding*

To round off this discussion of Gadamer, there are two further comments to make about presuppositions. Firstly, despite his polemics

---

[45] A fuller discussion of these linguistic points would soon take us back once more to Schleiermacher's views on parallel passages.

[46] Which does *not* mean 'once the ambiguities have been resolved', but rather, 'once they have been recognized and carefully delineated as ambiguities'.

against Cartesian epistemology, Gadamer sometimes shows himself to be unduly oriented towards 'the lone knower'. Although (in contrast to Descartes) he stresses that understanding occurs within a tradition, he largely vitiates this important insight by conceiving of tradition as a uniform stream which the individual is more or less locked into:

> [H]istory does not belong to us; we belong to it. Long before we understand ourselves through the process of self-examination, we understand ourselves in a self-evident way in the family, society, and state in which we live. . . . The self-awareness of the individual is only a flickering in the closed circuits of historical life.[47]

This badly neglects the multiformity of tradition, and hence the wealth of *alternative* presuppositions that are potentially available to the interpreter. Even at the level of popular enculturation, which Gadamer is principally concerned with here, most people know that within a given society there are different political outlooks, alternative moral standards, etc.; so that on many issues it would be far too simplistic to speak of, say, 'the British attitude towards . . .'.[48] This is even more the case when someone becomes a specialist in a particular discipline, as it is then part of their professional competence to be acquainted with the different approaches within that field. Thus someone writing a biblical commentary, for example, will be aware of the different kinds of interpretation advocated by, say, Alter, Barth, Childs, von Rad, Stendahl, and Zimmerli; moreover, as their research progresses they will become familiar with the differing interpretations that have been made of specific passages, and the grounds upon which each has been argued. It would therefore be far too simplistic to envisage the commentator as 'starting from his or her own presuppositions', as though they provided a single, unified perspective. Rather, a well-prepared interpreter will be aware from the outset that there are alternative presuppositions, and that they need to be critically tested against the text.

---

[47] *TM*, p. 276.

[48] A similar point can also be made with reference to the Elijah example considered above. Despite Prickett's sweeping statements about what 'modern English' requires, there will generally be a significant *variety* of outlooks among any reasonably-sized group of people. Thus Prickett himself, as a specialist in English literature, is naturally more sensitive to the positive contribution that literary ambiguity can make than some of his more scientifically-minded contemporaries might be, who would perhaps tend to see it merely as an obstacle to clear communication. This point can obviously be generalised to many other kinds of presupposition as well.

The interpreter's outlook can be broadened still further by delving into the history of scholarship, and thus becoming familiar with exegesis that proceeded from cultural, religious, and scientific presuppositions very different from his or her own. Childs himself points out the value of this, in explaining the purpose of the 'History of Exegesis' sections in *EC*:

> The history of exegesis is of special interest in illuminating the text by showing how the questions which are brought to bear by subsequent generations of interpreters influenced the answers which they received. No one comes to the text *de novo*, but consciously or unconsciously shares a tradition with his predecessors. This ['History of Exegesis'] section therefore tries to bring some historical controls to the issue of how the present generation is influenced by the exegetical traditions in which we now stand.[49]

Although it has rightly been pointed out that attempting such a history within the confines of a commentary tends to make it too brief and fragmented, and too directly tied to the concerns of the particular passage that is being exegeted, for its full value to be realized,[50] Childs' examples nonetheless give some useful pointers to how a history of interpretation can be illuminating.

The second point to make about presuppositions is that they can have a variety of epistemological statuses, and that these may change quite drastically as interpretation proceeds. So, for example, the modern prejudice against ambiguity which Prickett identifies is (on his account) a widespread but largely unconscious cultural presupposition; whereas when Bultmann claims that a Troeltschian version of historical criticism is an indispensable presupposition for exegesis he is recommending the conscious adoption of a principle for which, he believes, there are strong arguments. Or different again is Kuhn's initial realization that Aristotle's subject was change-in-general, which came to him in a sudden flash of insight. At first this was no more than a tentative hypothesis; yet it subsequently grew considerably in epistemological stature as Kuhn discovered that it illuminated numerous passages which had previously baffled him.

The important methodological point is that although there is one sense in which 'all understanding inevitably involves some prejudice'[51]—

---

[49] P. xv; cf. *BTCri* p. 145.
[50] See Barr, *HS* p. 164; cf. Brett, *Crisis?* p. 57 // *CAOTS* p. 133.
[51] *TM* p. 270; cf. p. 293.

namely, that interpretation does not successively eliminate our presuppositions until our mind becomes a *tabula rasa*—there is another
very important sense in which Gadamer is completely wrong: Our
presuppositions *are* successively eliminated from their *status* of being
'merely presupposed'. As interpretation proceeds they are critically
tested. Those that are found wanting are replaced; but a presupposition which is repeatedly borne out by the text thereby grows in
status. Therefore what began as an unconscious assumption or a
speculative conjecture may gradually become a reasonable belief and
then a well-established fact. Thus through critical evaluation, 'prejudiced interpretation' is steadily transformed into assured knowledge.

### 7. *Implications for Childs*

We began our discussion of philosophical hermeneutics by summarizing a number of possible connections between the thought of
Gadamer and Childs. Most of these have now been reviewed, and
the conclusions have generally been more negative than positive. Thus
on the one hand, we have seen that Gadamer offers a valuable critique of a 'hermeneutics of suspicion' which becomes so preoccupied
with the cultural or psychological factors which influenced the text's
production that questions about the truth-claims of its contents are
hardly even considered. This, we suggested, has significant parallels
with some of the objections which Childs raises against the standard
critical approach to the Old Testament. On the other hand, however, we have argued that Gadamer's rejection of objectivism (particularly in relation to texts having reader-independent meanings),
together with his views on the fusion of horizons, agreement concerning truth, and application, are badly flawed. *Contra* Gadamer,
we have argued in favour of objective meanings, and hence for a
Hirschian distinction between meaning and significance. For Childs'
programme to be methodologically sound, therefore, it must be based
upon an objectivist hermeneutics which is almost diametrically opposed
to Gadamer's. On these issues, Schleiermacher is a much better guide
than Gadamer.

There are two further points of comparison which I now wish to
consider, the first of which concerns Gadamer's views on classic texts.
This has been explored particularly by Mark Brett, who suggests that
a text being a classic, in Gadamer's sense, is 'analogous' to Childs'

idea of a biblical text being canonical.[52] Brett finds the point of comparison in the text's continuing to 'make a claim' upon successive
generations; but unfortunately Gadamer's notion of the classic is deeply
implicated in the problematic aspects of his theories about 'truth-
claims', and of the concomitant bifurcation of 'agreement' into a strong
and a weak form. As I shall now argue, this leaves little in Gadamer
that is of any value for Childs' programme.

Summarizing Gadamer's notion of a classic text, Brett suggests that

> The classic . . . continually demonstrates its value through the vicissi-
> tudes of time, taste, and criticism, and if any particular work does not
> continue so to prove itself, it can no longer be called classical. (p. 137)

Thus as Brett construes it—and clearly there are strands in Gadamer's
hermeneutics which support this reading—a text's being classical is
an *a posteriori*, contingent matter, which is closely related to Warnke's
Hegelian sense of agreement. Successive generations come to the text
with questions, values, and interpretative concerns that are characteristic of their own age: if the text 'continue[s] to demonstrate its
truthfulness in new situations to those who have been transformed
[by it]' (p. 146) then it is a classic; but if it does not (or if it eventually ceases to) 'demonstrate its truthfulness' in this way then it is
not accorded (or loses its) classic status.

There are two comments to make on this. Firstly, this weak version of 'agreement concerning the truth', in which it is an open
question as to whether or not a particular text gives us true insight,
is not a specifically Gadamerian idea—on the contrary, we have seen
that his distinctive, Heideggerian, principles lead instead into the strong
version of agreement. Whatever value there may be, then, in this
weaker notion of the classical, it cannot serve as bridge by which
Gadamer's hermeneutics may come to the aid of Childs' canonical
approach. But secondly, this idea of the classical seems in any case
to be of limited application in the theological field: 'The Bible in the
modern world' is a problem for the church precisely because significant portions of it have largely *failed* to display the contemporaneity
which the church expects of its Scriptures. Leviticus and Numbers
are often cited as examples of this; and yet in the wake of the
*religionsgeschichtliche Schule* there has been a growing sense that even
the central writings of the Bible, such as the Gospels, are products of

---

[52] *Crisis?*, p. 6.

an alien environment which is far removed from our own. But if this is our present situation, then describing the canonical books as classic texts seems appropriate only as an expression of what the church has traditionally thought they ought to be, rather than expressing what it now in fact finds them to be. Yet it is then difficult to see how this notion of the classical might assist Childs in defending his own Canonical Principle.

There is also another strand running through *TM*, however, in which the classical is associated with Gadamer's 'strong programme'. This is particularly the case when the idea of the classical as normative and truth-revealing comes to the fore. When this happens the perception of the classical as continuing to demonstrate its truthfulness takes on rather more of an *a priori*, necessary, character; and concomitantly, as Warnke explains,

> [H]ermeneutics becomes simply that which rescues the truths of the past from oblivion and allows their validity to be seen. The point of a hermeneutics of the classical is to demonstrate the continuing truth of classical texts. Hermeneutic consensus then refers . . . to the capacity to see that object's superiority. (p. 105)

Clearly this is very different from the weaker notion of the classical. The weaker notion depends on there being a critical distance between text and reader, so that one can make a reflective evaluation of its claims. As we have seen, however, in Gadamer's strong programme the relationship between reader and text becomes (as Thiselton aptly remarks)[53] reflexive rather than reflective, with fusion and agreement between 'then' and 'now' occurring simply in virtue of the past being understood through the prejudices of the present. Now clearly *this* hermeneutical theory would add substance to Childs' claim that the ('classical') texts of the Old and New Testaments are normative Scriptures; but since these conclusions derive entirely from the general hermeneutical theory rather than from anything specific to the biblical texts, one would likewise have to accept as normative the truth-claims of the *Almagest* and *Mein Kampf*. A notion of the classical which leads to this conclusion, however, is clearly of no use to Childs.

Finally in this chapter, something further can be said about Childs' Faith and Reason dilemma. We saw in section 2.2 that Childs advocates a unified 'interpretation in faith' which respects both of the

---

[53] See note 15 above.

following principles: (1a) It proceeds from a very specific hermeneutical starting-point, namely, from the faith-stance of the Christian tradition, which accepts the biblical writings as authoritative Scripture; and yet (2a) It is to produce results which are of general validity, at least to the extent that they are not open to charges of being merely sectarian or fideistic. We also saw, however, that Childs' repeated attempts to explain how this might be achieved invariably fell into an unstable oscillation between a faith-interpretation which looked suspiciously fideistic and an account of the descriptive task which marginalized faith.

As many readers will by now have realized, our discussion of Gadamer's hermeneutics has led to a very similar conclusion. Like Childs, Gadamer also wishes to hold together the following two principle: (1b) Interpretation proceeds from a very specific hermeneutical starting-point, namely, from the 'prejudices' associated with standing at a particular historical point within the evolving social-cultural traditions; and yet (2b) It is to produce results which are of general validity, at least to the extent that they are not open to charges of being merely parochial or subjectivistic. Now if Gadamer had found a way of simultaneously satisfying both these principles then he might have been able to help Childs resolve his Faith and Reason dilemma; but in fact Gadamer suffers from a very similar dilemma himself. Drawing upon Heidegger's analysis of understanding as thrown-projection to explicate its historically-conditioned character immediately raises the problem of subjectivism: If 'understanding' is essentially 'understanding through one's historically given fore-structures', how can this be prevented from degenerating into each interpreter finding in the text just what matches his or her own preconceived ideas (i.e., from becoming radically 'opportunistic', in Warnke's sense)? Gadamer tries to overcome this problem by stressing that our fore-structures must be critically revised by 'the things themselves'; yet he is also aware that for Schleiermacher critical revision did this so successfully that it *overcame* historical situatedness, yielding (allegedly) the objective meaning of the text itself. This, however, would mean that Gadamer had established his second principle (i.e., that which I labelled [2b]) only by reducing the first (i.e., [1b]) to no more than a *starting* point, which does not finally affect one's conclusions. To guard, therefore, against critical revision turning into Schleiermacherian convergence Gadamer further argues (i) that the tradition, and hence our fore-conceptions, is continually evolving, rather than converging towards a 'true understanding'; and (ii) that coherence is too loose a criterion to yield objectively correct understanding. Yet both these points 'save' Gadamer from a Schleiermacherian objectivism only by limiting the extent to which our fore-conceptions *can* be critically revised, thus resurrecting once more the subjectivism from which criticism was supposed to save him. In other words, there is an unresolved tension in Gadamer's hermeneutics which is remarkably similar to that which plagues Childs' work.

In view of this similarity, it is worth analysing more fully what the source of Gadamer's problem is. In discussing how, in view of a text having to be understood through the interpreter's preconceptions, it can 'be protected against misunderstanding from the start',[54] Gadamer offers the following explanation:

> A person trying to understand something will not resign himself from the start to relying on his own accidental fore-meanings, ignoring as consistently and stubbornly as possible the actual meaning of the text until the latter becomes so persistently audible that it breaks through what the interpreter imagines it to be.... But this kind of sensitivity [to the text having something to tell one] involves ... the foregrounding and appropriation of one's own fore-meanings and prejudices. The important thing is to be aware of one's own bias, so that the text can present itself in all its otherness and thus assert its own truth against one's own fore-meanings. (p. 269)

Unfortunately for Gadamer, however, he is here advising the interpreter to do a number of things which, if his own claims about the historically conditioned character of understanding were consistently applied, would be quite impossible. Thus it makes no sense, for example, to put forward 'the actual meaning of the text' as a hermeneutical check or control unless one is willing to allow that textual meaning has a sufficient degree of independent 'thereness' to stand over against the reader's prejudices and correct them, rather than itself being invariably reinterpreted to agree with them. Yet from a consistently Gadamerian perspective this is impossible, because it is a fundamental premise of his hermeneutics that meaning is always meaning *as understood through the reader's prejudices*, so that for it to be perceived as a meaning of the text it must already be a meaning coloured by the reader.

Gadamer, in fact, is guilty here of wanting both to have his cake

---

[54] *TM*, p. 268.

and it eat. If his claim that all understanding is prejudiced under-standing constitutes a valid argument against objectivism, then it provides an entirely general refutation of *all* forms of objectivism. This means, however, that the more radical tendencies of this 'preju-dices' argument cannot then be curtailed by falling back upon objec-tivist appeals to 'the actual meaning of the text'.

Nor, again, is there any point in Gadamer warning the interpreter against '*ignoring* as consistently and stubbornly as possible the actual meaning of the text', because what often divides interpreters (espe-cially when fundamentally different readings are at stake) is not that one ignores 'the actual meaning of the text' while the other pays it close attention but that each has a different notion of what it is to pay close attention. Thus even as extreme a case as Fish's attempted reading of 'Jacobs-Rosenbaum . . .' as a religious poem, which many would surely regard as a paradigmatic example of 'ignoring as con-sistently and stubbornly as possible the actual meaning of the text', appears from Fish's own point of view as a quite natural way of reading the text once one has decided to pay it a *certain kind* of close attention—namely, that which is appropriate when employing this particular interpretative strategy, which requires one to pay close attention to the possible religious connotations of the words. Fish cannot be refuted, therefore, simply by being told to stop ignoring the obvious, because he would in turn reply that what is 'obvious' is itself relative to an interpretative community. What one has to do, rather, is to show that Fish's own notion of paying close attention leads to *internal* inconsistencies. Once again, then, Gadamer has vio-lated his own fundamental principles by implicitly assuming that there are universally agreed conceptions of 'ignoring . . . the actual mean-ing' and of paying close attention to the text which have somehow escaped all taints of cultural and historical situatedness.

Similar comments also apply to Gadamer's remarks about bias. The problem, from a consistently Gadamerian perspective, with us '[being] aware of [our] own bias' is that it is precisely that—*us* being aware of our own bias. Gadamer fudges the issue here by speaking of the interpreter as an impersonal 'one'; but in fact the interpreter is always a situated *some*one, with situated notions, therefore, about his or her own biases.[55] Once again, then, Gadamer has violated his own fundamental principles by implicitly invoking an ahistorical 'pure

---

[55] Gadamer in fact seems to be merely playing with words here: 'Prejudices' which

reason' which supposedly enables an interpreter to identify biases in a way which is not itself biased.

An important general conclusion may be drawn from this discussion. Scholars in many different fields have in recent years used arguments which start from the premise that 'All understanding [knowing/reasoning/interpreting] is an understanding [etc.] through *our own* ideas . . .' to support relatively mild forms of anti-objectivism, such as that which Gadamer generally advocates. Our own analyses of Gadamer and Fish, however, suggest that it is actually much harder than most scholars have realized to prevent such arguments from passing over into into extreme versions of solipsism and relativism (regardless of whether 'our own ideas' is explicated in terms of membership of a Fishian community, or of a particular historical, social, or cultural milieux, etc.). The reason for this is simple: Whatever is put forward as a constraint which might halt the slide into solipsism must itself be construed, according to the initial premise, as no more than 'our own (socially/culturally/historically conditioned) idea' of what a valid constraint is; so that instead of *solving* the problem of relativism the proposed constraint simply provides another example of it. Or to put it another way, the reason why Fish's reader-centred hermeneutics is so much more radical than Gadamer's is that Fish is much more consistent in applying the fundamental principle which they both share: Whereas Gadamer tries to prevent things becoming too radical by falling back upon 'the actual meaning of the text', an ahistorical pure reason, and a generally attainable good will to apply it, Fish takes particular pleasure in debunking all such half-hearted relativists by pointing out that in positing something which stands 'over against' the interpreter as an independent or universally binding constraint, they are contradicting the premise from which their own anti-objectivist arguments begin.[56] In other words, Fish calls upon the half-hearted relativist to be more consistent, and therefore more radical; yet although such consistency is philosophically commendable, it also has, in this particular case, an unfortunate sting in its

---

ought to be corrected are arbitrarily relabelled as 'biases', and it is then assumed without further ado that a careful interpreter can make due allowance for them.

[56] See especially Fish's critiques of Toulmin, Habermas, and others in *Doing*, pp. 436–67; cf. pp. 342–55. For our present purposes the point is not, of course, whether or not the criticisms which Fish makes of these particular scholars are justified, but his insistence that, once a certain kind of anti-objectivist argument has been set forth, consistency demands that it cannot subsequently be constrained by covertly reintroducing elements of objectivism.

tail: As we saw in section 7.3, if Fish were himself only a little more consistent, and were to marshal his usual debunking arguments as rigorously against *his own* favoured constraint as he does against everyone else's, then he would quickly fall into total solipsism.

As it is, Fish remains the best illustration to date of the destination to which a fully consistent reader-centred approach leads. Clearly it is not a terminus at which Gadamer would care to arrive,[57] and yet he has no way of avoiding it, because, like Bultmann, he is unable to establish a stable, non-arbitrary 'stopping-point' between Schleiermacherian objectivism and eisegetical subjectivism. The logic of his Heideggerian starting-point ensures that, if it is followed out consistently, the 'opportunist' strand in his thought must triumph over everything else.

The implications of this discussion for Childs are clear and simple. Gadamer's 'oscillation' finally resolves itself into the secular equivalent of an extreme fideism, in which the initial faith-commitment so dominates the interpretative process that it is impossible for anything to count against it—all ostensible counterevidence is simply reinterpreted as further affirmations of the faith. Clearly this is of no help to Childs in overcoming his Faith and Reason dilemma.

---

[57] Nor, it should be repeated, would Fish welcome this conclusion, which constitutes a *reductio ad absurdum* of his own hermeneutics.

# CHAPTER TEN

# THE ILLUMINATION BY THE SPIRIT

When discussing Childs' views on 'interpretation in faith', we noted that one way in which he attempts to fill this out is through appealing to the role of the Holy Spirit in the modern church:

> The church's prayer for the illumination by the Holy Spirirt when interpreting Scripture is not a meaningless vestige from a forgotten age of piety, but an acknowledgement of the continuing need for God to make himself known through Scripture to an expectant people.[1]

Despite it being a recurring theme throughout his writings, however, Childs has never discussed this interesting suggestion at any length, although in *BTONT* he does briefly outline some of his main ideas: This illumination is necessary because human sinfulness has prevented God's revelation in the Bible from being understood; word and Spirit are not to be separated from or set against each other; yet this is not a plea for a 'spiritual sense' of the Scriptures beyond their 'literal sense'.[2] Childs clearly believes that the illuminating by the Spirit is indispensable for a proper understanding of the Scriptures, and in this he is making a significant departure from most of his critical colleagues. Unfortunately, however, his comments are extremely cryptic, and therefore difficult to assess. At a couple of points, however, he identifies the doctrine he is proposing with that of John Calvin;[3] therefore, following up this lead, the present chapter will consider whether Calvin's views might be helpful to Childs.

In *OTTCC* Childs appeals specifically to Calvin's discussion in the *Institutes of the Christian Religion* I.7; so as a first step towards assessing Calvin's possible value for Childs, I shall review this passage within the broader context of the discussion of the knowledge of God in

---

[1] *BTCri* p. 100; cf. *EC* p. xiii, *NTCI* p. 40, *OTTCC* pp. 12, 15; *BTONT* pp. 48, 67, 86, 87, 215, 722.

[2] See the references to *BTONT* in the previous note.

[3] *OTTCC* p. 12; *BTONT* p. 48.

*Institutes* I.1–9.[4] As Warfield has indicated (p. 31), Calvin's starting-point is his affirmation of a full natural revelation, which comes through the innate sense of God (a *sensus divinitatis* or *deitatis*) which all humans have, through God's created works of nature, and through his providential ordering of the affairs of men. Throughout his exposition of these topics, Calvin stresses the objective clarity and certainty of natural revelation—these phenomena unambiguously and unmistakably reveal the living God in his true character. Yet running throughout these same chapters is an equally firm conviction that natural revelation *never* brings anyone to a true knowledge of God, i.e., to a proper 'sense of the divine perfections' which results in 'reverence and love to God' (I.2.1). The reason for this is that humankind, as a fallen race, has lost the capacity to perceive rightly what God has thus revealed. Nonetheless, the Fall did not *completely* destroy humankind's ability to perceive and respond to God's natural revelation—if it had, then people would be contented atheists, able to exclude God from their life and thoughts without any qualms. In fact, however, humans generally are religious creatures, which in Calvin's view shows that they still have some perception of God's natural revelation; and yet because this revelation now impinges upon *fallen* men and women, it issues not in a true knowledge of God but in multifarious distortions of it—false religions, querulous atheism, and a bad conscience. Paradoxically, then, the effect of natural revelation is to render everyone culpable for their ignorance of God— his revelation is objectively adequate to make him known, but humankind has persistently misused it.

It is worth looking more closely at Calvin's views on 'the noetic effects of sin',[5] as they have important hermeneutical consequences. T.F. Torrance[6] comes to this subject after a lengthy examination of Calvin's doctrine of total perversity, of which 'sin of mind' is a particular part. '*Total* perversity' refers to humankind being corrupted in *all* their capacities, including their rational faculties. Torrance discusses this mainly in terms of the image of God having been lost; but as he points out (p. 88), there is an apparent contradiction here in that although Calvin repeatedly speaks of human corruption as

---

[4] These chapters have been thoroughly and perceptively analysed by B.B. Warfield in 'Calvin's Doctrine of the Knowledge of God', in Warfield, *Calvin and Calvinism* (Oxford: OUP, 1931), pp. 29–130.

[5] Warfield, p. 42.

[6] *Calvin's Doctrine of Man* (London: Lutterworth, 1949); cf. T.H.L. Parker's chapter

involving the loss of this image, he also affirms that something of the image still remains, albeit in a much-distorted form. Torrance (pp. 89–90) finds the solution to this problem in Calvin's distinction between humankind's natural gifts (such as judgement, will, moral capacity, etc.) and his supernatural, or spiritual gifts (e.g., faith, love for God, etc.): At the Fall the latter, which established humans in a proper relationship with God, were withdrawn. The former, however, although corrupted by the Fall, were not withdrawn; nor indeed could they be without the human race ceasing to be human and descending to the level of the beasts.

What Calvin maintains here concerning humankinds's faculties in general, he essentially repeats again when he comes to the particular case of the mental capacities. In *spiritual* matters, such as 'the knowledge of God [and] the knowledge of his paternal favour towards us ... men otherwise the most ingenious are blinder than moles' (II.2.18). Yet despite this, Calvin recognizes and admires humanity's considerable intellectual achievements in such fields as politics, medicine, and the mechanical and liberal arts (II.2.13–17).

One further aspect of Calvin's doctrine of sin to be noted here is that, for the fallen mind,

> a lawless element is in control which Calvin calls *concupiscence* or the element of proud self-will which is at enmity to God. Every action of the perverted reason partakes of this self-will or perversity, and every action is against the truth of God.[7]

Calvin speaks of 'the violent lawless movements' in humanity's desires that 'war with the order of God' (II.3.12); of the 'perversity in us [which] never ceases, but constantly produces new fruits' (II.1.8); and, more comprehensively still, of the fallen mind as 'corrupted with contempt for God, with pride, self-love, [and] ambition'.[8]

Returning with this in mind to *Institutes* I.1–9, it is clear that since humankind is so implacably hostile towards God, natural revelation cannot bring it to a true knowledge of him; therefore Calvin next explains the further provisions that God has made. Firstly, he has given a new revelation, through the Scriptures. This differs from natural revelation both in its scope (showing God not only as Creator

---

on 'Vanitas Mentis' in his *Calvin's Doctrine of the Knowledge of God* (Edinburgh: Oliver & Boyd, 1969).

[7] Torrance, p. 116.

[8] Commentary on Gen. 8:21.

but also as Redeemer) and in its clarity—Calvin likens the Scriptures to spectacles provided for someone with defective eyesight, who before could hardly make out the words but can now read plainly (I.6.1). Scriptural revelation is thus fitted to humanity in its fallen condition; yet such is human corruption that even this would not, of itself, bring men or women to a true knowledge of God. This leads on, therefore, to God's second provision for fallen humanity: the Holy Spirit.

The Spirit is the principal subject of the next chapter of the *Institutes*.[9] As Warfield has pointed out, however (pp. 70–71), although the preceding argument leads us to expect it to deal with the Spirit's overcoming of humanity's concupiscence, which prevents it from benefitting from God's revelation, Calvin in fact entitles this chapter, 'The Testimony of the Spirit [is] Necessary *to Give Full Authority to Scripture*' (italics added). Warfield offers this summary of it:

> Calvin's formula here is, The Word and the Spirit. Only in the conjunction of the two can an effective revelation be made to the sin-darkened mind of man. The Word supplies the objective factor; the Spirit the subjective factor; and only in the union of the objective and subjective factors is the result accomplished. . . . But when they unite, knowledge is not only rendered possible to man: it is rendered certain.[10]

This, I think, summarizes *some* aspects of Calvin's discussion very well; and yet a closer reading of I.7 seems to suggest that Calvin's position is more problematic than Warfield has realized, particularly regarding the role of human reason vis-à-vis the work of the Spirit. I shall therefore re-examine chapter 7 with this issue specifically in mind.

One way in which Calvin presents his views is through the metaphor of a special, Spirit-enabled perception:

> As to the question, How shall we be persuaded that [the Scriptures] came from God without recurring to a decree of the Church? it is just the same as if it were asked, How shall we learn to distinguish light from darkness, white from black, sweet from bitter? Scripture bears upon the face of it as clear evidence of its truth, as white and black do of their colour, sweet and bitter of their taste. (I.7.2)

This metaphor suggests a position which is non-rational and yet not irrational—standing in front of a post-box in broad daylight one does not *reason* one's way to the conclusion that it is red; and yet seeing

---

[9] I.7, to which Childs specifically refers in *OTTCC*, p. 12.
[10] P. 83; by 'knowledge' here Warfield means (see pp. 75–76) not a merely intellectual apprehension but a knowing that lives in vital communion with God.

it under optimal viewing conditions makes it reasonable to believe this. There is an additional complication, however, in applying this metaphor to Scripture, in that 'being of divine origin and/or authority' are not qualities that can be directly perceived; therefore in the passage I have just quoted Calvin claims that what the Bible 'bears on its face' is not its divine authority as such but 'evidence of its truth'.[11] Nonetheless, it is the authority of Scripture that Calvin is really concerned to establish, so he would presumably envisage some sort of *inference* being drawn from this 'evidence'. Thus from a closer consideration of how Calvin's perception-metaphor actually bears upon the issue at hand, it emerges that we are not dealing with a case of non-rational, direct justification after all, but with an *argument* which proceeds from certain alleged features of the Bible—Calvin mentions such things as the heavenliness of its doctrine and the harmony of all its parts—to a conclusion about its authority. Moreover, Calvin is confident that, in principle, this argument could be carried through so successfully that even 'the craftiest despisers of God' could be silenced (I.7.4)—i.e., he believes that these arguments are effective and should carry weight even with those who are not illuminated by the Holy Spirit. The Spirit's role, rather, is to take one beyond this sort of intellectual assent, into, as Warfield puts it, 'such an attestation as takes hold of the whole man in the roots of his activities and controls all the movements of his soul'.[12]

What emerges from this analysis, then, is that reason and the Spirit are each assigned a distinct role. Calvin clearly intends the two to go together; yet the separateness of their respective functions seems to threaten the coherence of Calvin's account. If so much is conceded to unaided, natural (i.e., fallen) reason as to allow it to produce intellectual assent to the divine origin and authority of the Scriptures, then the further operation which goes beyond this to vital, living knowledge becomes irrational and subjectivistic, because all the rational moves have already been made at the first stage. In other words, Calvin has distinguished reason and Spirit in such a way as to leave little natural cohesion between them; thus each can break free from the restraining influence of the other, leading either into subjectivism ('true life is in the Spirit, who works in ways that *surpass*

---

[11] Or more precisely, they bear on their face something (unspecified) that functions as 'evidence'; 'bears' seems to lack a direct object.

[12] Pp. 74–75; cf. Calvin's discussion in I.7.5, especially the addition in the French edition.

reason'),[13] or into rationalism ('the role of the Spirit is *merely* to add conviction to what is known already by reason alone').

A similar problem emerges once more when Calvin eventually comes to his discussion of the Spirit's illuminating of the fallen mind. This is included in his chapter on faith,[14] where it becomes clear that what Calvin is proposing is a twofold renewing by the Spirit of heart and of mind. Although the two run very much in parallel, Calvin nonetheless keeps them distinct from each other. This is perhaps clearest in III.2.36:

> What the mind has imbibed [must] be transferred into the heart. The word is not received in faith when it merely flutters in the brain, but when it has taken deep root in the heart. . . . But if the illumination of the Spirit is the true source of understanding in the intellect, much more manifest is his agency in the confirmation of the heart.

Moreover, this twofold renewing is paralleled by a similarly bifurcated account of man's fallen condition. This is particularly clear in his commentary on 1 Corinthians where, in discussing 1 Cor. 2:14, Calvin explicates the rejection of the gospel by 'the natural man' both affectively, in terms of human pride and presumption, and noetically, in terms of human rationative limitations:

> Although Paul here tacitly blames human pride for the fact that men presume to condemn as foolishness what they do not understand, at the same time however he shows how great is the feebleness, or rather the dullness, of the human mind, when he says that it is not capable of spiritual understanding. For he teaches that it is due not only to the stubborn pride of the human will, but also to the impotence of the mind, that man by himself cannot attain to the things of the Spirit. He would have been saying no more than the truth if he had said that men do not wish to be wise, but he goes further, and says that they do not have the power.

In summary then, as both heart and mind have been corrupted by the fall, and since both enter into the apprehension of the gospel, both must therefore be illuminated by the Spirit if true understanding is to be attained.

---

[13] Calvin could sometimes go a surprisingly long way in this direction: 'Enlightened by [the Spirit], we no longer believe, either on our own judgement or that of others, that the Scriptures are from God; but, *in a way superior to human judgement*, feel perfectly assured . . . that it came to us . . . from the very mouth of God. We ask not for proofs or probabilities on which to rest our judgement, but we subject our intellect and judgement to it as too transcendent for us to estimate' (I.7.5, italics added).

[14] See III.2.33–36.

Deferring the 'heart' side of his dichotomy for later discussion, there are a number of comments to make on Calvin's theories about the mind. Unfortunately it is far from clear what an illumination of the mind might actually consist in. Presumably this could not involve any changes in its basic rationative processes—one and the same argument cannot be both a *non sequitur* and a valid syllogism, depending upon whether the mind is illuminated by the Spirit. More plausibly, it might be suggested that the illumination of the mind has to do with reshaping its values and standards. Thinking is not just a matter of logical inference but also involves judgement and evaluation; but the standards of valuation are sometimes very different for the believer and the atheist. Yet this explanation does not seem to be satisfactory either. If the different evaluations are not simply gut-reactions, then the way for the believer and atheist to make progress would be for them to argue through the question of which standards were better. (As we have seen, there are ways in which people who start from very different principles can still have a reasoned argument about which of them is right.) But since, as I have just argued, the basic rationative faculties are common to both the believer and the atheist, an illumination of the mind again seems superfluous to such an argument. In fact, appealing to the Spirit when arguing with an atheist would open the way to a highly undesirable subjectivism—if all that the believer can ultimately say to an unbelieving critic is, 'I know that my standards of evaluation are correct because the Spirit has shown this to me; but I cannot prove this to you because your mind has not been illuminated by the Spirit', then faith has surely moved far too close to the anarchic state where everyone believes what is right in their own eyes. It seems, then, as though Calvin's distinguishing between the rationative and the affective leads to a dilemma: To allow that the mind does not need to be renewed would clearly not fit in with Calvin's beliefs on human corruption; and yet attempting to explicate the illuminating of the rationative faculties leads to irrationalism.

There are other places, however, where Calvin does not draw his heart/mind distinction so firmly, but instead envisages a noetic transformation *which is founded upon a moral transformation*. When discussing his views on the fallen mind, I drew attention to the part that such moral qualities as pride and high-handedness play in Calvin's explanation of why man does not come to a knowledge of God through natural revelation. This is repeated in his *Commentary on 1 Corinthians*;

and with this as background, he then offers the following explanation of the gospel:

> The characteristic work of the Gospel is to bring down the wisdom of
> the world in such a manner that, deprived of our own understanding
> we become completely docile, and do not consider knowing, or even
> desire to know, anything but what the Lord teaches.[15]

This strand in Calvin's thought comes out particularly clearly in
*Concerning Scandals*,[16] especially in his discussions of 'scandals' that arise
from the intrinsic character and teaching of the gospel. These, of
course, do not arise from any fault in the gospel itself; rather, human
perversity is such that when Christ is preached people 'run into scandals' (p. 9), because

> instead of quietly giving their assent to [Christ], in their obstinacy they
> rush upon him with blind fury. We realise, therefore, that such illwill
> or badness is rooted in human nature. (*ibid.*)

One of Calvin's many examples of this is the scandal caused to human
reason by the doctrine of the Incarnation. Calvin could, he says,
give to those who are offended by it a clear proof from the Scripture; yet this would be quite pointless, since 'they reject the whole of
Scripture [because] whenever it does not happen to please them,
they take up the attitude that it is absurd' (p. 18).

Clearly, then, the fundamental problem that people have with
Christian doctrine (according to this strand in Calvin's thought) is
not intellectual but moral. Therefore the basic solution which he proposes is also moral: they must learn humility before God. To those
who cavil at the Incarnation the only remedy that Calvin offers is

> that we learn to become fools in this world in order to become capable
> of the heavenly wisdom (1 Cor. 3:18). . . . Do not let anyone bring
> trust in his own mental resources or his learning into the school of
> Christ; do not let anyone be swollen with pride or full of distaste, and
> so be quick to reject what he is told, indeed even before he has sampled
> it. Provided that we show ourselves to be teachable we shall not be
> aware of any obstacle here. (pp. 18–19)

The fear of the Lord is the beginning of wisdom!

So then, in marked contrast to the overwhelming trend in Western

---

[15] On 1 Cor. 1:17.
[16] Edinburgh: St. Andrew, 1978. A 'scandal', in this context, is an occasion for
stumbling, or an obstacle to the acquisition and progress of true faith.

philosophy, in which epistemology has almost invariably been an enquiry into the capacities of an abstract, impersonal rationative faculty, Calvin sees it as a highly moral, affective, emotionally-charged subject, in which it is impossible to study human reason in isolation from the whole gamut of human life. It is clear, then, that for someone to understand the gospel there must be a correcting of their affective faculties; and this brings us back to the 'heart' side of the illumination by the Spirit. This, I think, is far more defensible than Calvin's comments on the regeneration of the mind; in fact, it brings an important theological dimension to the hermeneutical issues discussed in previous chapters. Understanding advances, we have seen, through critically testing and revising one's presuppositions; and although I have so far been mainly concerned with the logic of this process, there is nonetheless a vital affective factor implicit in this methodology, which will necessarily be important in its implementation. The critical spiral implies that progress will only be made if the investigator can admit that he or she is wrong, and is willing to forsake previous (perhaps strongly held) opinions in favour of the insights that more recent research has uncovered. In other words, for the critical methodology to actually work in practice, the interpreter must possess certain affective qualities, such as teachableness and humility in the presence of the texts that one is trying to interpret.

It further needs to be asked, however, why it should be necessary to appeal to the illumination by the Spirit when discussing *biblical* interpretation. The critical spiral, we have seen, is a *general* methodological principle, and yet no-one suggests that we need the Spirit's aid when interpreting *Macbeth*. But Calvin can reasonably argue that theology is a special case, in that the presuppositions involved here are, by their very nature, liable to be far more deeply ingrained than would generally be the case in other disciplines. For Calvin, 'the natural man' has a high estimate of his own goodness, but the gospel tells him that this is a dreadful delusion; he sets a high value on his autonomy, but the gospel says that his foremost duty is to make every thought captive to God; etc. The issues at stake here are far more momentous—and far more personally related to the interpreter's own self-estimation—than anything that would arise in interpreting *Macbeth*. Revising these presuppositions would mean changing one's views on issues that touch a person's self-estimation at its very core; so that moving someone to make such a fundamental revision will be extremely difficult. In fact, there seems to be a strand in *Scandals* which suggests (at least implicitly) that even rational argument will often be insufficient to achieve this, not because the argument will never be more than moderately plausible but because 'the natural man' is so in love with his own views of himself, and finds the gospel's estimation so abhorrent, that he simply will not *allow* himself to be persuaded, no matter how conclusive the argument might be.[17]

Although the illumination by the Spirit is not discussed in *Scandals*, this is presumably what Calvin would appeal to as the ultimate reason why believers accept the gospel; and if we give preference to the close interconnection of the affective and the rational of *Scandals*, rather than to the sharper heart/mind dichotomy of the *Institutes*, then the various elements fit together well: There *is* a common rationative faculty in believers and unbelievers alike, and therefore there can be reasoned argument between them over such questions as what the Scriptures teach and whether or not it is true; and furthermore (the believer claims) a rationally defensible case for the gospel *can* be made out. Yet the unregenerate will never allow themselves to be persuaded by it—they will always procrastinate, or retreat behind specious cavils, or break off the discussion prematurely, rather than admit that the gospel is true. Ultimately, they would rather be irrational than be 'converted'. But the illumination by the Spirit saves them from their own irrationality—not through operating upon the rationative faculties as such but by renewing the heart. The role of the Spirit is to instil humility and teachableness, in order that reason be allowed to work as it should. In such a state it may be persuaded by the gospel, and thus attain to a faith that is founded upon sound reason. Thus faith is not irrational, nor a mysterious leap beyond the rational; but neither is it a purely human achievement. It is only by the Spirit that people are able to see the truth, yet they see it in a properly rational way.

It seems, then, that although Childs is somewhat over-optimistic in claiming that the illumination by the Spirit 'has been developed so thoroughly by Calvin as to make further elaboration unnecessary',[18] it can nonetheless be reworked in ways that are theologically and hermeneutically interesting while yet retaining strong affinities with Calvin's own teaching. Moreover, this appears to offer Childs a way of filling out his claim that interpretation must proceed from a faith

---

[17] *Scandals*, however, is not entirely consistent on this, as Calvin sometimes concedes that the gospel *is* a mystery that surpasses rational arguments (e.g., p. 18).

[18] *OTTCC*, p. 12.

commitment, while also avoiding subjectivism: That an interpreter is illuminated by the Spirit is shown not through confessions of the 'inner light' which guides his or her exegetical labours, but through these labours consistently producing interpretations that (i) are theologically penetrating, and (ii) can be established as legitimate interpretations through rational, exegetical arguments, without appealing to 'spiritual intuition'. That a Christian faith-commitment is (as Childs claims) a necessary precondition for such exegesis would be shown by the fact (if it is a fact) that it is successfully carried out only (or at least, primarily) by interpreters who have this faith. Childs has in fact suggested that

> It is rare to find penetrating theological exegesis of the New Testament by one who shares little or nothing of the faith reflected by the literature. A different scale of priorities within the exegetical task usually leads these scholars into different concerns with the text. The hermeneutical issue at stake is . . . the willingness to work within a received context of faith.[19]

According to Calvin, this 'willingness' must be produced by the Spirit.

Yet despite the potential advantages that Calvin's doctrine offers Childs, it is not altogether clear whether Childs would be willing to pay the theological 'price' needed to appropriate them. As we have seen, Calvin's views on illumination are tightly bound up with a number of other doctrines, especially his particularly severe views on human corruption. Childs' own theological reflections on this subject, however, are not so pessimistic. In his *Old Testament Theology* the closest Childs comes to discussing this subject is in the chapter on 'Life Under Threat'; but as this title implies, its main focus is upon various *external* factors that disrupt human existence (the primaeval chaos, the serpent of Genesis 3, the curses of the Mosaic covenant, etc.). In the *Biblical Theology*, however, Childs considers human sinfulness more directly. Summarizing the Old Testament witness, Childs observes that 'the human problem' arises from the unwillingness to respond to God faithfully, and describes sin as 'an offence directed against Yahweh himself' which 'derives from a crooked heart'. Sinners 'hate' God, and are 'insolent and accursed'.[20] Like Calvin, then, Childs

---

[19] *NTCI*, p. 39.
[20] See *BTONT* pp. 574–75. This occurs in an 'Old Testament Witness' section, and it may be significant that it has little influence on the corresponding Biblical Theology and Dogmatics sections (pp. 587–94).

recognizes the affective dimension of sin, and can sometimes portray this in language similar to the Reformer's. Yet when Childs' writings are considered as a whole, his description of human sinfulness is much less severe than Calvin's portrayal of humankind's implacable hatred of God. Since, however, the purpose of the Spirit's illumination is precisely to overcome this hostility, it would become largely superfluous if Calvin's doctrine of sin were toned down or denied.

A further theological reason why Childs might find Calvin's views on illumination problematic is that they naturally lead on to a very stern doctrine of election:[21] If there is no salvation apart from a knowledge of the gospel, and the latter is impossible without the Spirit, then it becomes ultimately God's own choice as to whom he grants this illumination that determines who shall be saved and who shall be lost. Again, it is far from clear whether Childs would wish to accept this; yet it is a conclusion that might be difficult to avoid if he were to accept Calvin's doctrine of illumination.

The implications of this chapter for Childs' work, then, are somewhat equivocal: Within the context of Calvin's theology, his doctrine of the illumination by the Spirit does seem a viable way of filling out the idea of interpreting the Scriptures 'in faith'. Whether this can be transplanted into Childs' programme, however, is not altogether clear.

---

[21] This is brought out very clearly in Warfield's discussion.

# CHAPTER ELEVEN

# CANONICAL EXEGESIS

Our discussions of literary theory and philosophical hermeneutics have thus far set out some quite general principles for the interpretation of biblical texts. In addition to this, however, a number of further issues are raised by Childs' belief that the Christian theologian should interpret the Bible at the 'pan-canonical level'—or more specifically, that by reading the Old Testament in the context of the New, or in the light of the divine reality to which the New Testament points, we can hear in these pre-Christian writings a witness to Christ.

That the Scriptures should be read pan-canonically was already an important element in Childs' thought when he wrote 'Interpretation in Faith',[1] and has subsequently remained central to his conception both of Old Testament Theology and of Biblical Theology. In each case the success of these projects is crucially dependent upon Childs being able to read the Old Testament as, in some appropriate sense, Christian Scripture, and doing so in ways that cannot be accused of arbitrarily imposing Christian beliefs upon it. In other words, Childs needs to show that he really is hearing the witness *of the Old Testament* to Christ. Unfortunately, however, we have seen that his interpretative examples in *BTCri*, and especially in *BTONT*, are open to serious doubts at precisely this point.

In the present chapter, then, I wish to discuss a number of issues relating to the Christian interpretation of the Old Testament. Before considering the problem more generally, however, I shall first look at one particular aspect of it—namely, at the ways in which the Old Testament has been interpreted by the authors of the New Testament.

## 1. *The Old Testament in the New*

Childs' main discussions of the relationship between the Testaments occur in *BTCri*, *NTCI*, and *BTONT*. For the first of these, however,

---

[1] Recall once more his first two hermeneutical circles, 'IF' pp. 438–43.

there is little that needs adding to what was said in section 2.3. Although, since *BTCri* is an essay in theological methodology, it has much to say about the normative/constructive questions that we are considering here, we have argued that Childs' handling of Psalm 8 invites a number of standard critical objections to which neither this particular example nor his other discussions in *BTCri* provide an adequate response. Nor is there much to be said here about the New Testament *Introduction*, since it deals with descriptive rather than normative issues. *NTCI* is concerned with the Old Testament insofar as it is a factor in the canonical shaping of the New Testament, and therefore includes a number of interesting discussions of how the various New Testament writings regard the Old Testament and draw upon it. *NTCI* has little to say, however, about the normative/constructive questions of how the Old Testament relates to the New *as witness*, since this falls within the province of Biblical Theology rather than Introduction. It is to *BTONT*, therefore, that we must now turn.

We have already reviewed a number of *BTONT*'s christological interpretations of the Old Testament and suggested that they are not altogether convincing, so this again needs no further comment here. Instead, I would like to consider Childs' important methodological discussion of Paul's use of the Old Testament.[2] Citing examples from Philo, Qumran, and elsewhere, Childs begins by arguing (as, of course, would most critical scholars) that there were 'strong lines of continuity' between Paul's approach to exegesis and that of his contemporaries (p. 237). Applying these allegorical and midrashic techniques to the Scriptures, however, meant that Paul often showed little regard for their original context and meaning, and sometimes even went so far as to change the wording and disregard the syntax. Not surprisingly, this has evoked a largely negative evaluation from modern scholars. Reviewing a number of examples which 'stand out as especially grievous to modern sensibilities' (p. 238), Childs suggests that there are two questions to be addressed: (i) Have Paul's modern critics really understood what he was doing?; and (ii) What hermeneutical issues does this raise for the relationship between the Testaments? (p. 240). Childs takes up each question in turn:

(i) Firstly, Paul's exegetical practices must be understood in their historical context—an argument which seems rambling and confused when judged by modern standards can often be seen as quite logical

---

[2] *BTONT* pp. 237–44; cf. pp. 225–27, 553–54, 704–706.

and coherent when it is recognized as an example of a well-known rabbinic technique (*ibid.*). Secondly, Paul's exegesis must be related to his theology. For Paul the Scriptures were the oracles of God, and he therefore did not consider himself at liberty to twist them for his own ends. What he offered, rather, were interpretations which were meant to be convincing; yet they were interpretations which proceeded from '[t]he event of Christ', because he believed that the Scriptures bore witness to Christ.[3] And thirdly, Paul believed that what God had spoken in the past continued to speak today; and it spoke primarily about the gospel (pp. 241–42).

(ii) Considering next 'the larger hermeneutical issues', Childs summarizes a number of points with which we are already familiar: Paul's witness must be heard in concert with the rest of the canon; because both Testaments point to the same divine reality the Old is to be interpreted in the light of the New, and *vice versa*; etc. (pp. 243–44).

Clearly there are some interesting observations here; yet I cannot see that Childs has really got to grips with what the fundamental problem is. This comes out well in the following remark:

> For a modern biblical critic it is axiomatic that genuine exegesis depends on recovering a text's true historical context. For Paul genuine interpretation depends on its bearing witness to its true subject matter, who is Christ. . . . That Paul is not following modern exegetical rules is clear, but this acknowledgement is far from saying that he is wilful, inconsistent, or irrational. (p. 241)

Unfortunately this largely misses the point, because it fails to consider *why* modern scholars hold these views. Hearing a text in its original (or more precisely, intentional) context is not merely a modern prejudice, which can be taken up or set aside as one will. Rather, it is *an essential precondition for understanding the meaning of the text*; and conversely, midrashic and other techniques which disregard the intentional context, rearrange the wording, ride roughshod over the syntax, etc., will generally not hear the meaning *of the text*, but will hear some other meaning. Now of course this is an appeal to 'modern standards'; yet the nature of the argument—and more specifically, of Childs' own programme—is such that it must appeal to these standards. Childs wishes to hear the witness of the Old Testament; and since it bears its witness through its meaning, one has to ask which techniques

---

[3] Pp. 240–41; it will be recalled that Childs has adopted similar principles as part of his own methodology.

*really do* help us understand its meaning. To this, however, we cannot but give a 'modern' answer—to be intellectually honest we must respond in terms of the best insights that are presently available, which in practice means either accepting the currently established views or mounting an independent argument against them. Either way, however, it will be *modern* insights that finally count—even if one were successfully to argue that midrash is a legitimate technique,[4] it would then become an acceptable method for Old Testament interpretation because a modern assessment had led to this conclusion, not because Paul interpreted the Scriptures in this way.[5]

What Childs' arguments establish, then, at most, is that Paul sincerely intended to hear the witness of the Old Testament, and tried to do so through methods which, in his own day, were regarded as reasonable and rational. The crucial question for Biblical Theology, however, is whether Paul *really did* hear the Old Testament; and I cannot see that Childs has made any progress towards either reversing modern scholarship's adverse judgement on this matter or showing that it does not have serious negative implications for his own programme. Moreover if this is so, then the further theological and hermeneutical considerations which Childs raises in his discussion of Paul can likewise be seen to carry little weight: Even if we accept that Paul was motivated by a sincere (and, in his day, reasonable) belief that the Scriptures bore witness to the gospel, that they should be interpreted in the light of one's encounter with Christ, etc., a question-mark must still be put against the apostle's contribution to constructive theology if the techniques by which he implemented these principles are not ones that *we* can accept as methodologically legitimate.

The New Testament's use of the Old Testament, then, remains a highly problematic aspect of Childs' work. Yet the problems are even broader than this, because it is fundamental to Childs' own conception of Biblical Theology that *the modern interpreter* is likewise to hear

---

[4] This, of course, is *not* what Childs is trying to argue.

[5] Similarly, I think it is inadequate for Childs simply to argue that the development of Israel's traditions were motivated by primarily religious concerns without further assessing the reasonableness of the ways in which this was done (see section 6.3 above). Thus if, for example, the Chronicler interpreted the Deuteronomistic History by means of the various midrashic and harmonizing techniques which Childs (and most other scholars) attribute to him, then questions as to whether he *really did* hear the message of these texts, and how this affects our assessment of his own work, cannot be set aside.

the Old Testament as a witness to Christ, and one therefore needs
to ask Childs whether he has a sound methodological basis for this.
Unfortunately, Childs' answers have generally been extremely sketchy.
On the one hand, he has insisted that one cannot solve this problem
by imitating the midrashic practices of the New Testament writers;
and on the other hand, the modern interpreter is encouraged to read
the Old Testament in the light of the full divine reality, and not to
separate witness from subject-matter. Yet there is clearly a very wide
gulf between making these broad statements of principle and offering
a workable methodology; and as we saw in reviewing *BTONT*, Childs'
own interpretations of the Old Testament suggest that he is himself
still some way from discovering how to bridge this chasm. Unless
this hermeneutical problem can be resolved, however, Childs' theological claims are left hanging in mid-air, because without a workable methodology it is unclear as to how one is to hear the Old
Testament's christological witness. It seems, then, that Childs' conceptions both of Old Testament Theology and Biblical Theology run
into some fundamental problems here.

Fortunately it is possible, I believe, to do something towards resolve them; and in fact Childs has himself glimpsed the way forward
in his important essay on 'The Sensus Literalis of Scripture'. Our
next task, therefore, is to discuss this article in some detail.

## 2. *The* Sensus Literalis

We saw in section 2.4 that Childs is particularly attracted in 'SLS'
by Calvin's understanding of the *sensus literalis*, because the Reformer's
'literal' interpretations of the Old Testament enabled him to hear it
as '[a] witness to God's divine plan'.[6] Childs also goes on to note,
however, that this way of interpreting the Old Testament was subsequently displaced by the growth of historical criticism. The first
thing to do, therefore, is to look in more detail at how, in Childs'
view, this came about.[7]

From a careful reading of 'SLS' one discovers that Childs is using
*sensus literalis* here in connection with two different issues. Firstly, it
sometimes occurs in opposition to the 'allegorical' or 'spiritual' sense.

---

[6] 'SLS', p. 87.
[7] The following is based on my account in 'The *Sensus Literalis*', pp. 9–15.

This is clearly the case when, for example, Childs observes that

> Although Luther began his lectures on the Bible fully within the medieval tradition of the multiplicity of senses, his opposition to the allegorical method clearly intensified. Often as part of his polemic against the spiritualising of the text was his appeal to *ad literam*. (p. 86)

Or again, it is clear from the context that Childs has this understanding of *sensus literalis* in mind when he claims that 'A fundamental characteristic of the critical movement was its total commitment to the literal sense of the text' (p. 88). Childs is claiming that critical scholarship rejected the kind of the allegorizing interpretations that were common in the medieval church; and in this he is clearly correct. Modern biblical scholars are fully agreed that, in this sense, we must 'understand the Bible literally'.

Secondly, however, Childs also uses 'literal sense' in connection with *sensus historicus* and *sensus originalis*. In one significant but obscure passage, Childs makes the following claims:

> Among the Reformers the identity of the literal and the historical sense had been assumed and the terms *sensus literalis* and *sensus historicus* were often interchanged. In the new [i.e., critical] approach the identity of the terms was also continued, but the historical sense now determined its content. The historical sense of the text was construed as being the *original* meaning of the text as it emerged in its pristine situation. Therefore, the aim of the interpreter was to reconstruct the original occasion of the historical reference on the basis of which the truth of the biblical text could be determined. In sum, the *sensus literalis* had become *sensus originalis*.[8]

To elucidate this, one particularly needs to understand how the *sensus literalis* and *sensus historicus* were related by (i) the Reformers, and (ii) their critical heirs. These questions are reviewed at some length in Hans Frei's *Eclipse*, which Childs is largely following here; but without reproducing the details of Frei's discussion, the essential point for our present purposes is this: For the Reformers there was a natural coherence between the biblical texts and the 'subject matter' which made them religiously significant writings—to study, say, the Fourth Gospel's account of the life of Christ *was* to study the life of Christ, and hence to study what we ought to believe for our salvation. There was simply no 'critical distance' between these things; rather, the history and doctrine were directly rendered to the reader by the

---

[8] P. 89; Childs' italics.

canonical text.[9] This was the situation 'among the Reformers', then, to which Childs is referring in the passage I have just quoted. Subsequently, however, text and subject matter began to 'come apart'. For critical scholarship the Bible was a 'pointer' beyond itself to the essential subject matter, which different scholars variously took to be the actual historical events, the socio-cultural situation which gave rise to the text, the eternal truths of religion and morality, etc. Although the Bible was still indispensable as the primary source for our knowledge of these things, the subject matter itself was now regarded as independently significant in its own right.

For Childs, then, the orientation of critical scholarship towards the *sensus historicus* or *sensus originalis* signifies a quest for something *behind* the text, which is typically recovered by historical reconstructions and/or an investigation of original meanings or original contexts. This was clearly very different from what the Reformers meant by the *sensus historicus*. According to Childs, however, critical scholars nonetheless continued to identify 'the historical sense' with 'the literal sense', and thus engendered a correspondingly transformed understanding of what it means to 'interpret the Bible literally': For the Reformers this was a reading *of* the canonical text; for critical scholarship it was a reading *through* the text to recover something else behind it.

This discussion of the relationship between the literal and original senses apparently has little connection with our preceding observations on medieval allegorizing; yet in Childs' view they are closely interrelated.[10] Although the Reformers set the *sensus literalis* in opposition to allegory, it was not opposed to what Frei calls figural interpretation. On the contrary, the figural sense was seen as a natural extension of the literal, and in this way the Reformers were able to read the Old Testament as bearing witness to Christ.[11] The *critical* sense of 'literal', however, was set in opposition to both allegorical *and* figural readings—or perhaps more accurately, it was unable to recognize a

---

[9] As Frei remarks, 'History, doctrine, description of shape of life, all converged for [Calvin] and were held together by their common ingredience in the storied text of the scriptural word' (p. 21; cf. pp. 23–25).

[10] Again he is following Frei.

[11] Childs does not generally follow Frei in distinguishing between literal and figural senses (but see p. 93 for an important exception). Rather, he usually includes christological interpretations of the Old Testament within the Reformers' sense of 'literal' (as, for example, in his discussion of Calvin on p. 87).

figural sense distinct from an unacceptable allegorical sense. With the growth of critical scholarship, therefore, the figural reading of the canonical text was displaced by a 'literal' interpretation of its original/historical meaning.

One immediate consequence of this change was that the Reformers' christological understanding of the Old Testament was no longer considered to be viable. Whether this is to be regarded as a loss, however, or whether one should welcome it as a more consistent application of the Reformer's rejection of allegorizing, will obviously depend upon how figural interpretation is conceived.[12] For precritical scholars, according to Frei,

> [F]iguration or typology was a natural extension of literal interpretation. It was literalism at the level of the whole biblical story and thus of the depiction of the whole of historical reality. Figuration was at once a literary and a historical procedure, an interpretation of stories and their meanings by weaving them together into a common narrative referring to a single history and its patterns of meaning. (p. 2)

As we have seen, the Reformers believed that a historical event was rendered to the reader by the literal meaning of the text. Accepting this, figural interpretation made the further point that this could be done in such a way that the event not only 'signified itself' but signified some other event also, through the 'patterned' way in which the event was presented.[13] These patterns were not to be imposed upon the text by the reader, but discovered in the text itself; thus figural interpretation sought to bring together temporally separated events into a unified whole, through their literary presentation.

Clearly there are a number of ideas here which are potentially of some value for a canonical approach to biblical interpretation, and in the remaining sections of this chapter I shall consider how a christologically significant figural mode of interpretation might be reintroduced into biblical scholarship. To prepare the ground, however, we can first sharpen our perception of the problem by reviewing some further aspects of Frei's account of the demise of figural interpretation in the post-Reformation period.

---

[12] For this, Frei acknowledges his indebtedness to Erich Auerbach's *Mimesis: The Representation of Reality in Western Literature* (Princeton: Princeton University Press, 1968); also Auerbach's 'Figura', in Auerbach, *Scenes from the Drama of European Literature* (New York: Meridian, 1959).

[13] See especially Frei's quotation from Auerbach; *Eclipse*, pp. 28–29.

In addition to the refocusing of scholarly attention upon a positivity behind the text, which we have already discussed, there are two other factors to consider. Firstly, there were certain changes in how the nature of language was conceived, which Frei particularly associates with the philosophy of John Locke. For the Reformers, the literal sense was a *literary* sense; but for critical scholars it became 'literalistic':

> In the course of the eighteenth century ['verbal sense'] came to signify not so much a literary depiction which was literal rather than metaphorical, allegorical, or symbolic, but rather the single meaning of a grammatically and logically sound propositional statement.... In any case, 'verbal sense' was philological or 'grammatical-historical' (a common technical designation in the later eighteenth century, indicating the lexical in addition to the grammatical study of the words of a text) more than literary. (p. 9)

This literalistic conception of language greatly constricted the ways in which a text was allowed to communicate its meaning, restricting it, essentially, to the enunciation of semantic-grammatical statements. Figural interpretation was incapable of functioning under these constraints, which simply had no place in their scheme of things for literary patterning. As literalistic linguistics came to dominate biblical research, therefore, figuration was increasingly grouped with allegory as a method of interpretation which was not based upon the 'real' (i.e., literalistic) meaning of the text.

The second factor to consider is the (not unrelated) issue of multiple senses. We have already noted that the Reformers' insistence that the Scriptures must be 'understood literally' was, in part, a rejection of the allegorists' fanciful and speculative interpretations in favour of respecting the text's plain, straightforward sense. In the post-Reformation era, however, this self-restraint began to slacken:

> Pietist commentators were not nearly so completely wedded to the grammatical sense of the biblical texts as their more orthodox and scholastically-minded counterparts. While they affirmed a literal grammatical reading they also sought to transcend it. Indeed, the accusation of a plural sense given to single statements ... found its proper target ... in pietistic interpretation.[14]

With scholars such as Rambach insisting that there was a spiritual sense 'above' the plain, grammatical sense of the words, the interpreter's imagination was granted considerable licence; and some

---

[14] Frei, p. 38.

commentators stretched it to quite absurd lengths.[15] With 'typological' readings thus becoming virtually indistinguishable from fantasies, however, it was hardly surprising that a strong reaction eventually set in. Thus in the later eighteenth century the neological and rationalistic scholars

> insisted that there is *only one meaning* to a biblical as to any other proposition, and all interpretation ought to begin with as strict or faithfully reconstructed reading of the original text as possible.[16]

Adopting such a rule, however, could not but kill off *all* typology, whether of the extravagant or the restrained kind.

The changes which these various factors brought to biblical studies are well illustrated by Frei's discussion of Anthony Collins. The New Testament frequently refers to certain prophecies as being fulfilled in Christ; and yet (Collins observed) if these Old Testament texts are understood in their plain, grammatical sense they clearly refer not to Jesus but to events in ancient Israel. It must be, therefore, that they prefigure Christ through their typical or allegorical sense. Unfortunately the rules by which the apostles made these interpretations have long been lost; but now, Collins announces (tongue-in-cheek), modern research has recovered them. Collins then lists ten hermeneutical rules, of which Frei quotes the last as typical: 'Changing the order of words, adding words, and retrenching words; which is a method often used by Paul' (p. 69). In other words, the apostles had arbitrarily wrested the Old Testament to their own ends. For the orthodox defenders of typology, then, Collins' work posed an uncomfortable dilemma:

> One either admits the applicability of rules for literal interpretation in this instance, in which case the New Testament claims concerning the meaning of the Old Testament passages which they have quoted are demonstrably false; or one says that the rules governing the interpretation of the Old Testament prophecies in the New Testament are those for non-literal interpretation, which is equivalent to saying that the interpretation is meaningless because it has nothing to do with the words of the text of the prophecies.[17]

I do not intend to discuss Collins' work here, but the idea that a text has a single, semantic-grammatical sense has clearly been enormously

---

[15] See, for example, Frei's discussion of Cocceius (p. 49).
[16] Frei, p. 39; italics added.
[17] Frei, p. 70.

influential—much Old Testament exegesis has assumed, in practice, that once the text's grammatical meaning has been elucidated then the exegetical task is essentially complete (whatever else still needs to be done by way of theological reflection or application). Nor should one overlook the fact that, whatever we might think about Collins' own handling of the Old Testament, he does make a methodological point which is both valid and important. For the purposes of the present discussion this can be formulated as follows: For interpreters who wishes to pass beyond the semantic-grammatical meaning of a text to some kind of 'higher meaning', the onus rests with them to show that they are nonetheless proceeding in accordance with a reasonable set of exegetical criteria. Collins evidently believed that such criteria could not be found for the New Testament authors, and would presumably have thought it unlikely that a modern theologian might develop a legitimate typological interpretation of the Old Testament. On the whole, modern scholarship seems to have accepted this verdict. Overtly christological interpretations of the Old Testament have been generally frowned upon by critical scholars; moreover, as Childs has pointed out,[18] even when theologians of the stature of Eichrodt and von Rad have been favourably disposed towards typology, it has generally made little impact upon their exegetical work.[19] In practice, then, critical scholarship has been largely unsuccessful in reading the Old Testament as a witness to Christ.

In Childs' view this is highly unsatisfactory, and he ends 'The Sensus Literalis' with some cautious suggestions as to how modern scholarship can move towards a theologically more productive conception of the literal sense: The text and its subject matter must be studied together; the text must be studied as the Scriptures of a faith community; the canonical shaping must not be undone by a quest for historical reality; etc. (pp. 92–93). This, of course, has a familiar ring to it—as one might expect, Childs is essentially gathering together ideas which he has developed more fully elsewhere. These have mostly been discussed in earlier sections of this book, and we need therefore only recall that they have proved to be problematic in various ways. Thus although 'SLS' is very helpful in airing some difficult issues, it makes little progress, in my view, towards resolving them.

---

[18] See *BTONT*, p. 13.

[19] Karl Barth and Wilhelm Vischer are obvious exception; but precisely for this reason their work is looked upon askance by most critical scholars.

These subjects continue to be of central importance for Childs' work, however. His ultimate objective, it will be recalled, is to revitalize Old Testament Theology and Biblical Theology as *Christian* disciplines, and this is unlikely to be achieved unless he can develop an interpretative approach to the Old Testament which is both distinctively Christian and exegetically sound. In other words, Childs needs to make significant progress towards solving his long-standing problems of Faith and Reason, and to do so in a way that has concrete methodological consequences for what one might actually do in reading the Old Testament as Christian Scripture.

Since these problems become particularly pressing in the field of Biblical Theology, it is not surprising to find Childs returning to them at a number of points in *BTONT*. Compared to 'SLS', the diagnosis of the problem is much the same but Frei's notion of figural interpretation is now more overtly endorsed. The Reformers charged allegorical interpretation with subverting the plain, literal meaning of the text; but by the nineteenth century their concern for the literal meaning had been transformed into a historical quest for the single, original meaning. Against the latter, however, Childs now argues that

> [t]he role of canon as scripture of the church . . . is to provide an opening and a check to continually new figurative applications of its apostolic content as it extends the original meaning to the changing circumstances of the community of faith (cf. Frei, *Eclipse*, 2–16).[20]

In other words, Childs conceives the canonical sense as being, in part, a figural sense.

As is so often the case with Childs, these methodological prescriptions are better at setting out his goals than showing how they might be achieved. It is nonetheless clear, however, that Childs regards Frei's views on figuration as potentially of considerable value for his own work; and in this I think he is correct. In the following sections, therefore, I shall suggest how insights which have recently arisen from literary studies of the Old Testament can be used to 'fill out' Frei's ideas on figural interpretation.

---

[20] *BTONT*, p. 724; cf. pp. 14, 87–88, 520.

## 3. A 'New Typology'

We saw in the previous section that figural interpretation, as Frei and Auerbach conceive it, is essentially a 'literary device', which draws together different parts of a literary corpus through showing that there are significant structural parallels in the way that each is patterned. Now the recurrence of such patterns within the Hebrew Scriptures, and the contributions they make to our understanding of these writings, has recently been illuminated by Robert Alter's very perceptive work on biblical 'type-scenes'.[21] What I wish to do, therefore, is to consider how this can be used in developing a christological interpretation of the Old Testament. Needless to say, this is not the context in which Alter himself discusses type-scenes; his concerns, rather, are solely with the Hebrew canon, and are primarily oriented towards literary rather than theological issues. Nonetheless, his ideas and principles can also, I believe, be redeployed for other ends.

I shall begin, then, by outlining a couple of specific examples of 'typological' interpretation, which will then provide useful material for our methodological reflections. One type-scene which Alter himself unfolds in some detail is 'the encounter with the future betrothed at a well'.[22] Paradigmatic examples occur in Gen. 24:10–61; 29:1–20; and Exod. 2:15b–21; their common pattern is described by Alter in the following way:

> The betrothal type-scene ... must take place with the future bridegroom, or his surrogate, having journeyed to a foreign land. There he encounters a girl ... or girls at a well. Someone, either the man or the girl, then draws water from the well; afterwards the girl or girls rush to bring home the news of the stranger's arrival ... [and] finally, a betrothal is concluded between the stranger and the girl. (p. 52)

For our present purposes it is not necessary to review the diversified ways in which this pattern is instantiated in the Old Testament; instead, I shall turn directly to a notable example of the same type-scene in the Fourth Gospel.[23]

---

[21] See especially Alter's *The Art of Biblical Narrative*, chapter 3; also his 'How Conventions Help Us Read: The Case of the Bible's Annunciation Type-Scene', *Proof* 3 (1983), pp. 115–30.

[22] *Narrative*, p. 51.

[23] This has also been noted by Lyle Eslinger, 'The Wooing of the Woman at the Well: Jesus, the Reader and Reader-Response Criticism', *JLT* 1 (1987), pp. 167–83. Eslinger draws explicitly upon Alter's discussion of the betrothal type-scene, but even

In John 4 Jesus is journeying outside his own land, passing through Samaria. Coming to Sychar he stops beside Jacob's well to rest, and while he is seated there a Samaritan woman comes to draw water (vv. 1–7). This already introduces enough of the distinctive elements to identify this as a betrothal type-scene;[24] and true to form, the drawing of water quickly becomes the means of introducing the protagonists to one another. In the Old Testament this action is usually performed by the 'bridegroom', although in the Isaac story the author breaks with convention in order to convey something of Rebekah's character: Her 'continuous whirl of purposeful activity' as she draws water for Abraham's servant and for all his camels foreshadows her later taking of the initiative at a crucial juncture in the story.[25] John likewise handles this stereotyped element in a distinctive way. Jesus introduces the subject with a straightforward request for a drink (v. 7), to which the woman responds with an equally straightforward expression of surprise that Jesus should make such a request (v. 9).[26] In typical Johannine style, however, Jesus then moves the topic of conversation from the provision of literal well-water to his own identity as the giver of spiritual, 'living water' (v. 10). Unfortunately the woman—again in typically Johannine style—largely fails to comprehend this shift;[27] and with Jesus' intentions to reveal himself therefore thwarted, he abruptly alters the topic of conversation by telling the woman to call her husband (v. 16).

---

before Alter's work a number of scholars had identified some of the connections between John 4 and the pertinent Old Testament material; see Eslinger's bibliography on p. 180 n. 3.

[24] Cf. Alter's identification of another instance from similar elements in 1 Sam. 9 (p. 60).

[25] Alter, pp. 53–54.

[26] I am not convinced by Eslinger's arguments ('Wooing', *passim*) that the conversation in vv. 7–15 is laced with sexual double entendres. In my view Eslinger has given undue weight to the bare fact that, as he rightly argues, water imagery *can be* used in the Old Testament as a metaphor for sexual relations, without doing enough to show that, when the relevant expressions are read in the context of John 4, we are to understand them as having such connotations there. Eslinger's reading makes a high proportion of what both characters say largely irrelevant to what, in his view, their real motives are, and he therefore has to reduce it arbitrarily to feigned proprieties that are mouthed for the sake of appearances (e.g., p. 177). Eslinger is right to observe that 'Jesus seems to take an active . . . role in the unfolding of the pattern' (p. 175); but although this usually (though not invariably—recall Alter's discussion of 1 Sam. 9:11–12, pp. 60–61) eventuates in marriage, this is not a sound reason for expecting the type-scene itself to have sexual connotations.

[27] Her final comment in this section of the dialogue, indicating that possession of the 'living water' is attractive to her because she will then no longer have to come

This unexpected change of direction has occasioned much debate; but seen in relation to its Old Testament antecedents, its primary effect is suddenly to disclose, some way into a betrothal type-scene, that the female character is in fact totally unfitted for her role as bride! Again one finds the author shaping the stereotyped pattern for his own purposes. In his Old Testament models the lady's eligibility for marriage (together, in some cases, with an indication of her desirability) is made clear when she is first introduced into the story; but in retrospect we now recall that here the female character was introduced simply as 'a woman from Samaria' (*gynē ek tēs Samareias*).

The author's delay in communicating the highly pertinent information about her marriages, quite apart from its dramatic effect, is perhaps to prevent the reader's perception of his narrative as a betrothal type-scene from being subverted before it has been adequately established. As it is, this unexpected disclosure seems to break the type-scene off prematurely, since the conversation now turns, as Jesus had intended, to the question of his identity. Once he has revealed that he is the anticipated Messiah (v. 26), however, the betrothal pattern resumes. With the business at the well concluded, the next stage requires the prospective bride to hurry away to tell others of the remarkable events that have transpired there. For the marriageable maidens of the Old Testament this meant conveying the news to their immediate family. For the worldly Samaritan woman this has to be modified, but the same element is clearly visible in her returning to the city and telling the people about her meeting with Jesus (vv. 28–29).[28] And continuing the pattern further, this in turn leads to those to whom the news has been conveyed offering hospitality to Jesus, who stays with them for two days.[29]

Read at the grammatical level, John 4 recounts Jesus' progressive self-revelation as the Messiah to the Samaritan woman. Clearly this is not to be set aside; yet when one recognizes that it occurs within a literary setting which implicitly identifies Jesus as a prospective bridegroom and the Samaritan woman as his future betrothed its

---

to the well to draw (v. 15), makes it difficult to read her request for Jesus to 'give me this water' as a sexual invitation (*contra* Eslinger, p. 178, who again has to resort arbitrarily to 'feigned propriety').

[28] In this context the puzzling reference to her leaving her water jar at the well (v. 28), which has provoked many diverse explanations, is probably best understood as alluding to the 'haste' motif of this type-scene.

[29] V. 40; this is separated from the previous element by Jesus' conversation with his disciples (vv. 31–38), to which I shall return shortly.

significance is further extended. As Alter has pointed out, a betrothal type-scene usually gives important insights into the character of the main protagonists. We have already seen Rebekah characteristically taking the initiative; similarly Isaac, who elsewhere has a very passive role, is appropriately absent from his own betrothal;[30] Jacob 'the supplanter', whose constant striving against his circumstances is repeatedly associated with stones, removes a stone that is blocking the well (p. 55); Moses, who will deliver his people from slavery, saves Reuel's daughters from the hostile shepherds (p. 57). In John 4 Jesus' characteristic action is his lengthy conversation with the woman, in which he reveals his true identity. Jesus' self-disclosure is a major theme in this Gospel, but there is particular significance in him identifying himself specifically as the Messiah in this type-scenic setting. It presents this particular self-revelation as the very epitome of his career, inviting us to understand the whole in Messianic terms.

The Samaritan woman also plays a very prominent and active part in this episode, and it is appropriate to ask, therefore, if its presentation as a type-scene affects our understanding of her role. The woman's unusual personal history has sometimes been cited as a reason for seeing her as a symbolic figure, with her marriages to various men representing the hybrid character of Samaritan religion.[31] Schnackenburg is doubtful whether there is sufficient reason to see this woman as a symbolic figure unless one is going to regard all the characters in John as symbolic (p. 420); but although one can agree that interpretations which allegorize the details of her life should be avoided,[32] recognizing this passage as a type-scene does give a reason for thinking that this particular character, while certainly appearing in the story as a distinct individual, might also have symbolic overtones. The woman's tangled marital affairs make her, as we have mentioned, a highly unsuitable bride. Wrongful sexual liaisons are frequently a metaphor for false religion in the Old Testament, and it would be appropriate to see something similar here. The woman's conversation shows her to have a lively interest in religious issues, but she is slow to grasp the spiritual realities that Jesus reveals to her. Yet it is specifically to this unsuitable woman that Jesus comes

---

[30] See Alter, p. 53.

[31] For details see Rudolph Schnackenburg, *The Gospel According to Saint John* Vol. I (London: Burns & Oates, 1980), p. 433.

[32] As Schnackenburg (p. 433) and numerous others have argued, the details of the usual allegorization cannot in any case be worked out consistently.

as husband-Messiah. It seems difficult to deny that there is a degree of theological symbolism in this.

In the Old Testament exemplars it is characteristic of the male to draw the water, although Rebekah provides an exception. In John 4, however, neither Jesus nor the Samaritan draw any water; rather, this important motif is introduced at the expected point but then allowed to drop from the story as the conversation turns from literal to spiritual water, and to the identity of the one who provides this water. Similarly, the woman's water jar is finally 'left behind' as she becomes preoccupied with profounder things (v. 28).

By the time Jesus accepts the Samaritans' invitation to stay with them the reader is perhaps a little bemused. On the one hand, the point has been reached where a betrothal should now ensue. On the other hand, however, the narrative has itself forestalled this outcome— the disclosures about the woman's previous and current relationships put her in a completely different category from her Old Testament counterparts, and make it clear that Jesus is not about to embark upon married life. This tension finds a surprising theological resolution, however, in the narrative's final episode. At precisely the point where the Old Testament model leads us to expect a betrothal there occurs instead a declaration of belief (v. 42); and given that John 4 has carefully recapitulated each element from the Old Testament models in its due place,[33] this cannot be merely coincidental. On the contrary, it has been prepared for by the digression[34] in vv. 31–38 which, coming between the townspeople going out to see Jesus and their inviting him to stay, holds up the progress of the type-scene in order to anticipate its final episode. This is does through reintroducing the disciples into the story in the role of missionaries. Whatever implications vv. 35–38 may have for the church's post-resurrection mission, their application to the immediate situation is clear: Jesus has 'sown' the knowledge of his true identity in his conversation with the Samaritan woman, who in turn has conveyed it to the townspeople. Their interest and curiosity thus aroused they invite Jesus to

---

[33] With the exception of the woman's (in)eligibility for marriage. We saw, however, that there were special reasons for it being handled in this particular way, and it therefore does not detract from the impression which John 4 as a whole conveys of an author who is closely following his Old Testament models.

[34] This is formally signalled as such by vv. 28–30 being largely repeated in vv. 39–40, emphasizing the resumption of the main narrative line after the 'offline' (but, as we shall see, highly pertinent) episode in vv. 31–38.

remain with them, and thereby provide the disciples with an ideal missionary field, ripe for harvesting.

In the closing episode (vv. 41–42) the anticipated harvest is duly reaped. Understanding this as the culmination of the betrothal type-scene, the implicit imagery is not dissimilar from the Pauline metaphor of the church as the bride of Christ, with a union between bride-groom and bride being effected through faith in Jesus in his self-disclosed identity as the Messiah. At this wedding, the role of the bride is filled collectively by the townspeople.[35] Moreover, the blessings which, in a literal marriage, can be received only by one, are here enjoyed by all who believe; thus Jesus not only fulfils the Old Testament 'type' but far surpasses it. In sum, then, recognizing John 4 as a type-scene enables us to interpret it at a higher level than the semantic-grammatical, and thus to perceive significant theological themes which would otherwise pass unnoticed.

My second example of the New Testament's use of type-scenes brings us rather closer to classical typology. The Old Testament contains a number of strikingly parallel stories about a Rejected Deliverer, whose very rejection by his own people leads to him saving them:

(i) Joseph is sold into slavery by his brothers, and is thus brought to Egypt. Via Potipher's house and Pharaoh's prisons, however, he rises to second in the kingdom, from which position he masterminds a plan to mitigate the effects of the impending famine. When, therefore, the famine forces Joseph's own family to seek food in Egypt, it is as a direct consequence of his brothers' prior rejection of him that they are now saved from starvation.

(ii) Jephthah the Gileadite is thrown out by his half brothers, apparently with the connivance of the tribal elders. In direct consequence he becomes the leader of a band of brigands, and thus an experienced military chieftain; therefore when his tribe is threatened by the invading Ammonites he is well equipped to return as commander of the Gileadite army and thereby save his own people from catastrophe.

(iii) Seeking vengeance against Samson, the Philistines raid Lehi in Judah. The men of Judah therefore appease the Philistines by themselves binding Samson and handing him over to them. Samson promptly breaks his bonds, however, and improvising a weapon from

---

[35] Perhaps surprisingly, the Samaritan woman herself is never explicitly said to believe in Jesus. On the contrary, her use of *mēti* in asking the townspeople whether he is the Christ (v. 29) implies at least hesitation on her part.

the jawbone of an ass, inflicts a crushing defeat upon the Philistines.

(iv) Samson is again betrayed (this time by Delilah) into the hands of the Philistines, who keep him in prison. On the occasion of a great celebration, however, they bring him into the temple of Dagon when it is filled with the Philistine nobility. Pulling down the temple upon them, Samson inflicts his greatest defeat upon his people's oppressors.

These narratives also have a number of other features in common, of which the following are particularly notable:

(i) There is a death, either literal or virtual, associated with the rejected deliverer: Joseph's brother's originally intended to kill him, and deceive their father into believing that he has been slain; Jephthah's daughter dies as a result of her father's rash vow; Samson's exertions with the jawbone exhaust him to the point where he would have died if God had not miraculously provided water; and in his final destruction of the Philistines Samson destroys himself as well.

(ii) A sense of isolation attaches itself to the rejected deliverer as he brings about salvation: Joseph is in a foreign land, completely cut off from his family and kinsmen; Jephthah is reluctantly accepted as head of Gilead purely out of military necessity, with no true reconciliation between him and the elders;[36] Samson is literally a one-man army, invariably engaging the Philistines single-handedly.

The relevance of this type-scene to the New Testament's portrayal of Jesus hardly needs labouring, although for a full assessment of its significance one would have to look at the distinctive use which each Gospel makes of the pattern. Unfortunately this is beyond the scope of the present study; but we can round off our present discussion by noting a few points from Mark's passion narrative. The theme of Jesus' rejection is developed through three stages, which successively broaden the scope of those who reject him (and hence, implicitly, of those whom he will save). Firstly, he is betrayed by Judas to the chief priests, who have already determined to kill him. When Judas strikes his bargain with them he is described as 'one of the twelve' (14:12), stressing that Jesus' betrayer belongs to his inner circle of disciples. This is given even greater poignancy by Jesus announcing at the passover meal that his betrayer is 'one of the twelve, one who is dipping bread in the same dish with me' (v. 20; cf. v. 18); and

---

[36] See Alter's insightful discussion; 'Introduction', pp. 18–20.

when Judas brings the arresting party to Jesus he is again identified as 'one of the twelve' (v. 43). Secondly, Jesus is rejected by 'all the chief priests and the elders and the scribes' (v. 53), acting here in their official capacity as the leaders of the Jewish nation—Jesus' own people. (The people themselves play a part in Jesus' rejection in the next chapter when, at the instigation of the chief priests, they cry out for Barabas to be released and Jesus crucified, 15:6–15). The 'whole council' are assembled 'against Jesus to put him to death' (14:55), and it is a consultation of 'the whole council' that decides to hand him over to Pilate (15:1). Thus Jesus comes to be rejected, thirdly, by the official representative of the Roman Empire, the ruling world power. Although put under pressure by the chief priests and the crowd, it is finally by Pilate's own decision that Jesus is crucified (v. 15).

The theme of Jesus' isolation is also developed in a number of different ways. At the passover meal Jesus predicts that all the disciples will scatter from him, and in response to Peter's protestations he foretells that the latter will deny him three times (14:27–30). Passing on to Gethsemane Jesus withdraws from his disciples to pray alone; returning to them, however, he discovers that he is even more on his own than he intended because, instead of remaining watchful and praying, the disciples have fallen asleep. (This incident is repeated, with small variations, three times in vv. 32–41.) When Jesus is arrested the disciples, as predicted, 'all forsook him, and fled' (v. 50), as too did an otherwise unidentified young man in a linen cloth (vv. 51–52). Peter nonetheless does follow Jesus (though only 'at a distance', v. 54); but when others identify him as a disciple Peter too behaves as predicted, swearing that he does not even know Jesus (vv. 66–72). And finally, even the women who do accompany Jesus in his final hours only 'look on from afar' (15:40), and are not mentioned until after he has died.

It seems clear, then, that the authors of the Gospels wish us to perceive Jesus through the pattern of the Old Testament's Rejected Deliverer—in other words, to see Jesus as the 'antitypical' fulfilment of the Old Testament 'types'. This in turn has significant implications for how we understand the purpose of Jesus' career. The Old Testament deliverers, it will be recalled, were consistently portrayed as saving those who rejected them from a devastating catastrophe, and we are therefore meant to understand what Jesus accomplished in commensurate terms. Thus explaining Jesus' death, for example, in terms of his willingness to die for the truth rather than to compromise his principles clearly would not satisfy the pattern which the Old Testament establishes. Of course this is not to deny that Jesus' uncompromising affirmation of his beliefs was a significant causal factor in bringing about his death; yet the Old Testament background shows that something far more radical is involved than just 'standing up for what is right'. The Old Testament types did not merely set good examples or offer wise counsel but actually *accomplished* something, namely, the deliverance of those who rejected them from a catastrophic situation. Again we see, then, that recognizing the appropriate type-scene has important theological consequences.

### 4. *Reflections on the 'New Typology'*

Although a full discussion of typological interpretation is not possible here, something needs to be said about how the preceding examples avoid the well-known failings of classical typology.[37]

(i) The Old Testament text is taken seriously on its own terms, with the proper constraints of semantic-grammatical exegesis being fully observed: Joseph saved his family from famine, not from their sins; Jephthah did not fight against satanic hordes but against flesh-and-blood Ammonites. Or again, there is no speculative guessing about what the slaughtered Philistines 'really' stand for; they are simply themselves. In Childs' terms, the character of these texts as *Old* Testament witness is fully preserved, through them being described in a way that respects their original context and function.

(ii) There is a principled way of deciding from the Old Testament itself what is and is not typologically significant. Thus on the one hand, no attempt is made to give a Christian meaning to every detail of Samson's betrayal by Delilah; yet on the other hand, points are not picked out on the basis of a prior Christian conception of the doctrines one wishes to see exemplified. Rather, identifying a recurrent pattern means that there is a basis in the stories themselves for deciding which are their significant features.

---

[37] For a summary of the standard critical objections to typological interpretations of the Old Testament see R.N. Whybray, 'Old Testament Theology—A Non-existent Beast?', in Barry P. Thompson (ed.), *Scripture: Meaning and Method* (Hull: Hull University Press, 1987), pp. 170–72.

(iii) The Old Testament, then, has an independent integrity; and it is precisely because the new typology is able to respect this that it can make a genuinely original contributions to our understanding of the New Testament. The betrothal type-scene can be established from the Old Testament alone, and is thus an independent 'given' which a New Testament passage can be measured against. As we have seen, this can lead to important theological insights.

(iv) The concept of a type which I have been developing[38] is sufficiently precise for there to be fruitful discussion about their identification and fulfilment. One problem with classical typology, Frei observes, is that it

> had to convince less by a statement of an operative principle establishing a connection and more by sheer juxtaposition of the two occasions, noting the similarities in their constituent features. ... In effect this juxtaposition in itself exhibited—it was hoped in convincing fashion—the divine purpose that constituted the bond between the two occasions.[39]

Seeing an antitype, however, as a further occurrence of an established pattern means that there are several passages available for making cross-comparisons, thus adding a considerable degree of exegetical control. In sum, then, it apparently is possible to develop a form of typological interpretation which is both methodologically sound and theologically fruitful.

This is also an appropriate place to say something about the tangled terminology which this issue has spawned. Discussions of typological interpretation have produced numerous designations of the various 'senses' of the Bible which different schools have either commended or condemned: the literal sense, the plain sense, the historical (or grammatical, or historical-grammatical) sense, the original sense, the figurative (or figural) or typological sense, the spiritual sense, the allegorical, anagogical, and mystical senses, etc. This proliferation has surely now reached the point where it serves more to confuse than to clarify, especially since the basic issue can be stated without resorting to complicated terminology: The exegete's task is not to discover meanings that float 'above' the Scriptures or lie 'behind' them, or which, though grounded 'in' them, somehow pass 'beyond' them;

---

[38] I would not, of course, exclude there also being other legitimate forms of typology.

[39] *Eclipse*, p. 30.

rather, it is to discover the meanings *of* the Scriptures, i.e., to explicate what the Scriptures themselves objectively say. Such exegesis is not, of course, the *whole* task of biblical studies or of theology; on the contrary, besides this quest for (Hirschian) meanings there are also perfectly legitimate and important questions to be asked about, for example, the truth of their claims, and their modern-day significance. Unless, however, one restricts 'the meanings of the Bible' to what can be objectively demonstrated through sound exegetical procedures then the door is opened to all kinds of fanciful spiritualizings which, far from yielding a fuller insight into the Bible, only obscure what it says. This, of course, was one reason why the Reformers rejected medieval allegorizing, and was also part of the motivation behind the rise of the historical-critical approach. It is still a perfectly legitimate concern today.

Yet on the other hand, it is hardly less important to emphasize that 'sound exegetical procedures' must not be construed restrictively. One of Childs' principal criticisms in 'SLS' of the historical-critical approach is that it has frequently made this mistake, with 'sound exegesis' being equated with discovering the single, semantic-grammatical, meaning of a text in its original historical context. In this I think that Childs is correct. As previous sections have pointed out, there are in fact many ways besides the narrowly semantic-grammatical in which a text can convey meanings; thus there may, in principle, be several 'levels' of meaning within any particular text. Each, however, is an exegetically demonstrable meaning *of the text*.

The final issue to discuss here is the implications of these typological examples for the question of author's intention. I argued in chapter 7 that 'meanings which no-one meant' is not a viable concept; therefore searching for pan-canonical, Christian interpretations of the Scriptures is a sensible project only if one also posits an 'author' who intended such meanings. How, then, might this be done?

In his own discussion of type-scenes, Alter suggests that in ancient Israel they were (presumably quite familiar) literary conventions, so that being able to recognize a certain series of events as, say, the opening sequence of a betrothal type-scene was part of the educated Israelite's literary competence. Now if this were so, it would provide a perfectly adequate rationale for Alter's own 'canonical interpretations', in which, for example, the full meaning of Saul's encounter with the maidens only emerges when it is read in conjunction with the similar stories concerning Isaac, Jacob, and Moses. As literary *conventions*, type-scenes would be handled in the same sort of way as other conventional aspects of the language, such as its grammar. The author of the Saul story would, through his native acquaintance with the requisite conventions, be able to draw upon them in shaping his material; and an ancient Israelite reader of this story would likewise be able to understand it directly. We too can understand it, once we are aware of these conventions; but since we are not native readers we have to discover them by looking at the 'parallel passages' in Genesis and Exodus. For Alter's 'canonical' reading of type-scenes, then, human intentionality can provide the necessary rationale.

But granted this understanding of the Old Testament type-scenes, one still has to ask whether it would adequately account for their extension into the New Testament. One important difference here is that, in some cases at least, the New Testament authors are not simply using conventions 'off their own bat' which others (sc. the Old Testament writers) had also used. Quite apart from the historical question as to whether these conventions were in fact still generally known and/or used in the latter part of the first century A.D.,[40] it seems clear from such cases as John 4 that the author intends us to see his composition as a re-use of the Old Testament material. The story of the Samaritan woman does more than just employ the same type-pattern that is found in a number of Old Testament betrothals— as various commentators have pointed out, there are several clear allusions in John 4 specifically to the corresponding Old Testament passages: Jesus, like Moses, has embarked on this journey to escape the attentions of the authorities, which his immediately preceding actions have provoked;[41] like Jacob, he arrives at the well at noon;[42] etc. Such cases, then, raise questions concerning not the use of a common pattern but the conscious *re-use* of certain prior exemplifications of that pattern.

Seen in this way, the issues here are quite similar to those we discussed at the end of section 7.2. As we saw there, the kind of explanation which might prove adequate depends very much upon the extent and precision of the Old Testament's anticipations of the New. The Old Testament is a fairly sizeable and diverse collection,

---

[40] This could presumably be decided by looking at other Christian and Jewish writings from around that time.

[41] John 4:1–3; Exod. 2:11–15.

[42] John 4:6; Gen. 29:7.

and it would hardly be surprising, therefore, if a perceptive New Testament author could *occasionally* find in it something like the betrothal type-scene which, he realizes, can be put to a novel, Christian use. It would be a very different matter, however, if this and the Rejected Deliverer proved to be just the tip of a typological iceberg. That the Old Testament should contain numerous patterned presentations of its principal characters (or events, or institutions, or whatever) which 'just happened' to provide striking illustrations of the Christian doctrines of atonement, ecclesiology, eschatology, and the like, and which consistently lent themselves to giving apposite presentations of the life, death, and resurrection of Jesus of Nazereth, would be too convenient to be merely coincidental. If the Old Testament proved to be susceptible to this sort of *extensive* typological reading then one would again seem to be driven towards postulating some sort of divine inspiration, because only a divine intentionality would appear to be capable of 'writing into' the Old Testament the meanings which such an interpretation would read from it.

In summary, then, this chapter has argued that Childs' own discussions of the christological interpretation of the Old Testament, whether by the New Testament writers or by the modern biblical theologian, have not been altogether satisfactory. This is mainly due to him never having worked out an appropriate exegetical methodology for such cases. Because of this it is generally—at best—unclear whether the christological interpretations of the Old Testament which Childs offers in *BTONT* and elsewhere really are hearing the true witness of the Old Testament, or whether (albeit unintentionally) they are imposing an alien meaning upon it.

For a programme that wishes to reinstate Biblical Theology as a legitimate branch of academic theology this is a major deficiency. In the latter part of this chapter, however, I have suggested how one might start to rectifying it by developing one example of a methodology which appears to achieve what Childs needs. This, of course, by no means solves all his problems; there are no doubt many examples of the New Testament's use of the Old which cannot be explained in this figural way. It does suggest, however, that there may be fruitful avenues which have yet to be explored. If the typological examples I discussed above are exegetically sound, then apart from any contribution which they make in their own right, they further suggest that (at least some of) the New Testament authors were perhaps more subtle and perceptive readers of the Old Testament than has hitherto been realized. Perhaps the apostles *did* have 'rules' for interpreting the Old Testament figuratively, but of very different order from those on Collins' list.

We saw in discussing 'SLS' that what a programme such as Childs' needs to show is (i) that there are other ways of reading the Old Testament besides the historical-grammatical; and (ii) that by broadening one's range of 'reading strategies' it is possible to discover levels of meaning which transcend 'the literal' as critical scholarship has generally conceived it, and yet are still meanings *of the text*. Drawing on recent 'literary approaches', my typological interpretations have suggested one way in which the New Testament authors themselves did this. Whether further literary work on this problem will uncover additional examples, perhaps based on strategies quite different from the typological, remains to be seen. Clearly this is an area where more research is needed.

# CHAPTER TWELVE

# A CRITICAL RECONSTRUCTION OF
# CHILDS' PROGRAMME

Because of the complexity of Childs' canonical methodology the preceding chapters have had to traverse a lot of difficult and diverse ground. In this final chapter it is therefore necessary to draw together the different threads and to consider whether a viable biblical-theological programme can be based upon Childs' work.

## 1. *The Role of the Historical-Critical Tools*

This section can be brief, as it is only necessary to collect together points that have been discussed elsewhere. I argued in section 6.1 that although Childs thinks that the critical tools help him to understand the meaning of the text's final form, they are in fact intrinsically unsuited for this role. They are properly employed, rather, in investigating questions of historical referentiality, both of 'reference in' and 'reference behind' the text.

Although Childs sometimes takes an intentionalist and sometimes an anti-intentionalist stance,[1] we have seen that the latter is hermeneutically untenable: If the authors' intentions are (deliberately or inadvertently) disregarded then the interpreter will discover only degraded meanings; and if the motivations for writing these texts were predominantly political, or if they were collected simply as an anthology, then it is extremely unlikely that they will yield canonical meanings of any great religious significance. Childs ought therefore to maintain a consistently intentionalist stance, with respect to both motives and communicative intentions.

In his intentionalist phases, Childs does recognize that critical questions of 'what really happened' are relevant to the text's significance; thus his programme is *not* a covert regression to the pre-critical era, but is a genuinely critical theology. Unfortunately, Childs himself

---

[1] It will be recalled from section 3.2 that Childs covers issues both of author's/redactor's communicative intentions and motives under this rubric.

tends to obscure this by his sharp but diffuse polemics against historical referentiality, which have led some of his less perceptive readers to conclude that his programme has little or no place for historical-critical questions. A balanced consideration of all that Childs says on this subject, however, shows that what he is actually opposed to is such questions being pursued in ways that are unhelpful or even inimical to the understanding of the Bible as Christian Scripture.[2] When guided in this way by his Relevance Principle, these polemics often make a good point.

We also saw in sections 2.2 that in his earlier writings Childs argued that the supposed 'faith-neutrality' of the critical methods—which in reality imports an anti-theological bias into biblical studies—makes them intrinsically unsound tools for the biblical scholar. In his later work this charge has largely been dropped; yet some important aspects of Childs' earlier position have been vindicated by the discussion of historical methodology in chapters 4 and 5, where it was argued that certain applications of Troeltschian analogy and of the fact/interpretation dichotomy are, as Childs suspected, implicitly biased. I also argued that both these principles are inherently flawed, and developed a historical methodology, similar to that of Pannenberg and Collingwood, which avoids these (and other) weaknesses. Thus Childs' programme would, on this issue, be strengthened by him reverting again to his earlier position.

In the light of this, the characterization that I have just given of Childs' programme as 'a genuinely critical theology' needs to be further refined: Although this recognizes the legitimacy of critical questions about 'what really happened', it should nonetheless not be too readily assumed that the critical tools, as these are generally understood, necessarily provide us with the correct way of answering them. In some cases at least, the tools themselves need to be revised in order to avoid begging important theological questions.

## 2. *Stendahl's Dichotomy*

The discussion thus far has been generally favourable towards Stendahl's dichotomy, at least insofar as it parallels Hirsch's distinction between meaning and significance. Particularly in the light of Ben

---

[2] Childs gives some particularly clear examples of this in 'On Reading the Elijah Narratives', *Int* 34 (1980), pp. 128–37.

Ollenburger's thorough critique of Stendahl's methodology, however, more needs to be said about each of its main elements.

(1) 'What it meant'. As the past tense implies, Stendahl is primarily concerned here with a text's 'historical' meaning; yet the way in which he conceives this is, in certain respects, highly problematic. According to Stendahl, 'The question of meaning . . . always require[s] a subject (for whom?) and . . . a *Sitz im Leben* (when and in relation to what question or questions?)';[3] thus we might ask about what (say) Romans 7 meant for Calvin, or for Bultmann. Yet in addition to this, we surely also want to ask (as Ollenburger points out)[4] whether Calvin and Bultmann understood this text *correctly*—i.e., whether it really does have the meanings which these and other scholars have ascribed to it. Stendahl, in fact, is not unaware of this;[5] and (in line with his general characterization of meaning) he at one point explicates the descriptive task as 'ask[ing] what a certain writer meant', which he then glosses as 'what for example, Paul thought that he meant' (p. 199). As Ollenburger has pointed out, however,[6] this is open to some serious objections, both methodological and practical: Methodologically, one can still say of Paul, as one can of his readers, 'I accept that this is what he *thought* that Romans 7 means; but does it *really* mean this?';[7] and practically, the only information we have as to what Paul thought about the meaning of Romans 7 is Romans 7 itself. Stendahl's explication of 'what it meant', then, is not tenable.

Ollenburger is also unhappy with the contrasted tenses of 'what it meant' and 'what it means'. According to Ollenburger, this implies that in describing 'what the text meant' one is searching for a certain property (a 'meaning', M) which the text *used* to have at some time in the past (i.e., when it was first written) but which it does not have today. Ollenburger finds this objectionable for several reasons: It is unclear what could now be known about M, or how this could be discovered; it is unlikely that many would be interested in a property which the text no longer has; and (recalling Stendahl's analysis of

---

[3] 'Method', p. 200.

[4] 'What Stendahl Meant', pp. 68–69.

[5] A history of the 'meanings' that the Corinthian epistles had for their successive interpreters, Stendahl remarks, 'would not yield answers to the question, "what does this statement of Paul's mean?"' ('Method', p. 200).

[6] See pp. 69, 80–81.

[7] Paul, in effect, is being viewed as a reader of his own work, who is therefore subject to the same limitations as other readers. This point and the next, of course, have often been made in discussions of the Intentional Fallacy.

meaning as 'meaning *for* someone') M is just the first in a long series of such former properties.[8] On the basis of this discussion Ollenburger concludes that '[Stendahl's] meant/means distinction, which seems so straightforward and helpful at first glance, seems upon closer analysis to be problematic in fundamental ways' (p. 88).

There are a number of points that can be made in Stendahl's defence, however. Although his methodological discussions are not always as clear and precise as one might wish, there are good reasons for doubting whether Stendahl ever thought that the task of biblical theology is to describe the meanings which a text used to have but has now lost. Stendahl does not in fact give much space to explaining his conception of 'what it meant' in his 'Method' article (which Ollenburger is mainly considering); but this is primarily because he had already done so in 'Biblical Theology, Contemporary'.[9] To understand Stendahl's position, therefore, it is important to take full account of his earlier article, and in particular, to note the close connection which he draws there between the descriptive task and the *religionsgeschichtliche Schule*. According to Stendahl, the significance of the history of religions approach is that its thoroughgoing orientation towards historical investigations enabled scholars to make significant progress in describing the biblical texts 'on their own terms':

> Once freed from the anachronistic interpretations of their predecessors, and forced to accept the hiatus between the ideas and ideals in the biblical material, the theologically minded student of the Scriptures slowly found a new and deeper relevance in what the *religionsgeschichtliche Schule* described for him as the pre-Westernized meaning of sayings and events.[10]

Describing 'what it meant', therefore, was *already* an established part of biblical studies (according to Stendahl's account) well before he wrote 'BTCon'—it had emerged during the first two decades of the twentieth century as 'a mature outgrowth of the historical and critical study of the Scriptures'.[11] Thus in distinguishing between the descriptive

---

[8] See pp. 86–88.

[9] See Stendahl's comment in 'Method', p. 199 n. 8.

[10] 'BTCon', p. 419; there are several important references to description now being carried out 'on its own terms' in the section on 'The Descriptive Task' in this article (pp. 418–25).

[11] P. 418; cf. p. 422: '[O]ur only concern is to find out what these words meant when uttered or written by the prophet, the priest, the evangelist, or the apostle. . . . Such a programme is . . . a mature fruit of the historical method'.

and the normative tasks, Stendahl's intention with respect to the former was not to propose something new but to call attention to what was already being done, in order to emphasize its distinctiveness (it is different from the normative task) and to discuss its place within the broader theological enterprise (it is related to the normative task via a hermeneutics of 'translation').

If this is an accurate description of Stendahl's methodology, then Ollenburger's critique of the meant/means distinction largely misses the mark. There seems little reason to think that many scholars conceived of historical-critical exegesis as recovering a former property of the text which it had subsequently lost, or that Stendahl is trying to persuade us that it should be so conceived. Ollenburger appears to have read too much into Stendahl's tenses.

In the light of this discussion, it can be readily understood why Stendahl should have thought it appropriate to characterize the first part of his dichotomy as describing 'what it *meant*': Historical criticism has been concerned with finding the meaning that a text had in its original context. This is not to say, however, that the text only had this meaning when it was first written. The point, rather, is that critical scholars are seeking the meaning of the text, and believe that the correct way to discover it is to consider the text in relation to its original historical context. As I have argued in chapter 7, there is in fact a substantial measure of truth in this belief. Yet this is quite different from claiming that all one has discovered through a historical reading is (say) the first-century meaning of Romans.[12] What one has discovered, rather, is simply the meaning of Romans, because this is the (descriptive) meaning it will have for *all* who read it correctly (i.e., historically), whatever century they live in. In sum then, I believe that Stendahl's conception of the descriptive task is basically sound.

There are two points of qualification which need to be added, however. Firstly, the descriptive task is not necessarily neutral in the way that Stendahl claims. If, for example, one believes that the Rejected Deliverer type-scene was fulfilled in Jesus of Nazareth,[13] then

---

[12] Unfortunately, Stendahl's contrasting of 'meant' with 'means' can give this impression, although I do not think that this is what he is trying to say. Rather, the 'meaning' in 'what it means' is conceived by him as different in kind from the textual meaning that we are discussing at present; that, in large measure is the point of him contrasting them as descriptive and normative. I shall return to this below.

[13] This, it should be noted, is more than I argued for in section 11.3, which dealt

one way of describing these Old Testament stories is that they are prefigurements of Jesus' salvific death; and given our knowledge of human limitations in anticipating future events and discerning their theological import, such a description is not 'faith neutral'. And secondly, there is the question of *what* is to be described. For Stendahl this is (usually) the individual literary units (at various levels) in their original historical contexts; for Childs (from *IOTS* onwards) it is the final form of the text in its canonical context. Although these alternatives do not form a total antithesis (as we saw in section 11.3, even pan-canonical interpretations can still be historically rooted), they will clearly lead to quite different kinds of interpretation. Some sort of choice therefore needs to be made between them; but unfortunately neither Childs nor Stendahl appear to have made out a compelling case for their own preferred alternative being adopted as a general principle. On the one hand, Childs has given a number of persuasive reasons why, *in some cases*, going behind the final form would be a retrograde step; and building upon Moberly's work, I have further argued that the final form may *sometimes* be far less amenable to investigations into its prehistory than has generally been realized. On the other hand, I cannot see that Childs has thus far done nearly enough to justify his claim that it is invariably the final form which must be taken as the theologically significant level.[14] *Prima facie*, there are some cases in which the final form is marked not by subtle literary structuring or productive tensions but by unproductive obscurities and unliterary confusions. Unless such assessments can be overturned by a more careful exegesis, there seems little point in insisting that it is nonetheless the final form of these texts which is theologically normative.

In the current state of scholarship, and in view of the diverse character of the biblical literature, it is probably too early to adjudicate

---

only with the literary relationship between the Testaments.

[14] Cf. Douglas A. Knight: 'Childs, like Gunkel and von Rad before him, has identified for serious study a largely neglected phase in the development of the biblical literature but . . . also like them, he is overemphasizing the relative importance of this phase' ('Canon', p. 130). This is probably the most frequent criticism that is made of Childs' programme; see, for example, Barr, 'Childs' *Introduction*', pp. 12–13; James L. Mays, 'What is Written', *HBT* 2 (1980), p. 161; Robert B. Laurin, 'Tradition and Canon', in Douglas A. Knight (ed.), *Tradition and Theology in the Old Testament* (London: SPCK, 1977), p. 272. Some of Childs' critics, however, seem not to have appreciated that he has given strong reasons why the final form should at least *sometimes* be given priority.

between the claims of Childs and Stendahl on this point. At present an eclectic approach would seem to be more appropriate, with a scholar studying a text at whichever level appears (at the present time) to be the most fruitful for that particular text, while remaining open to the possibility that further research might show another level to be more appropriate. Here again Childs' Relevance Principle can provide useful guidance: Which level is 'the most fruitful' to study will depend, in part, upon the kind of fruit one is looking for.

(2) 'What it means'. As 'what it meant' signifies the descriptive pole of Stendahl's dichotomy, so 'what it means' signifies the normative. Here again, however, there are some points to be clarified.

The contrasting of the descriptive and the normative is another aspect of Stendahl's thought which Ollenburger finds highly unsatisfactory. The 'semantic rules' (Ollenburger points out, p. 74) governing the usage of 'descriptive' and 'normative' (and their cognates) are quite different; so they are not really an appropriate pair to set in opposition to one another. On the contrary, there are some cases at least in which a description is itself normative—a word-processor manual, for example, describes what I *must* do if the words I select are to appear on the printed page. In Ollenburger's view, therefore, the descriptive/normative distinction is 'dubious as Stendahl uses it'.

Without rehearsing more fully Ollenburger's arguments (with which I largely concur), his point can be illustrated for the case of biblical interpretation as follows: Insofar as someone offers an accurate description of, say, the theology of the canonical Amos, this description carries with it a certain normative force: Anyone else who wants to understand Amos' theology *ought* to believe this description.[15] This, in fact, follows from 'the logic of belief': To believe X is to believe that X is true; and an accurate description gives a true account of its object; therefore true descriptions are the ones that ought to be believed (if anything is to be believed).

But why, then, has Stendahl's opposing of the descriptive to the normative seemed evidently correct to most scholars? Ollenburger suggests that one reason is that 'descriptive' was implicitly understood to mean the kind of historical-critical descriptions which scholars

---

[15] In fact the situation is slightly more complicated than this: If someone were to produce a novel but accurate description of Amos and yet support it with inadequate or fallacious arguments then there may not be sufficient reason why another scholar ought to believe that description. It is unnecessary to consider this here, however.

standardly give of the biblical texts; and these were 'not [thought] of . . . as normative because we understand "normative" to refer . . . to prescriptive dogmatic claims' (p. 79). What Ollenburger appears to have overlooked, however, is that this is also how *Stendahl himself* understood these terms. As we have already noted, the descriptive task, for Stendahl, came into its own with the *religionsgeschichtliche Schule*, where the descriptions in question were those which emerged from the mature application of the historical-critical tools; and the normative task (or 'systematic' task, as he also calls it) is associated by Stendahl with various kinds of church-oriented theological activities, including academic system-building and reflection, proclaiming, confessing, and preaching.[16] Stendahl's purpose, then, is not (as Ollenburger apparently thinks) to oppose 'the descriptive' to 'the normative' *as such*, but to identify specific aspects of the descriptive and the normative where there is a danger of them wrongly becoming intertwined. Or in more concrete terms, Stendahl is warning us against a statement such as 'God is . . .' first being produced as a description of the theology of Amos, but then being recycled, without any further argumentation, as a normative theological statement of what we ought to believe about God. Stendahl's objection to this is that one is not justified in making a normative statement that is implied by (and implies) *one kind* of description when in fact one has only established *another kind* of description. Affirming 'God is . . .' as a theologically normative statement is equivalent to saying that 'God is . . .' is a true description of God; this, however, cannot be established simply by showing that 'God is . . .' is a true description of what Amos says about God. In other words, there is a difference in kind between the descriptions which biblical interpreters produce, and the descriptions which licence the normative claims of the systematic theologian. Stendahl's point, therefore, is that this difference should be overcome not by proceeding as though it does not even exist, but through a proper hermeneutical process of 'translation'. This, in my view, is a valid point.

Stendahl's 'what it means' is a special aspect of Hirschian significance—namely, the relationships which the text's meaning bears to other things, insofar as these relationships are relevant to the modern-day appropriation of the Bible. In previous chapters I have argued for the objectivity of a text's meaning; in contrast, however, no clear-cut answer can be given as to the objectivity of its significance.

---

[16] 'Method', pp. 202–203, 204.

A text may be significant in relation to many different things, with questions of objectivity entering into each in different ways. So, for example, we have seen Childs conceding that if Wellhausen's reconstruction of the priestly traditions is correct then this would largely undermine their religious value; and since the correctness of Wellhausen's reconstruction is an objective historical question, then so too is this aspect of their significance. On the other hand, if someone tells us that prayerful meditation upon these texts fills them with a profound sense of the Otherness of God, then they are testifying to a quite different aspect of the text's significance. This latter kind is clearly a much less objective matter—someone from another religious tradition might experience these same texts in a quite different way. So then, what one says about 'what it means' will depend very much upon the specific relationship(s) between the text and the 'now' that are being considered. I shall discuss further some aspects of this in section 5 below.

(3) 'Translation'. This is Stendahl's metaphor for the transition between 'what it meant' and 'what it means'. The descriptive task has shown (Stendahl claims) that the biblical writings are the products of a culture quite alien from our own, and are therefore permeated with questions, assumptions, and concepts that are far removed from those of modern man. Therefore a 'translation' of 'what it meant' must be made into the concepts and concerns of the modern world, so that we can comprehend 'what it means' for us today.[17]

There are two comments to make on this. Firstly, this concept of translation undermines the most valuable aspect of Stendahl's dichotomy, namely, its showing that there are *two distinct kinds* of questions that need to be tackled: (i) What did the biblical writers believe?; and, (ii) What ought we to believe? In distinguishing clearly between them Stendahl has shown us that one cannot, in general, answer the second question simply by reiterating the answer to the first;[18] yet his account of translation partly undermines this achieve-

---

[17] Stendahl even goes so far as to suggest that, as the biblical languages can be translated into any other language well enough to convey their message, so there are probably 'few philosophies, epistemologies, anthropologies, etc., which could not furnish the framework for a systematic theology by which the meaning of the Christian scripture could be stated' ('BTCon', p. 427).

[18] In practice, of course, this is a point which *everyone* accepts: Even the most literal-minded Fundamentalist does not apply, say, Leviticus to the modern church with a simple 'Go thou and do likewise'.

ment by obscuring the nature of the problems that arise in moving from 'them' to 'us'.

One particularly important aspect of this relates to the 'truthfulness' of 'what it meant'. Although Stendahl has himself drawn attention to the cultural gulf between the biblical world and our own, he has perhaps not altogether realized that the fundamental problem which this poses is not that 'what it meant' is now, like an untranslated tongue, virtually incomprehensible to us, but that it is no longer credible—we *could* learn to think once more of the universe as a three-decker structure with heaven 'up there' and Hades 'down there'; but modern astronomy has completely destroyed this cosmology, and has thereby raised serious credibility problems for any theological beliefs that presuppose it. Or again, the chief problem of modern application raised, for example, by 'God is love' is not that of finding an appropriate philosophical or anthropological explication of *agape* which would translate it into the modern idiom, but of deciding to what extent, if at all, we can still believe such a statement in a century that has witnessed far too many examples of human brutality, persecution, and spitefulness. In such cases as these, then, the basic difficulty to be dealt with is the credibility of the original claim. This, however, raises problems that are quite different from those of finding an adequate translation.

Since Stendahl points to Bultmann's demythologizing as an example of translation,[19] it (sc. Stendahlian translation) is presumably intended to cope with examples like this; yet it seems ill-equipped to do so. The point about a translation is that it aims to say *essentially the same thing* in a different language, whereas the real problem is that questions can arise as to whether in fact we do want to say the same thing, whatever philosophical 'language' we might use to say it, or whether we might value demythologizing precisely as a way of *avoiding* having to affirm things which the biblical writers believed (such as the three-decker cosmology) but which we cannot. Insofar, then, as demythologizing offers some help with these problems it does so precisely by *not* providing a translation, and thus illustrates the shortcomings of Stendahl's metaphor.

When questions of credibility arise, then, it seems that something quite different from a translation will be needed to handle them. But

---

[19] 'BTCon', p. 422.

secondly, even when such problems do not occur, there are still other ways of effecting a transition between 'then' and 'now' besides recasting the biblical material into a modern conceptual idiom. In particular, there are two alternatives which (for reasons that I shall return to in section 6 below) are of some importance for Childs: (i) 'Nominal Translation': Sometimes one might wish to reaffirm the biblical claims. If, for example, the original meaning of 1 John 1:5 is accurately expressed by 'God is light, and in him there is no darkness at all', then one possible way of transforming it into a modern affirmation is simply to explicate the pertinent associations of 'light' and 'darkness'. Of course, in the light of Stendahl's articles one would not *naively* reaffirm the original sense without being aware that, in putting it forward as a normative theological affirmation, one is making a statement which is different in kind from that of someone who offers the same sentence as no more than a ('descriptive') rendering of ancient Greek into modern English. There is nothing in Stendahl's argument, however, that methodologically precludes us from reaffirming descriptive statements as normative ones when it is appropriate to do so. The point, rather, is to be aware that a *re*affirmation is being made, and to have sufficient reasons for making it.

(ii) 'Internal Translation': Sometimes one might appeal to intracanonical indices for guidance in making the transition from 'then' to 'now'. This, of course, is closely related to Childs' views on actualisation, which will be discussed more fully in section 5 below.

In summary then, although the 'meant'/'means' dichotomy makes a distinction which, in itself, is sound, some of the ways in which Stendahl explicates it are not. But once these are cleared up, I cannot see that anything remains which could damage Childs' programme—on the contrary, it could help him significantly in clarifying and ordering the diverse elements in his own work. In this connection there are two brief comments to make. Firstly, one might wonder if Childs' opposition to Stendahl's dichotomy stems in part from him conceiving it in unnecessarily narrow terms. Childs himself sets 'the normative' and 'the descriptive' firmly against each other when he asks us to consider

> whether the discipline [of Old Testament Theology] strives in some sense for theologically normative appraisals of the biblical literature for the life of the church, or whether the discipline entails primarily an objectively historical description of an aspect of ancient culture whose

method of research is shared with the study of any ancient Near Eastern religion.[20]

Childs, of course, opts for the first alternative; and *when 'the descriptive' is set out in these terms,* one can understand why Childs feels he needs to oppose it: *this* kind of historical-descriptive work has often yielded little theological fruit. Nor is it difficult to see why Childs is then led to reject Stendahl's dichotomy—Stendahls' lengthy discussion in 'BTCon' of 'what it meant' is in fact largely concerned with this kind of historical description. Yet we have seen that Stendahl can nonetheless sum up the descriptive side of his methodology as studying 'the actual theology and theologies to be found in the Bible';[21] and although one might justifiably complain that the rest of Stendahl's discussion neglects this aspect, he has nonetheless identified here an objective, descriptive task which, far from being inimical to normative theological construction, provides its foundation.

Secondly, Childs' rejection of Stendahl's dichotomy often betrays him into making the unwarranted transition which Stendahl warns us against. Throughout *OTTCC* and *BTONT* especially, Childs seems too readily to assume that his descriptions of the biblical material at the canonical level are themselves a quite direct contribution to normative theology. Of course, in saying this one must not give an unduly simplistic presentation of his work. Childs' acute awareness of the heterogeneity of the biblical materials generally keeps him well away from harmonistic summaries of 'the message of the Bible'; on the contrary, his discussions (particularly in *BTONT*) are frequently characterized by a careful comparing and contrasting of the different strands of tradition. And yet despite all this (in a certain sense) critical sifting, the move from biblical text to divine reality is often assumed just to happen,[22] without the critical issues which Stendahl has highlighted ever being addressed. Or to put it another way, questions along the lines of 'Yes, I can see that the Old Testament bears witness to a Greater David who is yet to come; but is this witness *true*?' seem largely to lie, in practice, beyond the horizons of Childs' thought.

---

[20] *OTTCC*, p. 5.

[21] 'Method', pp. 198–99.

[22] In this connection one wonders whether there is a significant ambiguity in Childs' use of 'witness', with (for example) 'John's witness to Christ' tending to mask an unmarked transition from descriptive statements about John to normative statements about Christ.

This does not mean, of course, that his programme is fundamentally flawed (he is not methodologically precluded from widening his horizons); nor does it pose a problem that is peculiar to Childs' work, but one that needs to be tackled by all who offer a normative theology.[23] They do, however, bring to light a significant lacuna which needs to be filled.

## 3. *Inspiration and Exegesis*

At several points in our discussions we have reached conclusions which, although potentially of some value to Childs' programme, could only be sustained if his hermeneutics were supplemented by some kind of doctrine of 'biblical inspiration'. It is appropriate, therefore, in this final chapter to consider more fully how this might be done—and in particular, how a belief in inspiration might be combined with an exegetical methodology which pays due regard to 'original meanings' and 'original contexts'.

Although biblical inspiration is too broad a subject to permit a general discussion here,[24] the distinction that was drawn in section 2.3 between its material and its formal aspects can now be used to focus attention upon the issues which are particularly pertinent to Childs' programme. In the light of our discussions of author's intention, we can now see that Childs' Canonical Principle of interpretation (i.e., that the meaning of each text should be found through interpreting it in the context of the completed canon) is formally equivalent to believing that the Bible is so inspired as to be ultimately the work of a single Author: Since a text will only yield its maximal meaning if it is interpreted in relation to its intentional context, Childs' Canonical Principle is implicitly claiming that the completed canon is (a part of) the intentional context for each of its parts; and since the only kind of intentionality which can be exercised with respect to the canon as a whole is that of a divine will, the Canonical Principle is equivalent to the Bible being divinely inspired.

---

[23] One might wonder, however, whether Childs' Canonical Principle puts him under such tight constraints as to make it particularly difficult, if not impossible, for him to address these questions satisfactorily. I shall consider this in section 6 below.

[24] For recent surveys see the entries in Coggins and Houlden (eds.) *A Dictionary of Biblical Interpretation* under 'Inspiration' and 'Verbal Inspiration' (written, respectively, by John Goldingay and John Barton).

Unfortunately Childs has given little indication as to how his Canonical Principle should actually be applied, and this leaves some cardinal issues obscure—in particular, it is far from clear how canonical context should be related to original (historical) context (or equivalently, how divine and human intentionality are related). In order to clarify these points, therefore, I shall suggest a formal model for the character of the Bible which develops the Canonical Principle in ways that have significant implications for biblical exegesis. These will then be explored more fully in the latter part of this section.

The formal model, then, which I am proposing is that the biblical canon be construed as analogous to the 'collected works' of a single author. This (divine) author wrote them (over a considerable period of time) by assuming a variety of authorial *personae*, each with its own distinctive character, historical situation, etc. As one moves, therefore, from one book to another one encounters a diversity of 'implied authors', each of whom must be understood on their own terms; yet behind them all is a single, controlling intelligence, working to an overall plan. Because of this, these diverse works therefore can—and for a full understanding, must—be read together as a unified canon.

The point of this model is to suggest that there are significant parallels between the exegetical problems posed by a divine-human biblical canon and those which we already know how to handle in a secular context (e.g., in taking account of the respective roles of the implied author and the real author in interpreting a modern novel); therefore applying appropriate considerations from the latter situation to the former can guide us in making novel yet hermeneutically responsible interpretations of the Bible at the pan-canonical level. Before exploring this further, however, there are some possible misapprehensions that must be cleared up. Firstly, it must be emphasized that what I have proposed is only a *formal* model, whose purpose is to suggest various interpretative procedures which might be fruitful; it is not a material model, and is therefore not intended to have any implications as to *how* the Bible was 'inspired'. Thus, for example, when speaking of God 'assuming a variety of authorial *personae*' this is intended only as a metaphorical pointer towards what needs to be done in interpreting the Bible (i.e., that certain human *and* divine factors must be taken into account, in ways that will be discussed below); it is not meant to suggest that, say, Isaiah was merely a passive channel through which God spoke in an Isaianic voice, nor to propose any other theory about the 'mechanics' of how God, through Isaiah, brought about the writing of certain texts. Questions such as these, though certainly important, concern the material aspects of inspiration, and therefore fall outside the scope of the present discussion.

Secondly, it should be recalled from our discussion of the (auto)biographical fallacy that author's intention does not relate to textual meaning as something to be sought behind or apart from the text, but functions as a regulative principle. This applies as much to divine as to human intentions—even in the case of divine authorship, claims about what the author intended the text to mean can always be rendered exegetically irrelevant (even when, on the basis of the external evidence, we have good reasons to believe that they are true) by pointing out that such a meaning cannot be found in the text itself. Thus my canonical model in no way countenances interpretations of the Bible that appeal to extra-biblical indices of 'what God really intended to say', such as the church's traditions or creeds, or the interpreter's ineffable intuitions that his reading is guided by the Holy Spirit.[25] What (if anything) may be learned about God's intentions by such means is quite distinct from what he meant (i.e., succeeded in meaning) in a certain biblical passage. Thus any such claim as 'the canonical portrayal of David foreshadows Jesus' can be substantiated only by a proper exegesis of the text, not through any kind of external authority.

With these points clarified, I shall now consider the implications of this model for canonical exegesis. Firstly, the starting point for all exegesis must be the text in its original[26] historical context: If one takes seriously the fact that God spoke *through Isaiah*, then what was said must be understood, in the first instance, in terms of the state of the language in Isaiah's day, and his allusions explicated with reference to the social and religious institutions with which Isaiah would have been familiar. But secondly, if one takes seriously the fact that *God spoke* through Isaiah, then discovering the original meaning can be *only* the starting point of exegesis, not the full task. Isaiah's knowledge was limited to the affairs of his own day, but God's was

---

[25] Although it would be methodologically permissible to appeal to such things for heuristic reasons, in the same way as one might find it helpful consult the private correspondence of a human author.

[26] How 'original' would have to be decided on the merits of each particular case. This is the 'final form versus underlying traditions' issue again, which has already been discussed at some length.

not; thus a model of the canon which posits God as its ultimate author at least opens up the possibility that the book of Isaiah speaks of things beyond the natural knowledge of the historical prophet—for example, that it anticipates the birth and death of Jesus.

This raises the question as to whether a distinctively Christian interpretation of the Old Testament could be exegetically viable. Could it avoid degenerating into Christian eisegesis? And how might it proceed? There are many things that one might discuss here, but the following pages will particularly look at some 'canonical procedures' which are related to various well-established exegetical practices. Since they are therefore already familiar, they provide a natural point of departure for further exploration.

Firstly, then, although the original meaning of a text is the proper *starting* point for exegesis, one should also consider whether its meaning is semantically altered when it is read within the context of the canon. That semantic meaning is dependent—sometimes dramatically so—upon exegetical context is generally recognized; and from the viewpoint of a canonical model that regards the whole Bible as the intentional context for each of its parts, it is natural to ask (as Childs' Canonical Principle directs us to) about the meaning of the individual text in its broader context. How the meanings which might be discovered at the canonical level would relate to the meanings which the same texts have in their original contexts cannot be answered in general terms, but depends very much upon the details of the individual case. The typological meanings which we found, for example, in the Rejected Deliverer narratives when they were read together pan-canonically do not displace or invalidate the meanings which have been found when the Jephthah or Samson stories are each read as a separate text; rather, the canonical reading builds upon, and thus affirms, the individual meaning of each, yet shows that in addition to this there is a further stratum of canonical meaning. Or again, we have largely missed the point of John 11:49–50 unless we perceive the different meanings which Caiaphas' saying has in its (purported) original context and in its Christian context, since their divergence makes a significant contribution to the irony of the canonical Gospel. By contrast, Childs has cited various instances (usually relating to a reconstructed context that is far removed from canonical traditions) in which one might agree that the original meaning was very different from that of the final form, but where little or nothing of the former has been preserved within the canon.

Childs' Relevance Principle then offers a good reason why a Christian interpreter should not be concerned to restore it.

Perhaps the main reason why the 'original context' versus 'canonical context' problem is particularly difficult is that one is implicitly having to adjudicate between the claims of different authors, whose intentions may not entirely coincide. Yet there is a significant parallel to this in something which is already an accepted part of biblical exegesis—namely, the allowances that must be made for an author using words with special connotations of his or her own. Although the interpretation of Romans must begin from the common usages of first-century Greek, some passages nonetheless call attention to themselves as problematic through failing to yield adequate meanings when interpreted by this principle alone. One solution is to postulate special Pauline senses for some of the words, such that the passage then makes coherent sense within its broader context, and parallel passages are also illuminated. Thus although the prevailing common usage provides the starting point for interpretation, allowances can also be made for a supervening Pauline intentionality. Similar methodological considerations can also be invoked, however, in arguing for pan-canonical meanings. Although the original context, with its prevailing conventions, must be respected as the starting point for exegesis, an argument for canonical meanings that cannot have been intended by the original author can nonetheless be mounted by showing that they make the best sense of the canonical text taken as a whole. In principle this would be subject to the same sort of exegetical safeguards as apply when arguing for special Pauline meanings in Romans.

A second factor relevant to pan-canonical interpretations is that a text may have more than one referent. Childs' messianic interpretation of 2 Samuel is a good example of this: While obviously not denying that the text's primary reference is to king David, Childs argues that it also points beyond itself to an ideal king who is yet to come; and in the context of the completed Christian canon, this can only be a reference to Christ.

Of course, claims that a text has a second referent must be exegetically justified; and in this respect Childs' interpretation of 2 Samuel is perhaps not altogether adequate. That the text portrays an idealized kingship which jars with its own depiction of David is a plausible reason (if we accept this exegesis) for claiming that it points beyond him; yet Childs too readily assumes that what it points to is

Christ. This defect could be remedied, however, through (i) discussing more fully which aspects of David's kingship are presented in 2 Samuel as prefigurements of the Ideal Ruler, and (ii) showing that these aspects were realized in Jesus. If this could be done, then Childs would have good exegetical reasons for interpreting David as a prefigurement of Christ. In contrast, however, it seems difficult to accept John Sawyer's claim that the virgin birth is part of the canonical meaning of Isa. 7:14, when the only reason he offers for this is that Matt. 1:23 interprets it in this way. Sawyer comments on this example that 'one passage provides a way of understanding the other';[27] but the exegetically and theologically important question, I would argue, is whether Matthew 1 *has* understood Isaiah 7, or whether it has imposed an alien meaning upon it. To vindicate the Matthean interpretation one would have to show that there are independent exegetical grounds for reading Isaiah 7 as anticipating a supernatural birth. Nonetheless, if the temptation to settle such questions *a priori* on Troeltschean grounds is resisted, there does not seem to be any methodological reason why an Old Testament text should not be interpreted as referring to Jesus, provided that there is exegetically demonstrable warrant for this in the text itself. Of course, the human authors could not, of themselves, have written proleptically of Christ; but positing God as the ultimate author of the canonical books provides the necessary epistemological underpinning.

Thirdly, there are a number of comments to make on Barth's Christian interpretations of Genesis 1–2, which we reviewed in section 3.6 above. From the viewpoint of my canonical model, it would not be surprising to find outline sketches in the Old Testament of matters which are set out fully only in the New: An author may well adumbrate in an early work something which he intends to fill out later. Once again, however, although the exegetical issues which this raises are complex, they are already an accepted part of scholarly interpretation: Someone studying an early Platonic dialogue knows that a fully developed doctrine of the Forms must not be read back into it, but that one might nevertheless argue that Plato's earlier work anticipates his later thought. The key to resolving these problems, as usual, is careful attention to the details of the text.

A number of further issues are highlighted by Barth's vividly christological reading of Genesis 2. It is perhaps this style of inter-

---

[27] 'A Change of Emphasis', p. 246.

pretation which, more than most, is likely to provoke charges of
Christian eisegesis; yet although Barth often expresses himself in ways
that are disconcertingly paradoxical, one can still discern here the
kind of principles that would constitute exegetical 'checks and controls' (although it has to be said Barth does not always observe them
very rigorously). Firstly, interpretation must start from, and never
lose sight of, a careful consideration of the Old Testament text on its
own terms.[28] Whatever else one might say about the meaning of
Genesis 2, it is first and foremost a narrative account of human origins,
which recounts certain events occurring in a particular temporal
sequence, and with certain interconnections between them. A Christian interpretation of this chapter (if such can be given) must therefore be consistent with this perception of its character; otherwise it is
difficult to see how it could be called an interpretation *of Genesis 2*.

Secondly, a legitimate christological interpretation of the Old Testament must be consistent in *how* it finds Christian meanings in any
particular text—if (as is the case with Barth's interpretation of Genesis 2) they are found in some of its fine details then either they
must be found in *all* such details, or else reasons must be give from
the text itself to justify the particular selection that is made.[29] And
thirdly, whatever Christian meanings are found within a particular
Old Testament text must 'hang together' as a coherent and cogent
whole. As we have seen, Barth interprets Eve's creation out of Adam
and her 'marriage' to him as a prefiguration of the church's creation
out of and union with Christ; therefore the Christian meanings which
he finds in the details of Genesis 2 ought to fit naturally within this
overall interpretation. If this constraint is not observed then interpretation can quickly become arbitrary and unilluminating. Thus one
important reason why Stanley Fish's interpretation of 'Jacobs-
Rosenbaum . . .' as a religious poem had to be rejected, it will be
recalled, was that on this reading the text degenerated into a con-
ceptual/thematic mess; and by the same token, if a Christian interpretation of an Old Testament passage amounted to little more than
a loose jumble of disparate ideas then this would provide strong
grounds for suspecting that it was being read 'against the grain'. Yet

---

[28] Compare Childs' insistence that, while the Old Testament bears witness to
Christ, it does so precisely as the *Old* Testament.

[29] Our study of the Rejected Deliverer has illustrated one way in which this could
be done; there might, of course, be others.

if, on the other hand, there were an overall congruence between the natural sense of the Old Testament text and its Christian reinterpretation then the possibility is opened up that former might afford new insights into the latter. (Again this can be illustrated from our study of the Rejected Deliverer.) So then, whether or not one is persuaded by Barth's own interpretation of Genesis 1–2, it does give some important pointers as to how an overtly Christian exegesis of the Old Testament could be made. Such an interpretation need not be subjectivistic or arbitrary—there are stateable principles by which the legitimacy of a proffered interpretation can be objectively assessed.

To round off this section, there are a few comments to make on the issues of canon and inspiration in relation to dogmatic theology. Childs has given an interesting outline of the changing role of the canon within Old Testament Introduction,[30] the gist of which is that in the post-Reformation period the conception of the canon shifted from being primarily a *theological* affirmation that a certain unified body of writings was the normative Scripture of the church, to it being a *historical* affirmation that certain writings had been accepted by the church as authoritative. For a growing number of scholars, an obvious corollary of this was that one could not be bound by these ecclesiastical decisions; rather, each book should be considered on its own, in its original historical context, without regard for the place it had been assigned in the canon, or for the traditional views concerning its authorship.

The decisive shift from a theological to a historical conception of the canon seems to have occurred with J.S. Semler and J.D. Michaelis. A discussion of their work cannot be undertaken here,[31] except to note Michaelis' clear perception that the historical study of the Scriptures and the question of their inspiration are not independent issues:

> If the parts of the New Testament are inspired, they make collectively a single entire work, in which the doubts arising in one passage are fully explained in another: but if the several parts of the New Testament are not inspired, the chain by which they hang together is destroyed, and the contradictory passages must occasion anxiety and distrust.[32]

According to Kümmel (p. 73), these considerations led to Michaelis'

---

[30] *IOTS*, chapter I.
[31] For this see W.G. Kümmel, *The New Testament: The History of the Investigation of its Problems* (London: SCM, 1973), pp. 62–73.
[32] Michaelis, as quoted in Kümmel, p. 71.

348 CHAPTER TWELVE

historical investigations being seriously hampered by doctrinal questions; but J.G. Eichhorn, 'breaking with ... Michaelis', pointed the
direction for subsequent research in his New Testament Introduction, where he became

> the first seriously to maintain that the investigation of the conditions
> under which the New Testament and its writings came into being has
> completely to disregard the question of inspiration.[33]

This, of course, has subsequently become established as an indisput-
able axiom of virtually all modern biblical scholarship.

In this connection the Enlightenment has often been lauded as the
time when theology became free to investigate the Bible on its own
terms, without being fettered by prior ecclesiastical decisions as to
what it ought to say;[34] but while there is an important element of
truth in this, care must be taken in applying it to the issues of inspiration and the canon. A good example of how to go wrong here is
provided by Wilhelm Dilthey's brief history of hermeneutics. Reviewing
how Semler and Michaelis reoriented biblical studies towards 'the
original context', Dilthey remarks that '[a]t this point the liberation
of exegesis from dogma was complete; the grammatico-historical school
was founded'.[35] Yet in my view, this is true only in a much more
restricted sense than Dilthey apparently intends. Semler and Michaelis
were indeed influential in 'liberating exegesis' from the 'dogma' that
the Bible should be interpreted as an inspired canon; yet this was *not*
a move towards 'dogma-free' biblical studies—or, in a less loaded
terminology, towards presuppositionless exegesis. What they brought
about, rather, was the replacement of one presupposition by another.
That the Bible is *not* divinely inspired, or that one canonical book is
to be interpreted without regard for the others (except insofar as
there are historical connections) is just as much of a 'dogmatic commitment' as the Reformers' doctrine of inspiration. In fact, it is logically

---

[33] Kümmel, pp. 86–87; cf. *IOTS*, p. 36.
[34] Thus James Barr: 'Freedom is the central concept of criticism when applied to
the Bible. Criticism ... has generated various methods, but it is not itself a method. ...
Criticism means the freedom, not simply to *use* methods, but to follow them wher-
ever they may lead. Applied to theological problems, this means: the freedom to
come to exegetical results which may differ from, or even contradict, the acceptable
theological interpretation' (*HS* pp. 33–34; Barr's italics).
[35] 'The Rise of Hermeneutics', *New Literary History* 3 (1972), p. 239. For a fuller
account of Dithey's views on the history of hermeneutics, see Gadamer, *TM* pp.
153–56.

impossible for the exegete to proceed at all without making *some* presuppositions in relation to these issues—if one has no views at all
about such matters as human vis-à-vis divine authorship, it is impossible to identify the correct intentional context, and hence to decide
basic exegetical questions about the proper historical and literary
contexts of the passage being studied. Thus the divergence of exegesis after Semler from that of the Reformers consists not in it having
less of a theological commitment, but in being committed to the denial
of certain doctrines which the Reformers affirmed. In this respect at
least, Childs seems well-justified in suspecting that the supposed neutrality of the historical-critical methods actually masks a definite anti-
theological bias.

This is also an appropriate point at which to say something about
Benjamin Jowett's dictum that the Bible should be interpreted 'like
any other book'. Jowett's 'any other' implies that a fair, even-handed
approach is to be adopted which treats every book in the same way;
yet in fact it conceals an implicitly anti-canonical bias that makes it
incapable even of handling certain kinds of *secular* literature adequately,
and which, when applied to the biblical books, makes a number of
theological assumptions that a canonical approach might well want
to challenge. As I have argued elsewhere,[36] Jowett meant by this
dictum that a book should be interpreted solely in relation to its
original circumstances. In fact, however, this is often quite inadequate:
Few would assert, as a matter of hermeneutical principle, that Hume's
*A Treatise of Human Nature* should be interpreted without reference to
his *Enquiries concerning Human Understanding and concerning the Principles of
Morals*; or that *Crime and Punishment* should be read as though it were
the only literary work that Dostoevsky had ever written. Such works
must obviously be read as integral parts of the Humean and Dosto-
evskian canons, because, in view of their common authorship, the
language, themes, and ideas of one member of the canon can often
illuminate another. And on the basis of the formal model of biblical
inspiration proposed above, similar considerations also apply in the
case of the Bible. In this respect, interpreting the Bible 'like any
other book' would be a good summary of *Childs'* position, provided
that the 'other books' were, for example, the collected works of Plato
or Shakespeare.

In summary then: To see the Enlightenment doctrine of Scripture

---

[36] 'The *Sensus Literalis*', pp. 6–7.

as being, in itself, a more liberated belief than that of the Reformers would be a grave hermeneutical error. Insofar as the new doctrine promoted a better understanding of the Bible (through, for example, making it easier to recognize the diversity of its contents) then it is obviously to be applauded; yet if further exegetical work shows that Barth's trinitarian interpretation of Genesis 1, or Childs' messianic interpretation of 2 Samuel, or my typological interpretation of Israel's Rejected Deliverers, are representative of how the Old Testament as a whole can be read as Christian Scripture, then the new doctrine will perhaps have to be faulted for blinding several generations of scholars to significant aspects of the Bible's meaning. Whether the Enlightenment doctrine, then, is an advance or a backwards step cannot be decided by the rhetoric of freedom and liberation, but through the alternatives being subjected to a thorough exegetical testing.[37] In this matter, freedom means that each position is given a fair hearing on its own merits, rather than being castigated for 'betraying our Reformed heritage', or for 'undermining two hundred years of critical scholarship'.

## 4. *Interpretation in Faith*

Although Childs has done little to substantiate his claim that biblical interpretation should proceed from a specifically Christian faith-commitment, preceding sections of this book have suggested two ways in which Childs might substantiate his position without falling into subjectivism or fideism. The first relates to faith as a disposition of humility before God and dependence upon him. In discussing Calvin's doctrine of the illumination of the Spirit we saw that, with a certain amount of restructuring, it could bring a significant theological dimension into the hermeneutical discussion. Nonetheless, it also appeared that there was a price to pay for this in terms of the further beliefs that one was thereby committed to, concerning human corruption and divine election. Whether, in the light of this, Childs would still wish to appropriate Calvin's doctrine of illumination is at present unclear.

The second—and less ambivalent—way in which faith may have

---

[37] I intend to discuss the Rejected Deliverer and other similar examples more fully in future publications. In my view, the Rejected Deliverer is only one of many such typological appropriations of the Old Testament by the New.

a legitimate role in theological studies concerns faith as an affirmation of overtly theistic beliefs. When discussing the historical methodologies of Pannenberg and Harvey I argued that there can, in
principle, be no objection to a historian starting from a specifically
Christian faith-commitment (such as a belief that the Christian God
can, and in certain specific instances has, intervened in history to
bring about occurrences that are contrary to the natural order). This,
we saw, need not degenerate into fideism, because such claims can
be critically evaluated through assessing the internal coherence of
the historian's 'reconstructions in faith'. In this way rational discussions between the supernaturalistic and the atheistic historian can
still occur,[38] yet without either of them having to compromise their
own ultimate principles in order to secure common ground on which
to argue.

Although this argument was developed for the specific case of
historical reconstruction, it should be clear, in the light of our subsequent hermeneutical discussions, that a similar case could also be
made for the legitimacy of biblical interpretation beginning from a
Christian faith-commitment. It has long been recognized by Childs
himself that such a commitment is involved in his claim that both
Testaments together bear witness to God; and yet the ways in which
he has filled this out have often been unsatisfactory. His problems
are well illustrated by the following passage:

> The juxtaposing of the two Testaments to form a new context [for
> interpretation] rests on a faith claim. Its validity cannot be demonstrated.
> Nevertheless, the truth claim of this assertion has not been abandoned.
> The interpreter is anxious to show the nature of the logic of faith. The
> joining of the two Testaments does not result in an arbitrary construct . . .
> but there is a compatibility between witnesses. This reveals itself in
> characteristic approaches to divine reality, commensurate imperatives,
> and a sustained level of seriousness respecting the major questions of
> life and death.[39]

Although this makes some important points, they are seriously undermined by Childs' unsatisfactory views on Faith and Reason. That
canonical unity is a claim of faith immediately entails for Childs that
'it cannot be demonstrated'; and yet—presumably from a (well-
grounded!) fear that this is too fideistic—he then indicates the ways

---

[38] And, by the same token, between those with other faith-commitments also.
[39] *BTCri*, p. 112.

in which a reasonable demonstration *could* be given (namely, through showing a coherence of content between the Testaments). Yet faith now seems to have been completely displaced by reason.

My own handling of the Faith and Reason issue has been very different from Childs'. Firstly, I have identified a specific faith-affirmation that is implicated in making a Christian interpretation of the Old Testament, namely, that the viability of such interpretation is premised upon it being divinely authored; but secondly, I have suggested a formal model of the canon in which divine authorship has an integral role, and have developed this model in such a way that it has concrete exegetical consequences. These consequences can then be rationally debated both by those who have and those who lack the faith-commitment which engendered them. One does not need a special faith-commitment to assess Barth's interpretation of Genesis; as we have seen, there are faith-independent criteria for assessing whether a proposed exegesis is acceptable. Yet if such exegetical testing confirms that specifically Christian ideas *are* in fact adumbrated in this and many other Old Testament texts, then this provides cumulative, 'inductive' evidence from 'the phenomena of the Bible' for the Old Testament being divinely inspired—given our conclusions about author's intention, it is extremely difficult to explain how else such meanings could be found there.[40] Thus my canonical model both guides one in how to attempt a Christian interpretation of the Old Testament, and yet is itself open to being tested and modified by these attempts. In this way the claims of both faith and reason are given their due place.

It should also be clear by now why Childs must adopt an objectivist hermeneutics if he is to avoid fideism. If one's interpretations are to proceed from specifically Christian presuppositions but not degenerate into fideism then there must be some way of critically testing and, where necessary, revising one's starting-point. An anti-objectivist hermeneutics, however, cannot endorse sufficiently strong principles of critical correction without interpretation becoming convergent and thus ceasing to be anti-objectivist. But within an objectivist framework, there can be rational debate between supernaturalists and atheists, or between 'inspirationists' and 'non-inspirationists', as to which approach yields the better interpretations. On this basis, then, it

---

[40] Strictly, of course, this is an abductive rather than an inductive form of argument.

appears that one of Childs' most distinctive and most radical claims can be realized.

## 5. *The Present-Day Significance of the Bible*

We have seen that one of Childs' central concerns is that the Bible should be heard as the Scriptures of the contemporary church; so given that Stendahl's dichotomy marks a genuine distinction, something needs to be said about how the gulf between 'then' and 'now' might be crossed.

One classical solution to this problem is that the Bible teaches various 'eternal truths' about God and man which, once discerned in the ancient Scriptures, are therefore directly applicable to the modern world. Childs, however, has consistently maintained that this is *not* an adequate solution, with his objections being set out most fully in *EC*:

> Although the Decalogue has been continually treated as if it . . . were timeless and unchanging in value, the cultural conditioning of the interpretation appears with the greatest clarity right at this point. No one can read the Reformers' interpretation of the commandment to honour one's parents as a warrant for obedience to the state without sensing that an inherited, cultural concept of government played a role in shaping the exegesis. . . . However, the fact that every interpretation reflects a large amount of cultural conditioning . . . is not evidence to justify a theory that all exegesis is purely a subjective endeavour. . . . Rather, it belongs to the essential function of biblical interpretation that it does share the thought patterns and language of its age, while at the same time . . . seeking to shape these patterns through an encounter with the biblical text. The mistake lies in assuming that there is such a thing as a timeless interpretation. The challenge to hear the Old Testament as God's word in a concrete definite form for one's own age carries with it the corollary that it will soon be antiquated. (pp. 437–38)

To my mind, however, this is a good example of the confusion that arises when Hirsch's distinction is overlooked. On the one hand, the last sentence makes an important point about a text's *significance*: The Decalogue, and the Bible generally, makes no reference to such modern phenomena as nuclear warfare and embryo research; consequently, any attempt to consider these matters from a biblical perspective will necessarily be framed in distinctively late twentieth century

terms, and will therefore inevitably become 'antiquated' by the march
of time. On the other hand, the *meaning* of a text does not change.
'Honour your father and your mother' does not and never did mean
'Obey the State', even when interpreted in its full canonical context.
That is clearly an eisegetical interpretation; and although the current
cultural climate may help us to recognize this, it was just as true at
the time of the Reformation. Thus however one might apply the
Decalogue to modern political and social issues, the starting-point, if
one is to avoid eisegesis, is the fixed, objective, meaning of the text
itself; and this already suggests that 'eternal truths' are going to play
some role in passing from 'then' to 'now'.

Another objection that Childs brings against a timeless truths approach is that it is not true to the character of the Bible: 'God has
revealed his will, not in timeless universal truths, but in concrete
manifestations of himself, restricted in time and space, and testified
to by particular witnesses'.[41] Put as baldly as this, however, Childs'
contrast is surely overdrawn—there are significant instances where
the prophetic and apostolic witness clearly *is* expressed through timeless, propositional truths.[42] Nonetheless, Childs is right to point out
that *most* of the biblical material does not obviously fall into this
category, but consists, rather, of accounts of specific historical occurrences, and of reactions to and reflections upon them.

Childs' point can perhaps be expressed more accurately by observing
that attempts to draw eternal truths from specifically 'situated' material have generally tended to leave out precisely those aspects of the
text which are most distinctive, and thus to devalue (often large)
proportions of it. So, for example, Conyers Middleton claimed that
the meaning of Genesis 1–3 is 'that this world had a beginning and
creation from God; and that its principal inhabitant man, was originally formed to a state of happiness and perfection which he lost';[43]
yet if this were all that it meant, why does it employ a carefully
structured six-day pattern in chapter one, have a second account of
the creation in chapter two, etc.? In other words, an eternal truths
approach seems to pass over what, on any natural reading, constitutes

---

[41] *BTCri* p. 105; cf. *ibid.* p. 101, *OTTCC* pp. 13–14.
[42] E.g., Prov. 1:7; John 1:1–5; 3:3, 16–21; Rom. 6:23; 2 Cor. 5:21; etc. For an
analysis of different senses of 'proposition' and their varying relationships to eternal
truths, see Paul Helm, 'Revealed Propositions and Timeless Truths', *RelStud* 8 (1972),
pp. 127–36.
[43] Quoted by Frei, *Eclipse* p. 5.

much of the real substance of the passage, reducing it to merely the decorative packaging in which the abstract ideas are wrapped.

Another scholar who has pointed to the temporally conditioned character of the Bible as an objection to the timeless truths approach is David Clines;[44] moreover, Clines has proposed two alternative ways in which the Bible can have 'a *contemporary* religious function that respects its *past* religious function' (*ibid.*) These he discusses under the headings of Story and Promise. For the former (on which I shall concentrate, as it brings out the methodological points most clearly) Clines observes that

> What is offered in a story is a 'world'—make-believe or real, familiar or unfamiliar. To the degree that the hearer or reader of the story is imaginatively seized by the story, to that degree he or she 'enters' the world of the story.... The Pentateuch as a story therefore performs the function of creating a 'world' that is to a greater or lesser extent unlike the world of the reader, and that invites the reader to allow the horizons of his own world to merge with those of that other world. And to respond to that invitation is to allow oneself to be worked upon, influenced, by the story.[45]

Since this 'fusion' occurs through conscious reflection upon the 'world' offered by the text, it is (fortunately) more akin to Gadamer's Hegelian practice than to his Heideggerian theory; and as we have seen in chapter 9, once the latter has been discarded, the former has some useful insights to offer. Building on this, Clines' recognition of a narrative's ability to render a 'world' makes an important contribution to understanding the contemporary relevance of the Old Testament, because this gives one a way of handling the *complexities* which inevitably arise in discussing any realistic situation. To take just one example: When is it morally permissible for me to use force in achieving my goal? In defending myself, or my family, or my property, or my country? (And from what?) In upholding an ethical principle? (The right of free speech? The abolition of apartheid? Animals' rights?) In resisting state persecution? (On account of my religious beliefs? Or because I belong to an ethnic minority?) As a punitive measure? (Against a persistently anti-social individual? A terrorist group? A

---

[44] *The Theme of the Pentateuch* (JSOTS 10; Sheffield: JSOT Press, 1978), p. 101.

[45] P. 102; this has clear affinities with Hans Frei's idea that the gospels 'tell a story of salvation, an inalienable ingredient of which is the rendering of Jesus as Messiah, and that whether or not he was so in historical fact, or thought of himself as Messiah ... are different questions altogether' (*Eclipse*, p. 133).

barbarous nation?) Such examples raise a serious problem for an 'eternal truths' approach, as this is normally conceived: Any attempt to give a concise statement of such truths is only too liable to fall into pat, abstract generalisations which fail to do justice to the complexity of real life.

The value of a 'story' approach is well illustrated from Childs' discussion of Moses' slaying of the Egyptian taskmaster.[46] Asking what bearing this has on the contemporary problem of 'using physical violence as a means for social change',[47] Childs observes that the Old Testament itself does not moralize upon Moses' violence. Nonetheless, there is still much that is ethically significant in the Exodus account. Firstly, Childs draws attention to the *ambiguity* of the killing. Moses acted from a selfless love for his oppressed people, and thought they would recognize him as their deliverer. Yet the man who was maltreating his fellow Hebrew, while indeed recognizing Moses' claim to authority, saw it as a threat to himself and therefore impugned his motivation: 'Who made you a ruler over us?'. Secondly, Childs notes how the story stresses the furtiveness of Moses' deed, and wonders 'whether an act of justice can really be done under these circumstances' (p. 183). It leaves him so vulnerable that, once the act is known, he has to flee like any other political fugitive. The repercussions of Moses' deed are left for others to deal with; no deliverance has been effected. Thus Childs concludes:

> Our text does not provide one clear answer to the complex problem of using violence for the sake of justice. But it does raise a whole set of issues that are inherent in such action. By uncovering the ambiguities in the act of violence, the reader is forced to confront rather than evade those basic factors which constitute the moral decision. (*ibid.*)

Of course, it must also be added that the text itself gives considerable guidance as to *how* this 'set of issues' should be 'confronted', through bringing the salient features of this story to the careful reader's attention. Thus although one does not carry away a neat moral at the end, someone who has understood this and other such stories will be better placed to evaluate the use of violence in the modern world, because through wrestling with these ancient texts one gains pertinent insights into (among other things) the unexpected misunderstandings and hidden consequences that such actions can have.

---

[46] *BTCri*, chapter 10 // *EC* section III.
[47] *BTCri* p. 182.

In other words, someone trying to make a Christian assessment of, say, the morality of an international peacekeeping force intervening in a civil war, is not reduced to the desperate expedient of finding a biblical example of 'just the same sort of thing', from which an appropriate moral can be drawn. Rather, through immersing oneself in the biblical world, which is constructed through grappling with the many and various stories from the Old Testament and the New, one becomes aware of the appropriate questions to ask, and the relevant concepts with which to make a Christian evaluation, even in situations that are far removed from any biblical parallels.[48]

Clincs' 'story' approach, then, makes a valuable contribution to our understanding of how the Bible can address the modern world; yet it is not (as Clines thinks) an *alternative* to the 'eternal truths' approach, but a more sophisticated version of it. Although it would be simplistic to sum up the moral of Moses' slaying the Egyptian as, say, 'Violent actions can be misconstrued, and this may have serious consequences', nonetheless, one can only expect these ancient stories to illuminate modern problems if there is an essential continuity in 'the nature of violence'—i.e., in the sorts of issue it raises about ambiguity of motivation, the possible consequences of acting covertly, etc.—between the narrative's age and our own; and this is tantamount to bridging the gulf between 'then' and 'now' through an appeal to eternal truths. I would argue, therefore, that there is no *intrinsic* fault in appealing to eternal truths; the flaw lies, rather, in thinking that such truths can be distilled out of a narrative into a neat series of cut-and-dried propositions. What the preceding discussion has shown, I think, is that such propositions, while not without some value in giving a general orientation, are liable to be simplistic; and that what is needed, therefore, is a more sophisticated way of expressing these truths. Clines has made a notable contribution to showing how this can be done.

I shall end this section with some more general considerations. Firstly, although we have been discussing moral examples, very similar principles would also apply to the theological application of the Old Testament. Here too it is difficult to see why one should expect the Old Testament to be of much theological significance for the modern church unless there is a significant degree of continuity between the

---

[48] In 'A "Balanced" Reading of the Rape of Dinah' (*BI*, forthcoming, 1996) I have likewise argued that this is how Genesis 34 functions.

substantive theological affirmations of the Bible and the faith that we confess today. But to accept such continuity is tantamount to accepting that there are timeless truths about God; thus the real problem is to find a non-simplistic way of expressing them. Again a 'story' approach seems very promising.

But secondly, this approach can only be applied to a limited part of the Bible, because a significant proportion of it is not narrative. Clines is aware of this, and has also pointed to Promise as a further way in which the Bible can have contemporary significance. Promise, on the one hand, 'binds man to the future'[49] by raising expectations of what Yahweh will yet accomplish; and on the other hand, 'it also binds [man] to the past',[50] since the promise is given and grounded in the concrete particularities of Israel's history. The interval between past and future is a period of tension (p. 116).

It can be objected to Promise as to Story that again it is not applicable to major portions of the Old Testament; but Clines' point can be generalized to the observation that the future orientation of this literature is already a major concern of the Old Testament itself. The modern interpreter, therefore, should be concerned not so much with finding how the Bible can be made to 'speak' to the modern world, but with investigating how the Bible itself looks beyond its own time; and with this we are very close to Childs' views on actualization. Childs does not tie himself to specific categories, such as Story and Promise; nor does he generalize about how historical books or prophetic literature addresses the future. This, however, gives him a significant advantage over Clines, because it leaves him free to examine the details of how the problem of future-relatedness arises for each individual book, and thus to uncover the surprising variety of ways in the Old Testament tackles this problem. It is unnecessary to analyse actualization in detail, since much of what has been said about Story applies here also: However the transition is made, an actualization which takes the historical situatedness of the text seriously enough to avoid eisegesis and yet finds it to have a contemporary relevance, is implicitly assuming a significant degree of similarity between 'then' and 'now', and is thus a form of the 'eternal truths' approach. Through careful attention to the canonical shape, however, it can avoid the simplistic abstractions or arid generalizations

---

[49] Jürgen Moltmann; quoted by Clines, p. 111.
[50] Clines, p. 115.

which have sometimes characterized this approach.

In summary, then, actualization is not an alternative to the eternal truths approach but a more sophisticated version of it. By relating it to the canonical shape of the final text, and thus suggesting that actualization can occur in many different ways, Childs has made a valuable contribution to theology.

## 6. *The Coherence of Biblical Theology*

So far this chapter has been arguing that the distinctive elements in Childs' canonical approach are, on the whole, methodologically defensible, and that in some cases at least, they make significant contributions to modern biblical studies. But granted this, it still has to be asked whether Childs has assembled these parts into a coherent whole. To answer this, I wish first to review James Barr's argument that the earlier Biblical Theology Movement was fraught with certain internal inconsistencies which made it a self-contradictory enterprise, and then to consider whether Childs' programme is open to similar objection.

While praising Childs' *BTCri* as a good historical delineation of the American Biblical Theology Movement, Barr nonetheless thinks that Childs has misunderstood the nature of the crisis into which biblical theology fell. This, according to Barr, lay 'in its loss of status, its loss of prestige, the loss of its power to persuade'.[51] These losses came about through it having to justify itself 'against *theology*',[52] i.e., against scholars who specialized in systematic and dogmatic theology. Although it had expected to be attacked by historical critics, the theological criticisms caught it quite unprepared; and when it therefore began to fall into crisis, most systematicians, Barr tells us, were relieved and delighted.

According to Barr's account, the basic reason[53] why these scholars

---

[51] 'The Theological Case Against Biblical Theology', in Tucker *et al.* (eds.), *Canon, Theology, and Old Testament Interpretation*, p. 4. Barr has previously discussed similar ideas in *HS*; see especially pp. 116–22, 126, 136–39.

[52] 'Case', p. 5; Barr's italics.

[53] Barr also suggests a further reason in that while Biblical Theology brushed aside the traditional interests in natural theology and apologetics as illegitimate, it nonetheless dabbled covertly in these things itself (p. 9). This does not need to be discussed here, however.

were so opposed to Biblical Theology was that they resented its attempts to dominate the whole of theology:

> For [Biblical Theology], the only target, the only horizon, the only
> criterion, and the only arbiter must be the Bible. . . . Almost inevitably
> this meant that any sort of theology for which there existed any sort of
> authority, any sort of consideration at all, apart from the Bible or along-
> side the Bible, must be uneasy in its relations with biblical theology.
> (p. 6)

The Biblical Theology Movement did not, of course, deny that systematic theology also had an important role; and yet its own intense
focusing upon the Bible meant that it was incapable of handling many
of the classical theological issues, such as the doctrinal controversies
of the patristic age. Therefore although these matters continued to
be of considerable interest and importance to the systematicians, they
were nonetheless seriously neglected when the theological agenda came
to be dominated by Bible-centred issues and Bible-centred arguments.

The earlier Biblical Theology, then, proved to be an exclusivist
theology, which ruled out of court any kind of theological investigation which did not proceed within its own, Bible-centred, terms of
reference. It therefore suffered a very severe blow when scholars began
to feel that

> biblical theology at its best was still not really *theology*. It was a mode
> of organizing and interlinking the biblical material that differed indeed
> from the historical mode; but that in itself did not make it theology.
> Theology . . . must be the construction, criticism, and refining of *our*
> concepts of God in Christ and in the church.[54]

Theologians increasingly came to see Biblical Theology as not being
equipped to handle these constructive and critical tasks. To do so it
would have to engage in various kinds of *extra-biblical* arguments (concerning, for example, the different philosophical and sociological
analyses of religion), whereas Biblical Theology focused on the Bible
alone (pp. 10–11). In other words, these constructive matters clearly
belong within the province of systematic and philosphical theology;
therefore if Biblical Theology shuns their kinds of arguments then it
necessarily ceases to be a legitimate form of *theology*, but offers instead no more than a certain kind of description of the biblical
materials. And yet if it does engage in philosophical and sociological

---

[54] P. 9; Barr's italics.

arguments, then it loses it purely biblical focus. In sum, then, 'biblical theology' appears to be a self-contradictory concept.

Barr, it should be noted, does not himself apply this critique to Childs' programme; nor would this be possible without at least adding some important qualifications, because, as our discussions of historical referentiality have shown, Childs does not in fact regard the Bible as 'the only target, the only horizon, the only criterion, and the only arbiter' of his theological reflections—questions of 'what really happened' are also of cardinal importance to him. Nonetheless, there are clearly some significant parallels between Childs' position and that which Barr criticizes.[55] Thus in his long-standing disagreement with Stendahl, Childs has always insisted that biblical theology is not to be merely descriptive but is also to engage in (as Barr puts it) 'the construction, criticism, and refining of *our* concepts of God'. In other words, biblical theology should be a normative discipline, which is therefore necessarily concerned with the formulation of *truth*-claims (i.e., with the question of what we can affirm about God). Moreover, Childs has clearly shown his affinities with the earlier Biblical Theology Movement in attaching his concept of normativity particularly to the canonical Scriptures; and although Childs has never set this in total opposition to extra-textual realities, canonical normativity has frequently led to him taking a very negative attitude towards, for example, existentialist or Hegelian philosophies, or to the reconstruction of a 'positivity behind the text'. In the light, therefore, of Barr's critique of the earlier Biblical Theology Movement, the question that needs to be put to Childs is whether his Canonical Principle can at the same time both be sufficiently 'narrow' to preserve his distinctive emphasis upon the normativity of *the canonical text*, and yet be sufficiently 'broad' to allow him to engage with whatever extrinsic matters are necessary for maintaining the *normativity* of the canonical text.

To help resolve this question, I shall first introduce some useful terminology. In the subsequent discussion, calling a theology 'genuine' will mean that it is methodologically equipped to do all that a theology ought to do; in particular, this will indicate that it encompasses adequate means of assessing the truth of its substantive claims. Calling a theology genuine is therefore to be clearly distinguished

---

[55] This, of course, is entirely to be expected, since Childs made it clear in *BTCri* that his aim is to develop a new biblical theology which, while avoiding the problems of the earlier movement, pursues very similar goals.

from describing it as 'true'—i.e., from affirming that its substantive theological claims are actually correct. As a methodological investigation, this book has been primarily concerned with the *genuineness* of Childs' programme. To decide whether Childs has given us a *true* theology, however, would need an entirely different kind of investigation, oriented towards resolving concrete exegetical and historical issues. The question being discussed in the present section, then, is whether an argument similar to Barr's can show that Childs' canonical approach cannot be a genuine theology but can only describe the biblical materials.

As a further preliminary, I would suggest that 'systematics' covers (at least) two very different kinds of activity, which need to be distinguished from one another. These two kinds are: (1) 'Methodological systematics', i.e., critical reflections upon the methods and procedures of theological studies (or of a particular theological programme); and (2) 'Substantive systematics', i.e., 'the construction, criticism, and refining of *our* concepts of God in Christ and in the church'. What Barr is claiming, then, is that any genuine theology must engage with methodological systematics. This is doubtlessly correct; but Childs *can* meet this requirement (I shall argue) without substantially altering the character of his programme. In contrast, Childs *would* have to substantially modify his programme if it could be shown that, to offer a genuine theology, he also had to engage in certain kinds of substantive systematics—for example, if in constructing his normative concept of God it were necessary for him to draw upon both the biblical witness and the independent testimony of the natural world. There appears to be no compelling methodological reason, however, why Childs should need to do this. Within the context of Childs' programme, therefore, 'biblical theology' does appear to be a coherent concept, and Childs' work *is* a genuine theology.

Theological studies is a very broad field, which encompasses many different kinds of scholarly investigations. Rather, therefore, than attempting to develop the preceding points in general terms, I shall instead discuss a number of specific instances to clarify these ideas and illustrate their application. From this is should become clear that, at the very least, Childs' programme is not obviously guilty of the incoherence which Barr finds in the earlier Biblical Theology Movement. I begin, then, with some comments on the straightforward but methodologically significant case of using extra-biblical linguistic factors in the exegesis of the canonical text.

In discussing the canonical shapes of the various biblical books, Childs has doubtless made extensive (implicit) use of BDB and other such tools. These, in turn, are based in part upon many extra-canonical texts, including some that are in languages other than Hebrew; moreover, the uses that were made of such materials in compiling the standard lexica and grammars, and the ways in which Childs used these aids, were guided by various linguistic considerations of a methodological/philosophical nature (concerning, for example, the identification of parallel passages). Yet no-one, presumably, would on these grounds alone contend that what Childs has given us is not really *canonical* interpretation, but only a canonical shape which is the hybrid product of, say, the canonical Genesis plus a mass of other ancient literature plus a certain linguistic philosophy. Such an objection would clearly be misguided, because the whole purpose of a lexicon (and thus of the extra-biblical texts and the linguistic considerations that went into its production) is to assist one in understanding *the meaning of the canonical texts themselves* more accurately. Or to generalize the point: Identifying instances where Childs does, or even (for practical and/or methodological reasons) must, draw upon extra-canonical data and ideas does not of itself show that he has fallen away from his principle of canonical normativity. The crucial question that has to be asked, in each such case, is *how* he has drawn upon these data and ideas. If Childs were to turn to the Ras Shamra texts for extra-biblical information about the Canaanite gods, and were then to feed it into his substantive-normative theological affirmations, then he would clearly have violated his own Canonical Principle. Such would not be the case, however, if he were to use these texts only to improve his understanding of biblical Hebrew, and were to derive his theological affirmations only from the (now more fully comprehended) biblical texts. Merely pointing to extra-canonical factors in Childs' work, then, is far from sufficient grounds for convicting him of inconsistency. The crucial question is *how* they enter his work.

Similar observations can also be made about the various methodological issues discussed in this book. In assessing Childs' programme, previous chapters have raised numerous extra-canonical, philosophical questions about objectivity, historical methodology, author's intention, etc., and it would clearly be right for Barr to insist that, to be a genuine theology, canonical hermeneutics must enter into these debates. Yet there is no reason to think that this would necessarily compromise its character as a biblical theology. These are debates about correct methodology, and as we have reiterated a number of times, the whole point about a valid methodology is precisely that it does *not* make any substantive contribution to its field, but allows the subject-matter to speak for itself.[56] Thus a Childsian programme must enter fully, for example, into assessing the alternative hermeneutical theories of Schleiermacher and Gadamer if it is to qualify as a genuine theological programme. Yet in fact it can do this without compromising its canonical character because, as these are methodological debates, their successful resolution does not lead to substantive theological conclusions being based upon philosophical arguments. Rather, it shows how such conclusions can be based more accurately upon the canonical texts. Or again, it is methodologically consistent of Childs to be wary about existentialist philosophies being drawn into biblical interpretation, because insofar as these bring with them their own substantive analyses of human existence they would compromise the canonical character of the resultant theological constructs.[57] So then, Childs' canonical programme does not have to take an 'all or nothing' approach to philosophical discussions; rather, there are considerations which allow it to engage with those aspects that are essential to it being a genuine theology without it having to cease being a canonical theology.

Further issues are raised by the various kinds of historical referentiality that we have discussed. Insofar as Childs were to draw upon archaeological evidence to elucidate biblical references to a certain custom or institution with which the reader is presumed to be familiar, it is difficult to see why this might be regarded as problematic—on the contrary, this is methodologically very similar to the use of Ugaritic texts to further our understanding of biblical Hebrew. Of course, it would be a different matter if he were to draw upon such evidence to reconstruct, say, a sacrificial cultus which is unattested in the biblical writings, and were then to draw substantive theological conclusions from this construct. This, however, would be

---

[56] So, for example, this is why Troeltschian analogy was rejected as an illegitimate methodological principle.

[57] This is not, of course, to say that such views can just be ignored—on the contrary, to be a genuine theology the canonical approach must be able to interact critically with views which are substantively different from its own (whether these stem from a philosophical or from some other basis). How this can be done will be discussed below.

an example of basing one's theology on a 'positivity behind the text', which Childs has always rejected. Methodologically, it is perfectly consistent for him to do so, and he therefore cannot be faulted on this account.[58]

Another aspect of referentiality concerns biblical references to historical persons and events. Childs has sometimes been reluctant to face up to these extra-canonical commitments, but we argued in section 4.2 that these are often unavoidable because the canonical theology cannot generally be detached from the concomitant history without being theologically devalued. Thus a 'canonical approach' which based its theology solely on a literary study of the biblical text would certainly run into methodological problems at this point. Such an approach would not be representative of Childs' better thoughts on these matters, however—as we have seen, Childs does affirm (at least when pressed) the importance of the real events of space and time, even though he generally shows little further interest in them. At least in principle, then, Childs does seem to commit himself sufficiently to historical investigation for his programme to qualify as a genuine theology.

It should nonetheless be added that questions of historical referentiality do pose very major problems for Childs' programme—unless Old Testament scholarship changes direction quite radically, it seems that Childs will have to get to grips with the fact many of the historical affirmations which are made by the biblical writers, and to which they have tied their theologies, cannot be re-affirmed today. There are also, however, some further factors to be mentioned. Firstly, the problems here are not methodological but substantive: If historical investigations showed, for example, that Israel's origins had no connection with an escape from Egypt this may have significant implications for the theological truth-claims that can be made, but it does not undermine the genuineness of Childs' theological programme. Secondly, Childs' views on the variable referentiality of the biblical texts means that his historical commitments are limited to those which the Bible itself makes—although on any natural reading of the texts, this is still a very substantial (and problematic) commitment.[59] And

---

[58] Again, the further question of how Childs can critically interact—as he clearly must—with those who claim that our substantive theological conclusions *should* be based upon such underlying 'positivities' will be discussed below.

[59] Of course, Childs is not the only theologian for whom this is a problem, although his unswerving commitment to the final form limits the ways in which he might resolve it.

thirdly, it is also worth recalling that Childs' commitment to history does retain a distinctively canonical orientation, as we discussed in section 5.3 above. In summary, then, although referentiality does not pose any significant methodological problems for Childs, it remains an open question as to whether the dependence of theology upon history and the prevailing historical scepticism of modern biblical studies may yet combine to rob Childs' programme of much of its theological fruit, thus leaving him with a programme which is methodologically viable but theologically unproductive. Clearly this is an area where much more research is needed.

Returning, however, to the methodological coherence of Childs' programme, another aspect of this can be drawn out through some further comments on Stendahlian translation. We saw in section 2 that Stendahl points to Bultmann's demythologizing as an example of such translation; however, this way of passing from 'what it meant' to 'what it means' would render problematic Childs' claims for the normativity of canonical theology. The logic of demythologizing runs as follows: (1) The Bible utilizes the common beliefs of its cultural milieu (e.g., in conceiving the universe as a three-decker structure); (2) some of these are no longer credible; but (3) the essential theme of the Bible is the being of humankind; and (4) this has been thoroughly analysed by Heidegger; therefore (5) 'translating' the gospel into existentialist terms both preserves the substance of the kerygma while freeing it from an outmoded world view. Clearly the second step in this argument brings in extra-canonical beliefs, such as the discoveries of modern astronomy, in ways that affect the substantive content of the theological affirmations.[60] However, we have seen that there are (at least) two other ways of passing from 'then' to 'now' (namely, Nominal and Internal translation). Neither of these brings in external factors, and Childs could therefore use them in discussing the contemporary witness of the Scriptures without compromising his canonical principle. Of course, it would be an embarrassment to him if the normativity of the canon then entailed that we ought to

---

[60] Childs apparently suspects the third and fourth steps of also doing this, although Bultmann would presumably claim that existentialist categories are only articulating what the canon itself presents as its essential message. In Childs' view, however, it is at most true that only *some* strands in the New Testament can be satisfactorily rendered in existentialist categories; therefore they in fact function as an external authority that decides which parts of the New Testament are authentic (see *BTONT* p. 81).

believe in a three-decker universe;[61] but this would again be a problem concerning the substantive content of his programme, not its methodology.

Although the preceding is by no means an exhaustive survey of the kinds of activities in which theologians engage, it is sufficient to show that Childs' programme is by no means bereft of the critical and evaluative resources that are essential to a genuine theology. There is another aspect of Barr's argument against the Biblical Theology Movement which needs to be considered in relation to Childs' work, however, namely, that it was untenably exclusivist in ruling out of court modes of theologizing which differed from its own. As Barr remarks at one point,

> Suppose we were to say that the defining horizon of biblical theology is the Bible, but the defining horizon of theology as such is God in Jesus Christ? . . . At least in principle these might be very different. They would easily coincide only on one assumption, namely, that the circle defined by the Bible and the circle defined by God are identical. In other words, there are *no* factors other than the Bible itself that count in the understanding of God. This position might in itself be true but it undoubtedly excludes the possibility of many kinds of theology.[62]

These observations are highly pertinent to Childs' work. Childs himself thinks that our theological affirmations should be exclusively based upon the canonical witness; yet there are other scholars who would claim that a substantive contribution might also be derived from other sources, such as natural theology or religious experience. If the canonical approach is to qualify as a genuine theology then it must have the resources to interact critically with these alternative programmes.

Once we consider how such an argument would be conducted, however, it soon appears that Childs is well equipped to handle it. Suppose, for example, that another scholar were to maintain that, *contra* Childs, theology has both a natural and a revealed dimension; then clearly this is another example of disputants arguing from different fundamental premises, and should therefore be prosecuted in the way

---

[61] Although some scholars have claimed that this sort of spatial language was used only metaphorically by the New Testament writers themselves, who were therefore not committing themselves to a particular cosmology; see Colin E. Gunton, *Yesterday and Today* (London: DLT, 1983), pp. 111–13; F.F. Bruce, 'Myth and History', in Colin Brown (ed.), *History, Criticism, and Faith* (Leicester: IVP, 1976), pp. 85–86.

[62] Pp. 6–7; Barr's italics.

we discussed in section 5.2: Each disputant pursues the two-pronged strategy of developing a coherent theological programme based upon his or her own fundamental principles, while showing that one's opponent is unable to do the same. Now clearly this would deeply immerse both parties in a wide variety of philosophical and methodological arguments (e.g., in assessing whether the Cosmological and Teleological arguments lead to substantive theological insights); but we have already seen that there appears to be no intrinsic reason why Childs could not engage in these discussions without compromising his canonical principles. For Childs to contend, for example, that his opponent's natural theology is open to philosophical objections $O_1$, $O_2$, and $O_3$ does not entail that his own substantive theological claims are themselves based upon the canon plus philosophy. Of course, if the opponent were able to answer these objections and further show that substantive knowledge of God *can* be derived from reflecting upon the natural world then this might well pose problems for Childs; but again they would not be problems concerning the *genuineness* of his theology.

To summarize, then: If the whole sum and substance of a 'canonical approach' consisted in just the explication of the canonical texts, then (for the reasons which Barr discusses) it would certainly not qualify as a genuine theology; but in fact Childs has never presented his work in this way, and there seems to be nothing in his Canonical Principle which would restrict him to such a narrow focus. If, then, one nonetheless wished to argue that Childs' programme is guilty of the inconsistencies with which Barr charges the earlier Biblical Theology Movement, one would have to show both (i) that there is some particular 'X'—a commitment to natural theology, perhaps, or to a specific philosophical premise—such that Childs needs to affirm X if his work is to qualify as a genuine theology; and yet (ii) that such an affirmation would lead him into substantive theological commitments which go beyond the theology of the canon alone. In fact, however, there seems to be no reason to fault Childs' programme in this respect.

This discussion has nonetheless underlined once more the significance of the fact that, despite Childs' insistence that biblical theology is a normative discipline, his own work is mostly at the descriptive level—i.e., that he has done little to show us that the descriptions that emerge from his canonical exegesis are a *true* witness to God. Barr's article helpfully reminds us that there are important questions here that need to be addressed if canonical hermeneutics is to qualify as a genuine theology. There seems little reason to doubt, however, that Childs' programme is methodologically equipped to do this.


## 7. *Concluding Summary*

This book has argued that although there are fundamental weaknesses in Childs' own conception of his programme, it can be recast in a form which appears capable of achieving nearly all of his major goals.[63] The principal elements in a revised canonical hermeneutics for which I have argued are:

(i) A much greater orientation towards historical questions of 'what really happened';

(ii) A revised historical methodology, which (1) allows the Christian historian to start from a specific faith-stance, (2) rejects the distinction between fact and interpretation, and (3) rejects Troeltschian analogy as a critical principle, replacing it with a principle of coherence;

(iii) An acceptance of Stendahl's dichotomy, insofar as this recognises that there are two quite different kinds of question that theologians need to tackle;

(iv) An objective, reader-independent conception of textual meaning, with the reader's 'situated' presuppositions being tested and corrected through a convergent hermeneutical spiral;

(v) The acceptance of author's intention and intentional context as exegetical criteria;

(vi) The recognition that a text can have a multiplicity of meanings, and that 'literary approaches' to the Bible can be of considerable assistance in discovering them;

(vii) A formal model of biblical inspiration which (1) justifies the search for pan-canonical and Christian meanings of an Old Testament text, and (2) gives exegetical guidance to such a search; and

(viii) A new form of typological interpretation, as one example of such exegesis.

No doubt these and other methodological issues raised by Childs' work will continue to be discussed. It is no less important, however,

---

[63] The main exception is that, in the current state of biblical scholarship, I can see no adequate grounds for *invariably* giving priority to the final form of the text, although Childs certainly gives strong reasons why we should *sometimes* do so.

for the evaluation of Childs' programme that concrete historical and exegetical work be undertaken from a canonical perspective. There are two reasons for this. Firstly, the most that a methodological discussion can establish is that canonical hermeneutics is a genuine theology; it cannot show that it is a true theology. The former is a precondition for the latter, and yet it would be of little significance to show that there are methodologically sound ways of interpreting the Old Testament christologically if detailed exegesis then discovered that these writings do not in fact say anything about Christ. And secondly, the methodological arguments are unlikely to develop fruitfully unless they are conducted in the context of concrete historical and exegetical work. As we have noted before, the whole point of a sound methodology is that it allows the subject-matter to 'speak for itself'; therefore methodological proposals need to be tested out by seeing if they do in fact handle their subjects in an illuminating way. Without this safeguard, it is all too easy for methodological discussions to drift into *a priori* analyses of how interpretation ought to proceed, which follow very plausibly from their author's prior philosophical commitments but make little contact with the realities of historical and exegetical practice. Hermeneutical reflections and interpretative practice, then, need to make progress together, through each reflecting critically upon the other.

In summary, then: I believe that Childs has made a contribution to biblical studies of the highest significance, both in raising a host of fundamental methodological issues and in reorienting historical and exegetical work towards an important set of new questions.

# BIBLIOGRAPHY

Abraham, William J., *The Divine Inspiration of Holy Scripture* (Oxford: OUP, 1981)
——, *Divine Revelation and the Limits of Historical Criticism* (Oxford: OUP, 1982)
Abrams, M.H., *The Mirror and the Lamp: Romantic Theory and the Critical Tradition* (Oxford: OUP, 1953)
Achtemeier, Paul J., *The Inspiration of Scripture* (Philadelphia: Westminster, 1980)
Ackerman, James S., 'Joseph, Judah, and Jacob', in Kenneth R.R. Gros Louis with James S. Ackerman (eds.), *Literary Interpretations of Biblical Narratives II* (Nashville: Abingdon, 1982) 85–113
Alter, Robert, *The Art of Biblical Narrative* (Hemel Hempstead: George Allen & Unwin, 1981)
——, 'How Conventions Help Us Read. The Case of the Bible's Annunciation Type-Scene', *Proof* 3 (1983) 115–30
——, 'Introduction', in Robert Alter and Frank Kermode (eds.), *The Literary Guide to the Bible* (London: Collins, 1987) 11–35
Anderson, Bernhard W., Review of *Tradition and Theology in the Old Testament*, *RelSRev* 6 (1980) 104–10
——, Review of *Introduction to the Old Testament as Scripture*, *TToday* 37 (1980–81) 100–108
Auerbach, Erich, *Mimesis: The Representation of Reality in Western Literature* (Princeton: Princeton University Press, 1968)
——, 'Figura', in Auerbach, *Scenes from the Drama of European Literature* (New York: Meridian, 1959)
Barr, James, *The Bible in the Modern World* (London: SCM, 1973)
——, 'Childs' *Introduction to the Old Testament as Scripture*', *JSOT* 16 (1980) 12–23
——, *Holy Scripture: Canon, Authority, Criticism* (Oxford: OUP, 1983)
——, 'Jowett and the "Original Meaning" of Scripture', *RelStud* 18 (1982) 433–37
——, 'Jowett and the Reading of the Bible "Like Any Other Book"', *HBT* 4 (1988) 1–44
——, 'The Literal, the Allegorical, and Modern Biblical Scholarship', *JSOT* 44 (1989) 3–17
——, *Old and New in Interpretation: A Study of the Two Testaments* (London: SCM, Second edition 1982)
——, Review of *Biblical Criticism in Crisis? The impact of the canonical approach in Old Testament studies*. By Mark G. Brett, *JTS* 43 (1992) 135–41
——, 'The Theological Case Against Biblical Theology', in Tucker *et al.* (eds.), *Canon, Theology, and Old Testament Interpretation* 3–19
Barth, Karl, *Church Dogmatics* III.1 (Edinburgh: T & T Clark, 1958)
Barth, Markus, 'Whither Biblical Theology?', *Int* 25 (1971) 350–54
Barthes, Roland, 'The Death of the Author'; reprinted in Lodge (ed.), *Modern Criticism and Theory* 167–72
Barton, John, *Reading the Old Testament: Method in Biblical Study* (London: DLT, 1984)
——, 'Verbal Inspiration', in Coggins and Houlden (eds.), *A Dictionary of Biblical Interpretation* 719–22
Bauckham, Richard, Review of Childs, Brevard S., *Biblical Theology of the Old and New Testaments: Theological Reflections on the Christian Bible*, *BI* 2 (1994) 246–50
Bernstein, Richard J., *Beyond Objectivism and Relativism: Science, Hermeneutics, and Praxis* (Oxford: Basil Blackwell, 1983)

Betti, Emilio, 'Hermeneutics as the General Methodology of the *Geisteswissenschaften*', in Bleicher (ed.), *Contemporary Hermeneutics* 51–94

Bleicher, Josef (ed.), *Contemporary Hermeneutics: Hermeneutics as Method, Philosophy, and Critique* (London: Routledge, 1980)

Bloch, Marc, *The Historian's Craft* (Manchester: Manchester University Press, 1954)

Brett, Mark G., 'Against the Grain: Brevard Childs' *Biblical Theology of the Old and New Testaments: Theological Reflections on the Christian Bible*', *Modern Theology* 10 (1994) 281–87

——, *Biblical Criticism in Crisis?: The Impact of the Canonical Approach on Old Testament Studies* (Cambridge: CUP, 1991)

——, *The Canonical Approach to Old Testament Study* (Unpublished Ph.D. thesis; Sheffield University, 1988)

——, 'The Future of Reader Criticisms?', in Watson (ed.), *The Open Text* 13–31

——, 'Four or Five Things to Do with Texts: A Taxonomy of Interpretative Interests', in Clines *et al.* (eds.), *The Bible in Three Dimensions* 357–77

——, 'Motives and Intentions in Genesis 1', *JTS* 42 (1991) 1–16

Bruce, F.F., 'Myth and History', in Colin Brown (ed.) *History, Criticism and Faith* (Leicester: IVP, 1976) 79–100

Bultmann, Rudolph, 'Is Exegesis Without Presuppositions Possible?', in Mueller-Vollmer (ed.), *The Hermeneutics Reader* 242–8

——, 'The Problem of Hermeneutics', in Bultmann, *New Testament and Mythology* (London: SCM, 1985) 69–93

Calvin, John, *Concerning Scandals* (Edinburgh: St. Andrew, 1978)

——, *The First Epistle of Paul the Apostle to the Corinthians* (Edinburgh: Oliver & Boyd, 1960)

——, *Institutes of the Christian Religion* (Grand Rapids: Eerdmans 1983)

Carroll, Robert P., 'Canonical Criticism: A Recent Trend in Biblical Studies?', *ExpTim* 92 (1980) 73–78

——, Review of *Introduction to the Old Testament as Scripture*, *SJT* 33 (1980) 285–91

Childs, Brevard S., *Biblical Theology in Crisis* (Philadelphia: Westminster, 1970)

——, *Biblical Theology of the Old and New Testaments: Theological Reflection on the Christian Bible* (London: SCM, 1992)

——, 'The Canonical Shape of the Prophetic Literature', *Int* 32 (1978) 46–55

——, 'Critical Reflections on James Barr's Understanding of the Literal and the Allegorical', *JSOT* 46 (1990) 3–9

——, 'The Exegetical Significance of Canon for the Study of the Old Testament', *VTSup* 29 (1978) 66–80

——, *Exodus: A Commentary* (OTL; London: SCM, 1974)

——, 'Interpretation in Faith: The Theological Responsibility of an Old Testament Commentary', *Int* 18 (1964) 432–49

——, *Introduction to the Old Testament as Scripture* (London: SCM, Second edition 1983)

——, *Isaiah and the Assyrian Crisis* (SBT Second Series 3; London: SCM, 1967)

——, 'Karl Barth as Interpreter of Scripture', in D.L. Dickerman (ed.), *Karl Barth and the Future of Theology: A Memorial Colloquium Held at Yale Divinity School January 28, 1969* (New Haven: Yale Divinity School Association, 1969) 30–39

——, *Memory and Tradition in Israel* (SBT 37; London: SCM, 1962)

——, *The New Testament as Canon: An Introduction* (London: SCM, 1984)

——, *Old Testament Theology in a Canonical Context* (London: SCM 1985)

——, 'On Reading the Elijah Narratives', *Int* 34 (1980) 128–37

——, 'A Response [to James Mays *et al.*]', *HBT* 2 (1980) 199–221

——, 'Response to Reviewers of *Introduction to the Old Testament as Scripture*', *JSOT* 16 (1980) 52–60

——, Review of *Holy Scripture: Canon, Authority, Criticism*, by James Barr, *Int* 38 (1984) 66–70

——, Review of *The Past, Present and Future of Biblical Theology*, by James D. Smart, *JBL* 100 (1981) 252–53

——, 'The Sensus Literalis of Scripture: An Ancient and Modern Problem', in Herbert Donner (ed.), *Beiträge zur Alttestamentlichen Theologie. FS für Walther Zimmerli zum 70. Geburstag* (Göttingen: Vandenhoek & Ruprecht, 1977) 80–93

——, 'Some Reflections on the Search for a Biblical Theology', *HBT* 4 (1982) 1–12

Cioffi, Frank, 'Interpretation and Intention in Criticism', in Newton-De Molina (ed.), *On Literary Intention* 55–73

Clines, David J.A., 'Story and Poem: The Old Testament as Literature and as Scripture', *Int* 34 (1980) 115–127

——, *The Theme of the Pentateuch* (*JSOTS* 10; Sheffield: *JSOT* Press, 1978)

—— and J. Cheryl Exum, 'The New Literary Criticism', in J. Cheryl Exum and David J.A. Clines (eds.), *The New Literary Criticism and the Hebrew Bible* (*JSOTS* 143; Sheffield: Sheffield Academic Press, 1993) 11–25

——, S.E. Fowl, and S.E. Porter (eds.), *The Bible in Three Dimensions* (*JSOTS* 87; Sheffield: Sheffield Academic Press, 1990)

Coggins, R.J. and J.L. Houlden (eds.), *A Dictionary of Biblical Interpretation* (London: SCM, 1990)

Collingwood, R.G., *The Idea of History* (Oxford: OUP, 1961)

Corliss, Richard L., 'Schleiermacher's Hermeneutics and Its Critics', *RelStud* 29 (1993) 363–79

Danto, Arthur C., *Narration and Knowledge (including the integral text of Analytical Philosophy of History)* (New York: Columbia University Press, 1985)

Dilthey, Wilhelm, 'The Rise of Hermeneutics', *New Literary History* 3 (1972) 229–244

Dulles, Avery, 'Response to Krister Stendahl's Method in the Study of Biblical Theology', in Hyatt (ed.), 210–16

Dunn, James D.G., 'Levels of Canonical Authority', *HBT* 4 (1982) 13–60

Eslinger, Lyle, 'The Wooing of the Woman at the Well: Jesus, the Reader and Reader-Response Criticism', *JLT* 1 (1987) 167–83

Evans, C. Stephen, 'Critical Historical Judgement and Biblical Faith', *Faith and Philosophy* 11 (1994) 184–206

Evans, Gareth, 'Identity and Predication', *JPhil* 72 (1975) 343–63

Fish, Stanley, *Doing What Comes Naturally: Change, Rhetoric, and the Practice of Theory in Literary and Legal Studies* (Oxford: Clarendon, 1989)

——, *Is There a Text in This Class?: The Authority of Interpretive Communities* (Cambridge, MA: Harvard University Press, 1980)

Fowl, Stephen, 'The Canonical Approach of Brevard Childs', *ExpTim* 96 (1985) 173–76

Frei, Hans W., *The Eclipse of Biblical Narrative: A Study in Eighteenth and Nineteenth Century Hermeneutics* (New Haven: Yale University Press, 1974)

Gadamer, Hans-Georg, *Philosophical Hermeneutics* (Berkeley: California University Press, 1977)

——, 'The Problem of Language in Schleiermacher's Hermeneutics', *JTC* 7 (1970) 68–95

——, 'On the Problem of Self-Understanding', in Gadamer, *Philosophical Hermeneutics* 44–58

——, 'On the Scope and Function of Hermeneutical Reflection', in Gadamer, *Philosophical Hermeneutics* 18–43

——, 'Semantics and Hermeneutics', in Gadamer, *Philosophical Hermeneutics* 82–94

——, *Truth and Method* (London: Sheed and Ward, Second, Revised Edition 1989)

——, 'The Universality of the Hermeneutical Problem', in Gadamer, *Philosophical Hermeneutics* 3–17

Goldingay, John, 'Inspiration', in Coggins and Houlden (eds.), *A Dictionary of Biblical Interpretation* 314–16

Gottwald, Norman K. 'Social Matrix and Canonical Shape', *TToday* 42 (1986) 307–21

Gunn, David M., *The Story of King David: Genre and Interpretation* ( *JSOTS* 6; Sheffield: *JSOT* Press, 1978)
—— and Danna Nolan Fewell, *Narrative in the Hebrew Bible* (The Oxford Bible Series; Oxford: OUP, 1993)
Gunton, Colin E., *Yesterday and Today* (London: DLT, 1983)
Hanfling, Oswald, *Logical Positivism* (Oxford: Blackwell, 1981)
Hanson, Norwood Russell, *Patterns of Discovery* (Cambridge: CUP, 1958)
Harrelson, Walter, Review of *Introduction to the Old Testament as Scripture*, *JBL* 100 (1981) 99–102
Harvey, Van Austin, *The Historian and the Believer* (London: SCM, 1967)
Hasel, Gerhard, *Old Testament Theology: Basic Issues in the Current Debate* (Grand Rapids: Eerdmans, Revised 1975)
Heidegger, Martin, *Being and Time* (Oxford: Blackwell, 1962)
Helm, Paul, *The Divine Revelation* (London: MMS, 1982)
——, 'Revealed Propositions and Timeless Truths', *RelStud* 8 (1972) 127–36
Hesse, Mary B., 'Theory and Observation', in Hesse, *Revolutions and Reconstructions in the Philosophy of Science* (Brighton: Harvester, 1980)
Hilberath, Bernd Jochen, *Theologie zwischen Tradition und Kritik: Die Philosophische Hermeneutik Hans-Georg Gadamers als Herausforderung des Theologischen Selbstverständnisses* (Düsseldorf: Patmos, 1978)
Hirsch, E.D., *The Aims of Interpretation* (Chicago: Chicago University Press, 1976)
——, 'Meaning and Significance Reinterpreted', *Critical Inquiry* 2 (1986) 627–30
——, *Validity in Interpretation* (New Haven: Yale University Press, 1967)
Hoy, David Couzens, *The Critical Circle* (Berkley: University of California, 1978)
Hoyningen-Huene, Paul, *Reconstructing Scientific Revolutions: Thomas S. Kuhn's Philosophy of Science* (Chicago: University of Chicago Press, 1993)
Hume, David, *Enquiries concerning Human Understanding and concerning the Principles of Morals*, edited by L.A. Selby-Bigge and P.H. Nidditch (Oxford: OUP, Third Edition 1975)
——, *A Treatise of Human Nature*, edited by L.A. Selby-Bigge and P.H. Nidditch (Oxford: OUP, Second Edition 1978)
Hyatt, J.P. (ed.), *The Bible in Modern Scholarship* (London: Carey Kingsgate, 1966)
Janzen, J. Gerald, 'The Canonical Context of Old Testament Introduction', *Int* 34 (1980) 411–14
Jowett, Benjamin, 'On the Interpretation of Scripture', in *Essays and Reviews* (London: J.W. Parker 1860)
Kimmerle, Heinz, 'The Afterword of 1968', in Schleiermacher, *Hermeneutics* 229–34
——, 'Editor's Introduction', in Schleiermacher, *Hermeneutics* 21–40
——, 'Hermeneutical Theory or Ontological Hermeneutics', *JTC* 4 (1967) 107–21
Kittel, Bonnie, 'Brevard Childs' Development of the Canonical Approach', *JSOT* 16 (1980) 2–11
Knight, Douglas A., 'Canon and the History of Tradition: A Critique of Brevard S. Childs' *Introduction to the Old Testament as Scripture*', *HBT* 2 (1980) 127–49
—— (ed.), *Tradition and Theology in the Old Testament* (London: SPCK, 1977)
Kuhn, Thomas S., *The Copernican Revolution* (Mass.: Harvard University Press, 1957)
——, *The Essential Tension* (Chicago: Chicago University Press, 1970)
——, *The Structure of Scientific Revolutions* (Chicago: Chicago University Press, Second Edition, Enlarged 1970)
Kümmel, W.G., *The New Testament: The History of the Investigation of its Problems* (London: SCM, 1973)
Landes, George M., 'The Canonical Approach to Introducing the Old Testament', *JSOT* 16 (1980) 32–39
Laurin, Robert B., 'Tradition and Canon', in Knight (ed.), *Tradition and Theology in the Old Testament* 261–74
Lentricchia, Frank, *After the New Criticism* (London: Methuen, 1983)

Lodge, David (ed.), *Modern Criticism and Theory: A Reader* (London: Longman, 1988)

Mays, James L., 'What is Written', *HBT* 2 (1980) 151–63

McEvenue, Sean, 'The Old Testament, Scripture or Theology?', *Int* 35 (1981) 229–42

Melugin, Roy F., 'Canon and Exegetical Method', in Tucker *et al.* (eds.), *Canon, Theology, and Old Testament Interpretation* 48–61

Mitchell, Basil, *The Justification of Religious Belief* (New York: OUP, 1981)

Moberly, R.W.L., *At The Mountain of God: Story and Theology in Exodus 32–34* (*JSOTS* 22; Sheffield: *JSOT* Press, 1983)

——, 'The Church's Use of the Bible: The Work of Brevard Childs', *ExpTim* 99 (1988) 104–109

Morgan, Donn F., Review of *Introduction to the Old Testament as Scripture*, *ATR* 64 (1982) 383–92

——, 'Canon and Criticism: Method or Madness?', *ATR* 68 (1986) 83–94

Morgan, Robert with John Barton, *Biblical Interpretation* (The Oxford Bible Series; Oxford: OUP, 1988)

Muilenburg, James, 'Form Criticism and Beyond', *JBL* 88 (1969) 1–18

Mueller-Vollmer, Kurt (ed.), *The Hermeneutics Reader* (Oxford: Basil Blackwell, 1986)

Newton-De Molina, David (ed.), *On Literary Intention* (Edinburgh: Edinburgh University Press, 1976)

Noble, Paul R., 'A "Balanced" Reading of the Rape of Dinah: Some Exegetical and Methodological Observations', *BI* (forthcoming, 1996)

——, 'Hermeneutics and Postmodernism: Can We Have a Radical Reader-Response Theory? Part I', *RelStud* 30 (1994) 419–36

——, 'Hermeneutics and Postmodernism: Can We Have a Radical Reader-Response Theory? Part II', *RelStud* 31 (1995) 1–22

——, 'Fish and the Bible', *HeyJ* (forthcoming, 1996)

——, 'The *Sensus Literalis*: Jowett, Childs, and Barr', *JTS* 44 (1993) 1–23

——, 'Synchronic and Diachronic Approaches to Biblical Interpretation', *JLT* 7 (1993) 131–48

O'Collins, G.G., 'Revelation as History', *HeyJ* 7 (1966) 394–406

Oeming, Manfred, *Gesamtbiblische Theologien der Gegenwart* (Stuttgart: Kohlhammer, 1985)

Ollenburger, Ben C., 'What Krister Stendahl "Meant"—A Normative Critique of "Descriptive Biblical Theology"', *HBT* 8 (1986) 61–98

Pais, Abraham, *Inward Bound: Of Matter and Forces in the Physical World* (Oxford: OUP, 1986)

Palmer, Richard E., *Hermeneutics: Interpretation Theory in Schleiermacher, Dilthey, Heidegger, and Gadamer* (Evanston: Northwestern University Press, 1969)

Pannenberg, Wolfhart, *Basic Questions in Theology* I (London: SCM, 1970)

——, 'Dogmatic Theses on the Concept of Revelation', in *RaH* 123–58

——, 'Hermeneutic and Universal History', in *BQT* I 96–136

——, *Jesus—God and Man* (London: SCM, 1968)

——, 'Kerygma and History', in *BQT* I 81–95

——, 'Redemptive Event and History', in *BQT* I 15–80

——, 'The Revelation of God in Jesus of Nazareth', in James M. Robinson and John B. Cobb, Jr. (eds.), *Theology as History* (New Frontiers in Theology III; New York: Harper & Row, 1967) 101–133

—— (ed.), *Revelation as History* (London: Sheed, 1979)

Parker, T.H.L., *Calvin's Doctrine of the Knowledge of God* (Edinburgh: Oliver & Boyd, 1969)

Polk, David P., 'Brevard Childs' *Introduction to the Old Testament as Scripture*', *HBT* 2 (1980), 165–71

Popper, Karl, *Conjectures and Refutations: The Growth of Scientific Knowledge* (London: RKP, Fourth edition (revised) 1972)

——, *The Logic of Scientific Discovery* (London: Hutchinson, Tenth impression (revised) 1980)

——, *Objective Knowledge* (Oxford: OUP, revised 1979)

Porter, Stanley E., 'Why Hasn't Reader-Response Criticism Caught On in New Testament Studies?', *JLT* 4 (1990) 278–92

Prickett, Stephen, *Words and* The Word (Cambridge: CUP, 1986)

Priest, John F., 'Canon and Criticism: A Review Article', *JAAR* 48 (1980) 259–71

Quine, Willard Van Orman, *Word and Object* (Mass.: MIT, 1960)

Rad, Gerhard von, *Genesis: A Commentary* (OTL; London: SCM, Revised 1972)

———, *Old Testament Theology* I (London: SCM, 1975)

———, *Old Testament Theology* II (London: SCM, 1975)

Ray, William, *Literary Meaning: From Phenomenology to Deconstruction* (Oxford: Blackwell, 1984)

Rendtorff, Rolf, 'Between Historical Criticism and Holistic Interpretation', *VTSup* 40 (1988) 298–303

———, *Canon and Theology: Overtures to an Old Testament Theology* (OBT; Minneapolis: Fortress, 1993)

———, *The Old Testament: An Introduction* (London: SCM, 1985)

———, 'The Paradigm is Changing: Hopes and Fears', *BI* 1 (1993) 34–53

Rossiter, A.P., 'Political Tragedy', in B.A. Brockman (ed.), *Shakespeare: Coriolanus* (Basingstoke: Macmillan, 1977)

Sanders, James A., *Canon and Community: A Guide to Canonical Criticism* (Philadelphia: Fortress, 1984)

———, 'Canonical Context and Canonical Criticism', *HBT* 2 (1980) 173–97

———, *Torah and Canon* (Philadelphia: Fortress, 1972)

Sawyer, John F.A., 'A Change of Emphasis in the Study of the Prophets', in Richard Coggins *et al.* (eds.), *Israel's Prophetic Tradition* (Cambridge: CUP, 1982) 233–49

Scalise, Charles Joseph, *Canonical Hermeneutics: The Theological Basis and Implications of the Thought of Brevard S. Childs* (Unpublished Ph.D. thesis; Southern Baptist Theological Seminary, 1987)

Schleiermacher, F.D.E., 'The Academy Addresses of 1829', in Schleiermacher, *Hermeneutics* 175–214

———, 'The First Draft of 1809–10', in Schleiermacher, *Hermeneutics* 67–90

———, 'Hermeneutics: The Compendium of 1819 and the Marginal Notes of 1828', in Schleiermacher, *Hermeneutics* 95–151

———, *Hermeneutics: The Handwritten Manuscripts* (Atlanta: Scholars, 1986)

———, 'A Loose Page from 1810–11', in Schleiermacher, *Hermeneutics* 91–93

———, 'The Marginal Notes of 1832–33', in Schleiermacher, *Hermeneutics* 215–27

———, 'The Separate Exposition of the Second Part', in Schleiermacher, *Hermeneutics* 161–73

Schnackenburg, Rudolph, *The Gospel According to St. John* I (London: Burns & Oates, 1980)

Schökel, L. Alonso, 'On Methods and Models', *VTSup* 36 (1985) 3–13

Segrè, Emilio, *From X-Rays to Quarks: Modern Physicists and Their Discoveries* (San Francisco: W.H. Freeman, 1980)

Sheppard, Gerald T., 'Barr on Canon and Childs', *Theological Students Fellowship Bulletin* 7 (1983) 2–4

———, 'Canon Criticism: The Proposal of Brevard Childs and an Assessment for Evangelical Hermeneutics', *Studia Biblica et Theologica* 4 (1974) 3–17

Skinner, Quentin, 'Motives, Intentions, and the Interpretation of Texts', *New Literary History* 3 (1972) 393–408

Smart, James D., *The Past, Present, and Future of Biblical Theology* (Philadelphia: Westminster, 1979)

Spina, Frank A., 'Canonical Criticism: Childs Versus Sanders', in W. McCown and J.B. Massey (eds.), *Interpreting God's Word For Today* (Indiana: Warner, 1982) 165–194

Sternberg, Meir, *The Poetics of Biblical Narrative: Ideological Literature and the Drama of Reading* (Indiana Studies in Biblical Literature; Bloomington: Indiana University Press, 1985)

Stendahl, Krister, 'Biblical Theology, Contemporary', *IDB* I (1962) 418–32
——, 'Method in the Study of Biblical Theology', in Hyatt (ed.), *The Bible in Modern Scholarship* 196–209
Suleiman, S.R., 'Varieties of Audience-Oriented Criticism', in Suleiman and Crosman (eds.), *The Reader in the Text* 3–45
—— and I. Crosman (eds.), *The Reader in the Text: Essays on Audience and Interpretation* (Princeton: Princeton University Press, 1981)
Suppe, Frederick, 'The Search for Philosophical Understanding of Scientific Theories', in Suppe (ed.), *The Structure of Scientific Theories* (Urbana: University of Illinois Press, 1974) 1–241
Thiselton, Anthony C., *The Two Horizons: New Testament Hermeneutics and Philosophical Description with Special Reference to Heidegger, Bultmann, Gadamer, and Wittgenstein* (Exeter: Paternoster, 1980)
——, *New Horizons in Hermeneutics* (London: Harper-Collins, 1992)
Tompkins, Jane P. (ed.), *Reader-Response Criticism: From Formalism to Post-Structuralism* (Baltimore: Johns Hopkins University Press, 1980)
Torrance, T.F., *Calvin's Doctrine of Man* (London: Lutterworth, 1949)
Tracy, David, *The Analogical Imagination* (New York: Crossroad, 1981)
Troeltsch, Ernst, 'Historical and Dogmatic Method in Theology', in Troeltsch, *Religion in History* (Edinburgh: T & T Clark, 1991) 11–32
Trotti, John B., 'Brevard Spring Childs: A Bibliography', in Tucker *et al.* (eds.), *Canon, Theology, and Old Testament Interpretation* 329–36
Tucker, Gene M. *et al.* (eds.), *Canon, Theology, and Old Testament Interpretation* (Philadelphia: Fortress, 1988)
Warfield, Benjamin Breckinridge, 'Calvin's Doctrine of the Knowledge of God', in Warfield, *Calvin and Calvinism* (Oxford: OUP, 1931) 29–130
Warnke, Georgia, *Gadamer: Hermeneutics, Tradition, and Reason* (Cambridge: Polity, 1987)
Weinsheimer, Joel C., *Gadamer's Hermeneutics: A Reading of Truth and Method* (New Haven: Yale University Press, 1985)
Westermann, Claus, *Genesis 1–11: A Commentary* (London: SPCK, 1984)
——, *Genesis 37–50: A Commentary* (London: SPCK, 1987)
Wharton, James A., 'Splendid Failure or Flawed Success?', *Int* 29 (1975) 266–76
Watson, Francis (ed.), *The Open Text: New Directions for Biblical Studies?* (London: SCM, 1993)
Whybray, R.N., 'Old Testament Theology—A Non-existent Beast?', in Barry P. Thompson (ed.) *Scripture: Meaning and Method* (Hull: Hull University Press, 1987)
Wimsatt, W.M., 'Genesis: A Fallacy Revisited', in Newton-De Molina (ed.), *On Literary Intention* 116–38
Wimsatt, W.M. and Monroe C. Beardsley, 'The Intentional Fallacy', in Newton-De Molina (ed.) *On Literary Intention* 1–13

# INDEX OF AUTHORS

# BIBLICAL INTERPRETATION SERIES

ISSN 0928-0731

1. VAN DIJK-HEMMES, F. & A. BRENNER. *On Gendering Texts.* Female and Male Voices in the Hebrew Bible. 1993. ISBN 90 04 09642 6
2. VAN TILBORG, S. *Imaginative Love in John.* 1993. ISBN 90 04 09716 3
3. DANOVE, P.L. *The End of Mark's Story.* A Methodological Study. 1993. ISBN 90 04 09717 1
4. WATSON, D.F. & A.J. HAUSER. *Rhetorical Criticism of the Bible.* A Comprehensive Bibliography with Notes on History and Method. 1994. ISBN 90 04 09903 4
5. SEELEY, D. *Deconstructing the New Testament.* 1994. ISBN 90 04 09880 1
6. VAN WOLDE, E. *Words become Worlds.* Semantic Studies of Genesis 1-11. 1994. ISBN 90 04 098879
7. NEUFELD, D. *Reconceiving Texts as Speech Acts.* An Analysis of 1 John. 1994. ISBN 90 04 09853 4
8. PORTER, S.E., P. JOYCE & D.E. ORTON (eds.). *Crossing the Boundaries.* Essays in Biblical Interpretation in Honour of Michael D. Goulder. 1994. ISBN 90 04 10131 4
9. YEO, K.-K. *Rhetorical Interaction in 1 Corinthians 8 and 10.* A Formal Analysis with Preliminary Suggestions for a Chinese, Cross-Cultural Hermeneutic. 1995. ISBN 90 04 10115 2
10. LETELLIER, R.I. *Day in Mamre, Night in Sodom.* Abraham and Lot in Genesis 18 and 19. 1995. ISBN 90 04 10250 7
12. TOLMIE, D.F. *Jesus' Farewell to the Disciples.* John 13:1-17:26 in Narratological Perspective. 1995. ISBN 90 04 10270 1
13. RYOU, D.H. *Zephaniah's Oracles against the Nations.* A Synchronic and Diachronic Study of Zephaniah 2:1-3:8. 1995. ISBN 90 04 10311 2
14. PORTER, S.E. & J.T. REED. *The Book of Romans.* A Grammatical-rhetorical Commentary. In Preparation. ISBN 90 04 09908 5
15. SELAND, T. *Establishment Violence in Philo and Luke.* A Study of Non-Conformity to the Torah and Jewish Vigilante Reactions. 1995. ISBN 90 04 10252 3
16. NOBLE, P.R *The Canonical Approach.* A Critical Reconstruction of the Hermeneutics of Brevard S. Childs. 1995. ISBN 90 04 10151 9